NEW DESIGNS FOR ELEMENTARY CURRICULUM AND INSTRUCTION

SECOND EDITION

John U. Michaelis
Professor of Education
University of California, Berkeley

Ruth H. Grossman
Professor of Education
The City College of the City University of New York

Lloyd F. Scott
Professor of Education
University of California, Berkeley

175
176

206
207
208
209
219
↓30

1975

McGraw-Hill Book Company
New York St. Louis San Francisco Auckland Düsseldorf Johannesburg
Kuala Lumpur London Mexico Montreal New Delhi Panama Paris São Paulo
Singapore Sydney Tokyo Toronto

NEW DESIGNS FOR ELEMENTARY CURRICULUM AND INSTRUCTION

1234567890 DODO 798765

This book was set in Press Roman by Allen Wayne Technical Corp.
The editors were Stephen D. Dragin and Phyllis T. Dulan;
the cover was designed by Anne Canevari Green;
the production supervisor was Judi Frey.
The drawings were done by Eric G. Hieber Associates, Inc.
R. R. Donnelley & Sons Company was printer and binder.

Library of Congress Cataloging in Publication Data

Michaelis, John Udell, date
    New designs for elementary curriculum and instruction.

    First ed. published in 1967 under title: New
designs for the elementary school curriculum.
    Includes bibliographies.
    1. Education, Elementary—Curricula. I. Grossman,
Ruth H., joint author. II. Scott, Lloyd F., joint
author. III. Title.
LB1570.M5   1975   372.1'9   74-26549
ISBN 0-07-041772-5

Contents

Preface

At the present time, curriculum evaluation and planning are being undertaken in many school systems, contributions to curriculum are being made by curriculum planning centers outside the school systems, and academic and commercial production of new programs and materials are also being made. In view of this vast activity, a need arises for a clarifying focus on the essential features of the emerging curriculum. Also, a need arises for guidelines which will facilitate the continual analysis, evaluation, development or adaptation, and utilization of new curriculum designs and materials in the programs of elementary and middle schools.

In response to these needs, this volume addresses those who wish to improve the elementary and middle school curriculum. As in the first edition, the authors have provided a model for analysis, planning, and evaluation of curriculum. In this second edition, the model has been revised to include all components essential to current principles of curriculum development. The use of this model is enhanced by an expanded discussion of each part in separate chapters. The chapters on each subject area have been brought up to date in regard to recent trends and developments, and have been organized around the revised model.

The organization of this volume provides a framework that may be used to analyze, develop, and evaluate curriculum. Part One provides an analytic model, Part Two provides for application of the model, and Part Three provides for evaluation. Chapter 1 outlines significant historical elements related to the development of current philosophies of education, goals and objectives, teaching strategies, and other elements vital to consideration of the curriculum as represented by the model introduced here in outline form. Emerging developments with impact on curriculum, such as increased attention to early childhood learning, use of performance objectives, and bilingual education are discussed. Chapters 2 and 3 provide an expanded analysis of philosophical, social, psychological, and disciplinary foundations of curriculum. Chapter 4 presents broad goals and guidelines for determining objectives. Guidelines for organization of the curriculum are discussed in Chapter 5, organization of classes, school organization, and instructional media are analyzed in Chapter 6. A detailed presentation of teaching strategies follows in Chapter 7. To complete the model, Chapter 8 provides guidelines for evaluation and accountability.

In Part Two Chapters 9 through 17 provide examples of use of the model in each subject area, beginning with subjects in which symbolic skills are developed (reading, language arts, mathematics), proceeding to areas of the curriculum that expand self-knowledge and knowledge about the world (science, social studies, health education), and concluding with subjects that develop motor skills and aesthetic expression (physical education, art, music).

In Part Three, Chapter 18 discusses balance in the curriculum to provide for all these areas of learning and integration of curriculum to provide for development of understandings, skills, and attitudes that cut across subject areas. Chapter 18 also builds on all the preceding chapters to summarize procedures for utilizing the model in curriculum analysis and development and discusses problems and challenges in curriculum planning and implementation.

An important feature of this edition is the use of the taxonomies of cognitive and affective objectives in the construction of evaluation devices. Every effort has been made to identify the conceptual structures and modes of inquiry in new curriculum materials and to present both substantive and process components of the curriculum. The introduction to each chapter provides guides for its use, with applications of chapter material provided in suggested follow-up questions and activities.

This volume has been written and organized to be used in courses in elementary or middle school curriculum and instruction as well as advanced work in curriculum planning for students in the fields of curriculum, instruction, supervision, or administration. It is also intended as a tool for in-service preparation for teachers, supervisors, administrators, and others who participate in curriculum development or who are involved with the implementation of new designs. When used in a course in curriculum and instruction, the model as explicated in Chapters 1 through 8 provides a guide for analysis of observed programs, while Chapters 9 through 17 provide information about curriculum trends and guidelines for teaching strategies. Chapter 18 then aids the reader in viewing the total program experienced by children in elementary and intermediate schools. When used in a course in curriculum development, the model presented in Chapters 1 through 8 may be analyzed by all students, followed by different patterns of use for Chapters 9 through 18. Individuals or groups might apply the model to development of curriculum in one subject area, using the relevant subject chapter and guidelines in Chapter 18. Two or more subject chapters might be used by those planning a "core" program of related subjects such as aesthetic education, health and physical education, mathematics and science, and so on. Use of all the chapters in Part Two would be appropriate for those involved in planning the complete program for a class, grade level, or school at the elementary or middle school level. For development of curriculum in departmentalized middle schools, Chapter 18 provides a guide to ensure that relationships between subject areas are not overlooked.

Acknowledgment is made of the contributions of theorists, project staffs, and elementary school teachers whose efforts to improve curriculum have resulted in written materials. A special acknowledgment goes to David Wright, School of Education, University of California at Los Angeles, for contributions to the sections on philosophical and psychological foundations. The authors are grateful for the responsive dialogue with students, elementary school teachers, and colleagues that has served to sharpen our perceptions. Special thanks are given to those who gave permission to quote material in the text.

John U. Michaelis
Ruth H. Grossman
Lloyd F. Scott

Part One

A Model for Curriculum Development

Chapter 1

A Model for the Elementary Curriculum in Historical Perspective

Curriculum has frequently been defined in educational literature as all the learning experiences of the child under the auspices of the school. This definition encompasses both the planned and the "hidden" curriculum. In this book the planned curriculum is defined as broad goals and specific objectives, content, learning activities, use of instructional media, teaching strategies, and evaluation—stated, planned, and carried out by school personnel. The "hidden" curriculum includes learnings in the cognitive, affective, and psychomotor domains that are acquired concurrently with the planned curriculum but come about as a result of conditions or experiences not deliberately planned or set forth in advance. For example, in a classroom where reading groups are designated by names of members but members are dispersed for other learning activities, children may learn that each classmate has a unique set of talents, skills, and weaknesses, and may learn to respect each other because each is treated equally by the teacher. In another classroom where the "Airplanes," "Jets," and "Rockets" remain seated in their reading groups for other activities, children may learn to classify people according to arbitrarily valued

1

characteristics or to treat with less respect those classmates who seem less valued by the teacher.

This book deals primarily with the planned curriculum, but this focus is not intended to imply that the "hidden" curriculum is less important in its impact on children. In fact, curriculum planners who take cognizance of factors that affect the "hidden" curriculum can develop planned content and learning experiences that will be conducive to desirable "hidden" outcomes. For example, study of family life in countries around the world may suggest to children both that there is similarity across cultures as well as understandable and acceptable diversity and that other people are worthy of attention. On the other hand, study of family structures and lifestyles only in the student's own culture might suggest that these are the forms that are "right," that people in other cultures are less worthy of attention or consideration, or that they ought to be evaluated in terms of their resemblance to the student's culture.

As defined above, the planned curriculum includes several interrelated components. The process of curriculum development involves a consideration of each of these elements in a larger framework which includes factors that underlie and affect curriculum decisions and implementation. This framework or system for curriculum development is presented below as "A Model for Curriculum Development and Analysis." The historical antecedents of each component in the model are discussed later in this chapter. Each component is then elaborated in Chapters 2 through 8 in terms of current and emerging developments.

A MODEL FOR CURRICULUM DEVELOPMENT AND ANALYSIS

The development of models for curriculum development has progressed from the consideration of such components as subject matter, methods of instruction, and views of learning to a consideration of a complete set of factors related to the design of instructional programs. The model presented in this section includes the components generally recognized to be essential to curriculum development. It is designed to be used in two ways. First, it may serve as a guide to the development or revision of the curriculum. The various components may be considered in the order in which they are presented, or the order may be varied in terms of immediate concerns and problems, but all components should be given attention at some point in the development process. Second, the model serves as a guide for the review and analysis of the curriculum. In the later chapters of this book in which specific areas of the curriculum are reviewed, selected components of the model are used to organize the presentation of current practices and new developments.

Foundations of the Curriculum

There are five major sources of ideas that serve as the foundations for curriculum planning. The historical foundations are useful in putting problems, issues, and practices in perspective. The philosophical foundations may be drawn upon to develop a framework of values and beliefs related to the goals, selection and use of knowledge, means and methods, and other dimensions of education. The social foundations are sources of information of societal values, changes, problems, pressures, and forces that merit consideration in curriculum planning. The psychological foundations contain ideas about child growth, development, and learning on which the program may be based. The disciplinary foundations serve as sources of information about concepts, generalizations, supporting data, and modes, methods, and processes of inquiry that may be used in developing the curriculum and planning instruction.

Goals and Objectives

Related to analysis of the foundations are major goals of education that give direction to planning at all levels and in all areas of the curriculum. Objectives must be consistent with goals but more specific so that immediate direction is obtained for instructional planning and evaluation. General goals should be cooperatively developed by school personnel and laymen and generally acceptable in the community. Objectives should be defined by school personnel with assistance from experts in areas of the curriculum, evaluation, and the formulation of objectives so that they will be optimally useful in planning and appraisal activities.

Contributions of Areas to Goals Each area of the curriculum should be analyzed to identify its specific contributions to major goals. This step is helpful in developing a coherent curriculum in which all areas or fields of study are viewed as contributing to common goals. It is also helpful in identifying the unique contributions that each area can make to goals and thus makes possible the design of a complete and balanced program of instruction that incorporates aesthetic and other unique contributions as well as intellectual contributions.

Objectives of Areas of the Curriculum Objectives of each area may be viewed as a detailed elaboration of contributions to major goals. Their function is to provide specific direction to program planning. Four sets of interrelated objectives that include the cognitive, affective, and psychomotor domains are as follows: conceptual objectives, thinking or inquiry process objectives, skill objectives, and affective objectives. Special categories may be used to highlight contributions of some areas, for example, visual/tactile objectives, creative expression objectives, and aesthetic judgment objectives in art education. However, within such special categories one may find conceptual, process, skill, and affective objectives. Detailed specification of objectives in behavioral or performance terms is done to facilitate unit and lesson planning and to evaluate instructional outcomes.

Organization of the Curriculum

Decisions must be made about organization of the curriculum, units within areas of the curriculum, unit organization, and unit planning procedures. Scope or breadth of the curriculum must be determined and special attention must be given to learning sequences that provide for cumulative learning and integration of learning. Other decisions must be made about curriculum development procedures, broad fields or other patterns of organization, roles of curriculum personnel, and design of curriculum guides.

Organization and Extension of the Learning Environment

School organization must be considered in terms both of the movement of students from level to level (vertical organization) and of the grouping of students and placement of teachers at various levels (horizontal organization). Attention also needs to be given to individualized and personalized instruction, grouping for instruction, organizing and sequencing group work, and interaction analysis. A variety of ways of extending the learning environment merits consideration, ranging from open education, time and spatial extensions, and use of the community as a laboratory for learning.

Instructional media should be analyzed and selected in terms of criteria because of their fundamental importance as key ingredients in the learning environment. The full range of educational technology, including hardware such as equipment and software or courseware such as instructional materials, should be examined and selected in terms of multiple criteria. Provision should be made for instructional media that are useful in all areas of instruction and special media that are needed in particular areas. A variety of printed materials, audio-visual materials, community resources, learning packages, multimedia sets of materials, and multilevel materials should be considered.

Instructional Support Services

The implementation of new or revised programs of instruction requires a variety of support services. The quality of leadership essential to sound curriculum development is also essential to implementation. Consultant and supervisory services are needed to assist in solving general problems and problems related to areas of instruction. Other needed services include those related to instructional media, special education programs, diagnosis and correction of learning difficulties, evaluation, and in-service education of the instructional staff.

Teaching Strategies

A variety of teaching strategies should be selected or designed for use in the instructional program. There is need for inductive strategies that include moves from the particular to the general and deductive strategies that include moves from the general to the particular. Discovery strategies in which students find out on their own and teacher-directed strategies in which students are guided systematically to attain stated objectives are needed along with strategies that call for varying degrees of teacher guidance. Combinations of the preceding strategies may be used to develop and apply concepts, clarify values, and attain other objectives as various media are used in different areas of the curriculum. In addition, consideration should be given to guidelines or principles of instruction for each area of the curriculum.

Evaluation and Accountability

Diagnostic, formative, and summative evaluation are needed to determine needs of students, assess progress toward objectives during instruction, and appraise outcomes of instruction at the end of a given period. A broad and comprehensive program of evaluation is needed in which a variety of instruments and techniques are used to evaluate conceptual, process, skill, and affective outcomes of instruction. Accountability systems should be conducted in ways that contribute to a sense of professional integrity on the part of the school staff and keep the developing child and his learning in central focus. In addition to evaluation of children's learning, consideration should be given to systematic evaluation of areas of the curriculum so that continuing improvements can be made.

HISTORICAL FOUNDATIONS OF CURRICULUM

The curriculum of elementary and middle schools of today has not evolved in a vacuum. At first glance there is much that is different in the content and instructional strategies of American schools of the eighteenth, nineteenth, and twentieth centuries, but a closer examination reveals that each succeeding change in education, while representing a response to changing social conditions, to advances in knowledge, or to new views of the learning process and nature of children, also reflects elements of preceding educational practices, and, in turn, establishes models available for subsequent changes. An examination of the historical foundations of curriculum points up threads of continuity as well as instances of rejection of precedents and illustrates the way in which curriculum, at any point in time, is also a product of that time. So too is the curriculum of today and the curriculum that will be planned for the needs of tomorrow.

The historical outlines that follow generally are organized around five periods to provide a focus for comparison of conditions and educational developments that represent significant changes. The first is the colonial period, during which the foundations of elementary education were established, and the persistent goal of universal literacy was first expressed. During the early national period, from the American Revolution to 1870, public education was established and extended, and new needs, goals, content, and strategies evolved. The period from 1870 to 1920 saw rapid and dramatic advances in psychology, in academic fields of knowledge, and in education as a profession. "Progressive education," "child-centered curriculum," and interest in schooling as an agent for social change characterized the period from 1920 to 1955. From 1955 to the present there have been extensive efforts at curriculum revision with renewed attention to contributions of the academic disciplines. This period has also been characterized by development of a variety of forms of school and intraclass organization and of a concern for the role of schooling in racial integration. Although division into periods provides a useful framework for discussion, the dates that divide periods must be considered somewhat arbitrary; they do not, of course, represent a demarcation between two vastly different sets of conditions. Development of American education has been a continuing process; in each period, characteristics of preceding and following times may be discerned as well.

Philosophical and Social Foundations of Education

During America's colonial period, elementary education had two major purposes. One, most fundamental to common education, was the development of literacy for religious purposes. Literacy has remained a persistent value in elementary education, for reasons that changed in relation to changing needs of later periods. The other purpose was provision of basic learnings leading to education for the roles and occupations of a privileged class. Children of lower socioeconomic levels left schooling early to enter the work force. Those boys whose family situations enabled them to remain in school acquired skills needed for commerce or prepared for study leading to law, medicine, or the ministry. Later critics of education noted that tracking of pupils in different programs in the early twentieth century perpetuated socioeconomic differences. More recently, others have suggested that class distinctions are fostered in schools that emphasize the values of a limited segment of the population.

The strength of religious beliefs may be seen in the passage of an act in Massachusetts in 1647 that required towns to establish schools to teach reading in order to thwart the designs of the "old deluder Satan." However, education continued to be minimal for the next 130 years. Girls had little formal schooling beyond learning to read; boys might learn computational arithmetic for business skills or go on to grammar schools to study Latin and classical literature. No formal provisions existed for education of black children.

New needs arose with the American Revolution. Those eligible to participate as citizens and officeholders required a knowledge of the structure of their new form of government. The new egalitarianism extended education to a broader spectrum of classes. Literacy and knowledge of government were regarded as requisites for a free, self-governing people. Practical and commercial skills needed in the independent nation necessitated education in computing and use of language. Public elementary education developed slowly at first, along with religious school systems. Some church groups provided elementary education for free blacks in Northern cities, but education of blacks was prohibited in Southern states.

During the first half of the nineteenth century as suffrage was extended, an increasing proportion of the male population required elementary education. After the War Between the States, common elementary education, including study of American history, was viewed as a means of developing national unification and good citizenship. This was extended to black males, usually in segregated schools. Of course, needs for child labor had the effect of keeping many children out of school altogether, and many others attended only long enough to acquire the rudiments of reading and computing. Those who remained in school might go on to an academy to study practical subjects for commerce, including mathematics, modern languages, or navigation, reflecting an early essentialist view, or they might attend grammar schools to study Latin, Greek, and classical literature, the carriers of civilization valued by early perennialists.

Extensive and increasingly accelerating changes in social conditions after 1870 led to changing priorities in the purposes of education. Increasing industrialization and urbanization reduced family roles in education. Special interest groups began to form and to exert influence on education. Veterans' groups promoted inculcation of patriotism through legislation requiring flag ceremonies and teaching of American history. Labor groups pressed for compulsory education laws to remove children from the crowded work force and for vocational training to replace the earlier, declining apprenticeship system of learning a trade. Business groups called for the teaching of commercially useful skills for potential employees. Increased immigration from Latin and Slavic countries and compulsory education laws resulted in a larger and more varied pupil population, presenting many challenges to the school. Changes in social roles and views of women led to recognition that some education was needed for girls. Primary education was coeducational, but differences in roles and citizenship eligibility led to separate classes for boys and girls in upper elementary grades.

As social problems were identified, schooling was viewed increasingly as a means of overcoming disadvantages. Vocational education, supported by federal funding, was accepted as part of public education. In fact, increased costs of education during the twentieth century extended the funding base from local taxes to state and federal grants. Funding from these sources reflected current social, philosophical, or political values as funds were provided, or reduced, for such purposes as free lunches, breakfast programs, purchase of instructional materials, development of curriculum in specific areas, provision of bilingual-bicultural programs, establishment of Headstart programs, and so forth.

During the first half of the twentieth century, there developed educational philosophies that saw education as preparation for social and occupational roles, as a means of enhancing children's developmental needs, or as a means for effecting change in society by educating children to analyze problems and assume responsibilities. These philosophies of essentialism, progressivism, and reconstructionism are discussed in Chapter 2.

Concern about threats to democracy in the mid-1930s gave added emphasis to the continuing role of education in developing democratic values and citizenship skills. Extension of voting rights to women ended needs for differences in elementary education, although some secondary schools remained segregated by sex. Increasing social responsibility extended public education to handicapped learners. The Supreme Court decision on integration of schools in 1954 focused attention on the question of equality of educational opportunity. Controversy about integration of schools continues to the present. Curriculum planners have been challenged to provide programs, and forms of pupil organization, that promote intergroup understanding. Existentialism, also discussed in Chapter 2, developed during this time, but the impact of its focus on individual self-responsibility was not very evident in education until recently, as attention is being given to development of positive self-concepts and individual value clarification.

Since 1955 increasing attention has been given to suggestions for action-oriented education relevant to societal needs. Higher education is accepted as the right of all students, not just those in certain socioeconomic groups or intellectual levels. Mass media have put young learners in touch with more information at earlier ages. The increasing participation of women in the work force is one of the reasons for extension of early childhood and nursery programs. Another impetus has been the view that some formal learning experiences before the kindergarten level would provide compensatory education for children who might otherwise enter school with the disadvantage of limited preparation for academic skills.

Some current social conditions having an impact on the curriculum include ethnic-group inequalities, environmental crises, the women's liberation movement, and concern about drug abuse. Ethnic studies, the study of environmental problems, and the dangers of drug abuse are being implemented in elementary and middle school programs. Textbooks and teaching practices are being scrutinized for treatment of minorities and perpetuation of stereotyped male and female roles. Continuing concern for social change is manifested in many ways, including attention to career education. At the elementary level this involves the developing of children's awareness of the many possibilities available to them. The question of home versus school responsibility is highlighted in controversies over whether schools should provide sex education.

Most recently, critics such as Silberman, Kozol, Holt, and others, concerned about development of individuals in impersonalized educational systems, have described the "joyless" atmosphere of schools in which standardized curricula and instructional practices seem inconsistent with informed views of education today. Others such as Illich have gone further and questioned whether the institution of schooling itself is a valid setting for learning in the emerging future.

Over the past three hundred years, increasing democracy and diversity in American society have led to acceptance of public elementary and secondary education and, in many areas, higher education for every child. Increasing social concern has led to views that education can be a means for social change and a means of preparation for the future, although there is much divergence in defining what changes are desirable or how schools may effect them. Educators today are challenged to continuously evaluate and modify goals and priorities of education and the curriculum by which schools implement these goals.

Psychological and Discipline Foundations

In colonial times, religion provided a framework for educational theory. The view of children relevant to education was that they were born sinful and were saved or civilized through education; that is, by learning to read the Bible and liturgy. Childhood was seen as a preparation for adult life.

Knowledge of mathematics was limited. Children who learned computational skills did so by rote memorization. Learning was seen as a matter of observing, imitating, or memorizing.

In the early years of the new nation, ideas of Rousseau, Pestalozzi, Froebel, and Herbart about the unique nature of childhood and about learning processes began to receive some attention. The theory of faculty psychology—the notion that the brain consists of specific skills or faculties, each of which could be developed through the study of specific subjects—developed. It was also believed that study of a difficult subject, such as Latin, had the transfer value of "strengthening" thinking ability in general. Language learning was extended to include spelling, grammar, speech, and handwriting. Science was in its infancy and was represented in the curriculum as nature study, primarily a matter of observation and classification. World geography, U.S. government, and U.S. history were based on the limited descriptive level of social science at that time. Later in the nineteenth century, educators began to examine methods of

teaching. The first normal schools were established, providing high school grad-
uates with some pedagogical techniques. Teaching developed into a profession; the
forerunner of the National Education Association (NEA) was organized in 1857.

From 1870 to 1920 the development of all fields of knowledge accelerated.
As the ideas of European educators began to have more impact through the
study and efforts of Horace Mann, Henry Barnard, and others, study of the
child and the learning process was given impetus. As the field of psychology
emerged and rapidly advanced, study of learning was made with the now very
diverse student population, and this study led to the proposals of Dewey,
Kilpatrick, Montessori, and others. Education was recognized as a field of
knowledge with the first university chair in education in 1879. Specialized professional teacher organizations were formed, and teacher education was extended
to the college level. Appreciation of developmental needs of children impelled
the establishment of kindergartens in some city school systems in the 1870s,
the beginning of a movement for increased attention to early childhood education that has continued for the past hundred years.

In the last half of the nineteenth century the development of academic
disciplines also accelerated. Physics, biology, and chemistry developed as distinct
fields of knowledge, and each of these in turn fostered branches of knowledge
that expanded into new disciplines. History evolved from chronicling to analysis
of human behavior over periods of time. Political science, sociology, anthropology, and economics developed as separate disciplines. From 1870 to 1920 school
programs reflected these developments by the addition of new subjects or updating of content. Drawing, vocal music, and manual training were also introduced as these began to be recognized as useful in children's total development.
Education was no longer limited to intellectual development or knowledge
acquisition.

From 1920 to 1955 child study and the ideas of Dewey particularly influenced refinement of educational procedures. Childhood was recognized as a
period distinct from later development, with concerns, interests, and developmental needs not necessarily related to preparation for adult life. These interests
and needs were to be met through appropriate learning experiences. This led to
a search for content relevant to children's needs, to the development of the
"project method" of Kilpatrick, and to the unit plan, in which topics of interest
to children became the center of organization of learning experiences. Dewey
stressed development of each child's thinking abilities through use of the "scientific method," or problem-solving sequence, as a model for the child's acquisition of knowledge. Another trend was to identify children as "slow," "average,"
or "gifted" in academic learning and to provide three differing programs, on
the assumption that these were immutable differences and determined the occupational options available to each group.

Ideas about the learning process led from correlation of some related subject matter in the late nineteenth century to fusion of related subjects after 1920, such as general science, social studies, and language arts. In some programs, all subject areas were related through a core curriculum. Often this meant topics based on children's interests, such as the circus, the supermarket, or the harbor, with language, mathematics, and science learnings developed in terms of application to study of the core topic. A greater variety of learning experiences were utilized, many of which involved children in constructing, measuring, drawing, dramatizing, or participating in field trips. Emphasis on these participatory experiences was referred to as the "activity movement," although definitions of "activity" varied. Drill and rote memorization persisted, but they were given less emphasis.

After 1955 academic scholars began to participate directly in curriculum development, narrowing the gap that had developed between the state of knowledge in the disciplines (linguistics, mathematics, science, the social sciences) and the elementary and secondary curriculum. These scholars provided guidelines for substantive and methodological structures of each discipline as frameworks for curriculum content. Examples are discussed in Chapter 3. Curriculum projects developed by groups of educators and academic scholars became available to schools.

Recent psychological influences on curriculum have included the idea that early learning is crucial because most of the factors that affect a child's complete intellectual development are determined by the time he is four. This has added impetus to development of programs for three- and four-year-olds that vary from undirected play experiences, to informal learning and manipulation of varied learning materials, to formal and prescribed learning experiences. The work of Piaget is having impact on selection and grade placement of learning experiences from early childhood through middle school years. Attention is being given to the development of self-concept as an essential factor in effective learning. Significant current views of child development and learning are discussed in Chapter 3.

Over the past three hundred years, changes in academic disciplines and increased knowledge of child development and learning processes have brought American elementary education from a limited emphasis on rote learning of reading and computing for a few children to a broad and varied curriculum, developed through a variety of learning experiences, for all children.

Goals of Education

Goals of American education have always been derived from philosophical, social, psychological, and academic foundations. During the colonial period, the goal of literacy was an outgrowth of religious views. In the early nineteenth century, this was augmented by the goals of development of good moral character and good citizenship for eligible males. The theory of faculty psychology was a foundation for the goal of development of reasoning abilities. Occupational skills could be considered a goal for some, but this was limited to the ministry, law, medicine, and some mercantile occupations. Craft skills were developed through apprenticeship, not under school auspices.

From 1870 to 1920 increased immigration and diversity of population led to emphasis on "Americanization" of children as a major goal. Education for citizenship became increasingly important as suffrage was extended to all citizens. Increasing social concern and advances in knowledge about child development led to expansion of the scope of school responsibilities, as expressed in the 1918 statement of the Cardinal Principles of Education: good health, mastery of fundamental processes, worthy home membership, vocational skills, citizenship, worthy use of leisure time, and development of ethical character. The second, fifth, and last goals, long established in American education, were augmented by newer goals that took into account the varied and extensive personal and social needs of the diverse school population.

Twenty years later another statement of major educational goals reflected further social and philosophical changes, as well as developments in child study and learning. The seven Cardinal Principles were still viewed as valid, but they were reorganized in a way that emphasized new priorities. The goal of self-realization subsumed those of health, ethical character, and mastery of fundamental processes, all of which were viewed as inseparable aspects of a child's total development. Worthy home membership was extended to the goal of effective human relations, reflecting social concerns in an interdependent world on the verge of global war. The goal of vocational skills was subsumed under economic efficiency, which also included consumer education, a goal receiving increasing attention today. The goal of civic responsibility extended the goal of citizenship to include concerns for conservation, social action, and world citizenship, goals that have been reemphasized in the 1970s.

After 1955 Bloom, Harrow, Krathwohl, and others defined taxonomies or levels of cognitive, affective, and psychomotor goals, providing guidelines for clear definitions of thinking skills, physical skills and development, and value development. Accelerating changes opened up the "space age," and priorities of educational goals were revised to give more attention to knowledge and learning skills needed for the changing technological world of the present and future. One reflection of this was a reaction to the broad scope of responsibilities accepted by schools in the first half of the twentieth century, expressed in the 1961 NEA statement that the central purpose of education, as distinguished from other institutions, was development of thinking ability. A detailed discussion of current goals of education and behavioral definitions of specific objectives is found in Chapter 4.

Although there is much divergence of opinion today, there is no question that American schools have moved from goals related to limited academic needs to today's comprehensive programs designed to implement a broad range of personal, social, ethical, and intellectual goals.

Organization of the Curriculum

During the colonial and early national periods, greatest emphasis was given to the teaching of reading and computing. Dame school teachers used the hornbook as their initial reading curriculum. The mathematics curriculum was an assemblage of number facts and computational processes to be memorized. As nineteenth century school systems were organized, principals or superintendents determined curriculum by providing subjects that implemented contemporary goals and selecting textbooks which, in effect, determined curriculum content and sequence.

From 1870 to 1920 new subjects were introduced as academic disciplines developed, knowledge about learning and children's needs advanced, and various interest groups suggested curriculum directions. Near the end of this period, "social utility" became an important criterion. Surveys were made of adult activities to determine which language and mathematical skills were actually utilized in personal or work activities and therefore should be developed in the curriculum.

After 1920 Dewey's influence and the idea that learning must begin with life-related, direct experiences before moving to more abstract levels led to more active participation by pupils and less reliance on textbooks as the total curriculum. Every classroom teacher was now a curriculum planner, because curriculum decisions had to be made to meet the differing needs of each particular class or group. Separate subjects gave way to core topics, usually from science or social studies areas, with language and mathematics skills developed in relation to study of the core topic. "Progressive" education was not universal and varied in practice, but in theory it reflected much of the best thinking in education during this time.

After 1955 reactions to this approach suggested that learning had become too incidental; much content was omitted or lacked logical sequence. Participation of academic scholars tended to move curriculum into subject areas again, although active participation of learners and direct experiences were still seen as appropriate learning strategies. Less emphasis was given to "interests" or "problems" as primary determinants of content. Federally funded curriculum projects gave much attention to revision of programs in mathematics, science, and social studies. However, many school systems continue to place heavy emphasis on reading and mathematics in the elementary grades, sometimes devoting the entire morning schedule to these two areas.

Another trend with important curricular implications is the open education or "integrated day" approach. These terms apply to programs, largely based on recent British infant school models, in which effort is made to provide learning experiences that relate several curriculum areas. No time is allotted for separate subjects. The teacher must devise a separate curriculum, sometimes on a day-to-day basis, for each child, in the context of a program which provides each child with alternative choices of activities at various times. Proponents of this approach point out that each child learns best when enabled to learn at the pace, and in a sequence, that meets his unique needs. Critics suggest that children can become sidetracked in activities that lack educational value and that some essential content or skills may be neglected as the teacher strives to plan, guide, evaluate, and record the progress of thirty pupils following thirty different programs.

Increased attendance of three- and four-year-olds in day-care or nursery programs raises important questions. To what extent should planned learning activities be provided for these age groups? How should these "preschool" experiences be related to elementary education? What changes should be made in kindergarten or early grade programs for children with "preschool" experience? More and more school systems now plan curriculum content in a nursery through high school sequence.

Another recent development is bilingual-bicultural education. Children usually of Hispanic-American, Chinese-American, or Haitian-American backgrounds are enrolled, in some school systems, in programs that provide a curriculum related to their dual cultural heritage. Content includes study of their ethnic history, culture, and countries of origin. Language objectives include development of proficiency in both English and their home language. Children dominant in the home language are initially taught all subjects in that language, with time provided for instruction in English as a second language. As oral skill develops, reading in English is introduced, and some instruction is carried out in this language as well, until a goal of 50 percent of instruction in each language is reached. Attempts were made in the 1950s to introduce foreign languages in the elementary school, but this movement never achieved high priority. However, if bilingual-bicultural education proves viable and is extended, schools may be in a position to offer a second language to English-dominant children.

Table 1-1 offers an outline view of the scope of the elementary curriculum at various periods and the sequence of changes in each particular area from colonial times to the present. Chapter 5 discusses current trends in curriculum organization, and Chapters 9 through 17 elaborate curriculum development in each subject area.

During the past three hundred years, the curriculum of the elementary school has expanded from reading and mathematics to a broad spectrum of interrelated subjects. Curriculum has often been determined by textbook content. Even today, curriculum in a subject area may be determined by a packaged program produced commercially or by a committee of educators and academic scholars.

However, as more attention is given to individualizing education, each classroom teacher is becoming more responsible for curriculum decisions, which also involves skill in evaluating and adapting the great variety of instructional materials and programs available.

Organization of the Learning Environment

The Temporal-Physical Environment During the colonial period reading instruction was often conducted in the home of the instructor. The first common schools were usually bare rooms in town halls or rectories or small one-room buildings where children of many ages learned reading or mathematics at different levels, seated on long benches, sometimes without benefit of desks.

As schooling became more systematic and widespread during the early national period, small schoolbuildings were erected with desks and seats, and a new invention, the chalkboard, was sometimes installed. The school calendar in an agrarian nation began after fall harvest and ended in time for summer farm activity. In recent years suggestions have been made for year-round schooling, but few school systems have done this at the elementary level.

After the middle of the nineteenth century, the increasing school population in urban centers necessitated development of a large building with many classrooms to house pupils who were now organized by age into grade levels. Such buildings were able to include specialized facilities such as large open halls on the ground floor for physical exercises and auditoriums for school assemblies. Late nineteenth-century classrooms had individual or paired desk-seat combinations designed to the contours of different age groups and bolted to the floor in rows, focusing pupils' attention on the teacher's desk at the front. This arrangement often supported the practice of seating the brightest or best-behaved students in the front of each row, although the honor was sometimes extended to the short and nearsighted.

After 1920 architects broke away from reproduction of earlier buildings to design on the basis of the functions of a building and the characteristics inherent in twentieth-century building materials and techniques. The imitation Gothic, Tudor, and Renaissance palaces that served as schools were gradually replaced with buildings that reflected changes in teaching strategies. Larger rooms were provided for activities in early grades. Formal assembly halls gave way to multipurpose rooms with cafeteria facilities, and library rooms were included. Furniture was movable; teachers could set up any variety of arrangements and could move around the room instead of lecturing from the front.

Schoolbuildings constructed today are usually one or two stories to allow for pupil mobility. Libraries have been enlarged to serve as educational media centers with spaces for study carrels and multimedia equipment accessible to

Table 1-1 Scope of the Elementary Curriculum

	Reading	Language arts	Mathematics	Science
Colonial period	Most important subject, taught with a phonic approach	Some study of grammar and elocution for a few advanced pupils	"Ciphering"—learning number facts and basic operations; optional	None
Early national period 1780–1870	Continued emphasis on reading, taught with New England Primer, a standard method for all pupils	Grammar, spelling, elocution, and handwriting for all elementary pupils, taught as separate subjects	Computing skills taught to all pupils; math skills for practical applications and mental discipline	None at first; some nature study by mid-century, often for younger pupils
1870–1920	Continued emphasis on reading, still mainly phonic approach; introduction of reading materials related to children's interests	Language skills still taught as separate subjects, but with some attempts at correlation	Continued emphasis on drill and memorization	Nature study; observation and classification
1920–1955	Introduction of reading readiness programs and visual aids; use of sight word approach in instruction; use of basal readers	Language skills taught as interrelated language arts; attention to social and occupational uses of language	Emphasis on practical applications of mathematics; introduction of visual aids; word problems used	Broad range of topics, often based on pupils' interests; use of models; plants and pets in the classroom
1955–Present	Variety of teaching strategies used; refinement of diagnostic techniques to determine pupils' particular problems in learning to read; multimedia programs produced commercially, less use of textbooks; some use of linguistically based approaches to instruction	Influence of linguistics on approaches to grammar and spelling; language arts related more closely to early reading instruction; introduction of bilingual instruction and teaching of English as a second language	Mathematics taught for meaning; curriculum based on structure of mathematics and logical learning sequences, rather than social utility; use of visual and manipulative materials	Topics based on structure of sciences; emphasis on processes of inquiry instead of acquisition of facts; variety of curriculum projects available

Social studies	Vocational and career education	Physical and health education	Aesthetic education
Some reading of ancient and British history for advanced pupils	None	None	None
Study of forms of U.S. federal and state government; readings in U.S. history; some observational geography in early grades	Some instruction in commercial arithmetic, navigational geography, and other occupational skills; no trade education	None	None
Local geography in early grades, world geography in upper elementary grades; civics (local government) introduced; study of Indians and holidays in early grades; U.S. and European history in upper grades	Beginning of vocational training at secondary level; manual training for boys, "domestic science" for girls at elementary level	Beginning of physical training; primarily exercises, folk dancing, some games	Some drawing and vocal music introduced, largely teacher-demonstrated and directed; some art and music "appreciation" to inculcate tastes
Sequential social studies program, usually in "expanding horizons" sequence of family, community, state, nation, and western hemisphere; unit topics based on human activities rather than separate subjects	Manual skills, crafts, shopwork often part of core curriculum activities; social studies giving attention to "community workers"	More informal physical activities; less exercise, more attention to games; rhythm activities in early grades; some formal health education	Cooperative art projects and construction integrated in core curriculum; vocal and instrumental music as separate subjects and core experiences
Curriculum organized around generalizations and concepts from the social sciences; attention to processes of inquiry; focus on value clarification, environment, cultural pluralism, and study of all areas of the world	Some manual activities for boys and girls; study of tasks involved in a variety of occupations to develop awareness of career possibilities	Little time allotted for physical education in total program; recent attention to movement education as physical expression and part of total development; attention to drug abuse education and sex education	More attention to development of individual creativity; greater variety of visual art media employed by pupils; simple composing in music activities; encouragement for creative expression not dependent on "talent"

children. Some schools provide large open spaces shared by several learning groups in place of separate, enclosed classrooms.

Organization for Instruction In the colonial period and early nineteenth century, school population was limited, and each community's school was small. One teacher usually was responsible for instruction of all the children, so learners of different ages would be found in the same schoolroom. Older children sometimes tutored younger ones. Public school systems that developed in the mid-nineteenth century provided education for children from the ages of six or seven to twelve or thirteen. As school populations increased, children were grouped by age level. In schools with semiannual promotions the age range was six months. Grade designations from first through eighth were applied. The curriculum in any class was the same for all pupils. The size of a class, usually forty or more pupils, was determined by the teacher-pupil ratio a school system could afford.

Later in the nineteenth century, public secondary education was established. Eventually, educators identified special learning needs and developmental characteristics that distinguished children of twelve to fifteen from those in younger and older groups, and developed the junior high school as a transition for grades 7 through 9. More and more school systems adopted this organization during the first half of the twentieth century. More recently, educators have reexamined the needs and characteristics of children in today's society and have redefined children from ten to fourteen as "transcesents." The junior high school, modeled on the senior high, is being questioned as an appropriate setting for this age group. Instead, some school systems are moving to an organization of a primary school for kindergarten through fourth or fifth grade, a middle or intermediate school for fifth or sixth through eighth grade, and a four-year senior high school, as a more appropriate vertical organization for age groups with distinctive needs. There is little consensus, however, on the organization of pupils within the middle school. Some schools have departmentalized programs and sometimes group pupils into achievement levels within each grade. Others utilize multisubject cores with teams of teachers responsible for large groups or several classes. Still others follow the elementary school model of the self-contained classroom. The middle school movement is posing a challenge to curriculum planners to identify learning needs of this newly defined age group and to articulate programs with those of the primary and senior high schools.

During the first half of the twentieth century, various forms of organization were explored in an attempt to meet learning differences. Homogeneous grouping separated classes on the same grade level according to pupils' reading levels, although this had little effect on reducing any other intraclass differences. Continuous progress, or the nongraded plan, provided a setting in which each pupil could progress through sequential learning experiences at his own rate, without having to conform to a schedule of annual grade promotions.

Since 1955 other approaches to grouping have been proposed and evaluated. The dual progress plan suggested graded or ability grouping for reading and mathematics, with heterogeneous, ungraded grouping in other subject areas. Multigrade grouping, reminiscent of the one-room schoolhouse, places children of three or four grades or ages in one class. Team teaching, which can be utilized in a variety of organizational forms, usually involves a small group of teachers, each with special skill in one or more subjects, who are jointly responsible for planning and carrying out instruction for several classes or an entire grade. In schools with self-contained classrooms, special teachers of music, science, or other subjects may work with pupils during various scheduled periods. In all these forms of organization, curriculum development becomes the responsibility of a group of teachers working together to plan and evaluate children's experiences.

Much attention is being given to open education plans, which range from individualized learning in a self-contained classroom, to "open corridor" plans in which pupils in adjacent classrooms engage in multigrade activities in the corridor or any of the participating rooms, to "open school" plans with no interior walls, permitting pupils to move to different areas for different activities. Another important trend is to view the entire community as a learning environment. In the elementary grades, community resources are usually utilized through teacher-directed study trips or classroom interviews of resource people. At the secondary level, some schools have developed plans in which students engage in learning experiences in museums, social agencies, and commercial institutions, sometimes without direct teacher supervision. Similar experiences at the middle school or junior high level tend to involve whole-class projects with teacher supervision.

The past three hundred years have seen schoolbuildings evolve from small and limited environments to large, specialized, multiequipped settings. Pupils in early schools often received individualized instruction in multiage groups. As school populations increased and grades were organized, pupils either followed the same curriculum or were tracked into programs for different ability levels. The influence of Dewey and of "progressive" educators set in motion efforts to individualize instruction that have continued to the present. Open education plans at the elementary level and alternative school plans at the secondary level are recent movements in this direction. Chapter 6 discusses in detail the curricular implications of current forms of organization of the learning environment.

Instructional Media

Colonial children learned to read with the aid of hornbooks, which were single sheets of paper inscribed with the alphabet, some consonant-vowel combinations, and the Lord's Prayer, attached to a wooden paddle and protected with a covering sheet of transparent horn. When individual slates were available, letters and words could be written as each pupil progressed. With increasing population and establishment of more schools in the late eighteenth and early nineteenth century, a market was available for textbooks. The famous *New England Primer* with its religious verses was the ubiquitous instructional tool of elementary education until well into the nineteenth century. During the early national period, as new subjects were introduced, textbooks were produced which presented content in an expository manner. Noah Webster's "blue-backed speller" was widely used, and readings in American history and government were provided. Periodically revised maps of the new nation's expanding territory were studied, along with descriptive geography texts.

Later in the nineteenth century, textbook writers utilized the catechism approach to motivate learning; that is, texts were written in the form of a series of questions and answers. Learning involved memorizing the answers. Computing was originally taught without books, but later textbooks were introduced to standardize the curriculum—an early attempt at "teacher-proof" materials. Indeed, although teacher education remained limited to little more than mastery of the content to be taught, textbooks provided both the curriculum and the instructional procedures of eighteenth- and nineteenth-century schools.

After 1870 a greater variety of instructional materials were produced as educators recognized a need for visual aids in teaching a diverse pupil population. Globes and scientific models were introduced. Pestalozzi had earlier recommended the use of real objects to facilitate learning. Drawings, and later photographs, were added to textbooks.

Technological developments led, after World War I, to production of records, slides, and films for school use. Recognition of the importance of children's interests led to increase in production of children's literature and nonfiction trade books. In recent years, a tremendous volume of audio-visual material has been developed, augmented by tapes of television programs. Educational television is utilized in many schools. Study carrels are equipped with "talking typewriters" and other responsive computer-based media. Games are produced in many subject areas. Many are board games with directions for moves, but some are played on computer terminals or through role playing and involve open-ended or varied alternatives. Textbook publishers are moving to multimedia packages that include a variety of audio-visual materials that supplement or replace a conventional textbook. Implementation of activities based on the theories of Piaget or the programs of Montessori necessitates a variety of real and manipulative materials. Open education programs depend upon availability of a quantity of instructional materials handled directly by the learner with little or no teacher intervention.

In addition to the wealth of commercial materials, learning experiences today include pupil preparation of charts, games, models, tape recordings, films, and videotapes of their own, as means of recording, organizing, and extending their observations of their environment or their learning in various areas. This necessitates development of pupils' skills in use of media as part of the elementary curriculum. Chapter 6 discusses utilization of instructional media in curriculum development.

Teaching Strategies

Colonial children learned to read by learning the names of the letters and then their sounds, putting letter sounds together to sound out syllables, and finally sounding out words. Irregular constructions had to be memorized. Arithmetic computations were demonstrated by the teacher and practiced by pupils. Number facts were memorized through repetitive drill.

Influence of the work of Pestalozzi was a factor in establishment of early teacher-training schools. The first normal school opened in 1826, eleven years before the first state board of education, that of Massachusetts, was established. Although the number of normal schools increased, such training was not universally required, and many teachers had no education beyond some mastery of the subjects they taught. In the early nineteenth century a British educator, Lancaster, proposed the monitorial system adopted by some American schools. This system involved hundreds of boys assembled in a large hall under the surveillance of one teacher. Most of the instruction was carried out by pupils who were the monitors for each row. This system was, of course, very economical and was used as an argument for the establishment of public education.

However, once public education was well under way in the mid-nineteenth century, increasing numbers of educational leaders studied the theories of Comenius, Pestalozzi, Herbart, and Froebel. Through normal school training, now more widely required, and through publications or school superintendents' directives, teachers were introduced to a greater variety of instructional strategies.

The development of psychology and child study after 1870 and the concurrent increase and diversity in school population led to an acceleration of efforts to develop more effective teaching/learning strategies and more suitable forms of vertical and horizontal grouping. Herbart had earlier urged more emphasis on *understanding* meaning, rather than rote memorization. Dewey, Montessori, and others offered ideas on child-centered, rather than subject-centered, approaches to teaching. From the end of World War I to the mid-1950s, the progressive movement influenced use of more active participation of pupils in the learning process and more direct, firsthand experiences for learners. Sometimes, of course, this approach was poorly understood and led to activity for its own sake, with a resultant loss of attention to the quality of children's learning. A greater variety of instructional media added variety to instructional techniques. Patterns of unit teaching necessitated more curriculum responsibility for each teacher, with less reliance on textbooks as sources of curriculum. In-service education was increasingly utilized to acquaint teachers with new materials or methods. A baccalaureate degree was increasingly required for teacher certification, and after mid-century some states began to require graduate work for permanent certification. Since 1955, educators have developed refined techniques for analysis of teacher-pupil interaction as a means for assessment and improvement of teaching skills. Videotaping of classroom activities has provided a tool for self-analysis of teaching style.

Over the past three hundred years teaching has developed from a limited range of expository techniques to a broad repertoire of strategies, many of which involve the teacher in providing materials and situations for learning, doing less "telling" while guiding children to work out their own conclusions. Teaching strategies are described in detail in Chapter 7.

Evaluation and Accountability

In a sense evaluation of pupil progress in colonial times was performance-based; if a child could not sound out a letter or syllable, more instructional effort was applied. During the early national period, written tests and oral examinations revealed what pupils had memorized. Spelling bees were used for evaluation as well as entertainment. In dame schools and grammar schools, accountability was a direct matter between teacher and parent. If the parent was dissatisfied, the pupil could be removed to another school or tutor.

As public school systems developed in the nineteenth century, teachers were hired and periodically evaluated by school administrators on the basis of classroom control, pupil progress, and any other tasks considered part of the teacher's role. School superintendents generally made annual reports to their boards which included some references to pupil progress. Written tests of memorized facts continued to be a major tool for evaluation. School systems set specific criteria for promotion to the next grade level. To some extent, pupils were considered accountable for their own learning; those who were unable to learn dropped out of school. In general, nineteenth-century parents, often having little education themselves, tended to view education as a means of economic improvement for their children. Immigrant parents saw the "Americanization" process of schooling as a means toward social acceptance as well. Schools were viewed as being capable of providing these opportunities through curricula and methods rarely questioned by parents. The burden was on the child to take advantage of what was offered.

From 1870 to 1920 techniques of "scientific" measurement were developed. School surveys provided a means of making school boards or administrators accountable to taxpayers. As standardized achievement tests were developed, these too provided a means for comparison of pupil progress from school to school or system to system. In the early twentieth century intelligence tests were developed. Sometimes results were used to track children into different programs for "slow," "average," or "bright" learners.

From 1920 to 1955 changes in teaching strategies necessitated greater variation in evaluation techniques. Observation of children's actions, collections of
children's work, and checklists of social behavior or study skills supplemented
paper-and-pencil tests. Evaluation criteria also had to be developed to enable
educators to assess the increasing variety of textbooks and other instructional
media being produced.

Since 1955 use of intelligence tests has been questioned. Some studies have
demonstrated that changes in environment or instruction produce increases in
children's scores, leading to challenges to the assumption that "intelligence" is
an inherent and unchangeable characteristic. Various minority groups have also
challenged intelligence tests, pointing out that many questions relate to a cultural
context familiar to middle-class white children but unfamiliar to those whose
frame of reference is a rural or minority-group ethnic culture. Changing goals
necessitate new evaluation techniques. For example, attention to development
of the child's independence as learner calls for self-evaluation and joint teacher-
pupil assessment through conferences. In addition, standardized tests are being
questioned as inadequate indications of individual pupil achievement. Criterion-
reference tests, which do not involve grade-level norms, are being suggested as
more suitable alternatives.

Parents educated in more traditional settings sometimes have questioned
the purposes or effectiveness of educational innovations after 1920. Taxpayers
have questioned increasing costs of equipment, teacher salaries, or new building
needs. More recently, members of minority groups have questioned whether
schools described as "middle-class oriented" have been effective learning environments for all children. There are demands that teachers be directly accountable
to the community for pupil achievement. The move for accountability has led
to some use of performance contracts, in which a group of teachers or, more
often, a commercial manufacturer of instructional media, contracts with a school
system to raise the achievement of a designated percentage of pupils to a predetermined level within a specified amount of time to receive payment. One
criticism of performance contracting has been that children may be taught to
pass certain tests which are taken to represent achievement, but in effect no
real or worthwhile learning may be accomplished. Another approach to accountability is the voucher plan, in which parents are given a voucher for each school-
age child amounting to the per pupil sum expended by the local school system.
The voucher can be presented to any public school in the system and sometimes
to a private school. Thus, as in the colonial period, parents may withdraw a
child from a school that is not meeting their expectations and place him elsewhere. Proponents claim this open-market system would stimulate instructional
improvement, but opponents suggest it would weaken public school systems by
depriving them of funds and could lead to establishment of segregated private
schools. Both performance contracting and the voucher plan raise questions

about priorities of educational goals, about who should be responsible for determining such goals, and whether stress on accountability fosters emphasis on limited but easily evaluated cognitive objectives.

Over the past three hundred years evaluation techniques have increased in variety to keep pace with development of diverse teaching strategies. Computer scoring has made possible comparative achievement testing on a nationwide basis. As the educational level and taxpaying burden of the population have increased, and as curriculum and teaching strategies have undergone extensive changes from one generation to the next, there has been an increasing demand that school personnel be accountable to their supporting communities for pupil achievement. In some school systems, cooperative efforts are under way to develop criteria and procedures for constructive evaluation of instruction. Procedures of evaluation and accountability are discussed in Chapter 8.

FOLLOW-UP ACTIVITIES AND PROJECTS

1 Make a comparative analysis of the model for curriculum development presented in this chapter and the ones included in the references below by Saylor and Alexander and by Taba. Or you may select two other models. Note similarities and differences and any special items of emphasis that you think should be included in a model. Finally, make a short outline of components that represent your view of what should be included in a model for curriculum development.

2 Examine curriculum bulletins of your local school system to identify major goals, statements of specific objectives, outlines of curriculum content and organization, and provisions for evaluation. In what ways do each of these components reflect the historical development of curriculum as outlined in this chapter? Identify historical antecedents or current influences that you believe have had a role in determining each of these components in the local elementary curriculum.

3 Examine your own classroom practices, or those you observe in an elementary classroom for a week or two, and identify ways in which these practices reflect historical or current trends. For example, how is classroom space utilized? How are pupils grouped? What kinds of instructional media are really utilized? What teaching strategies are employed? What subjects or types of learning activities are given greatest attention or allotted the greatest amount of time? What learning outcomes are evaluated, and what evaluation techniques are employed?

4 Obtain copies (in the local school district professional library) of local curriculum bulletins of the late nineteenth century, the 1920s or 1930s, and the present. Compare goals, curriculum content and sequence, and evaluation techniques. What changes have occurred? How do each of the curriculum outlines compare with trends or practices typical of American education at each time? Or you may obtain copies of an elementary textbook published before 1940 and one in the same subject published recently. Compare content, sequence of

topics, format of the books, and suggestions for teaching. What is the same? Why is this unchanged? What is different, and what accounts for the changes? What other instructional media are available to supplement or replace textbooks in this subject?

5 Visit schoolbuildings in your community. When were they constructed? In what ways have older buildings been modified to meet changing needs? In what ways do the newest buildings meet, or fail to meet, current educational practices? Compare the ambience you notice in three or four different buildings. What characteristics of each building contribute to its particular atmosphere? How does your own classroom, or one that you have observed, meet educational needs you consider important? What modifications would you make to enhance the effectiveness or atmosphere of the room? Do pupils feel the room belongs to the class as a whole, or is it the domain of the teacher? What responsibilities do pupils have for classroom maintenance, decor, and seating or equipment arrangements?

BIBLIOGRAPHY

Cook, Ruth C., and Ronald C. Doll. *The Elementary School Curriculum.* Boston: Allyn and Bacon, 1973. Chapter on evolution of the elementary curriculum.

Good, Harry G., and James D. Teller. *A History of American Education.* New York: Macmillan, 1973. Trends in the development of American education.

Goodlad, John I., M. Frances Klein, and Jerrold M. Novotney. *Early Schooling in the United States.* New York: McGraw-Hill, 1973. Current theories and practice in early childhood schooling.

Goodlad, John L., and Harold G. Shane. (Eds.) *The Elementary School in the United States.* 72nd Yearbook, National Society for the Study of Education, Part II. Chicago: University of Chicago Press, 1973. Essays on history, status, and needed changes.

Gordon, Ira J. (Ed.) *Early Childhood Education.* 71st Yearbook, National Society for the Study of Education, Part II. Chicago: University of Chicago Press, 1972. Essays on history and current developments in early childhood education.

Hass, Glen, Joseph Bondi, and Jon Wiles. *Curriculum Planning: A New Approach.* Boston: Allyn and Bacon, 1974. Comprehensive treatment of various phases of curriculum development.

Henrie, Samuel N. (Ed.) *Sourcebook of Elementary Curricula Programs and Projects.* Washington: Government Printing Office, 1972. Review of programs in aesthetic education, affective education, career education, drug education, early childhood education, environmental education, ethnic studies, and all areas of the curriculum.

McClure, Robert M. (Ed.) *The Curriculum: Retrospect and Prospect.* 70th Yearbook, National Society for the Study of Education. Chicago: University of Chicago Press, 1971. Essays on the past, present, and future of curriculum development.

Overly, Donald R., Jon R. Kinghorn, and Richard L. Preston. *The Middle School: Humanizing Education for Youth.* Worthington, Ohio: Charles A. Jones Publishing Co., 1972. Overall treatment of the middle school.

Ragan, William, and Gene D. Shepherd. *Modern Elementary Curriculum.* New York: Holt, 1971. Chapter on historical influences.

Saylor, J. Galen, and William M. Alexander. *Planning Curriculum for Schools.* New York: Holt, 1974. Chapter on theories of curriculum planning.

Spodek, Bernard. *Teaching in the Early Years.* Englewood Cliffs, N.J.: Prentice-Hall, 1972. Treatment of all phases of early childhood education.

Squire, James R. (Ed.) *A New Look at Progressive Education.* Yearbook of the Association for Supervision and Curriculum Development. Washington: Association for Supervision and Curriculum Development, 1972. Essays on the continuity and relationships of major progressive education ideas with current and emerging educational theories and practices.

Taba, Hilda. *Curriculum Development: Theory and Practice.* New York: Harcourt Brace Jovanovich, 1962. Discussion of curriculum theory and guidelines for planning.

Chapter 2

Foundations of Curriculum Development: Philosophical and Social

The foundations of curriculum development are rooted in five broad areas of study. History of education provides a backdrop on past developments, highlights of which are needed to understand certain features of the elementary curriculum today as illustrated in the preceding chapter. Philosophy of education provides points of view and systematic procedures for use in clarifying issues and problems and making decisions at many points in curriculum planning. The social foundations provide information on societal values, changes, problems, and conditions that are requisite in program planning. The psychological foundations provide guidelines related to child growth, development, and learning. The disciplinary foundations provide data, concepts, and generalizations, along with modes, techniques, and processes of inquiry for use in areas of the curriculum.

An understanding of the foundations of the curriculum is helpful in several ways. First of all, it helps directly in the planning of curriculum and instruction as the program is attuned to philosophical viewpoints, psychological principles, social requisites, and material drawn from the disciplines. Second, insight into the foundations helps teachers understand how various forces and factors touch the lives of children and their parents. Better guidance can be provided and interpretation and accountability to parents and other laymen can be improved. Third, a grasp of the foundations helps teachers and other school personnel to put problems and issues in perspective and to devise changes and improvements that are consistent with basic values and other factors illuminated by historical, philosophical, psychological, social, and disciplinary studies. Finally, direct contributions are made to one's working philosophy of education, an outcome that has innumerable practical as well as theoretical applications in curriculum development.

Three approaches are usually followed in clarifying the foundations of curriculum development. One is the direct use of studies and reports prepared by experts in the various foundations or by curriculum specialists. A second is the use of consultants to curriculum committees who indicate ways in which a program can be improved by considering the foundations. A third approach is an informal one in which issues and problems as they arise in the process of curriculum planning are used in going to the foundations to search for bases for decision making. It is the authors' view that all three should be used. Their use will be improved by keeping in mind various fundamental considerations in each of the foundations, to which we now turn. Philosophical and social foundations are considered in this chapter, followed by psychological and disciplinary foundations in Chapter 3.

PHILOSOPHICAL FOUNDATIONS

All of us involved in curriculum development have a philosophy of education even though we may not have engaged in formal study of philosophy. Our philosophy becomes evident to an astute observer as we make comments and decisions related to goals and means of education, the nature of children and childhood, and other basic considerations such as the content of greatest value in curriculum development. This is so because our philosophy serves as a general framework for decision making.

This section is designed to summarize viewpoints on selected topics, to present current directions as we see them, to aid readers in clarifying their own beliefs, and to illustrate a procedure for considering the philosophical foundations of the curriculum.

There are several approaches to [the] clarification of one's philosophy of education in general and the philosophy of curriculum development and instructional planning in particular. One approach is the direct study of different schools of educational philosophy. Another is the analysis of issues and problems followed by the formulation of beliefs or viewpoints related to them. A third, which the authors have found to be helpful, is the consideration of highlights of the positions of individuals in various schools of educational philosophy on a few topics of interest in curriculum development. This approach is followed by a short review of emerging viewpoints as we see them and follow-up analysis and discussion in which participants state and explain their own views.

This approach to the clarification of philosophical viewpoints can be illustrated by considering five different views of the goals of education: knowledge and subjects of greatest worth, means and methods of education, and decision making in education. Perennialism with its emphasis on the cultivation of reason and essentialism with its emphasis on accumulation of knowledge as preparation for life have been selected because they represent conservative and traditional philosophies. Progressivism with its emphasis on learning by doing and reconstructionism with its emphasis on improving society have been selected because they represent reactions to traditional viewpoints. Existentialism has been selected because of its emphasis on individual decision making and responsibility, even though many existentialists believe that children are too immature to benefit greatly from the application of their views.

Our approach is intended to serve as a practical springboard to clarification of one's beliefs related to topics of importance in curriculum development and to further study of schools of educational philosophy. Readers are urged to check their own views against those abstracted from different schools and those presented as current trends, to note agreements and disagreements, and to note changes that should be made to represent their position. Remaining sections of this chapter and subsequent chapters contain viewpoints on critical issues and problems which should be checked in the same manner. The outcome should be a more useful and explicit formulation of a working philosophy of education for curriculum development and instructional planning, along with the ability to use and to improve a procedure for the clarification of philosophical positions.

Goals of Education

Major philosophical issues related to goals of education hinge upon views of ultimate outcomes of education and the degree on certain ones. The range of positions on ultimate goals of education varies from educating children to use reason and to preserve great ideas, to the preparation of children for life and the equipping of children to reconstruct society. Individuals of most philosophical views agree that thinking ability, reading and other skills, and knowledge are important, but they differ on ultimate ends to be served by education. For example, many perennialists stress development of reason and preservation of great ideas; essentialists stress preparation for life, whereas progressives emphasize learning to deal with the ever-changing environment; reconstructionists stress improvement of society, and existentialists hold for development of the realization on the part of children that they are responsible for their own lives.

Views of ultimate goals of education are also related to views of the educated person. Perennialists set as their model the individual who has mastered disciplines of knowledge and uses reason in all things. Essentialists believe that the educated person is one who has mastered basic subjects, is well prepared for life, and maintains cherished traditions. Progressives believe that the educated person is one who intelligently handles problems as they arise in the continuing effort to adapt and change the environment. Reconstructionists set as their ideal the individual who works to rebuild society through organized political action and persuasion. Existentialists take as their model the person who directs his own life by making choices and accepting responsibility for them.

As developed in more detail in Chapter 4, most current statements of goals of education include attention to thinking ability, development of each individual's potentialities, human relationships, civic and economic competence, and learning how to learn. Within the context of these broad goals one may find a mixture of the above philosophical views, with varying degrees of emphasis and at times wide deviation from a purist position. For example, reasoning ability is frequently mentioned as a major goal along with thinking ability; knowledge is stressed but more in the context of growing and changing knowledge than as immutable and unchanging truth; the cultural heritage is stressed along with learning to deal with the environment now and in the future; social problems and conditions and issues in need of social action are included, but the involvement of students in action programs to reconstruct society is not endorsed; and helping students to become responsible and to accept consequences for their actions may be noted, but not in as complete a context of freedom as some existentialists hold to be important.

Knowledge and Subjects of Greatest Worth

No school of educational philosophy places low value on knowledge, but there are great differences in viewpoints on the kinds and uses of knowledge and the value of various areas of knowledge. Many perennialists favor such subjects as mathematics, grammar, classics, history, science, literature, and languages because they are helpful in developing reasoning ability, and knowledge gleaned from them is one of the hallmarks of an educated person. Essentialists place high priority on basic education that emphasizes reading, arithmetic, language skills, civics, history, and content from other areas that prepare students for life. Progressives tend to select content from any area that will be useful in handling problems, topics, and issues that arise as children interact with their environment. Reconstructionists emphasize the selection and use of knowledge in relation to social problems and processes of social action and change. Existentialists place high premium on content that can be used in making diverse interpretations and developing insight into interpersonal relations and self-awareness.

A fairly consistent view of knowledge and the worth of various subjects may be noted in current programs. High premium is placed on the function of knowledge in human affairs, the increasing need for depth of education in the disciplines, the changing nature of society and knowledge, and the importance of both scientific and humanistic approaches to the extension of knowledge. There is an emphasis on ways in which man creates conceptions of reality, builds structures of knowledge about reality, and makes interpretations of experience. Knowledge is viewed as dynamic and changing, and high value is placed on invention, discovery, and restructuring of knowledge in new patterns. Openness to experience and logical consistency are brought together and focused on the use of concepts to build knowledge out of interpreted experience.

An aspect of social change that has been given great attention is scientific advancement—the explosion of knowledge—and its impact on human affairs. Scientific literacy is regarded as essential to an understanding of contemporary issues and problems. Economic, political, and social problems are intimately related to scientific and technological developments. And the scientific study of human problems—local, national, and international—is viewed as a critical need that must be given increasing emphasis.

At the same time, thoughtful consideration is given to other ways of knowing and studying, not only to the scientific. Insights, feelings, aspirations, and viewpoints expressed through humanistic studies and writings and through art and music are a part of a complete curriculum. The narrative of history and the changing and differing interpretations of events and processes provide understandings and appreciations that can be attained only in a complete curriculum, which includes material drawn from the humanities as well as the natural and social sciences.

The importance of *learning to live intelligently* in a rapidly changing world has been emphasized with a new look at what is most significant both for now and for the future. The search for the most significant learnings has led to the identification of durable ideas, durable in the sense of having lasting value in promoting continuing learning. A basic assumption is that the key concepts, themes, generalizations, models, and theories that form the structure of disciplines are the durable ideas that should be emphasized. And they should be emphasized in the context of how they are produced, how they have changed, and how they will continue to change. The goal is to enable students to develop the competencies needed to learn on their own in a self-directive manner. Significant knowledge for living in our times, therefore, consists in key concepts and generalizations supported by critically selected content and in a grasp of rational processes of inquiry that facilitate independent learning.

As to subjects of greatest worth, highest premium is placed by most educators and laymen on reading instruction. This high valuation is evident in the time, effort, and money expended, and in the many pre-service and in-service education activities devoted to reading along with the large membership in professional associations that focus on instruction in reading. Arithmetic is highly valued along with such language arts as oral and written expression and spelling. Science education has been given increased attention in recent years, and the social studies continue to be viewed as a part of general education for all students. Some individuals tend to give somewhat lower priority to art, music, and physical education, although health and fitness are universally desired and most educators and laymen support those who point out the values of these areas of curriculum. The general trend is to provide a balanced program, a complete curriculum, even though some individuals tend to place areas of study in an order of priority.

Means and Methods of Education

Viewpoints related to educational procedures may be viewed on a continuum ranging from strict discipline and rigorous training to guided discovery and freedom of choice on the part of students. Perennialists hold for strict discipline and the training of reasoning ability through arithmetic and other difficult subjects. Essentialists believe that well-organized and systematic instruction should be provided in basic subjects under the direction of subject-oriented teachers. Progressives emphasize the active involvement of students and place high premium on creative activities, meeting individual differences, and making the classroom a laboratory for democratic living. Reconstructionists want students to be actively involved in social-improvement activities under the guidance of teachers who provide direction and at the same time develop the ability of students to work together to solve problems. Existentialists want openness and freedom so that students can make choices and learn to take responsibility for their choices.

In new programs of instruction there is a clear tendency to stress teacher guidance and direction so that specified objectives can be attained. This is especially true of developmental programs in reading, other language arts, and in mathematics education. Provision is also made for creative and problem-solving activities in which students have a wide range of choices. Active involvement of students is recommended for psychological as well as philosophical reasons, and various teaching strategies are used to get involvement and to guide learning toward objectives. Many of the strategies for value clarification offer freedom and openness so that students can make choices and weigh consequences without intervention by the teacher. In some alternative or free schools and open schools high premium is placed in freedom of choice in the selection of learning activities.

Decision Making in Education

In spite of the reality of basic decision making in education, views vary greatly among individuals in different philosophical camps. The hard-core perennialist believes that decision making should be handled by those with the best education, which of course includes authorities or scholars in basic areas of knowledge. The essentialists tend to hold for decision making by competent community leaders as overall policy makers and professional educators with subject specialization as day-to-day decision makers who carry out basic policies. Progressives opt for cooperative approaches involving elected board members, teachers, parents, and administrators, and group decision making in the classroom through teacher-guided group planning, doing, and evaluating by children. Some reconstructionists want students to be involved actively in decision making related to reconstruction of the school, which is a microcosm of society in many ways. Existentialists tend to take the position that only students and teachers should make decisions because the relationships between students and their teachers are of basic importance and should not be disturbed or unduly influenced by outside decision makers.

Currently recommended views include overall policy making by elected members of state and local boards of education with professional school personnel carrying out the policies and making day-to-day decisions. In this general framework cooperative decision making on matters of curriculum and instruction is recommended with teachers playing a central role along with individuals in charge of curriculum development and specialists in various areas of the curriculum. Laymen should be involved at both the local and state levels. At the classroom level students should be involved in making decisions within a framework that is consistent with their experience and capabilities so that they will develop decision-making abilities and the program will be more meaningful and significant to them.

A Mixture of Viewpoints in Classroom Activities

The way in which classroom practices reveal a mixture of viewpoints may be illustrated by giving a few examples of activities that are consistent with various views. Requiring all members of the class to complete the same assignments and homework is consistent with perennialism. Emphasizing the value of certain learnings is preparation for life is consistent with essentialism. Providing for interaction with a rich environment in an open classroom is consistent with progressivism. Working with students in campaigns and action programs to improve safety and other aspects of community living is consistent with reconstructionism. The use of open-ended valuing strategies in which teachers play a nondirective role is consistent with existentialism.

Notice that the phrase *is consistent with* is used in each example. This phrase is inserted deliberately because most teachers provide learning activities that will help to attain objectives without deliberately considering the philosophical viewpoint behind the activities. Hence the phrase *is consistent with* is used to indicate a relationship but not to imply that the action is based on philosophical reflection or analysis.

The same point can be made about eclecticism in which several viewpoints are brought together in a working philosophy. Few of us in education have developed a truly eclectic philosophy based on an analysis and synthesis of differing viewpoints. Most of us, however, provide activities that are quite consistent with several different philosophical views. Hopefully, we will take the next step and work out a synthesis that will be useful in curriculum development and instructional planning. With this objective in mind let us turn to suggested activities and additional readings that will be helpful in this regard.

FOLLOW-UP ACTIVITIES AND PROJECTS

1 Make a list of five or six goals of education that you believe should be given high priority in the schools. Discuss your list with fellow students, noting points of agreement and disagreement. How might differences be reconciled?

2 What knowledge do you believe is of greatest worth to students? What subjects, if any, should have highest priority? Discuss and defend your position with fellow students.

3 Which of the views on means and methods of education and decision making, as presented in this chapter, do you accept? What alternative views do you think should be considered? Check them with others and find out if they agree.

4 Reexamine the positions you have taken in each of the three activities immediately above. How do you and how do others classify you as to philosophical camp? Perennialist? Essentialist? Other? Or a mixture of several?

5 Evaluate the authors' procedure for clarifying philosophical beliefs. How was it helpful? How can it be improved? Outline a procedure you might use with a group of teachers.

BIBLIOGRAPHY

Beckner, Wildon, and Joe D. Cornett. *The Secondary School Curriculum.* Scranton, Pa.: Intext Educational Publishers, 1972. Philosophical foundations in terms of viewpoints on issues and schools of philosophy.

Brubacher, John S. *Modern Philosophies of Education.* New York: McGraw-Hill, 1969. Essential features of current philosophies.

Cook, Ruth C., and Ronald C. Doll. *The Elementary School Curriculum.* Boston: Allyn and Bacon, 1973. Chapter on different schools of philosophy with checklist on functions of education.

Kneller, George F. *Introduction to the Philosophy of Education.* New York: Wiley, 1971. Review of various philosophies of education.

Morris, Van Cleve. *Existentialism in Education.* New York: Harper & Row, 1966. Discussion of viewpoints applied to education.

Pratte, Richard. *Contemporary Theories of Education.* Scranton, Pa.: International Textbook Company, 1971. Detailed treatment of five philosophies of education.

Wirsing, Marie E. *Teaching and Philosophy: A Synthesis.* Boston: Houghton
    Mifflin, 1972. Schools of philosophy in relation to values, thinking, content,
    objectives, and evaluation.
Wingo, Max. *Philosophies of Education.* Lexington, Mass.: Heath, 1974. Discus-
    sion of essentialism, progressivism, perenialism, and existentialism.

SOCIAL FOUNDATIONS

Education and other social institutions reflect the values, social changes, pressures, and forces that impinge upon them, even though at times it may seem as
if some institutions are as immutable as the Rock of Gibraltar. Tradition and
change operate as two opposing forces, but change is as inevitable in institutions
as it is in other aspects of life. And continuity is also fundamental in social
institutions so that their basic functions can be carried out in ways that serve
human welfare.

Of particular importance to curriculum workers are several aspects of the
social foundations of education that bear upon tradition and change in instructional planning. Basic societal values serve as overarching guidelines or standards
for human behavior and exert both a conserving or traditional influence and a
changing influence, a conserving influence when used to defend practices and a
changing influence when used to argue for improvement. Social and cultural
changes along with social pressures operate to influence curriculum planning
directly and indirectly. Legal requirements and various rules and regulations tend
to have a conserving or traditional impact on instruction. Neighborhood and
community values, changes, and pressures are usually a mixture of forces
working for tradition and change.

A procedure we have found helpful in examining the social foundations is to
keep forces of tradition and change in mind as direct attention is given to the following: values and beliefs in our society, social and cultural changes, social pressures and forces, and study of the local setting. It is helpful to begin with democratic values and beliefs and clarify them in much the same way suggested for
philosophical values in the preceding section. This may be followed by a review
of social and cultural changes and an appraisal of them in terms of democratic
values. Next, attention may be given to social pressures and forces that impinge
on the curriculum with further appraisal in light of democratic values. Finally,
the local community should be examined because it is in the community that
the foregoing have their direct impact on children and teachers.

DEMOCRATIC VALUES AND BELIEFS

Deeply embedded in the democratic way of life are certain values and beliefs
that serve as ideals. Even though ideals are not fully attained in any society, they
serve as guides to behavior in all spheres of human activity in a democracy. The
following are generally accepted as being basic in our society and as being of

primary importance in overall educational planning, as well as in the development of curricula and programs of instruction.

Respect for the individual and concern for the general welfare

Freedom of speech, thought, press, religion, association, and petition coupled with the responsible exercise of freedom

Equality of opportunity, justice, and due process of law in all spheres of activity regardless of sex and racial, ethnic, national, or religious background

Regard for majority rule, minority rights, and property

Consent of the governed in a system of government by, of, and for the people

Individual rights, responsibilities, independence, creativity, and self-direction

Free play of intelligence on all problems and use of persuasion based on reason

Openmindedness, fair play, and consideration of the views of others

Faith in the ability of people to govern themselves with rationality, morality, and practicality

A belief in progress and change through constructive action

A note of caution is in order regarding the danger of disillusionment that may emerge in the minds of some individuals because of the great disparity between the real and the ideal. When this occurs, it is possible that the function of values and beliefs has not been kept clear. Their primary function is to provide a framework which in a way "sets the rules of the game," or more formally, sets the standards which should be used in human affairs.

Democratic values serve as standards for curriculum workers in several ways. They are directly related to major goals of education as indicated in Chapter 4. They serve as guidelines for the maintenance of human relations in the school and the classroom. They serve as focal points for the study and analysis of our American heritage in selected portions of units of instruction. They serve as standards for the assessment of individual and group actions and proposals, in situations ranging from the community to the national and international level, both in the past and the present. They are also useful in appraising social and cultural change and related problems which may be serious deviations from the ideals we profess to cherish.

SOCIAL AND CULTURAL CHANGE

The inevitability and rapidity of change have long been recognized as characteristics of modern society. Social change takes place in institutions, social structure, and social interaction; for example, in the family, in positions held by individuals, and in such forms of interaction as cooperation, competition, and conflict. Cultural change is evident in emerging values, customs, ideas, and patterns of living; for example, new ideas in science, new technological developments, and new artistic expressions.

Change takes place as a result of invention, discovery, borrowing, and diffusion. Modern science and technology have accelerated invention, and the mass media have accelerated the diffusion of new ideas. Diffused ideas may be further changed as adaptations are made in terms of values, needs, and varying conditions. And some changes have a chain effect; for example, the invention of television led to new industries, governmental regulations, and changes in family life.

Responses to change vary greatly among individuals and between generations. Some individuals are shocked by change and resist it, while others accept it and still others attempt to guide and direct it. Children growing up today take for granted television and space travel, while to many adults these are amazing developments. Those who plan and guide the learning of children should be able to view change from both the child's and the adult's standpoint and devise programs that put change and the consequences of change in perspective.

Major Changes and Problems

Keeping abreast of societal changes and problems is essential in curriculum development. This may be done by focusing on long-term changes under which may be subsumed a variety of new developments. The following include those that are relatable to the lives of students, to areas of the curriculum, and to resources available to students and teachers.

The geographical setting of the community, land use, major zones, nearby areas, natural resources, and changes made in them

Historical development of the community from settlement to the present and changes and problems that follow in perspective

Scientific and technological changes and their impact on ways of living, the human condition, and the environment

Transportation changes with accompanying problems of congestion, mobility and movement of people, and use of energy

Communication changes and problems with special attention to the influence of mass media, the credibility of individuals and groups, and efforts to maintain freedom of expression

Environmental changes, conditions, and problems in relation to social, economic, and political forces and factors as well as to ecological forces and factors

Urbanization at home and in areas around the world with accompanying problems of urban decay and renewal, metropolitan and intercity relationships, and uses of energy

Population changes and shifts and their impact on education, the family, community life, and social, economic, and political activities

Extension of freedom and equality at home and abroad, in education, justice, social, political and economic opportunity, for all groups and individuals regardless of sex and racial, ethnic, national, social class, or religious background

Institutional changes such as those in the family and its structure, in the church and programs for children, in recreation, in courts and their administration of justice, in government at local, state, and national levels, and in health, education, and welfare and their impact on children, their families, and others

Social problems such as intergroup and interpersonal relations, crime and delinquency, group prejudice, industrial conflict, unemployment, corruption in government, child abuse and desertion, and discrimination in social, economic, political, educational, and other spheres of human activity

Applications of knowledge that have a bearing on the health, education, and welfare of children, including drug use and abuse, changing views on sex, morality, and religion, family and community life, and the environment

Aesthetic changes in art, music, architecture, literature, other art forms, and the environment with special attention to the neighborhood and the community

Linguistic changes and new knowledge of language patterns with special attention to terms, expressions, and patterns that are useful in bilingual and bicultural settings

Implications of social and cultural change may be drawn for both the scope and sequence of the curriculum. The scope should be broad enough to include those changes and problems most significant in the lives of children. The sequence should be planned in accord with the capabilities of students and developmental programs of instruction in areas of the curriculum. An effective procedure is to embed instruction in change in units of work in the social studies, science education, health education, or other areas of the curriculum. At times interdisciplinary studies may be provided, for example, in units dealing with changes in the environment.

In addition to social and cultural change, curriculum workers should understand social pressures and forces that have an impact on curriculum planning. In fact, some pressures and forces may be viewed as change agents because of their direct impact on instruction, as shown in the following section.

SOCIAL PRESSURES AND FORCES

All institutions are subject to social pressures and forces. Education in general and elementary education in particular have been and will continue to be subject to pressures and forces because of the high value placed on education and the immensity of the educational system. Rather than decrying the situation, educators should take steps to understand current pressures and forces and to provide direction so that their impact will result in better education. And such direction should be given professionally and in the context of policies and procedures that have been made and can be changed by duly elected representatives of the people.

Subtle and Pervasive Forces

Some of the most potent forces are subtle but pervasive in their influence. Tradition, characterized as the "heavy hand of tradition" by some individuals, is evident in the classroom as some teachers do things as they have always been done, in resistance to needed change by both laymen and educators in laws and regulations made to solve problems of yesteryear, in values and beliefs that range from little red schoolhouse notions of schooling to child-centered education, and in countless other ways of doing things as they have been done in the past without reflection on whether or not change is needed. Recognizing that change merely for the sake of change should be avoided, traditional ways of doing things should be under continuing examination so that conventional wisdom will not prevail over ongoing study and analysis of ways to improve the curriculum and instruction.

Expectancies that are widely held for children growing up in our society constitute another pervasive force. One way of viewing these expectancies is in terms of developmental tasks that are set for children. For example, during infancy and early childhood education, children are expected to learn to talk, walk, control body wastes, adjust to immediate social and physical realities, relate emotionally to others, make judgments of right and wrong, begin their schooling with success, and adopt approved modes of behavior. During the elementary school years children are expected to learn to read and master other subjects, develop skills for a variety of games, get along with peers and adults in authority positions, develop boy and girl roles, develop approved attitudes and values, and make moral judgments (Havighurst, 1966).

The social or socioeconomic class in which a child is born and reared has a powerful influence on development in general and education in particular. Learning from interaction with peers and adults, educational aspirations of parents and their children, opportunities for recreation and travel, language development, participation in church and various community activities, medical and dental care, attitudes toward work and play and welfare, and a host of other background differences may be noted among children from lower-, middle-, and upper-class backgrounds. These differences and others make mandatory the provision of programs of instruction that meet the needs of all children—the disadvantaged and the advantaged, those with differing social class, ethnic, and other backgrounds, and those with differing social, emotional, intellectual, and physical makeup.

Overt and Direct Pressures and Forces

Demands of parents and others in the community constitute one of the most potent pressures on early childhood and elementary education. The concept of neighborhood school and community school includes the notion that parents will and should be involved and that school-community relationships will be nurtured. Beginning in preschool and extending throughout the elementary school, teachers and principals tend to keep close contacts with parents and to develop programs that are consistent with community wishes and conditions. Serious difficulties arise when there are conflicts over matters of curriculum and instruction which cannot be resolved through reasoned analysis, discussion, and negotiation. A sound procedure is to involve parents and competent laymen in committees, review groups, workshops, and other activities so that problems can be anticipated and difficulties can be resolved. Their involvement is of critical importance in handling issues in different areas of the curriculum; for example, family life education as a part of health instruction, phonics in the reading program, theories of evolution in science education, and issues in the social studies. As a general rule, continuing involvement should be obtained rather than spotty and haphazard involvement when a crisis or problem arises.

Community agencies such as the church, service clubs, patriotic organizations, environmental groups, ethnic groups, health organizations, industry and business, labor organizations, sports and recreational groups, and various special interest groups attempt to influence the curriculum and instruction. Their programs range from writing contests and awards to students to specific recommendations on content and attitudes that should be emphasized in instruction. Some of their suggestions or demands may be appropriate in terms of goals and objectives, whereas others may be clearly detrimental to the development of the curriculum. Their views should be reviewed with the same care and respect that is accorded all individuals and groups. And adoption of their recommendations should be based on the same criteria that are applied throughout the process of curriculum development.

Professional associations abound in education, and all of them exert direct or indirect influence on curriculum and instruction. Teachers' associations and unions have grown in stature and power in recent years and have a larger voice in curriculum and instruction today than ever before. Associations for supervisors, curriculum leaders, and principals work at the state and national level and at the local level in some areas to implement what they believe to be sound educational practices. Associations composed of school board members, superintendents, and other administrators give attention to the full range of educational problems. Special interest organizations such as those that focus on early childhood education, reading, the language arts, social studies, and other specific areas of the curriculum exert great influence on actual program planning.

The producers of instructional media attempt to develop materials that will meet criteria being used at the local and state level as adoptions are being made. Their writers and editors have views of curriculum and instruction and publishers' representatives feed in views of school personnel regarding the types of materials that are needed. This continuing interaction has led to improvement of both the quality and quantity of resources for use in instruction. Because the impact of adopted materials is so great the utmost care must be taken in applying criteria during the process of selection.

Governmental agencies exert powerful and direct influences on all phases of curriculum and instructional planning. Local and state boards of education set overall policy, requirements related to instruction, and budgetary support. State departments and local school administrative units are involved through regulations and various services. State legislatures have become increasingly involved in recent years through legislation bearing on instruction as well as through the provision of financial support. The federal government exerts influence through the funding of programs. Recent examples are Project English, Project Social Studies, various science and mathematics projects, compensatory education, Head Start, Right to Read, programs for the disadvantaged, bilingual and bicultural education, and the research and development laboratories. Various foundations have also had a similar impact through the support of curriculum development projects and others related to instruction.

Reports of groups set up to make special studies of various phases of curriculum and instruction may contain helpful suggestions and recommendations. Local surveys and studies under the auspices of the board of education, and statewide studies under the auspices of the state board, state department, or legislature contain material that should be reviewed by curriculum workers. Over the years a variety of national studies have been made under the auspices of foundations, professional organizations, and agencies of the federal government. Currently, reports are available on bilingual education, career education, environmental education, drug use and abuse, and many other topics. These are cited in subsequent chapters in relation to topics and problems in various areas of the curriculum.

There are several radical revisionist elements that need to be considered within the framework of social foundations.[1] Microcultures or subcultures within our pluralistic society are demanding schooling that includes attention to their values, language, and other unique cultural characteristics. The counterculture movement with its emphasis on meaningful personal relationships, more intimate group or community experience, and individual autonomy reflects the reaction of some youth to recent economic and social changes. Proposals for open education, alternative schools, and the deschooling of society reflect dissatisfaction with traditional educational practices and the need for a variety of

[1] For example, see Herbert R. Kohl, *The Open Classroom.* New York: Vintage Books, 1969; Charles E. Silberman, *Crisis in the Classroom.* New York: Random House, 1970; Ivan Illich, *Deschooling Society.* New York: Harper & Row, 1971; Jonathan Kozol, *Free Schools.* Boston: Houghton Mifflin, 1972; John Holt, *The Understanding School.* New York: Pitman Publishing Corporation, 1969; "Perspectives on Open Education," *National Elementary Principal,* November, 1972; "The Great Alternatives Hassle," *National Elementary Principal,* April, 1973; "Alternative Schools: Special Issue," *Phi Delta Kappan,* March, 1973; Robert Leeper (Ed.), *A Man for Tomorrow's World.* Washington, D.C.: Association for Supervision and Curriculum Development, 1970.

approaches to schooling. Future education with its emphasis on planning, predicting, and directing the future reflects current concerns about the rapidity of change and our need to plan for the future, not to be shocked by it. These and other revisionist elements represent accommodations and adaptations to change in our social/economic/political system (Gordon, 1974).

THE NEIGHBORHOOD AND COMMUNITY

The child's neighborhood and community are the setting in which values, changes, and pressures impinge directly on learning and teaching. And the community is the child's laboratory for learning. Each neighborhood and each community has a unique and distinctive quality that can only be grasped by direct study. Without a study of the local neighborhood and community there is danger of misapplying general notions of values, changes, and pressures. Specific adaptations must be made to fit the local setting.

Studying the Local Setting

An effective approach to study of the community is to use the values, changes, pressures, and forces noted above as an outline to guide direct investigation of the local setting. Such an outline serves two objectives: (1) it guides the collection of information directly useful by curriculum workers and (2) it further clarifies the uses of the social foundations in a concrete and practical fashion.

Useful procedures include informal talks with school personnel and laymen, planned interviews of experts on various topics, reviews of reports on various topics and special editions of the newspaper(s) in the community, and the keeping of notes and clippings related to various topics. Both individual and group investigation should be considered with assignment of specific topics allocated in terms of interest and background.

In a community survey care should be taken to gather information directly related to education in general and the teaching-learning process in particular. Because social changes and forces affect all institutions, it is possible to lose a focus on education and thus gather information that may not be directly useful in curriculum planning. The desired outcome is insight into community conditions that will lead to appropriate modifications and adaptations of the curriculum.

Another part of a complete survey is the identification of resources that can be used in instruction. Every community has resources that may be used to enrich teaching and learning, even though differences among communities are great in this regard. A search should be made for the following resources: field trips, resource visitors, radio and television, published materials, individuals to be interviewed, usable audio-visual materials, libraries and museums, and other resources children can use directly.

FOLLOW-UP ACTIVITIES AND PROJECTS

1 In what ways do the democratic values and beliefs outlined in this section operate as a conserving influence? A changing influence? Which values do you believe to be most important in planning curriculum and instruction? What changes, if any, do you think should be made in the list of values?

2 Which of the major changes and problems do you believe to be most critical in curriculum planning at the present time? How might the ones you selected be included in the curriculum?

3 Which of the social pressures and forces do you believe to be most potent? Least potent? Select three or four and outline ways in which they might be handled by curriculum workers.

4 Make a brief survey of your neighborhood or community, using a selection of values, changes, and pressures presented in this section. If feasible, do the survey in collaboration with three or four fellow students.

BIBLIOGRAPHY

Della-Dora, Delmo, and James E. House. (Eds.) *Education for an Open Society.* 1974 Yearbook. Washington, D.C.: Association for Supervision and Curriculum Development, 1974. Current issues and problems and suggestions for making progress in meeting them.

Goodlad, John I., and Harold G. Shane. (Eds.) *The Elementary School in the United States.* 72nd Yearbook. National Society for the Study of Education. Chciago: The University of Chicago Press, 1973. Chapters on social context, issues and opinions, sources of school practice, the school as socializer, and the urban elementary school.

Gordon, Wayne C. (Ed.) *The Uses of the Sociology of Education.* 73rd Yearbook, National Society for the Study of Education: Chicago: The University of Chicago Press, 1974. Essays on youth culture, ethnic integration, and other social trends.

Havighurst, R. J. *Developmental Tasks and Education.* (3d ed.) New York: McKay, 1972. Tasks faced by students with implications for education.

Herriott, Robert E., and B. J. Hodgkins. *The Environment of Schooling: Formal Education as an Open Social System.* Englewood Cliffs, N.J.: Prentice Hall, 1973. Social factors to consider in educational planning.

Hess, Robert D., and Doreen J. Croft. *Teachers of Young Children.* Boston: Houghton Mifflin, 1972. Chapters on school and family relations and social opportunity and educational achievement.

Hurwitz, Emanuel Jr., and Charles A. Tesconi, Jr. (Eds.) *Challenges to Education.* New York: Dodd, Mead, 1972. Readings on courts, politics, teacher power, ethnicity, and other major issues.

Margolin, Edythe. *Sociocultural Elements in Early Childhood Education.* New York: Macmillan, 1974. Social and cultural conditions and factors in relation to children's development.

Ragan, William B., and Gene D. Shepherd. *Modern Elementary Curriculum.* New York: Holt, 1971. Chapter on our changing society.

Saylor, J. Galen, and William M. Alexander. *Planning Curriculum for Schools.* New York: Holt, 1974. Chapter on sources of data for curriculum planning.

Chapter 3

Foundations of Curriculum Development: Psychological and Disciplinary

PSYCHOLOGICAL FOUNDATIONS

A broad definition of psychological foundations includes material from theories and studies of child development and learning and from studies carried on in classroom situations. Basic procedures for identifying useful aspects of the psychological foundations include review and analysis of studies and theories and use of special consultants. After central ideas are identified, curriculum workers face the task of deriving implications.

In this section attention is given to the following topics of current interest and usefulness in planning: selected characteristics of child growth and development, Piaget's theory of intellectual development, thinking, cognitive or inquiry processes, and guidelines from learning theories.

Developmental Characteristics and Stages

Planning in terms of child growth and development is essential in all areas of the curriculum. It should be recognized, however, that stages or levels are only descriptive points in a continuing pattern of growth and development. Distinctions should be made between stages or levels of development that are primarily a function of physiological and psychological development and those that are primarily cognitive and experiential and may be a function of planned educational experiences. Although a given stage may be descriptive of the general characteristics of a group of children, not all individuals in the group will be at the same point in the continuum.

Physical and psychological growth are key factors in the child's learning in all areas of the curriculum. For example, during early childhood education children in preschool and kindergarten need to move around, manipulate objects, make things, engage in a variety of physical activities, experiment with materials, take part in dramatic play, and participate in other activities that call for the use of large muscles. Their eye-hand coordination and use of fine muscles are not well developed. As they move through school, their attention spans increase, farsightenedness decreases, perceptual skills develop, and eye-hand coordination improves. They also give more attention to detail as they make things and engage in art activities.

Social growth is marked by several characteristics. Young children tend to be self-centered but need the security and stability that are provided by adults. There is a gradual transition from self-centered activities to partnership activities, to small-group activities, and to large-group activities. Peer influences and relationships become important to most children as they move into the middle grades. Sex cleavage, interest in team games, formation of groups to achieve common purposes, and group projects in the classroom are illustrative of ongoing social development. By the time children are in the upper grades they show a strong desire for group approval, a more critical selection of friends, and a strong move away from adult domination.

Kohlberg (1968) has outlined moral development in terms of the following levels. The first level is *preconventional*. The child responds to various rules and acts as good or bad or right or wrong. At first there is a punishment and obedience orientation associated with punishment and rewards. This level is followed by a stage in which fairness and sharing and other behavior are viewed as forms of reciprocity such as, "I'll share if you share." The next level is *conventional*. There is conformity and loyalty to rules, good behavior is viewed as that which pleases others, and approval is earned by sticking to rules and being nice. This is followed by a stage in which there is a law-and-order orientation. The third level is *postconventional*. Emerging in secondary school and further refined in adulthood, it is marked by a social-contract orientation in which right action is viewed in terms of standards or criteria that have been examined critically. Some individuals may reach the final stage in which there is a universal ethical-principle orientation in which right is viewed in terms of one's conscience and universal principles of justice and equality.

The child's emotional development is related to the meeting of basic needs that range from biological needs for food and rest to personal and social needs for affection and security. Beginning in early childhood education, attention should be given to the need each child has to find a place or status in social groups so that the move from home and family to school is made with a minimum of emotional stress. The child's growth from dependence to independence can be aided by guided experiences in working with small and large groups; working independently; being a leader and a follower; making and carrying out decisions in dramatic play, construction, and other activities; sharing objects and ideas with others; and taking various responsibilities in and out of the classroom so that there is increasing growth in self-direction. Feelings of security, satisfaction, and success should be a part of all learning experiences; they flourish in a classroom atmosphere that is *democratic* in the deepest sense of the term, that is, conducted in a manner consistent with the democratic values noted earlier. Also important are receiving and giving affection, learning to communicate and interact with others in positive ways, and facing and accepting reality.

Individual differences tend to increase as children grow and develop. Differences may be noted in social and emotional development as well as in physical and intellectual development. The meeting of individual differences may be handled by the following:

1 Basing instruction on a study of each child in terms of his background, interests, capabilities, achievement, and levels of development

2 Varying learning activities and learning materials to match each child's needs

3 Varying the time to complete learning activities in accord with rate of learning

4 Varying teaching strategies and techniques and the kind and amount of supervision given to each child

5 Providing opportunities for children to choose learning activities within an arranged environment

6 Teaching children how to individualize for themselves, for example, how to choose wisely, how to vary time, and how to use materials they can handle

7 Sub-grouping children with similar needs and interests in reading, arithmetic, social studies committees, or other groups

8 Providing opportunities for individual work, ranging from independent reading activities to investigation of special topics

9 Setting levels of skill and concept development and standards of evaluation in accord with the child's background and abilities

10 Using preplanned programs of instruction in reading, arithmetic, and other areas that include diagnostic, teaching, and other procedures for individualizing instruction

Intellectual development moves through several levels and stages that have been studied in depth by Piaget (1969). Because of the current interest in Piaget's work, the following section is devoted to his theory of intellectual development.

Piaget's Theory of Intellectual Development

Piaget developed his theory by presenting tasks and questions to children and relating findings to a logicomathematical framework, using clinical rather than other psychological methods. He found that processes of logical thought developed in a sequence that can be described in four major levels of intellectual development.

Sensori-motor During infancy to around eighteen months, the preverbal period of development, the child assimilates sensations as a result of touching, seeing, hearing, grasping, and manipulating objects. As the infant interacts with new objects, accommodation (the process of modifying internal schemas) takes place; for example, a baby accommodates its fingers to grasp a new rattle and muscular exertion to lift it. The new behavior is organized or integrated in a composite system or structure that combines grasping and lifting which will be followed later with higher-order systems or structures; for example, such patterns of behavior as pushing and shaking objects, imitating actions of others, anticipating events, searching for objects, producing new sounds, and developing new means of overcoming obstacles. The manipulation of objects to attain purposes is a primary mode of behavior.

Preoperational What the child perceives is important in making judgments from around one and a half to seven years of age. For example, if one of two pieces of clay of the same amount is rolled in a sausage shape, the child states there is more clay because it is longer. If the child is shown two glasses of equal size and shape containing the same amount of juice and the contents of one is poured into a wider glass the child states that it contains less juice because it does not come up so high. The child cannot handle class inclusion; for example, he cannot deal with a part and the whole at the same time in a task such as this: Are there more red roses or more yellow roses in the group containing ten red and five yellow roses. The ability to order or seriate is not present; for example, the four-year-old cannot place ten sticks of differing size in order from shortest to longest.

Children at this level make rapid growth in language development and use images and words to symbolize or represent objects and events. Symbolic play in which objects, such as a box, stand for real things, such as a house, is evident and has its parallel in many of the dramatic play activities used in preschool programs. The egocentric tendencies of the two- to four-year-old begin to give way to tendencies to share and play with others, as is evident among children in kindergarten and first grade. However, logical operations are not used; hence the designation of this level as preoperational.

Concrete Operations This period of development extends from around seven to around eleven when many children enter preadolescence. Decentering takes place as the child moves from centering or focusing on a single attribute or factor to the consideration of several at a time. Logical thinking operations are used as children move away from making judgments based on appearance. Additive composition is possible, for example, the concept of animals as including many types. Reversibility is evident as the child discovers ways to retrace thought processes, for example, subtraction as the reverse of addition and squaring 3 to get 9 and taking the square root of 9 to get 3. Associativity is evident as the child discovers that some things can be combined in different ways to get the same result; for example, several short sticks whose combined length is equal to a long stick can be arranged in several different ways and still match the length of the long stick. Identity is established by making one-to-one correspondence and thus the child recognizes identical sets, for example, ten beads grouped together and ten beads spread out on a line.

The concept of conservation emerges, but at differing times for the conservation of number, substance and length, area, weight, and volume. Conservation of number is developed around six to seven years of age; for example, the number of beads remains the same regardless of how they are arranged. The amount of substance such as liquid in different size glasses or clay in a ball or sausage is conserved at around seven to eight years; the length of a line or object also remains the same no matter how it is shaped. Conservation of area emerges about a year later, followed by conservation of weight at around nine to ten; last of all is conservation of volume in terms of the amount of water that is displaced by objects of equal size but different shape.

Formal Operations The use of logical reasoning and the application of rules in situations which are not concrete are evident around eleven years of age, beginning in early adolescence for many children. Children who are at this level are capable of reasoning deductively, stating formal hypotheses, devising ways to test hypotheses, testing them in a systematic fashion, and stating formal conclusions. They are able to consider general laws as well as specific situations, weigh possibilities as well as realities, keep several factors or variables in mind, and deal with combinations and probabilities.

Capabilities of children at this level may be illustrated by the pendulum problem. A pendulum consisting of a weight on a string is shown to the child. A demonstration is given on how to move the weight, change the length of the string, release the pendulum from various heights, and push it to exert greater force. The problem is to find out how to change the speed of the swing of the pendulum. The preoperational child uses a haphazard approach and does not develop a systematic plan of procedure. The concrete-operations child may discover that changing the length of the string is the solution, but does not use systematic and logical procedures. The formal-operations child considers different possibilities, plans a systematic procedure for checking them, records accurately, and concludes that length is the causative factor.

Four logical modes are used at this level. Conjunction is the relating of two recurring properties such as this rod is *glass* and it *breaks*. Disjunction refers to alternatives such as either this is the cause or that is the cause. Negation is the rejection of the idea that two attributes exist together or cause an effect, such as neither volume by itself nor mass by itself determines whether an object floats or sinks. Implication refers to the occurrence of a result given a certain variable such as the frequence of the pendulum changes in relation to length of string. Students at this level can handle these four modes abstractly as follows: conjunction—X and Y exist together or cause Z; disjunction—it is either X or Y; negation—neither X nor Y causes Z, or X and Y do not go together; implication—given X, then Y occurs, follows, or is true.

Piaget states that intellectual development is gradual and continuous and that there are developmental stages within each of the levels above which should not be viewed as discrete and separate periods of development. Four major factors are involved in children's growth from level to level. Maturation is an essential but not a sufficient condition. Experience is also necessary so that the child can perform operations on data, manipulate objects, and otherwise be actively involved in interacting with his environment. Social transmission of information is essential provided the child can assimilate it, act on it, and accommodate to it. Equilibration, the process of seeking equilibrium and balance in one's cognitive structures, is a self-regulating process used by the child to move from disequilibrium to states of greater equilibrium.

Piaget uses the concepts of organization and adaptation to explain aspects of the functioning of intelligence. Organization is used to refer to the tendency to organize processes into coordinated and efficient systems. Adaptation is considered primarily in terms of the two complementary processes of assimilation and accommodation. The child assimilates that which fits existing schemas and structures. The child accommodates by altering his schemas and structures to handle new situations. Put another way, assimilation is involved as the child handles situations in terms of existing structures, whereas accommodation is involved as structures are transformed in response to the environment.

Illustrative Implications

Piaget's levels or periods of development may be used as broad and general guides to sequential planning. Of particular importance in early childhood education is the preoperational period. Perceptual learning, language development, use of symbols to stand for objects, manipulation of objects, dramatic play, a variety of physical activities, construction, rhythmic movement, and other doing activities are needed. In short, motor and sensory activities are essential.

The period of concrete operations is of special importance throughout the elementary school as recognition is given to individual differences among children. Firsthand experience and active involvement continue to be important. A rotation of experiences is needed to provide for the assimilation of ideas into existing cognitive structures and the accommodation of new ideas into developing structures. False accommodation should be avoided and attempts to force accommodation should be avoided; for example, giving the child a solution or correct answer. Rather, children should explore, discover, and work out the solutions to problems and build the related thinking processes into their own cognitive structures. The pacing of instruction should be in accord with the child's own self-regulating (equilibration) processes. Activity and time should be provided for the child to organize and apply learning. Meaningful practice should be provided so that the child can assimilate and refine skills and processes.

The period of formal operations is of importance in planning intermediate- and middle-school programs for children who are moving into adolescence. Although they have the capability to engage in formal reasoning, it should be recognized that there is a transition from concrete to formal operations and that differences among children are great in this regard. Moving from the concrete to abstract still needs to be used as a guiding principle. Formal operations should be introduced in the context of meaningful experiences. Opportunities to lift thinking to higher and higher levels should be provided in all areas of the curriculum.

Specific implications may be drawn for the planning of learning experiences. For example, if hypothesizing is to be done during the period of concrete operations, attention must be given to concrete objects and events, not to abstract ideas. If classifying is to be done, rules and procedures need to be formulated in relation to concrete objects. The ability to conserve number, length, amount, weight, and volume should be kept in mind as experiences in mathematics and science are planned and as quantitative concepts are used in other areas. Additive composition, reversibility, associativity, and identity are useful concepts and operations in all areas of curriculum and are of particular importance in mathematics education. They are used in connection with the thinking or inquiry processes discussed in the next section.

THINKING, COGNITIVE, INQUIRY PROCESSES

Progress has been made in identifying thinking, cognitive, or inquiry processes that are useful in curriculum and instructional planning. General models of the structure of intellectual processes, processes for emphasis in areas of the curriculum, cognitive tasks faced by children, and strategies for developing processes have been proposed. Widely useful examples follow.

Guilford and Merrifield (1960) have proposed a model that includes processes or operations that range from cognition and memory to convergent production, divergent production, and evaluation. The ideas of convergent and divergent thinking have sparked interest in giving greater attention to the planning of learning experiences that lead to divergent thinking, when diversity and originality are prime objectives, and convergent thinking, when the objective is to focus on a key learning of central importance to a group of students. For example, divergent thinking may be emphasized in preliminary exploration of a problem and in various types of expressive activities in language and artistic expression. Convergent thinking may be emphasized in developing and extending key concepts and principles and in drawing conclusions from a set of data.

Taba (1965) has reported a study of three cognitive tasks: concept formation, the making of inferences and generalizations, and the use of generalizations or principles to provide explanations and to make predictions. Taba argues that concrete operations are essential to the attainment of high levels of cognition and that some students need far more concrete experience than do others. It is reported that less able students can develop high levels of abstract thinking if enough concrete experience is provided.

One of the most complete analyses of processes has been made in a science project (AAAS, 1965). Basic processes emphasized in the primary grades are observing, classifying, using space/time relations, using numbers, communicating, measuring, inferring, and predicting. Integrated processes emphasized in the intermediate grades are formulating hypotheses, controlling variables, interpreting data, defining operationally, formulating models, and experimenting. All the processes are viewed as basic activities for the learning of science. A discussion of each of the processes is included in the chapter on Science Education. These processes have many applications to other subjects that should be explored by curriculum builders.

A content analysis of processes recommended by various experts and groups has shown that the following include those of frequent and critical use in curriculum and instructional planning (Michaelis, 1973).

Recalling and observing
Comparing, contrasting, classifying, defining
Interpreting and generalizing
Inferring, hypothesizing, predicting
Analysing, synthesizing, evaluating

Both cognitive and affective dimensions are involved in the list above; for example, feelings may be a part of interpreting and other processes. Communication as an overarching process may be used to express what is recalled, observed, and so on. Application is to be used systematically in all the above, for example, using concepts to focus recall and to classify objects. All the above processes may be used in all areas of the curriculum and in different models of thinking as well as different types of thinking such as problem solving, critical thinking, and creative thinking. Examples of questions to include in teaching strategies for developing each process are presented in the chapter on Social Studies.

Using Learning Theories in Curriculum Planning

Learning theories have had a great impact on the planning of curriculum and instruction. From early notions of faculty psychology and the need to discipline the mind, we have moved to theories that are built around such concepts as stimulus-response, reinforcement, and conditioning at one extreme, and such concepts as configuration, cognitive field, perceptual field, and self-actualization at the other extreme. Ideas have been drawn from various theories and put to use in program planning. For example, in behavior modification as applied in some corrective and remedial programs, heavy reliance is placed on stimulus-response, conditioning, and immediate rewards as reinforcement. In other situations involving creative expression and divergent thinking, when a variety of outcomes are desired, emphasis is placed on self-actualization and the extension and clarification of the child's perceptual field.

A useful procedure is to synthesize ideas about learning so that they can be put to use in planning. This may be done from several vantage points. One is to consider the elements that should be included in a theory of instruction. A second is to get a view of types of learning arranged in a hierarchy. A third is to pull together a summary of guidelines from learning theories with specific attention to such factors as motivation, readiness, transfer, and others of primary concern to curriculum workers.

Elements in a Theory of Instruction Key elements to include in a theory of instruction have been recommended by a psychologist (Bruner, 1966). The first includes factors that predispose a child to learn effectively. The second element is the optimal structuring of knowledge so that basic concepts and generalizations are emphasized, basic in the sense of giving a notion of structure of the area under study. The third is an optimal sequence that provides for required, cumulative learning. The fourth is the nature and pacing of rewards so that continuing motivation is provided. Bruner states that the lure of discovery is a highly motivating factor.

Types of Learning One of the most helpful developments has been the ordering of types of learning into a hierarchy which can be used to plan sequences of instruction directly related to the nature of teaching-learning tasks that confront curriculum planners. Rejecting the view that there is one type of learning such as stimulus-response or problem-solving learning. Gagné (1970) has outlined eight types and arranged them in a hierarchy as follows:

Signal learning: development of a reflexive response to a signal by repeating a signal or stimulus in close proximity to an unconditioned stimulus; illustrated by responses to bells, automobile horns, and clap of hands to get children to pay attention

Stimulus-response learning: referred to as trial-and-error, operant, or instrumental learning by some writers; illustrated by the initial learning of words

Motor chaining: connection of a set of stimulus-response learnings; illustrated by printing letters, using science equipment, operating a model

Verbal chaining or association: learning of chains of verbal associates as in oral language activities; illustrated by learning sequences of sentence patterns, memorizing verbal expressions, reciting a poem

Multiple-discrimination learning: learning to make different responses to objects and events or to distinguish among them; illustrated by learning distinctions among shapes, colors, solids, liquids, and gases, or sets of words in a foreign language

Concept learning: learning to put objects or events into a class and responding to them as a group; illustrated by learning such concepts as cell, striated muscle, family, or legislature

The learning of principles: learning to link concepts together to show relationships as in generalizations and formulas; illustrated by "Round things roll," "Resources are used to provide food, shelter, and clothing," and "Find the area of a rectangle by multiplying length times width"

Problem solving: using principles to attain a goal and thereby learning a higher-order principle that changes the learner's capability; illustrated by using principles of addition, subtraction, or other processes to solve arithmetical problems, principles of line, space, form, color, and texture to solve art problems, or principles of supply and demand to solve economic problems

Gagné stresses the point that learning is cumulative; prerequisite conditions within the learner and external to the learner must be considered. Sequences of instruction should be planned in hierarchies to provide for the attainment of specified terminal behavior. For example, if the ability to classify objects is to be developed, a hierarchy of skills should be planned that begins with grouping in terms of one attribute (shape of such items as circles and triangles), and moves to grouping by less tangible attributes (such as texture or smoothness), to grouping by two attributes (shape and texture), to grouping by more than two attributes (shape, texture, and color). Examples of other sequences and more detailed description of the sequence for classifying are presented later in the chapter on Science Education.

Third force psychology with its emphasis on the individual's inner meanings and feelings must be considered along with other psychological forces and viewpoints. Various names have been given to the third force movement, including humanistic psychology, self-theory, phenomenological psychology, and self-actualistic psychology. Special emphasis is given to values, feelings, purposes, and personal meanings of the individual—areas that are neglected by behavioristic schools of psychology. Suggestions for giving attention to these areas of personal meaning and feeling have been outlined by Brown (1971), and by Weinstein and Fantini (1970).

Guidelines from Learning Theories and Studies

A mixture of learning theories may be found in actual classroom practices of effective teachers. For example, positive reinforcement of children's learning through immediate feedback of results is widely used in the language arts, mathematics, and other areas. The concept of positive reinforcement is emphasized in stimulus-response, conditioning, behavior modification, and similar theories of learning. On the other hand, many teachers at times emphasize self-actualization and self-direction with attention to social and emotional needs of children as well as intellectual and physical needs. Such an emphasis is characteristic of theories that can be grouped as humanistic psychology.

Presented below is a summary of guidelines or principles derived from a variety of theories and studies of learning. They are intended to serve as a framework for use in the planning of curricula and instruction.

Motivation is obtained by relating instruction to needs and interests of children, establishing clear objectives, providing for group planning, giving immediate feedback, providing rewards, using such drives as curiosity and desire to know and learn, and emphasizing intrinsic over extrinsic motivation.

Needs for security, belonging, affection, approval, and success should be considered at all levels of instructional planning in early childhood education and throughout the elementary school.

Readiness for learning should be planned both in terms of prior learning and development and in terms of experiences needed to develop readiness for learning specific skills, concepts, processes, and values in each area of the curriculum.

Discovery learning in which the child finds out on his own and goes beyond what is given to gain new insights should be provided, along with *guided learning* in which the child makes directed progress in developmental programs of instruction.

Thinking processes such as interpreting, generalizing, and hypothesizing, also referred to as cognitive and inquiry processes, should be emphasized because of their usefulness in all areas of the curriculum as well as in daily living.

Self-concept, *self-esteem*, and *self-evaluation* should be considered in all phases of curriculum planning and instruction so that each child will function

effectively in both individual and group activities and will develop positive attitudes essential to life-long learning and development.

Practice that is meaningful to the learner is essential to the development and
refinement of skills and the retention and transfer of learning.

Transfer of learning may be enhanced by making immediate applications in
new situations, emphasizing concepts and generalizations, identifying similarities
in different situations, organizing or structuring learning into models for use in
studying topics and problems, and guiding the discovery of applications by the
child.

Retention of learning may be aided by emphasizing personal meaning, value,
and usefulness to the learner, placing new ideas in context or perspective in
terms of prior learning, providing for the overlearning of basic skills and concepts, providing for completion of a unit of learning without the intervention
of interfering factors, and providing for meaningful practice.

Multiple learning should be recognized in all phases of instruction so that
objectives will be attained without such negative outcomes as undesirable attitudes, loss of interest, and decreased appreciation of the importance of the topics
under study.

Individual differences should be met by diagnosing needs, using a variety of
strategies, learning activities and materials, varying the time, providing for individual study, small-group study and individual tutorial, providing for partnership and team learning, and adjusting expectations and standards.

Classroom climate or atmosphere should be characterized by mutual trust
and respect, teamwork, fair play, openmindedness, and an absence of ridicule,
sarcasm, and disregard for the feelings of others.

Interaction with others and with a rich classroom environment promotes
learning provided there is active teacher guidance in group planning, group
activity and group evaluation, along with the use of materials and equipment to
attain objectives.

Inductive and deductive learning experiences are needed to develop thinking
ability so that children develop competence in moving from specific details to
general ideas and can apply general ideas in a variety of specific contexts.

Planned sequences of instruction are essential to effective learning in all
areas of the curriculum, yet flexibility must be provided to meet individual
differences and differing learning styles of children.

Evaluation of learning is needed to provide feedback for children and
information for the teacher that may be used to improve instruction.

FOLLOW-UP ACTIVITIES AND PROJECTS

1 List four or five implications of developmental growth characteristics that
you believe to be important for planning instruction for children at a given level.

2 Which ideas in Piaget's theory do you find to be most useful? How might
you put them to use in instructional planning?

3 Indicate how the cognitive or inquiry process can be put to use in instructional planning. For example, select four and five cognitive or inquiry processes or suggest questions and activities that can be used to develop them.

4 Select four or five guidelines from learning theories and studies and indicate ways in which they can be put to use in instructional planning.

BIBLIOGRAPHY

AAAS, Commission on Science Education. *Science: A Process Approach.* Washington: American Association for the Advancement of Science, 1965. Hierarchies of process charted in *An Evaluation Model and Its Applications.*

Brown, George I. *Human Teaching for Human Learning: An Introduction to Confluent Education.* New York: Viking, 1971.

Bruner, Jerome S. *Towards a Theory of Instruction.* Cambridge, Mass.: Harvard, 1966. Elements in a theory of instruction.

Gagne, Robert M. *The Conditions of Learning.* New York: Holt, 1970. Conditions for promoting eight types of learning.

Ginsburg, Herbert, and Sylvia Opper. Piaget's *Theory of Intellectual Development.* Englewood Cliffs, N.J.: Prentice-Hall, 1969. Review of main aspects of Piaget's theory.

Guilford, J. P. and Merrifield, P.R. *The Structure of Intellect Model.* Los Angeles: University of Southern California Press, 1960. A model of contents, operations, and products with suggestions for uses of the model.

Kohlberg, Lawrence, "The Child as Moral Philosopher," *Psychology Today*, 2, 25-30, 1968. Outline of stages of moral development.

Michaelis, John U. *Inquiry Processes in the Social Studies.* ERIC Listing ED080413, 1973. Analysis of cognitive processes with teaching strategies for each process.

Mussen, Paul. *The Psychological Development of the Child.* Englewood Cliffs, N.J.: Prentice-Hall, 1973. Concise review of major aspects of child development.

Snelbecker, Glenn E. *Learning Theory, Instructional Theory, and Psychoeducational Design.* New York: McGraw-Hill, 1974. Review of learning theories and approaches to instruction.

Taba, Hilda. "The Teaching of Thinking," *Elementary English,* May, 1965, Vol. 42, pp. 534-542. Study of cognitive tasks faced by students in elementary schools.

Thoresen, Carl E. (Ed.) *Behavior Modification in Education.* 72nd Yearbook, National Society for the Study of Education, Part I, Chicago: University of Chicago Press, 1973. Essays on various models and theories.

Weinstein, Gerald, and Mario D. Fantini (Eds.). *Toward Humanistic Education: A Curriculum of Affect.* New York: Praeger, 1970.

Wilson, John A. R., Mildred C. Robeck, and William B. Michael. *Psychological Foundations of Learning and Teaching.* (2d ed.) New York: McGraw-Hill, 1974. Cognitive, affective, and creative learning with material drawn from humanistic and behavioral as well as other research.

DISCIPLINARY FOUNDATIONS

All areas of the curriculum are directly related to disciplines in one or more fields of knowledge which include the natural sciences, the social sciences, the humanities, and mathematics. The other foundations of education are directly related to such disciplines as history, philosophy, sociology, anthropology, psychology, economics, and political science. The disciplinary foundations, therefore, merit consideration in depth by educators.

The search for knowledge of greatest worth has taken a new turn. No longer is it only a quest for information, although it is recognized that a critical selection of factual material is needed to develop concepts and other substantive elements. Efforts are being made to identify structural components in disciplines that can be used to design areas of the curriculum.

Persuasive arguments have been advanced in support of building the curriculum on structural components derived from the disciplines (Bruner, 1960; Phenix, 1964). Economy of learning is enhanced by the focus on fundamental ideas and the use of content to develop key ideas. Relationships among ideas are highlighted as a sense of structure emerges through the use of concepts and generalizations in active inquiry. Fundamental ideas are brought to bear upon the solution of problems, and current problems are used to extend understanding of key ideas. Transfer of learning is facilitated as concepts and generalizations of broad applicability are stressed. Curricula may be kept up-to-date because of the close liaison with scholars in the basic disciplines. Teaching strategies and basic study skills may be closely linked with ways of inquiring drawn from the disciplines. Motivation may be heightened as the lure of discovery characteristic of the work of inquirers is made a part of instruction. By using procedures that are tested and yet are being continually improved, students can get a grasp of fundamental approaches to knowing and to the means by which knowledge is extended. Better articulation can be achieved between instruction in elementary schools and instruction in secondary schools.

Many analyses of disciplines have been made to identify structures that can be used in curriculum planning.[1] At first attempts were made to identify *the* structure that could be used in planning, but it was soon discovered that experts proposed different structures. The outcome has been the selection of key elements from the disciplines and using them to structure the curriculum in ways that are most fruitful in moving students toward the attainment of stated objectives.

---

[1] For examples, see Paul D. Hurd, *New Directions in Teaching Secondary School Science.* Chicago: Rand McNally, 1969; John U. Michaelis, *Social Studies for Children in a Democracy.* Englewood Cliffs, N.J.: Prentice-Hall, 1972; American Association for Health, Physical Education, and Recreation, *Health Concepts, Guides to Health Instruction.* Washington, D.C.: National Education Association, 1967; and references in later chapters dealing with areas of the curriculum.

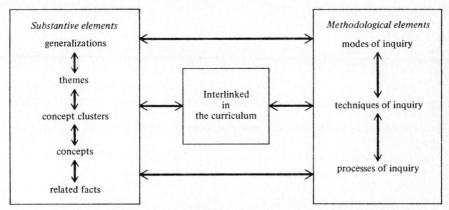

Chart 3-1 Relationships among substantive elements, methodological elements, and the curriculum

Of special importance in curriculum planning are two sets of elements—the substantive and the methodological. The substantive include the key concepts, concept clusters, themes, and generalizations along with the factual material needed to develop them. The methodological elements include the modes, techniques, and processes of inquiry that are useful in curriculum development. Interrelationships of these elements and the interlinking of them in the curriculum are shown in Chart 3-1.

Substantive Elements

The substantive elements are used to guide inquiry and to organize a vast body of information in convenient and usable form. Concepts and generalizations along with themes have been used for years by curriculum workers, and they are used extensively in newly developed materials because they constitute the essence or basic substance of what is taught. Concepts are categories or classifications—abstractions that apply to a class or group of objects, activities, or qualities that have certain attributes in common. Themes are two or more concepts joined together in a phrase, and generalizations are statements of broad applicability that indicate the relationships between two or more concepts. In between concepts and generalizations are concept clusters which consist of a root or key concept and the subconcepts that give depth and breadth of meaning to it.

At this point let us consider specific examples so that our use of concept cluster, theme, and generalization will be clear, and the importance of substantive elements may be illustrated in each area of the curriculum.

The language arts

Concepts
Word   Sentence   Paragraph   Verse   Meter   Essay   Poem
Concept Clusters
Prose: stanza, verse, refrain, meter, stress, rhythm, lyric, epic, narrative, sonnet, couplet, limerick
Language units: morpheme, grapheme, word, phrase, clause, sentence, paragraph
Themes
Changing language patterns, courage and diversity in literature
Generalizations
Reading material is oral language recorded in graphic form. The sentence is the smallest unit of complete expression.

Mathematics education

Concepts
Numbers   Operations   Measurement   Sets   Geometry   Relations
Concept Clusters
Numbers counting or natural, whole, integers, cardinal, ordinal, positive, negative, fractions, prime, composite, rational, irrational, real
Relations pairing, ordered pairs, ratio, percent, graphing, slope, intercept, interpolation, extrapolation, functional relationships, equivalence relations
Generalizations
Mathematical sentences may express equalities or inequalities. The sum or product of an addition or multiplication is unaffected by the order of the elements under these operations.

Science education

Concepts
Machines   Matter   Energy   Light   Cells   Rocks   Solar system
Concept Clusters
Simple machines: lever, pulley, wheel and axle, inclined plane, wedge
States of matter: solid, liquid, gas
Themes
Interaction of heredity and environment, adaptation to the environment
Generalizations
Simple machines make work easier and faster by overcoming inertia, gravity, and friction.
When matter changes from one form to another, the total amount of energy remains unchanged.

Social studies

Concepts
  Resources Production Role Interaction Society Government
Concept Clusters
  Resources: people, animal life, vegetation, soil, air, water, minerals
  Processes of government: legislative, executive, judicial
Themes
  The westward movement, taming the frontier, the growth of democracy
Generalizations
  How people use the resources in their environment depends in large part on
  their culture.
  Processes of government operate under a system of checks and balances in
  our society.

Health and physical education

Concepts
  Physical needs Basic foods Vitamins Fitness Coordination Posture
Concept Clusters
  Physical needs: food, water, rest, sleep, activity, protection from disease,
  care of the body
  Fitness: physical, mental, emotional, social, spiritual
Themes
  Basic foods for good health, timing and coordination, rhythm of activity and
  rest
Generalizations
  Nutritional needs of the body can be met through the eating of basic foods.
  Mental health is influenced by one's state of physical well-being.

Aesthetic studies
(art and music)

Concepts
  Design Line Style Criticism Tone Rhythm Form Texture
Concept Clusters
  Elements of design: line, color, light, form, space, texture, movement
  Elements of music: tone, melody, harmony, rhythm, form
Themes
  Form and function in art, the arts as expressions of values and aspirations
Generalizations
  People in all cultures express values and aspirations through the arts. Distinctive
  styles of art have been created in different times and places.

A critical selection must be made of substantive elements so that the most powerful and useful ones are included in the instructional program. The selection may be made by reviewing the recommendations of experts in various fields of knowledge and the reports of various professional groups. A basic source is the set of instructional materials to be used in a given program because they are the substantive elements students will be using in their own inquiries. The developers of instructional media take great care in selecting the substantive components that are most helpful in studying topics, problems, and issues in various areas of the curriculum.

Special attention should be given to the identification of concept clusters which are widely used in program planning in all areas of the curriculum. They help to indicate the scope of the teaching task. For example, the concept cluster *types of rocks: metamorphic, sedimentary, igneous* calls for instruction on all three types along with procedures for classifying rocks. A knowledge of clusters also helps in sequencing instruction. For example, the set of concepts related to *climate* may begin with temperature and precipitation as fundamental factors. As various land areas are studied, such concepts as elevation, latitude, mountain systems, winds, and ocean currents may be developed to round out the cluster and provide a model for studying the climate of different regions.

Methodological Elements

A useful way to view methodological elements drawn from the disciplinary foundations is in terms of widely applicable modes of inquiry that cut across areas of the curriculum, methods or techniques of inquiry that can be used in areas of the curriculum, and processes of inquiry that are basic to the use of both methods and modes of inquiry.

Three general modes or styles of inquiry are used in various areas of the curriculum and in daily activities—the generalizing mode, the integrative mode, and the decision-making mode (Michaelis, 1972). The generalizing mode involves analysis of several samples of information to arrive at a generalization about a topic or problem. For example, a teacher and a group of students may wish to analyze urban problems in several different cities in order to make a general statement about urban problems the cities have in common, or in health education the objective may be to formulate a generalization about the basic foods that are essential in a balanced diet for all people. The investigation is conducted so that several different sets of data are analyzed in order to have confidence in the generalization about basic food groups.

The integrative mode or style of inquiry is focused on the discovery of unique or special features of a particular event, place, person, or activity. Important details are brought together in a synthesis that gives one a picture, a feeling, a clear idea of the object or person under study. For example, if one is to find out what is special or unique about Chicago, pollution problems in a given area, the Civil War, the *Mona Lisa*, or any other item, then the focus must be placed on the item, not on cities in general, or pollution problems in general, or wars and paintings in general. Instead, significant details are brought together and organized in a way that highlights special characteristics.

The decision-making mode is focused on the making of decisions or judgments related to events, actions, and proposals under study. A basic feature of this mode is the clarification of standards or criteria for use in making the decision or judgment. Take, for example, such problems and issues as urban renewal, use of insecticides, improvement of health and safety in the community, rights of all groups to community recreational facilities, and criticism of different types of art and music. All the foregoing call for the clarification of standards that can be used to make a decision or judgment.

These three modes are currently in use in areas of the curriculum even though they are most frequently used implicitly without clarification of differences in emphasis among them. All areas, for example, provide opportunities to arrive at generalizations, to clarify particular objects or activities, and to make judgments or decisions. By making them explicit it is possible to obtain the desired kind of balance regarding the use of these modes in each area. The outcome should be increased competence on the part of students as they tackle different topics, problems, and issues both in school and in life.

The last point needs emphasis because all of us use these three modes whether we realize it or not. For example, think of all the generalizations we make around such topics as buying food, health care, government, transportation, and the like. Think of all the special and unique syntheses of ideas we make about such special places as our hometown, our favorite vacation spot, and the place where we bought the best bargain ever. Think of the innumerable decisions we make each day related to both personal and social activities of immediate concern as well as economic and political decisions of long-range concern.

A question that sometimes arises is how these three modes are related to problem solving. All of them may be carried out by using problem solving as it is usually defined to include clarifying the problem, gathering data related to the problems, evaluating and organizing data, and forming a conclusion based on the data. During clarification of the problem a decision should be made as to the need for analysis of a single topic in depth in order to arrive at a generalization, or the synthesis of data to highlight unique features, or criteria for use in making a decision or judgment. Once this is done, related data may be collected and organized in a form that is useful in arriving at the desired conclusion, whether it be a generalization, a synthesis, or a judgment.

Techniques of Inquiry

Adaptations of methods or techniques of inquiry and expression used in the disciplines have been used for many years in various areas of the curriculum.

Examples are experimentation in science education, interviews, and questionnaires in the social studies, and use of anatomical models in health education.
The following list includes those emphasized in recently developed instructional
materials.

Data Collection Techniques
Analysis of written materials such as letters, diaries, reports, and documents,
and orally transmitted materials such as ballads, legends, and folklore
Examination of art objects such as murals, tapestries, plaques, and ornaments
Examination of artifacts such as tools, utensils, instruments, and weapons
Observation of people at work, plant growth, changes in seasons and weather,
and other activities and phenomena
Interviews, polls, and questionnaires to gather data on topics and problems
in health education, social studies, science education, and interdisciplinary studies
such as environmental problems and urban problems
Role playing, sociodrama, and simulations related to clarification of decision
making, roles, and interaction in various situations
Use of charts, checklists, rating scales, and other evaluative devices

Techniques for Organizing and Presenting Data
Preparation of oral and written reports around concepts, concept clusters,
and generalizations
Construction of maps, charts, diagrams, tables, graphs, and models
Preparation of sketches, drawings, transparency overlays, slides, displays,
and exhibits
Preparation of tapes that contain data related to topics under study
Preparation of logs, diaries, and other systematic records

Processes of Inquiry

As noted earlier in the section on psychological foundations, there are basic
processes of inquiry that have widespread application in all areas of the curriculum. Recalling and observing are fundamental in the sense that they constitute the two avenues of data input. We all work with the data we can recall
coupled with data we can collect through the various forms of direct observation
that include seeing, touching, and use of other senses, and the intake of data
by reading, examining artifacts, and using other forms of indirect observation.
Comparing/contrasting, classifying, and defining are essential processes in ready-
ing data for interpreting, generalizing, hypothesizing, inferring, and predicting.
Analyzing and synthesizing of data are carried out at many points in the study
of topics and problems and are frequently used to formulate hypotheses, develop
a basis for making predictions, and process data needed to formulate generalizations. Evaluation is also used at many points in a given study to identify
strengths and weaknesses in techniques and processes being used, improvements
that should be made, and the ways in which products of inquiry can be improved.

Linking Substantive and Methodological Elements

A promising development is to link the substantive and methodological elements drawn from various disciplines and to put them to use in units of instruction. For example, each mode or style of inquiry calls for the use of concepts to guide inquiry, and each technique of inquiry should be used to collect data related to questions or hypotheses formulated around key concepts. Thus a study that is designed to develop a generalization about urban services that are common in all cities might be guided by such a focusing question as, What services (such as provision of education, government, transportation) are found in all cities? Students' use of techniques of inquiry as part of the basic process of observation is guided by the key concepts in the question. As a second example, a study in science education of the unique features of an invention might be guided by such a question as, How is this invention different in principle and usefulness from other inventions we have studied thus far? For a third example, a study of proposals for the improvement of safety in bicycle riding in the community might be guided by such a question as, Which proposal best meets the standards for bicycle safety as set by the city council?

The guiding principle is to link concepts and process together in inquiry-conceptual questions, as shown in the following examples.

How can we define the *role* of mayors? (defining)

How are the *inventions* of the telephone and telegraph alike and how are they different? (comparing/contrasting)

How can we group *foods* shown in the health chart? (classifying)

What can we say in general about the *theme* expressed in these pictures of murals in Mexico City? (generalizing)

Additional examples of inquiry-conceptual questions are presented in the chapters that deal with areas of the curriculum. The point to be emphasized here is that such questions bring together the substantive and methodological components of the disciplines in a manner that is useful for both students and teachers.

FOLLOW-UP ACTIVITIES AND PROJECTS

1 Examine recently published textbooks in two or three areas of the curriculum. Note the following:

(*a*) Five concepts	(*c*) Five themes
(*b*) Five concept clusters	(*d*) Five generalizations

2 Write three inquiry-conceptual questions based on the concepts or concept clusters. Use the root or basic concept for the questions based on concept clusters. Be sure to identify the process of inquiry for each question.

3 Reexamine the textbooks and find examples of the following:
(a) the generalizing mode   (c) the decision-making mode
(b) the integrative mode   (d) suggested techniques of inquiry
(e) examples of the use of processes of inquiry

Check the suggested activities for children in the textbooks and in the accompanying teacher's manual if you have difficulty identifying the above.

BIBLIOGRAPHY

Bruner, Jerome. *The Process of Education*. Cambridge, Mass.: Harvard, 1960. Views of structure and inquiry related to disciplines.

Educational Policies Commission. *The Spirit of Science*. Washington, D.C.: National Education Association, 1966. Values underlying scientific inquiry.

Hass, Glen, Joseph Bondi, and Jon Wiles. *Curriculum Planning*. Boston: Allyn and Bacon, 1974. Readings on the nature of knowledge.

King, Arthur R., Jr., and John A. Brownell. *The Curriculum and the Disciplines of Knowledge*. New York: Wiley, 1966. Procedures for designing curricula on the disciplines.

Michaelis, John U. *Social Studies for Children in a Democracy*. Englewood Cliffs, N.J.: Prentice-Hall, 1972. Chapter on concepts, concept clusters, and generalizations drawn from social science disciplines.

Phenix, Philip H. *Realms of Meaning*. New York: McGraw-Hill, 1964. Detailed treatment of uses of knowledge in curriculum planning.

Chapter 4

Goals and Objectives

Goals provide broad and general direction for education, whereas objectives serve as guides to instruction designed to attain major goals. Both are needed in curriculum planning. Goals help to clarify priorities by keeping central aims of education in focus, aims that are related to what is believed to be of greatest value to children and youth in our society. Objectives help to set the direction in each area of the curriculum and in units of instruction within each area.

Goals of education are discussed in the first section of this chapter. Attention is given to sources, functions, and criteria of useful goals, and to a procedure for formulating goals. This is followed by selected goal statements prepared in the past and a statement of six major goals believed to be of critical importance now and in the future. The remainder of the chapter deals with objectives. Attention is given to moving from goals to objectives, taxonomies of cognitive and affective objectives, and guidelines for stating objectives. Objectives of various areas of the curriculum are presented in subsequent chapters.

GOALS OF EDUCATION

Goals are general statements of purpose. They are long-range and broad, serving as ends that we aspire to attain. Goals give direction to policy making, to identification of contributions that areas of the curriculum can make to their attainment, and to the specification of objectives of instruction. Moreover, goals are indicative of key values in the philosophy underlying the total curriculum; they represent what we believe to be most important in the education of children.

In recent years there has been renewed interest in the development of statements of basic goals of education. Many school systems have appointed committees composed of laymen and school personnel to prepare goal statements as a first step in developing an accountability system. Of great value in such activity is the increased understanding participants obtain of the function of education, priorities in the educational process, the importance of education in our society, and their own philosophy of education.

The comment of a teacher in a curriculum development workshop highlights the value of a clear understanding of goals of education. Workshop participants had been working intensively on the revision of the elementary curriculum. During one evaluation session the teacher said: "Having major goals in mind is helpful in keeping a perspective on what is important in all areas of the curriculum. Our statement of goals helps me tie together the experiences we are planning for children."

There are several sources from which goals are derived. Three interrelated and widely used sources are societal values, conditions, and demands, the nature and needs of learners, and the disciplines of knowledge used to develop the curriculum. Operationally, one's own philosophy of education is a primary factor in determining what is most valued for children. A collection of goal statements made in the past is helpful to individuals and groups at work on the actual preparation of goal statements. All the foregoing should be considered as goals that are in the process of being formulated.

A statement of major goals of education should meet several criteria. First, goals should be consistent with cherished social values such as the equal moral worth of human beings, equality of justice and opportunity, concern for the general welfare, faith in human intelligence, individual freedom, majority rule and minority protection, and use of persuasion based on reason. Goals must be derived in terms of societal conditions and demands as represented by carefully made analyses and various laws and regulations. Goals should be communicable in terms that make them useful as overall guidelines to the development of curriculum and instruction. They should represent long-range and enduring directions of education on which there is fairly widespread agreement. They should be consistent with one another so that they provide a coherent sense of direction at all levels of instruction and across all areas of the curriculum. Finally, a statement of goals should reflect what is believed to be of highest priority in the education of children and youth in our times.

Various procedures are used to guide groups in the formulation of goals. One approach is to begin with a question such as, What are the chief reasons for getting an education? Or, What should be the characteristics of a person who has graduated from high school? Other more involved approaches may be used. One sponsored by Phi Delta Kappa has involved large numbers of laymen, educators, and students in the discussion and ranking of goals. Many school systems have prepared guidelines for use in involving laymen and school personnel in the formulation of goals as one phase of the development of an accountability system.

An approach that the authors have found to be fruitful is to begin with a question such as, What do you believe to be the major goals of education? After discussion of goals given by the group, statements prepared by others are handed out for study and analysis. This is followed by discussion of changes that might be made in the first statements offered by the group. Next, small groups of from three to five individuals are formed to prepare a concise statement of goals. Each group is urged to identify goals on which there is agreement and any on which there is disagreement. Each subgroup reports back to the total group, which attempts to identify goals generally acceptable to everyone. The final outcome for each individual in the group is a statement of goals which she or he supports. Examples of goal statements which have been used in this activity are presented in the following section.

ILLUSTRATIVE STATEMENTS OF MAJOR GOALS OF EDUCATION

In this section attention is given to statements of major goals of education proposed by different groups in the past. The statements have been selected because of their impact on the thinking of educators, the time at which they were published, and the consistency with which certain common themes appear.

Be critical as you read each statement, noting goals you endorse, ones you do not endorse, and any changes you think should be made in them. Note also any new goals that are introduced as you move from one statement to another. For example, the 1955 statement mentions lifelong learning and the 1961 statement stresses thinking ability. Finally, make a list of what you believe to be major goals of education so that you can check your list against the proposed set of goals suggested by the authors in the section that follows this one.

Seven Cardinal Principles, 1918

Although proposed as major goals of secondary education, the statement prepared by the Commission on Reorganization of Secondary Education in 1918 had great impact on elementary schools.[1] The seven goals were Health, Command

[1] Commission on Reorganization of Secondary Education, *The Seven Cardinal Principles.* Washington, D.C.: U.S. Bureau of Education, 1918.

of Fundamental Processes, Worthy Home Membership, Vocation, Citizenship, Worthy Use of Leisure, and Ethical Character. This statement reflected concerns of the time related to societal changes and needs, the nature and needs of students, and changes in educational theory. An attempt was made to move education from a narrow focus to a consideration of a broad set of goals. The need to continue the development of fundamental processes taught in elementary schools on through secondary schools was emphasized. To this day all the goals cited by the commission in 1918 will be found in one form or another in statements of major goals of education, as may be noted in the statements which follow.

Purposes of Education in American Democracy, 1938

A statement that has been used extensively throughout the country was prepared by the Educational Policies Commission and published by the National Education Association in 1938.[2] This statement postulated the fullest possible development of the individual within the framework of our democratic society as the basic goal of education. Emphasis was given to individual behavior and conduct that could be observed; this was an early accent on observable behavior that has become prevalent in recent years. This statement was organized around four major categories of goals related to the development of the individual, human relationships, economic competence, and civic responsibility. Each of the four goals was elaborated by stating illustrative aspects of behavior and conduct as follows:

Self-realization
The inquiring mind. The educated person has an appetite for learning.
Speech. The educated person can speak the mother tongue clearly.
Reading. The educated person reads the mother tongue efficiently.
Writing. The educated person writes the mother tongue effectively.
Number. The educated person solves his problems of counting and calculating.
Sight and hearing. The educated person is skilled in listening and observing.
Health knowledge. The educated person understands the basic facts concerning health and disease.
Health habits. The educated person protects his own health and that of his dependents.
Public health. The educated person works to improve the health of the community.
Recreation. The educated person is a participant and spectator in many sports and other pastimes.
Intellectual interests. The educated person has mental resources for the use of leisure.

[2] Educational Policies Commission. *The Purposes of Education in American Democracy.* Washington, D.C.: National Education Association, 1938, p. 41.

Esthetic interests. The educated person appreciates beauty.

Character. The educated person gives responsible direction to his own life.

Human Relationships

Respect for humanity. The educated person puts human relationships first.

Friendships. The educated person enjoys a rich, sincere, and varied social life.

Cooperation. The educated person can work and play with others.

Courtesy. The educated person observes the amenities of social behavior.

Appreciation of the home. The educated person appreciates the family as a social institution.

Conservation of the home. The educated person conserves family ideals.

Homemaking. The educated person is skilled in homemaking.

Democracy in the home. The educated person maintains democratic family relationships.

Economic Efficiency

Work. The educated producer knows the satisfaction of good workmanship.

Occupational information. The educated producer understands the requirements and opportunities for various jobs.

Occupational choice. The educated producer has *selected* his occupation.

Occupational efficiency. The educated producer succeeds in his chosen vocation.

Occupational adjustment. The educated producer maintains and improves his efficiency.

Occupational appreciation. The educated producer appreciates the social value of his work.

Personal economics. The educated consumer plans the economics of his own life.

Consumer judgment. The educated consumer develops standards for guiding his expenditures.

Efficiency in buying. The educated consumer is an informed and skillful buyer.

Consumer protection. The educated consumer takes appropriate measures to safeguard his interests.

Civic Responsibility

Social justice. The educated citizen is sensitive to the disparities of human circumstance.

Social activity. The educated citizen acts to correct unsatisfactory conditions.

Social understanding. The educated citizen seeks to understand social structures and social processes.

Critical judgment. The educated citizen has defenses against propaganda.

Tolerance. The educated citizen respects honest differences of opinion.

Conservation. The educated citizen has a regard for the nation's resources.

Social applications of science. The educated citizen measures scientific advance by its contribution to the general welfare.

World citizenship. The educated citizen is a cooperating member of the world community.

Law observance. The educated citizen respects the law.

Economic literacy. The educated citizen is economically literate.

Political citizenship. The educated citizen accepts his civic duties.

Devotion to democracy. The educated citizen acts upon an unswerving loyalty to democratic ideas.

Fourteen Goals, Whitehouse Conference on Education, 1955

At the Whitehouse Conference on Education in 1955 representatives of various groups across the country proposed the following basic goals for education:[3]

1 The fundamental skills of communication—reading, writing, spelling, as well as other elements of effective oral and written expression; the arithmetical and mathematical skills, including problem solving

2 Appreciation for our democratic heritage

3 Civil rights and responsibilities and knowledge of American institutions

4 Respect and appreciation for human values and for the beliefs of others

5 Ability to think and evaluate constructively and creatively

6 Effective work habits and self discipline

7 Social competence as a contributing member of his family and community

8 Ethical behavior based on a sense of moral and spiritual values

9 Intellectual curiosity and eagerness for life-long learning

10 Esthetic appreciation and self expression in the arts

11 Physical and mental health

12 Wise use of time, including constructive leisure pursuits

13 Understanding of the physical world and man's relation to it as represented through basic knowledge of the sciences

14 An awareness of our relationships with the world community

Thinking Ability, The Central Purpose, 1961

In a report published in 1961 by the National Education Association, the Educational Policies Commission stated: "The purpose which runs through and strengthens all other educational purposes—the common thread of education—is the development of the ability to think."[4] Members of the commission also stated that this was not the only goal of education, but that it was basic to the achievement of other goals. Civic responsibility and other goals stated by the commission in 1938 cannot be attained in the schools without developing the ability to think.

[3] *Proceedings, Whitehouse Conference on Education.* Washington, D.C.: Government Printing Office, 1955.

[4] Educational Policies Commission, *The Central Purpose of American Education*, Washington, D.C.: National Education Association, 1961.

Priorities and Joint Responsibilities, Project on Instruction, 1963[5]

In a major project on instruction carried on by the National Education Association, the following broad goals were identified in two categories, the first as priorities for schools, and the second as joint responsibilities of the school and other social agencies:

Priorities of the School

1 The teaching of skills in reading, composition, listening, speaking (both native and foreign languages), and computation
2 Ways of creative and disciplined thinking, including methods of inquiry and application of knowledge
3 Competence in self instruction and independent learning
4 Fundamental understanding of the humanities and the arts, the social sciences and natural sciences, and mathematics
5 Appreciation of and discriminating taste in literature, music, and the visual arts
6 Instruction in health education and physical education

Joint Responsibilities

1 Development of values and ideals
2 Social and civic competence
3 Vocational preparation

Eighteen Goals of Education, Phi Delta Kappa, 1973[6]

In a survey conducted by Phi Delta Kappa, a professional education fraternity, a random sample of over 1,000 members was asked to rank 18 goals as to importance. Presented below are the goals as ranked by 609 of the members who were representative of the total membership on several factors. Each goal is followed by descriptive phrases that have been excerpted from more detailed statements.

1 Develop reading, writing, speaking, and listening skills
(communication of ideas and feelings; skill in oral and written English)
2 Develop pride in work and a feeling of self-worth
(achievement and progress; self-understanding; self-assurance)
3 Develop good character and self-respect
(ethical and moral behavior; self-discipline; work, study and play constructively; values, goals and processes of a free society; standards of personal character and ideas)

[5] Ole Sand (Director), *Project on Instruction*. Washington, D.C.: National Education Association, 1963.
[6] Harold Spears, "Kappans Ponder the Goals of Education," *Phi Delta Kappa*, 55, 29–32, September, 1973.

4 Develop a desire for learning now and in the future
(curiosity and eagerness for lifelong learning; positive attitude toward learning and continuing independent education)

5 Learn to respect and get along with people with whom we work and live
(worth and dignity of individuals; minority opinion, major decision; cooperative attitude)

6 Learn how to examine and use information
(constructive and creative examination: scientific methods; reasoning abilities; logical thinking and proceeding)

7 Gain a general education
(numbers, sciences, mathematics, social sciences; information and concepts; special interests and abilities)

8 Learn how to be a good citizen
(civic rights and responsibilities; attitudes for citizenship in a democracy; respect for personal and private property; obligations and responsibility of citizenship)

9 Learn about and try to understand changes that take place in the world
(adjust to changing societal demands and a changing world and its problems; understand the past, identify with the present, meet the future)

10 Understand and practice democratic ideas and ideals
(loyalty to ideals; patriotism and loyalty to democratic ideas; rights and privileges in our democracy; understanding of American heritage)

11 Learn how to respect and get along with people who think, dress, and act differently (understanding of other people and cultures, other political, economic and social patterns; awareness of interdependence and processes of group relationships)

12 Understand and practice skills of family living
(group living principles; attitudes of acceptance of responsibility; awareness of future family responsibilities and skills needed to carry them out)

13 Gain information needed to make job selections
(self-understanding and self-direction in relation to occupational interests; use of information and counseling services; vocational information)

14 Learn how to be a good manager of money, property, and resources
(economic principles and responsibilities; personal buying, selling, investment; management of resources and the environment)

15 Practice and understand the ideas of health and safety
(individual physical fitness; understanding of good health and well being; sound personal habits and information; public health and safety)

16 Develop skills to enter a specific field of work
(skills for immediate employment; requirements for a specific type of work; appreciation of good workmanship)

17 Learn how to use leisure time
(productive use of leisure; variety of intellectual, physical, and creative activities; interests that lead to wise and enjoyable use of leisure)

18 Appreciate culture and beauty in the world
(expression of ideas and cultural appreciation—fine arts; beauty in various forms; self-expression through art, music, writing; special talents in art, music, literature, foreign language)

PROPOSED GOALS OF EDUCATION

The following six major goals of education are based on a review of those noted in the preceding pages and others cited in the references at the end of this chapter. The six goals include the four proposed by the Educational Policies Commission in 1938 because of their enduring importance and their relevance in terms of the current scene. To these four have been added thinking ability and learning how to learn because of their critical importance now and in the future.

The six proposed goals are broad enough in scope to include those noted above. They are of enduring value, are reflective of democratic values, and make possible the inclusion of new developments within categories of goals that give a sense of direction to overall curriculum planning. There is consistency among them and they are interrelated in a variety of ways. For example, thinking ability and learning how to learn run through the others, self-realization is nurtured in the context of human relationships which in turn may be enhanced by and may help to enhance growth in civic and economic competence. Yet there are distinctive features of each goal to which we now turn.

Thinking Ability Even though some have argued that this is not *the* central goal of education, it certainly is *a* central goal. It is basic to the attainment of other goals, as pointed out by the Educational Policies Commission. Subsumable under it are objectives related to development and use of modes, methods, and processes of inquiry, reasoning ability, critical and creative thinking, problem solving, use of concepts as tools of thinking, and attitudes and values such as openmindedness, thoughtful skepticism, and objectivity in use of evidence.

Self-realization The development of each individual's potentialities to the fullest has been prized for many generations. Subsumable under this goal are objectives related to development of reading, arithmetic and other basic skills, understanding of the social and physical environment, self-respect and wholesome self-concept, health and physical fitness, use of leisure time, ethical values and character, aesthetic interests, taste in literature, music, and visual arts, regard for one's ethnic and cultural background, ability to meet and cope with change, ability to clarify values, and personal enrichment through grounding in the sciences, humanities, and arts.

Human Relationships Of enduring importance is the quality of human relationships in settings that range from the home and community to those of national and international complexity. Included under this goal are the development of respect for humanity, intergroup relations, concern for general welfare and human dignity, minority pride and respect, regard for other groups and cultures, cooperative relationships in work and play, ability to deal with changing relationships and to foster effective relationships, competence in clarifying values in group decision making and using ethical means of group persuasion, and ability to live by democratic ideals, beliefs, and processes.

Economic Competence Over the years the schools of America have been called upon to provide experiences that will help to develop the competence needed for economic independence, a cherished aim of individuals and groups in our society. Related to this basic goal are such current concerns as career awareness, dignity of all types of work, regard for good workmanship, basic skills for occupational success, extension of equal opportunity to all individuals and groups, contributions of individuals and groups, role of labor and industry, consumer buying, protection, and judgment, management of money, property and resources, how to function in our economic system, and use of values to make and appraise economic decisions.

Civic Responsibility Schools have a central role to play in the development of civic responsibility, which is essential to the success of democratic government. Related to this goal are such long-standing and current concerns as civic rights and responsibilities, democratic ideals, ideas, and processes, social understanding, justice and activity, respect for law and property, ways to change the laws, ways of extending equal opportunity and justice to all individuals and groups, ways to improve the effectiveness of government, and participation in decision making and social action.

Learning How to Learn Ongoing lifelong learning has become both a personal and social responsibility if we are to keep abreast of the knowledge explosion and deal effectively with problems of change. Of more recent origin than the others, this goal has been receiving increasing emphasis through statements that refer to independent study skills, learning to use the methods of science, competence in self-instruction, discovery of ways of knowing through the arts, use of mass media and other resources for independent learning, learning how to examine and use information, positive attitudes of intellectual curiosity, and eagerness toward independent and lifelong learning.

FROM GOALS TO OBJECTIVES

A basic step in curriculum planning is formulation of objectives that are contributory to the attainment of major goals. One effective way of doing so is to analyze each major goal in depth and to specify related objectives. This may be done by identifying behaviors that students should develop if they are to attain the goal. The following examples are illustrative.

The goal to develop thinking ability includes problem solving, critical thinking, and creative thinking. Each of these modes of thinking may be broken down into various components. For example, problem solving includes such procedures as defining the problem, gathering data related to the problem, appraising, organizing, and interpreting the data, and stating a conclusion or solution to the problem. Each of these may be turned into a behavioral objective as shown in the following example that begins with the general goal.

To develop competence in problem solving so that the student is able to:

Define a given problem by stating it in his own words.

Collect data related to a problem by reading, interviewing, or observing films and making notes on items related to the problem.

Appraise data by checking one source against another and noting any differences which can be checked against another source.

Organize data by making an outline, table, or graph.

Interpret data by stating in his own words summary of findings and how they are related to the problem.

State a conclusion or solution to the problem by stating in his own words how the problem may be solved.

Notice in the examples above that each of the behaviors may be observed by the teacher. Also notice that only a sampling of behaviors, and not all behavior, related to problem solving has been identified. Two fundamental principles are involved here. The first is that objectives should indicate behavior, or a product of behavior, that can be observed. The examples above are directly observable instances of behavior. Notice that specific verbs such as stating and making notes (writing) were used rather than vague words such as "appreciate," "understand," or "know." In a situation in which a model, map, mural, or other product were to be the main outcome, then the product could be examined to determine if the objective had been attained. The second principle is that an adequate sampling of behavior should be identified so that the teacher can have confidence that a student who exhibits the specified behavior is moving toward the attainment of the objective. But it must be recognized that the specified behaviors are only a sampling and teachers should be alert to other behaviors that may be even more indicative of the attainment of a given objective.

Another basic consideration in moving from goals to objectives involves levels of complexity of learning and internalization of learning. Two taxonomies that are especially helpful in this regard are presented in the following section. Examples of behavioral objectives are given to further illustrate how goals may be transformed into objectives.

TAXONOMIES OF EDUCATIONAL OBJECTIVES

Two taxonomies that are widely used were originally prepared to classify objectives so that communication among examiners could be improved regarding the meaning of objectives, examples of different types of test items, and possible testing procedures (Bloom et al., 1956; Krathwohl et al., 1964). Since their publication educators have been able to use these taxonomies to identify objectives design questions, plan for evaluation, and classify objectives, questions, and activities. One taxonomy is focused on the cognitive domain, which includes intellectual abilities such as recalling information, interpreting data, and applying concepts and other learnings. The second taxonomy is focused on affective objectives related to attitudes, values, interests, and appreciations. The two taxonomies are interrelated in the sense that cognitive learnings do have accompanying affective dimensions and there is a cognitive element in affective learning.

The Cognitive Domain

Six categories in this taxonomy are organized according to level of complexity, beginning with knowledge and its recall and moving to evaluation. The ability of a student to function on higher levels is dependent upon mastery of preceding levels. A brief discussion of types of objective is included in each category and illustrative objectives follow.

Knowledge Included at this level are objectives related to the learning and recalling of specific terms and facts, conventions, trends, classifications and categories, methodologies, principles and generalizations, and theories and structures.

Illustrative Objective To describe five simple machines and state three reasons why they make work easier

Comprehension This level is a step more complex than learning and recalling knowledge. Objectives at this level are related to development of the student's ability to (1) translate what has been learned from one level of abstraction, verbal form, or symbolic form to another; (2) interpret what has been learned by relating parts, giving a summary, making qualifications, or explaining the essentials; and (3) extrapolate by extension to past and future situations.

Illustrative Objective To interpret a table showing population growth by stating in his own words the years in which growth was greater than 10 percent

Application Objectives at this level are related to the student's ability to apply what he has learned and comprehends in new tasks or situations. The student should be able to apply terms and concepts, generalizations, laws, models, and criteria.

Illustrative Objective To apply two concepts of civil liberties by stating or writing how they are involved in a recent action taken by the city council to protect the rights of minority groups

Analysis Going beyond the preceding levels, this category includes objectives related to breaking a whole into parts and identifying elements, relationships, and organizing principles.

Illustrative Objective To describe the two assumptions made by the writer of the environmental report and to state how the assumptions are related to his recommendations on reducing air pollution

Synthesis Next to the highest level of complexity, this category includes objectives related to putting parts together in a new form, producing a unique communication or plan, and other creative activities in which various elements are unified.

Illustrative Objective To construct a model that shows how water erosion takes place

Evaluation Objectives in this category are designed to develop the student's ability to make judgments of worth in terms of either internal or external criteria.

Illustrative Objective To distinguish between drawings which illustrate effective use of color and line to focus attention on a central feature and drawings that do not

Affective Domain

Included in this taxonomy are five categories of objectives that deal with values, attitudes, appreciations, and other affective dimensions of learning. The categories are arranged in hierarchical order according to degree of internalization.

Receiving This level is indicative of sufficient interest to attend or be aware and includes objectives designed to foster the development of a willingness to attend to what is presented or an initial interest in an activity or object.

Illustrative Objective To demonstrate an interest in music by listening to the first part of the *Peer Gynt Suite*

Responding Objectives in this category go beyond attention and awareness to include those designed to get students to respond in a preferred way (compliance), to respond willingly on their own, and to respond with a feeling of satisfaction.

Illustrative Objective To select books voluntarily for pleasure reading and to state ways in which they are interesting

Valuing Objectives at this level include behavior indicative of acceptance of a value, preference of a value, and commitment or conviction.

Illustrative Objective To demonstrate a conviction by writing a letter to the city council on the need to eliminate a safety hazard

Organization This level of internalization involves conceptualization of values, clarification of relationships among values, and organization of a value system.

Illustrative Objective To make and state judgments on issues and proposals related to extension of equality of opportunity to women

Characterization This is the highest level of internalization that is attained in adulthood. Objectives in this category are related to development of a generalized set of values and ultimately a philosophy of life.

Illustrative Objective To demonstrate in a variety of situations adherence to clusters of values that are rooted in a philosophy of life

Most relevant to curriculum planning at the elementary school level are the first three categories presented above. The last two may be given attention in secondary schools; for many individuals they are representative of lifelong goals that involve intensive reflection on value-laden issues and problems.

Psychomotor Domain

Although the individuals who developed the taxonomies for the cognitive and affective domains have not developed one for the psychomotor domain, a taxonomy has been prepared by Harrow (1972). Harrow's taxonomy includes six levels, beginning with reflex movements and fundamental movements and moving to perceptual abilities, physical abilities, skilled movements, and non-discursive communication. A brief description and illustrative objectives of the five levels emphasized in instruction follow.

Fundamental Movements Included at this level are objectives related to walking, running, jumping, pushing, pulling, and manipulating objects.

Illustrative Objective To demonstrate the ability to roll a ball to a classmate

Perceptual Abilities This level includes objectives related to kinesthetic, visual, auditory, tactile, and coordination abilities.

Illustrative Objective To demonstrate the ability to copy letters of the alphabet

Physical Abilities This level includes objectives related to endurance, strength, flexibility, agility, reaction-response time, and dexterity.

Illustrative Objective To demonstrate the ability to do five pullups

Skilled Movements This level includes objectives related to the skills involved in games, sports, dance, and the arts.

Illustrative Objective To demonstrate the ability to catch a fly ball

Nondiscursive Communication This level includes objectives related to expressive movement through posture, gestures, and facial expression, and to interpretive movement through creative expression.

Illustrative Objective To demonstrate the ability to create a rhythmic movement sequence and carry it out to a musical accompaniment

Because movement behaviors are so easily observed it is relatively less difficult to write objectives for them, and to evaluate their development, than it is for the other domains. Specific attention has been given to them in curriculum materials for many years as a part of the skill development program in physical education, handwriting, art, and music. For example, physical education guides include attention to gross and fine muscular movements, a variety of physical abilities, skills needed in various games and sports, and interpretive movement activities. In music education are such objectives as identifying higher and lower pitches, expressing emotion through movement, clapping to rhythm, and improvising melodies. Other examples are given in the chapters that follow under the heading of *skills*.*

*For other examples see: Elizabeth A. Simpson. *The Classification of Educational Objectives: Psychomotor Domain*. Urbana, Ill.: University of Illinois, Contract No. E 5-85-104, 1966; and Maxine R. Moore. *A Proposed Taxonomy of the Perceptual Domain and Some Suggested Applications*, Princeton, N.J.: Educational Testing Service, 1967.

Let us turn now to a detailed discussion of ways in which specific objectives can be stated so that they are useful in planning instruction and evaluating learning.

GUIDELINES FOR STATING OBJECTIVES

One approach to the writing of behavioral objectives that is widely used calls for attention to three characteristics of a clearly stated objective (Mager, 1962). The first is identification of behavior of the student that may be observed or a product of the student's efforts that may be examined. If the focus is on behavior, then terms such as *list, write, state, identify, name, order,* or *describe* may be used. If the focus is on a product, then terms such as make, *construct, design, produce,* or *prepare* may be used. For example, notice the behavior specified in the following objectives: The student will *describe* a covered wagon. The student will prepare a two-step outline.

The second characteristic of a clear objective is related to the conditions under which the student is to work. What materials are to be used? What activity is to be undertaken? Questions such as these help to pinpoint the conditions under which the student is to work. Adding conditions to the objectives noted above, we have the following: The student should describe a covered wagon after *seeing the film* on moving westward. The student should prepare a two-step outline after *study and discussion* of pages 58 and 59 in the language textbook.

The third characteristic of a clear objective is related to the level of performance that is desired of students. What percentage of accuracy is desired? How many items should be described, listed, and so on? What level of achievement is essential? Questions such as these help to identify the performance level. Adding performance level to the objectives above we have this statement: The student will describe at least *three features* of a covered wagon after seeing the film on the covered wagon. The student will prepare a two-step outline with at least *two major headings* and *two subheadings* after reading and discussing pages 58 to 59 in the language textbook.

The following objectives further illustrate the three characteristics noted above:

The student will demonstrate ¾ time (behavior) by moving in time with a recording (conditions) and do so without missing a beat (performance level).

The student will state (behavior) at least two causes of air pollution in our city (performance level) after hearing the committee report (conditions).

The student will make (behavior) a map that shows the three main travel routes westward (performance level) after reading pages 120 to 121 in the textbook (condition).

The student will describe (behavior) the three values that were prized by the pioneers (performance level), after seeing the film on pioneer life (conditions).

There are two other characteristics of clearly stated objectives that some teachers find helpful to keep in mind as they prepare objectives. The first is the time at which the students should be able to attain the objective. For example, should the objective be attained today, at the end of a unit, or at the end of the term or year? The second feature is the object of the behavior, being sure that it is clearly specified. The following objectives include the identification of these two added features:

By the end of the unit (time), the student will describe (behavior) at least two (performance level) values held by the pioneers (object), as presented in the film and reading materials listed in the study guide (conditions).

By the end of the semester (time), the student will make (behavior) a chart of four basic foods (object) out of pictures cut from magazines (conditions), showing at least four foods in each group (performance level).

Several other points should be kept in mind as behavioral objectives are written. The first point is related to the students who should be able to achieve the objective. Should all students? If not, which ones should? For example, the following illustrates the limiting of an objective to those students who are ready to move ahead: By the end of this lesson, those students who have completed their written reports will make a map that shows the location of the first three settlements in our state, using an outline map and pencils.

A second consideration is whether or not an open or closed objective is desired. A closed objective is one designed to develop the same behavior on the part of students; it is used when convergent thinking is being stressed. The examples above are illustrative of closed objectives. An open objective is designed to develop different types of behavior on the part of students; it is used when divergent thinking is desired. Here is an example: The student will draw a picture of a covered wagon that represents what he believes to be the most important features. A second example is: After studying models of Haiku poetry presented by the teacher, the student will write a Haiku poem that expresses any idea he believes is interesting.

Another point to consider is related to covert behavior and overt behavior on the part of students. Such important process behaviors as generalizing, inferring, and evaluating are covert behaviors; they cannot be observed directly.

The problem is to identify related overt behaviors of students which are related to the important covert behavior that is being developed. This problem is easily handled by stating the covert behavior first and then noting overt behaviors that may serve as observable indicators of the covert behavior. The following objective is illustrative: After seeing the film, the student will infer (covert behavior) how the pioneers felt when the scout failed to return by stating (overt behavior) at least two feelings and giving the reasons for them. As a second example: After studying the diagram showing zones of a city, the student will interpret (covert behavior) the map of our city by pointing to (overt behavior) at least three zones similar to those shown on the diagram. For a third example: After reading the assigned story, the student will generalize (covert behavior) by stating (overt behavior) in one sentence the main idea the author is conveying.

The procedure noted above may be used as a general guideline for writing instructional objectives. The principle is to state the covert behavior first and to follow it with an adequate sampling of overt behavior. This procedure is especially effective in moving from objectives of a general nature to those that are observable. Notice in the following examples that general objectives indicative of covert behavior do include terms that many teachers use in daily planning but that their meaning is not clear until the examples of overt behavior are read.

Students will develop concepts of people's need and provision for human shelter so that they are able to do the following:

State at least three reasons why people need shelter
Describe the type of shelter provided in at least three different climatic regions
List at least six different materials that are used to provide shelter

Students are to develop skill in creative writing so that they are able to do any one of the following by the end of the first semester:

Write at least two hundred words on a topic of choice
Write a dialogue between two people on a topic of choice
Describe the kind of person the student would like to be in ten years

Students are to develop and apply values such as equality and freedom of expression so that by the end of the year they are able to do the following:

State the freedoms in the Bill of Rights and give an example of how each one has been a key value in current or past event
Write a list of at least four actions an individual can carry out to provide for equality of justice
Describe two personal incidents in which they attempted to uphold freedom of expression

Special attention needs to be given to the writing of objectives in the affective domain. Attitudes, values, interests, and appreciations may be emphasized in objectives as noted in the following examples:

By the end of the first term, students will show an interest in reading by:

Selecting a story to read at least once a week during free time
Sharing during group discussion ideas discovered in reading
Describing the behavior of interesting individuals in stories

After completing the year's study of cultures in other lands, the students will demonstrate favorable attitudes toward people in other cultures by:

Stating at least three things discovered in another culture they would like to try to do, giving two reasons for their choices
Stating the reasons for at least three examples of behavior different from our own which they would not like to emulate
Describe how they might behave in at least three specific situations if they were to live in another culture of interest to them, giving a reason for each behavior they identify

By the end of this unit students will demonstrate an appreciation of the importance of values in people's behavior by:

Describing the actions taken by individuals who struggled to maintain freedom of speech in at least two historical events
Stating how a personal activity at home or in school was guided by a value such as concern for others
Listing at least three things a student can do in school to demonstrate the importance of respect for each individual

Notice in all the examples above attention is directed to aspects of behavior that are associated with the interest, attitude, or appreciation that is to be developed. The listed behaviors represent only a small sampling of behavior that may be associated with the interest, attitude, or appreciation. By observing behavior directly it may be possible to identify other behaviors that are even more indicative of the development of an affective outcome. For example, informal comments made by a child immediately after reading a selection may serve as an indicator of growing interest or a favorable attitude.

To summarize, the following may be used to write fairly complete performance objectives in any area of the curriculum:

Time. Indicate the time by which students should meet the objective: after completing this lesson . . . at the end of the unit . . . by the end of the year . . .

Who. Note whether all or certain students should attain the objective:
students who have completed . . . 80% of the students . . . all students should . . .
Behavior. Note the behavior to observe:
state . . . describe . . . list . . . name . . . arrange . . . construct . . . prepare . . .
Object. Note what is being studied, handled, or used:
the reasons for . . . an interesting character . . . steps in making steel . . . a map
of . . .
Performance level. Note criteria of performance that are desired:
at least three . . . 100% accuracy . . . three of the four main causes . . .
Conditions. Indicate related activities or materials that are essential:
given a ruler and pencil . . . using a dictionary . . . when given three choices . . .

A helpful device to facilitate consistency and completeness in the writing of
objectives is a model format which includes spaces for writing in each element
discussed above. The following model is illustrative:

Time
_____

Who
_____

Behavior
_____

Object
_____

Performance level
_____

Conditions
_____

A second example of a model format begins with a statement of a general
objective or covert behavior followed by observable or overt behavior as noted
in the examples presented above.

Write general objective or covert behavior
_____

_____

List related overt behavior
_____

_____

_____

When using this format, such elements as time, object, which students, performance level, and conditions may be identified along with the covert or overt
behaviors.

FOLLOW-UP ACTIVITIES AND PROJECTS

1 Three functions of education as an institution are (1) to transmit the cultural heritage, (2) to develop the potentialities of the individual, and (3) to promote social change in desirable directions. Review the goal statements presented in the first part of this chapter and identify those goals that relate to the first function. Next, identify goals that relate to the other two functions. Which statements include balanced attention to all three functions?

2 Prepare your own list of major goals and discuss it with others. On which goals is there agreement? Disagreement? How might the disagreements be resolved? Which of the three functions noted above are emphasized?

3 Analyze one of the major goals proposed by the authors, or one on your own list. Indicate specific behaviors that are observable on the part of students who are moving toward attainment of the goal, using the example on problem solving as a guide.

4 Use the guidelines and model formats for writing objectives at the end of this chapter to prepare eight to ten behavioral objectives. Do half of them on different levels of the cognitive domain and the other half on different levels of the effective domain.

BIBLIOGRAPHY

Baker, Robert L., and Richard E. Schutz (Eds.) *Instructional Product Development*. New York: Van Nostrand, 1971. Instructions for preparing objectives using five verbs: identify, name, construct, describe, order.

Bloom, Benjamin S. (Ed.) *Taxonomy of Educational Objectives: Cognitive Domain*. New York: McKay, 1956. Objectives and test items arranged by level of complexity.

Burns, Richard W. *New Approaches to Behavioral Objectives*. Dubuque, Iowa: Wm. C. Brown, 1972. How to write different types of objectives and to restate goals as objectives.

Ebel, Robert L., "Evaluation and Educational Objectives," *Journal of Educational Measurement*, **10**; 273-279, 1973. Critique of emphasis on detailed behavioral objectives and related problems.

Gagné, Robert M., and Leslie J. Briggs. *Principles of Instructional Design*. New York: Holt, 1974. Chapters on outcomes of instruction and defining performance objectives.

Harrow, Anita J. *Taxonomy of the Psychomotor Domain: A Guide for Developing Behavioral Objectives*. New York: McKay, 1972. Observable movement behaviors arranged from simple to complex.

Kearney, Nolan C. *Elementary School Objectives*. New York: Russell Sage, 1953. Objectives related to knowledge and understandings, skills and competences, attitudes and interests, and action patterns.

Krathwohl, David R., Benjamin S. Bloom, and Bert Masia. *Taxonomy of Educational Objectives: Affective Domain*. New York: McKay, 1964. Objectives and sample items arranged by degree of internalization.

Mager, Robert F. *Preparing Instructional Objectives*. Palo Alto, Calif.: Fearon, 1962. Procedures for writing behavioral objectives.

Maloney, Henry B. (Ed.) *Accountability and the Teaching of English*. Urbana, Ill.: National Council of the Teachers of English, 1972. Articles on the pros and cons of behavioral objectives and humanistic goals.

McAshan, H. H. *The Goals Approach to Performance Objectives*. Philadelphia: Saunders, 1974. Procedures for converting goals to objectives.

"NCSS Reports on National Assessment of Educational Progress," *Social Education*, **38**; 398–430, May, 1974. Articles on national assessment, illustrative objectives, procedures, and problems;

For a variety of examples of behavioral objectives, see the following sources:

Flanagan, John C., William M. Shanner, and Robert Mager. *Behavioral Objectives: A Guide for Individualizing Learning*. New York: Westinghouse Learning Press, 1971.

Instructional Objectives Exchange. Los Angeles: University of California at Los Angeles, Center for Study of Evaluation. Duplicated collections of behavioral objectives.

National Assessment of Educational Progress. Denver: NAESP, 822 Lincoln Tower, 1860 Lincoln St. 80203. Objectives for ten areas being assessed.

SCORE. School Curriculum Objective-Referenced Evaluation. Iowa City, Iowa: Westinghouse Learning Corporation, 1974. Bank of 8,000 objectives and 20,000 related test items.

Chapter 5

Guidelines
for Organizing
the Curriculum

Guidelines for use in organizing the curriculum are considered in this chapter in terms of several perspectives. The orientation to the structuring of areas of the curriculum is discussed in terms of three points of departure—subject matter or disciplinary, society, and the child. Of critical importance is the use of four key factors in organizing the curriculum: scope, sequence, cumulative learning, and integration of learning. Another critical task is the identification and selection of content of the curriculum, both substantive and methodological. Detailed attention is given to the planning and organization of units of instruction because it is through units that the curriculum emerges in the classroom. The final section is a review of emerging guidelines that have been and are being used in the development of new curricula. Specific attention is given to general procedures, systems approaches, patterns of organization, roles of various individuals, community involvement, and topics included in curriculum guides and frameworks.

ORGANIZATION OF AREAS OF THE CURRICULUM

Three different orientations, points of departure, or approaches have been used to organize areas of the curriculum. The most widely used in the past and today is the subject-matter or disciplinary orientation, which uses content from the disciplines on which areas of the curriculum are based as the point of departure and structures the content in a sequence that is compatible with child development characteristics. The content may be organized in broad fields such as social studies, language arts, or science education which include content from several different disciplines. Content may also be organized in separate subjects such as art, music, spelling, and physical education.

Varying degrees of emphasis on correlation and integration may be found in the approaches above. At times art, music, and other areas may be a part of social studies instruction as units about various cultures are under study. An interdisciplinary approach is used in the study of environmental, urban, and other problems, with content drawn from science, health, social studies, art, and other areas. At other times social studies and language arts may be interrelated to sharpen the applications of expressive skills. The guiding principle is to bring together content and skills from any subject that will help to attain objectives.

Another orientation takes society—conditions, changes, problems—as a point of departure. Content is selected and organized around persistent life situations confronted by students, or around social functions or areas of living such as government, education, health, recreation, making a living, and making a home. Developmental sequences of instruction are planned in accord with growth characteristics of children. Continuing analysis of society is needed along with continuing selection and transformation of content drawn from various disciplines so that the content can be fitted into the life situations or areas of living under study.

Still another orientation takes the child as the point of departure for planning the curriculum. Content is selected in terms of interests, felt needs, basic urges or drives, and concerns of children. The child-centered curriculum during the 1920s and some free schools and alternative schools of today are illustrative of this approach which has been carried out in a variety of forms. Other examples are the emerging curriculum, which is marked by teacher-pupil planning from day to day, and the "personal problems of living curriculum" in which problems confronted by students are the focus of instruction.

Several reasons for the continuing use of subject-matter orientation to development of areas of the curriculum have been identified. These range from tradition, preparation of teachers, and organization of basic knowledge to the need to structure programs in terms of disciplines, the continuing flow of new knowledge in various subjects, and the need for students to become grounded in basic areas of study. To these may be added the problems and difficulties that arise in making continuing transformations of knowledge from ongoing areas of study to fit life situations, social functions, felt needs, interests, and the like.

The use of a subject-matter orientation as the point of departure for planning areas of the curriculum will continue into the foreseeable future, but the other orientations need not and should not be disregarded. Useful ideas from other orientations should be incorporated within such broad fields as the social studies, science education, mathematics education, health and physical education, the language arts, and aesthetic studies. For example, children's interests and needs, significant life situations, social changes and problems, and teacher-pupil planning within a framework of developmental programs of instruction can be and, in fact, are being incorporated within broad fields of study. All three orientations—subject matter, society, the child—need to be kept in mind even though only one is used as the initial point of departure for structuring areas of the curriculum.

KEY FACTORS IN ORGANIZING THE CURRICULUM

There are four key factors to consider in organizing the total curriculum, an area of the curriculum, and units of instruction: scope or breadth, sequence of content and learning activities, cumulative learning on the part of students, and integration of students' learning.

Scope or Breadth of the Curriculum

Scope of the total curriculum should be designed to attain stated goals of education. This implies the inclusion of developmental programs of instruction in language arts, mathematics education, science education, health, safety and physical education, and aesthetic studies, including art and music. The neglect of any of the foregoing, which are derived in large part from the natural sciences, the social sciences, and the humanities, severely limits the contributions that can be made to the attainment of basic goals.

The scope of areas of the curriculum is related to objectives of each area and contributions each can make to major goals. The scope may be defined in terms of conceptual, process, skill, and affective objectives, main ideas or conceptual schemes, or basic activities. For example, generalizations about man's development of institutions to meet human needs are used in the social studies, conceptual schemes related to conservation of mass and energy and processes such as inferring and hypothesizing are used in science education, and such activities as painting and drawing are used in art education.

The scope of a unit of instruction is set in terms of the instructional objectives for the unit. The scope may be narrow as in units on a single topic or problem, such as air pollution in our city, or extremely broad in units that deal with a culture or several cultures, such as living in Mexico. As with areas of the curriculum, scope may be operationally set by concepts, processes, skills, and affective outcomes that are desired, or by generalizations, main ideas, or activities.

Sequence of Curriculum and Instruction

Sequence is planned to provide an order of instruction that optimizes children's learning and is consistent with the logic of the subject matter. Principles that combine psychological and logical ordering of content and learning activities include (1) moving from the simple to complex (decoding simple sound elements in reading followed by decoding increasingly complex ones), (2) planning in terms of prerequisite learning (addition facts and other learning prerequisite to column addition), (3) moving from whole to parts (the globe as a sphere representing the earth followed by such parts as land masses, water bodies, etc.), and (d) considering children's needs for personally and socially useful knowledge (safety in school and neighborhood followed by safety on bicycles, etc.). Underlying all the foregoing is the relating of sequences of instruction to children's developmental stages and backgrounds of experience.

Systematically planned sequences may be noted in the conceptual, skill, and process components of curricula. Sequences in reading, spelling, writing, and discussion skills are outlined in detail in language arts guides and instructional materials. Map and globe skills and time and chronology skills are sequenced in terms of increasing complexity in the social studies. The skills involved in using such processes as classifying, interpreting, generalizing, hypothesizing, and analyzing are outlined in science education and in some social studies programs. Art, music, and physical education programs include attention to performing and other doing skills in the psychomotor domain of learning. Mathematics programs include detailed sequences related to such strands as numbers and operations, measurement, and problem solving.

Cumulative Learning

Cumulative learning, or continuity of learning, is closely related to the planning of sequences, but it deserves special comment. Children need opportunities to apply and reinforce prior learning and to extend and enrich learning as they move from level to level. This may be accomplished by cycling or spiraling at various levels or grades such concepts as interdependence and adaptation, such skills as discussion and interviewing, and such processes as reviews of addition to assure depth, breadth, maintenance, transfer, and application of learning. The nurturing of interests and the development of such attitudes as openmindedness and such democratic behaviors as cooperativeness require recurring learning experiences on progressively higher levels of internalization.

Integration of Learning

Ways in which instruction can contribute to integration of children's learning is a fourth guidelines to keep in mind in curriculum planning. This may be accomplished within units of instruction, within areas of the curriculum, and across areas of the curriculum. For example, within units dealing with environmental problems, health and safety, other cultures, and current issues and problems, content from different fields of knowledge is needed; core processes such as interpreting and synthesizing are used; language, number, and other skills are essential; and openmindedness and other attitudes are involved. Integration within areas of the curriculum is evident in mathematics programs in which elements of algebra, geometry, sets, and measurement are fused with various aspects of arithmetic. Similarly, science education, social studies, and the language arts bring together materials from a variety of fields. Integration across areas of the curriculum is frequently done by focusing on large issues and problems which require content from a variety of fields of knowledge, for example, such problems as conservation of resources, urban renewal, and impact of technology on daily living. The social studies serve as an integrating core in some studies in which art, music, crafts, and other fields are drawn upon; this also is done at times in health education and selected units in the literature component of language arts programs. A continuing need in all approaches to integration is to give attention to processes, skills, and affective dimensions of learning as well as to conceptual dimensions.

IDENTIFYING AND SELECTING CONTENT

The content of the curriculum should be considered in terms of several different types that differ according to level of complexity, recognizing that all types are important and should be selected in terms of criteria. *Facts* such as number facts, dates, place names, directions, health and safety facts, and a host of others are needed in daily living as background for concept development and for other higher learning. *Concepts* such as role, force, tempo, and *concept clusters* such as types of rock (metamorphic, igneous, and sedimentary) are key organizers around which innumerable facts can be structured and which can be used to classify a variety of data; they are also useful in formulating questions to guide study and in formulating generalizations which combine two or more concepts. Themes which also contain two or more concepts are used to design units of instruction and to designate grade level emphases in areas of the curriculum. Examples are impact of science and technology, living in other cultures, the Westward movement, nutrition for healthful living, courage and diversity in literature, art as expression of feeling, and adaptation to environmental change. Main ideas, generalizations, and conceptual schemes are on a higher level and are widely used to structure areas of the curriculum and units of instruction. For example, "Living organisms are in constant change" and "The universe is in constant change" are used with others to structure science curricula.

In selecting content for an area of the curriculum, criteria such as the following are used:

Usefulness in contributing to the attainment of conceptual, process, skill, and affective objectives

Relevance to significant human activities, problems, and issues, and frequency and criticality of use

Reliability, authoritativeness, validity, and up-to-dateness

Adaptability in terms of children's capabilities and backgrounds

Usefulness in planning and organizing instruction, in generating questions and learning activities, and in making applications in a variety of situations

Usefulness in developing skills and modes, methods, and processes of inquiry

Usefulness in explaining a wide variety of phenomena and developing a sense of structure of the field of study

Usefulness in developing competence in clarifying values, attitudes, and value-laden issues and problems

Availability in textbooks, audio-visual resources, and other instructional media

Many analyses of content are available to curriculum workers. Various national education groups have made analyses and suggested concepts and generalizations for different areas of the curriculum. The nationally supported projects in mathematics, science, social studies, and the humanities have included attention to key concepts and generalizations. State and local curriculum committees have also made recommendations. Textbook series in different areas of the curriculum are based on content analyses of sources of information on up-to-date content. Appropriate references in later chapters are made to the various reports on content recommendations dealing with areas of the curriculum.

UNIT ORGANIZATION AND PLANNING

It is in units of instruction that the curriculum takes operational form. This is so because units contain in micro form the elements that are basic in curriculum planning. It is in units of instruction that specific applications of the foundations are made, contributions to goals are realized in the classroom, teaching strategies and instructional media are set in the context of learning activities, and direct evaluation of children's learning is accomplished.

Unit Organization

Several common elements may be noted in most units even though a variety of formats are used. These elements and examples of them are as follows:

The Title is descriptive of a major area of study, a topic, a problem, or a theme.

Example MEETING OUR NEEDS FOR FOOD

Background Information may be included to indicate concepts, main ideas, related information, special emphases, place of the unit in the program, and other information useful to the teacher.

Example This unit is part of a sequence that deals with ways in which people meet their needs for food, shelter, and clothing. Main ideas and related content are supported by available materials.

Main Idea Four basic food groups are needed for health.
  (1) milk, cheese, other dairy foods
  (2) bread, cereals
  (3) fruits, vegetables
  (4) meat, fish, poultry, beans, eggs

Objectives are stated specifically so that unique contributions of the unit are clear, guidelines are set for instruction, and evaluation is possible.

Example After completing this unit, children should be able to describe the four basic food groups and give at least three examples of each.

Initiation of the unit may be indicated by suggesting how to arrange the environment, how to relate the unit to a preceding one, questions that may be posed by the teacher, or a film or other resource that may be used to begin the unit.

Example Arrange a bulletin board that shows shoppers in a good store or the food section of a supermarket. On a table by the bulletin board place cans and packages that are illustrative of basic foods. Write the following question on a strip for placement on the bulletin board: What foods do all of us need?

Organizers in the form of main ideas to be developed, questions to be answered, or problems to be solved are used to group-related learning activities and instructional materials. Sections of the unit may be organized to include opening activities, developmental activities, and concluding activities.

Opening activities. Discuss the bulletin board arrangement and display, encouraging free response and reaction on the part of children. Ask: What are these people doing? Where are they shopping? Where does your family buy food?

Developmental activities. Show picture #45, *Schools, Families, and Neighborhoods*, and ask: What does this picture show? Why do we need food (for health, energy, warmth, growth)? What kinds of food are shown? How might we group them?

Begin a large chart to show main types of good. List types that are shown in the picture.

Concluding activities. Complete the chart showing main kinds of food. Have children summarize the main kinds that all of us need.

Culminating activities may be provided at the end of units to synthesize concepts, main ideas, and other outcomes.

Example The unit may be culminated by making a movie roll which depicts the main types of foods needed by everyone. Children should provide a commentary on why each type is important.

Instructional Materials that are needed to develop the unit may be noted as shown above in relation to learning activities, with a complete citation in the bibliography as shown below.

Evaluation is a part of ongoing activities as well as concluding and culminating activities.

Example Note children's responses to each question listed above, identifying correct and incorrect responses. Provide additional experience for those children who need help in identifying basic food groups and examples of each.

A *Bibliography* for teacher reference includes complete citations of materials for children and background materials for the teacher.

Example Grossman, Ruth H., and John U. Michaelis. *Schools, Families Neighborhoods. A Multimedia Readiness Program.* Menlo Park, Calif.: Addison-Wesley, 1972.

Examples of unit organization in other subject areas are noted in Chapters 8 through 16.

Unit Planning

Major phases of unit planning include the following, which may be carried out in variable order:

1 The unit to be planned is selected after checking the course of study, available instructional materials, and capabilities and developmental characteristics of children for whom it is intended.

2 A background of content is prepared by reviewing related instructional materials, references for teachers, and related teaching guides. The review is used as a basis for preparing main ideas, questions, or problems to be used as

organizers in the unit. If possible, the assistance of an expert is obtained to check the validity of the main ideas and the supporting content.

3 Objectives of the unit are outlined with specific attention to conceptual, process, skill, and affective outcomes. It is helpful to state objectives in performance or behavioral terms to facilitate planning and evaluation.

4 Learning activities are identified with special attention to a variety of types, including:

Intake experiences such as observing, reading, listening, using audio-visual materials, interviewing, interpreting maps and photographs, experimenting

Expressive experiences such as sharing, reporting, discussing, making charts, maps, murals and other materials, role playing, dramatizing, and expressing thoughts and feelings through art and music

Individual, small-group, and whole-group activities

5 A sequence of learning activities is planned with specific attention to the following:

a The initiation of the unit through an arranged environment, introductory discussion, related questions, and relationships to children's background of experience

b Placing main ideas, questions, or problems in order and sequencing learning activities and related instructional materials under each main idea, question, or problem

c Noting opening, developmental, and concluding activities for each main idea, question, or problem

d Possible culminating activities to provide for overall summarizing and integrating experiences

6 Ways of evaluating outcomes during the unit (formative evaluation) and at the end of the unit (summative evaluation) are identified.

7 A bibliography of materials for children and for teacher reference is prepared.

Unit Formats

Unit formats vary from single column arrangements in which objectives, activities, materials, and evaluation suggestions are listed in order to multicolumn arrangements on two-page layouts that show relationships among major elements in the unit. The examples on page 98 are illustrative.[1]

Excerpts from a Teaching Unit

The excerpt presented on pages 99 to 101, from a unit on map and globe skills, is illustrative of a format the authors have found to be helpful. It also illustrates how the methodological and substantive elements can be brought together as

---

[1] For a variety of examples, see John U. Michaelis, *Teaching Units in the Social Sciences.* (Three booklets, one for early grades, grades 2–4, and grades 5–6.) Chicago: Rand McNally, 1966; John U. Michaelis and Everett T. Keach, Jr., *Teaching Strategies for Elementary School Social Studies.* Itasca, Ill.: Peacock Press, 1972.

Content	Learning Activities	Resources

Content	Major Concepts	Skills	Activities	Resources

Generalizations (and other content)	Learning Activities and Materials	Evaluation

Goals and Objectives	Content	Teaching Procedures	Materials

suggested in Chapter 3 on the disciplinary foundations. It will be noted that this part of the unit begins with a focusing question, major understandings, and performance objectives. Notice that the objectives are directly related to the understandings. Inquiry processes are identified in the lefthand column; this is helpful in making sure that methodological elements are included in an appropriate sequence. The substantive elements—data, concepts, and generalizations—are identified in the righthand column. The teaching strategy brings the various elements together in the center column and includes introductory, developmental, and concluding activities. Notice that the key concept *directions* is emphasized throughout this section of the teaching unit.

Evaluation is handled in this section of the unit by observing children's behavior. For example, the way they point in response to questions related to different directions serves as an immediate and direct clue as to whether or not the objectives are being attained. Any children who have difficulties should be given additional instruction in small groups or on an individual basis.

I. HOW CAN WE TELL DIRECTIONS?

Major understandings

East, west, north, and south are fixed directions in the neighborhood. East and west are the directions in which the sun appears in the morning and evening.

Objectives

State that east is toward the early morning sun and west is toward the late afternoon sun.

State that when we stand with our backs to the sun at noon, our shadows are directly in front of us, pointing north.

State that we are looking south when we stand with the sun in front of us at noon.

Point or face east, west, north, or south when asked to do so.

State the direction in which they walk from school to home.

Note: Before introducing this lesson, have the class observe the location of the sun in the morning, at noon, and in the afternoon. Take them to the same spot in front of the school or in the school yard before classes begin in the morning, at noon, and at dismissal on the same day. At each observation, have the children locate the sun. Identify cardinal directions as indicated in the objectives above. After returning to the classroom (and before leaving for the day), have the children note the location of the sun from their room.

Teaching strategy

Inquiry processes	Questions and activities	Data, concepts, generalizations
	Introduction	
Recalling	Which way do we look to see the sun in the morning? Let's all point that way. Do we see the sun there every morning? (When it is not raining, of course.)	*Directions:* East is the direction in which the morning sun is seen, because the earth rotates toward the east.
Defining, classifying	What direction is that? We look east to see the morning sun. What streets are in that direction? (Identify two or three parallel streets, or roads in rural areas.) Who walks east to go home? Who walks along those streets to go home?	*Location; directions:* With the school as the point of reference, some streets, roads, or landmarks can be identified as being located to the east or west of the school.
Defining, classifying	(Follow the same procedure for west.)	*Directions:* West is the direction opposite east.
Classifying	If you live east of the school, raise your hand. If you live west of the school, raise your hand. Some children do not walk east or west to go home.	*Directions:* When you face the sun at noon, you are facing south. When your back is to the sun at noon, your shadow

Inquiry processes	Questions and activities	Data, concepts, generalizations
Classifying (continued)	(Call on some in this latter category.) Which way do you walk to go home? (Refer to directions faced at noon, to help children determine who lives north and south of the school. Some children might demonstrate directions within the classroom by walking east, etc., across the room.)	points north, in front of you. North and south are opposite directions.
Inferring	We use the words "east, west, north, and south" for directions to our homes. Can you use these words for directions if you move far away? Let's find out if people use these directions in other places.	*Directions:* Cardinal directions have the same definitions and use in all parts of the world.

Development

Observing	What is happening in this picture? Is it morning or afternoon? How can you tell? Where do you see the sun? Which way do we look to see the sun in the afternoon? Who can point to the children who are walking west?	*Directions:* In the afternoon, the sun appears to be toward the west.
Observing, interpreting	If you went to this school, which way would you look to see the morning sun? What direction is that? Where is the school bus? Which direction is it going?	*Directions:* In the morning, the sun appears to be toward the east.
Observing, interpreting	Where are the children on bicycles? Which way are they going? Pretend you are riding home with them. As you ride north, where do you see the afternoon sun? Is it on your left side or your right side?	*Directions:* When you face north, east is to your right, west is to your left. When you face south, the morning sun would appear to your left, afternoon sun to the right.
Contrasting, classifying	Which children are going east to go home? Which children are going west? Which ones are going north? Are any other children going home? Which way are they going?	*Directions:* South is the direction opposite north.

Conclusion

Classifying	Think of the way you go home. Who goes east? Who goes west? (Have a show of hands.) Find the children in the picture who go home in the same direction that you go. (Call on children to identify those in the picture who go in their direction.)	*Directions:* Motion on earth, or location of places on earth, can be identified by the cardinal directions of north, south, east, and west.

Concluding activities

Display a sign marked "East." Have children identify who walks east to go home. Have them point to the east in the classroom; post the sign on that wall. Each of the "easterners" might copy the word on a card of their own. Do this for each direction. When finished, call on a child to show his direction card and tell which way he goes home. He might then walk in that direction and tape his card to the appropriate wall. He can call on another child to do the same; each child calling on another until all have been included.

Take a walking trip around the school block just before noon. Have the children note the position of the sun, and ask them to identify the direction in which they are walking after they have turned each corner. If your school is not on a complete block, take the "trip" in the school yard.

As the children make maps or models of their neighborhood, have them indicate cardinal directions from the school. Place the map or model so that it is oriented in the same direction as your classroom.

EMERGING GUIDELINES IN NEW CURRICULA

The process of developing new curricula may be viewed in terms of two broad phases—development and implementation. The development phase may be characterized as the basic planning and design stage of curriculum development. Points of view are clarified and assumptions are made about the role of the school, teaching, and learning; objectives are clarified; organization is defined in terms of main ideas, conceptual schemes, or themes, modes, and processes of inquiry; and content is selected in accord with the objectives, assumptions, and organization. The implementation phase may be characterized as completion and refinement of the instructional program. A critical review is made of available materials of instruction, new materials are prepared if available materials are inadequate, strategies of teaching are selected and tested, and principles and techniques of evaluation are designed and used to assess outcomes. These phases are interlinked, and the steps within them are not followed in an exact order. For example, consideration may be given to problems of teaching and evaluation at many points in both phases.

General Procedures

The overall steps of procedure seem to flow somewhat as follows in complete curriculum development programs that begin with original development of materials and conclude with use at the local level:

Initial Planning
Staking out a domain of study to be given primary attention
Identifying the underlying structure of content and processes and selecting elements to include in instructional materials
Clarifying conceptual, inquiry process, skills, and affective objectives

Designing Units and Guides

Planning sequences of instruction for presenting content and processes

Preparing blocks or units of instruction in which to present the planned sequences of instruction and devising means of assessing instructional outcomes

Preparing related teacher's guides that include teaching strategies which are consistent with methods of inquiry stressed in the materials

Tryout and Revision

Engaging in a pilot tryout of materials and providing related in-service education of teachers

Revising units, evaluation devices, and guides as a result of feedback from the pilot tryout

Engaging in further tryout on a broader scale and providing related in-service education

Revising of materials followed by commercial publications for wide-scale adoption at the local level

Installation

Providing in-service education and supervision at the local level to promote effective use of the new program

Several feedback loops and a variety of assessment procedures may be used to get a flow of evaluative data that can be used to improve instructional materials. Preliminary evaluation may be obtained by setting up a feedback loop in which experts—scholars, teachers, curriculum specialists, psychologists— examine materials and make suggestions for improvement. A major feedback loop may be set up to get a flow of suggestions from schools in which teachers, pupils, and curriculum workers try out the materials. A third feedback loop, a subsystem within the preceding one, includes the teacher and students and is used to modify and adapt materials as they are used in the instructional program. Motion pictures, tape recordings, detailed records, and the observation of teachers' problems and students' difficulties may be made as materials are used in the classroom. Tests, checklists, and other evaluative devices are designed and used to assess achievement of students after completion of individual exercises, units of instruction, and the overall program.

Systems Approaches

A variety of systems approaches have been used to revise areas of the curriculum and to prepare instructional packages. Most have been associated with new developments in educational technology with a focus on development of a delivery system that includes the resources needed to meet predetermined needs. Others such as PPBS (Planning-Programming-Budgeting System) are broadly based, including needs analysis, goals and objectives, detailed programs, program budget structure, evaluation procedures, and cost-effectiveness analysis (Worner, 1973).

Intensive efforts have been put into the development of prepackaged individualized systems of instruction based on modules (units of instruction). These range from programs in a single subject such as reading and arithmetic to programs that include several areas of the curriculum. These programs differ from conventional class instruction in several ways. Instructional materials are designed so that there is less need for teacher direction of each lesson and more time for the teacher to diagnose, advise, and otherwise monitor learning. Students may work at their own pace, use different materials, study different topics, and approach topics in ways that fit their learning styles (Gagné and Briggs, 1974).

Of special interest to curriculum workers are the steps that are used in many systems approaches to the preparation of instructional materials (Gagné and Briggs, 1974). Although systems vary, in general the following steps or phases may be identified. The first phase involves the identification of needs, specification of related goals and objectives, and identification of alternative ways in which needs can be met, followed by designing the major components to include in the instructional system and a review of needed resources, available resources, and constraints such as rules and regulations related to instruction. The next phase includes the selection or the preparation of media and development of evaluation strategies. After field testing and revision, the instructional system is disseminated, appropriate teacher education is provided, and supervision is given as needed.

If a decision is made to produce needed materials for an instructional system, steps such as the following are taken: planning the design; deciding on method(s) of study, use of self-pacing and group-pacing, and types of activities for students; design of records of student achievement; clarification of the teacher's role; setting a schedule of group activities and related teaching strategies; establishing time limits; designing evaluation instruments; and working out procedures for providing guidance if options are offered to students.

Systems approaches may be used in all areas of the curriculum. The phases below are included in a system for developing learning packages for aesthetic education (Madeja and Kelly, 1971):

Package specification including content outline, workshop for staff, and classroom experiments

Procedural steps involving specification of objectives, activities, graphics, entrance and exit criteria, teaching/learning instructions

Evaluation procedures including development of items, and pre- and post-placement tests

Tryout and revision in classrooms resulting in package for pilot testing

Some have expressed concern about the possible mechanization of learning and curriculum planning through systems approaches. Although this may happen in any approach, including systems approaches, it need not and should not. The emerging view is that systems approaches, in fact all phases of educational technology, are tools to use as needed to improve both the quality and effectiveness of instructional planning. Humane approaches and the highest regard for students, teachers, and others involved in curriculum planning are of highest priority in all phases of curriculum development.

Principles and Patterns of Organization in New Programs

Many of the new programs, particularly in mathematics and science and to a degree in other areas, reflect certain principles and patterns of organization. A major difference between traditional and newer patterns of organization is in the degree of flexibility and latitude left to the teacher. In many current programs a definite sequence of instruction is proposed to develop the concepts, main ideas, modes of inquiry, and attitudes selected for study. The sequence is arranged in an order believed to be most efficient for promoting cumulative learning and the attainment of overall objectives of the program. Teachers at each level and for each unit of instruction are provided with guides and materials that are designed as part of a cohesive program of instruction. Training programs have been provided in some projects so that the teachers will use the materials properly. While optional or supplementary units may be suggested, provisions are made for basic units of instruction related to defined objectives, and optional units provide for the extension or enrichment of of basic ideas. In short, a clearcut pattern of organization is typical of many new curricula.

Another major difference in patterns of organization is to be found in the underlying rationale. In most new programs a direct analysis of the disciplines is made to identify the essentials to include in the curriculum. A pattern of organization is then structured in terms of the essential elements selected from the disciplines. It is not deemed necessary to devise a pattern of instruction around contemporary situations in which mathematics, natural sciences, or the social sciences are significant. Nor is it deemed necessary to devise a pattern in which current questions, interests, and problems of students are used as the basis for organization. Nor are community conditions, social functions, or persistent life situations used as a basis for organization. Rather the curriculum is organized to give direct attention to concepts, main ideas, and generalizations that are to be developed. A plan of organization based on such secondary analyses as are represented by the social functions, basic human activities, or day-to-day needs of the students diverts attention from the basic objectives of instruction. Furthermore, students may not obtain a grasp of the defined conceptual and inquiry components of structure when patterns of organization are based on secondary analyses. In summary, it appears to the authors that the following principles of organization are emphasized:

1   The scope of instruction is defined in terms of the concepts, main ideas, processes, or generalizations to be developed.

2   The sequence of instruction is organized in a logical-psychological order found through the tryout of units in the classroom to be effective in providing for cumulative learning of key ideas, methods of inquiry, skills, and attitudes.

3   Required units of instruction are designed to facilitate the attainment of objectives, and optional or supplementary units for enrichment of learning may be provided.

A variety of patterns of organization may be noted in the descriptions of programs presented in later chapters. First, some are *predisciplinary* in that concepts and methods of inquiry are emphasized in general contexts, not in the context of a discipline or group of disciplines. For example, some units in science education include concepts of interaction, system, and measurement without reference to specific disciplines. Second, some programs are based primarily on a single discipline; this is true in mathematics, in some science programs, in the arts, and in social studies programs in which history, geography, or other fields are singled out for emphasis. Third, some programs are *multidisciplinary* in that topics or problems are approached from the view of several disciplines. For example, in the social studies a given country or region may be studied in terms of geographic conditions, historical development, economic activities, and cultural achievements. Fourth, some programs are *interdisciplinary in that several specific* disciplines may be fused around key topics, concepts, ideas, themes, or problems. For example, some science units draw from several basic sciences and some units in the social studies draw from several social sciences in an effort to relate content and methods of inquiry to selected key ideas.

ROLES IN CURRICULUM DEVELOPMENT

The roles of many individuals can be described in general terms even though there is considerable variation from school system to school system and project to project. A promising development during the last decade that should be sustained is the involvement of scholars who have a critical role to play in identification and selection of content and processes. They also are needed to validate changes made in content of main ideas, generalizations, and conceptual schemes that are formulated for use in organizing units and curricula.

Teachers continue to play an essential role in all phases of curriculum development from initial planning and stating of objectives on through development, tryout, revision, and installation. There is no substitute for well-prepared teachers who are grounded in principles and procedures of curriculum development and instructional planning.

Curriculum leaders or coordinators play a decisive role in relating all phases of curriculum development and in coordinating the efforts of the many different individuals who are involved. Among their important responsibilities are assisting in the clarifying and stating of goals and objectives, exploring organizational patterns and principles that should be considered, identifying new instructional media and teaching strategies, and sharing new developments in evaluation and other aspects of education that have a bearing on curriculum development. Of critical importance is their work with laymen who are playing a larger role in curriculum planning.

Psychologists, measurement experts, and other specialists play varied roles ranging from sharing findings of relevant studies of child development and learning to assisting in the design of programs of evaluation. They may contribute directly to the specification of objectives, design of instructional sequences, development of teaching strategies, creation of evaluation devices, and the planning of in-service education programs and accountability systems.

COMMUNITY INVOLVEMENT

Community involvement is currently obtained in two basic ways. The first is through invited participation in which school officials ask laymen to become involved in various activities. The second is through accountability systems in which laymen have an assigned role to play in various activities. Both ways are used in most school systems.

Community involvement by invitation or initiation on the part of school personnel takes several forms. The first is consultative in which school personnel confer with laymen on issues and problems in order to get data needed to make decisions. The second is the establishment of committees to work on such problems or topics as family life education, the social studies, and ethnic studies. Laymen contribute their ideas as members of the committee and help to shape policies. The third is through a curriculum council in which laymen serve as members along with school personnel and participate in the formulation of district policies. The fourth is the obtaining of advice from parents at the individual school level by the principal and teachers.

Involvement through accountability systems such as PPBS (Planning-Programming-Budgeting-System) occurs at several points. One of the most fundamental is the formulating of goals and objectives in which laymen and school personnel work out a statement for the school system. A second is the designing of the curriculum and the consideration of various alternatives. A third is the analysis of costs of various programs and the comparison of costs with accomplishments. A fourth is the specification of program priorities and the relating of them to educational goals and values. A fifth is the consideration of innovative programs and curriculum revisions along with the funds, time, staff, and other constraints involved in their implementation. A sixth is the planning of ways in which public understanding of the educational program can be improved.

The curriculum council provides opportunities to obtain effective community involvement over extended periods of time. The typical council is made up of teachers, laymen, students, and administrative personnel, and chaired by the curriculum director. The council considers proposals in light of the district's philosophy, staff, budget, and various alternatives. Recommendations made by the council and approved by the Board of Education become district policies.

To be effective, community involvement should be widespread, the issues and problems under study should be vital, and it should extend from the district-wide level to the individual school level. Spotty and limited involvement turns out to be tokenism in most situations. Laymen as well as school personnel want to work on critical issues and problems and avoid trivial ones. District-wide groups are needed on overall policy planning, and involvement at the individual school level is of fundamental importance in attuning education to local needs.

Curriculum Guides or Frameworks

Curriculum guides or frameworks for various areas of the curriculum provide direction to teachers and other school personnel, make possible interpretation of the curriculum to laymen, and serve as a basis for getting feedback needed for continuing revision. Guidelines suggested in them must be adapted to meet neighborhood conditions and individual needs of students. They should include information on major components of the curriculum as shown in the following summary, which is illustrative of topics in recently developed frameworks.

1 *Introduction*
  Functions or uses of the framework
  Adaptation and implementation to fit local conditions
  Organization of the framework
2 *Importance of the Area of the Curriculum*
  Definition of the area
  Philosophical, social, psychological, disciplinary foundations
  Contributions to major goals of education
  Objectives of the area
  Characteristics of an effective program
3 *Organization of the Area of the Curriculum*
  Major strands or components
  Outline of sequence of instruction
  Themes, topics, and units by grade levels

4 *Instructional Media*
Selection of media
Guidelines for using media
Recommended media
5 *Approaches to Instruction*
Interdisciplinary, multidisciplinary, disciplinary
Variety of teaching strategies
Patterns and principles of organization
6 *Evaluation and Accountability*
Evaluation of learning
Evaluation of the program
Feedback for continuing revision
Accountability principles and procedures
7 *Staff Development*
Roles of school personnel
Pre-service education
In-service education

FOLLOW-UP ACTIVITIES AND PROJECTS

1 Examine a curriculum guide currently being used in your community. Select one in an area of the curriculum of your choice. Use the following questions to guide your analysis of it:

a What is the orientation—disciplinary, society, the child? In what ways, if any, is attention given to all three orientations?

b How is scope or breadth determined?

c How is the program sequenced? What provisions are made for cumulative learning and integration of learning?

d Examine the part of the guide that outlines content and apply the criteria for selection of content. Which criteria are met? Which are not?

2 Examine a unit of instruction related to a topic or problem of your choice. Analyze it in terms of the following:

a Plan of organization
b Statement of objectives
c Initiation
d Introductory, developmental, concluding activities
e Culminating activities
f Evaluation techniques

3 Design or adapt a unit format that you believe to be useful and prepare a section of a unit similar to the one presented in this chapter. Be sure to include both methodological and substantive components in whatever format you use.

4 Identify three or four of the guidelines in the last part of this chapter (that deals with emerging guidelines in new curricula) that you believe to be most useful. Identify one or two that you do not favor. Give reasons for your choices.

5 What topics do you think should be included in curriculum guides? Check those presented at the end of this chapter against those contained in locally available guides. How are they alike? Different? Make an outline that includes the topics you believe are of greatest importance.

BIBLIOGRAPHY

Cole, Henry P. *Process Education*. Englewood Cliffs, N.J.: Educational Technology Publications, 1972. Emphasis on materials based on processes of thinking and inquiring.

Current Curriculum Materials. Washington, D.C.: Association for Supervision and Curriculum Development, annually. Description of curriculum guides and other materials published each year.

Curriculum Materials Clearinghouse. Ann Arbor, Mich.: Xerox University Microfilms. Information on curriculum guides and related materials through various forms of publication.

Hass, Glen, Joseph Bondi, and Jon Wiles. *Curriculum Planning*. New York: Holt, 1974. Sections with articles on education for children, transescents, and adolescents.

Hertling, James E., and Howard G. Getz (Eds.) *Education for the Middle School Years: Readings*. Glenview, Ill.: Scott, Foresman, 1971. Articles on objectives, the early adolescent, the curriculum, model programs, physical facilities, and controversy.

Hess, Robert D., and Doreen J. Croft. *Teachers of Young Children*. Boston: Houghton Mifflin, 1972. Chapter on programs of early childhood education.

Hyman, Ronald T. *Approaches in Curriculum*. Englewood Cliffs, N.J.: Prentice-Hall, 1973. Selected writings of eleven curriculum theorists.

Lavatelli, Celia S., Walter J. Moore, and Theodore Kaltsounis. *Elementary School Curriculum*. New York: Holt, 1972. Comprehensive overview of the elementary curriculum.

Leeper, Sarah H., Ruth J. Dales, and Ralph L. Witherspoon. (5th ed.) *Good Schools for Young Children*. New York: Macmillan, 1974. Detailed treatment of various phases of childhood education.

Neff, Charles and Nancy. (Compilers) *Aids to Curriculum Planning: English Language Arts K-12*. Urbana, Ill.: National Council of the Teachers of English, 1973. Excerpts from curriculum guides related to philosophy, objectives, composition, media, reading and literature, and evaluation.

Overly, Donald E., Jon R. Kinghorn, and Richard L. Preston. *The Middle School: Humanizing Education for Youth*. Worthington, Ohio: Charles A. Jones Publishing Co., 1972. Sections on the curriculum.

Saylor, J. Galen, and William M. Alexander. *Planning Curriculum for Schools*. New York: Holt, 1974. Chapter on processes and roles in curriculum planning.

Spodek, Bernard. *Teaching in the Early Years*. Englewood Cliffs, N.J.: Prentice-Hall, 1972. Chapters on schools for young children and early childhood curriculum.

Spodek, Bernard. (Ed.) *Early Childhood Education*. Englewood Cliffs, N.J.: Prentice-Hall, 1973. Review of models and collection of readings on different models of childhood education.

Stephens, Lillian S. *The Teacher's Guide to Open Education*. New York: Holt, 1974. Procedures, illustrative activities, and suggestions for areas of the curriculum.

Taba, Hilda. *Curriculum Development: Theory and Practice*. New York: Harcourt, Brace, 1962. Section on curriculum theory.

Tyler, Ralph W. *Basic Principles of Curriculum and Instruction*. Chicago: The University of Chicago Press, 1950. Emphasis on purposes, experiences to attain purposes, organization, and evaluation; basis of many later curriculum models.

Chapter 6

Organization
and Extension
of the Environment
for Learning

The organization and extension of the environment for learning should be planned to facilitate development of each area of the curriculum. A broad view of learning environment includes the total environment in which children learn—the school setting, school organization, the full range of instructional technology, and the prevailing atmosphere or climate. All these elements should be brought together in ways that are conducive to optimum learning on the part of students.

The organization of the school is considered first in this chapter in terms of vertical and horizontal organization. Attention is given to graded and non-graded patterns of vertical organization and to several plans of horizontal organization which involve the placing of children in classes or groups for instruction and the assignment of teachers to instructional groups. Criteria for assessing plans of organization are presented for consideration and use by the school staff and others involved in developing an effective pattern of organization or a combination of patterns. The classroom environment is considered next with attention to a dynamic setting for learning, individualized and personalized instruction, group work, and interaction analysis. Open-space schools and other extensions of the learning environment are then considered and followed by instructional media and instructional support services that are essential to a complete environment for learning.

VERTICAL AND HORIZONTAL ORGANIZATION FOR INSTRUCTION

Over the years there have been many debates about plans of school and classroom organization. Advantages and disadvantages of various plans have been reported, and various individuals and groups have taken stands in favor of a plan or plans which they believe to be most effective in promoting the learning of students and improving or facilitating teaching. Several guidelines have emerged. First, no plan in and of itself is a panacea. It is what teachers do as they interact with children in teaching-learning situations that counts the most in quality education. A plan of organization should be designed to facilitate teaching and learning. It should be a plan that teachers have helped to formulate and should be consistent with goals and objectives, be interpretable to parents, and meet criteria such as those provided at the end of this section.

Two aspects of the organization of groups for instruction are vertical and horizontal organization. Vertical organization refers to the movement of children through the instructional program from level to level or grade to grade. Various plans of vertical organization have been proposed, the two currently receiving greatest attention being graded and nongraded plans. Horizontal organization refers to the placing of children in instructional groups or classes and the assignment of teachers at various levels or grades. Plans for horizontal organization range from the self-contained classroom with one teacher for all areas to departmentalization with a separate teacher for each area.

Graded and Nongraded Plans—Vertical Organization

Grades The dominant pattern of vertical organization is by grades. Curricula are planned in terms of grades and suggestions for teaching strategies, instructional media, and evaluation are included in grade level teaching guides. Textbooks, other instructional materials, testing programs, pupil promotion, and accountability systems are related to grade levels. At its best a graded plan of vertical organization can meet sound criteria; at its worst it results in a lock-step system, which is the antithesis of sound educational planning.

Patterns Typical patterns of grades within schools include primary and neighborhood schools with grades K through 3, intermediate or middle schools with grades 5 or 6 through 8, junior highs with grades 7 through 9, and high schools with grades 11 through 12. A variety of patterns for grade groupings have been proposed and used, including K-6, 7-9, 10-12; K-3, 4-6, 7-9, 10-12; K-8, 9-12; K-5, 6-8, 9-12; and K-12. Some of the foregoing plans have been based on sound criteria and planning, whereas others have been adopted as an expedient way of using existing buildings.

Neighborhood schools are designed to serve nearby children and most frequently include grades K through 3. Many have been integrated in recent years by busing children to provide for racial and ethnic balance.

The middle school represents an attempt to provide special and transitional learning experiences for children in grades 5 or 6 through grade 8. A claimed advantage is that they provide opportunities to give pre- and early adolescents a setting and program of instruction in accord with their development needs, interests, and capabilities. Various forms of team teaching, departmentalization, grouping, continuous progress, and individualization may be employed, or traditional approaches to teaching and learning may be used, depending upon the leadership and planning.

Nongraded Plans Based primarily on growth in reading, nongraded plans are used most frequently in grades 1 through 3 in around 10 percent of elementary schools. Emphasis is given to continuous progress, cumulative learning, and individualized instruction geared to each child's pace of learning. No time limits are set for learning, each child is placed in the program at his stage of achievement, and failure is not a threat or problem because each child progresses at his own rate. Detailed and continuing diagnosis of children's needs, specific planning of objectives and instruction to meet individual needs, systematic evaluation, and detailed recordkeeping are required. Effective means of communication between teachers and parents and among teachers as to children's level of achievement are also essential.

Several difficulties and disadvantages of nongraded plans have been reported. Reporting to parents may be time-consuming and difficult because they are accustomed to grade level indications of achievement and are confused by levels unless they are translated into grade equivalents. The intensive recordkeeping of individual progress is a burden to some teachers. The curriculum may be thrown out of balance because of emphasis on a single area, such as reading, which is typically used to plan levels of development. The profusion of levels, as many as fourteen or fifteen in reading, for example requires the continuous analysis of incoming materials for placement at appropriate levels. Children's learning may be limited by the planned sequence, the materials, and the related teaching strategies with a consequent neglect of children's involvement in planning, developing, and evaluating of learning experiences. The use of levels may add more lock-step hurdles for children, thus becoming a more rigid system than a graded plan.

Studies of children's achievement in nongraded and graded schools are inconclusive with no significant advantage for either plan (Cook and Doll, 1973). What goes on in the classroom seems to be more important than a plan per se. However, nongrading has brought home to many educators the importance of careful diagnosis and placement of children in planned learning sequences, the need for systematic recordkeeping and reporting, and the ways in which continuous progress of children may be fostered, particularly in the area of developmental reading instruction. If carefully planned and organized, a non-graded plan or organization can contribute much to the development of a sequential program of instruction that promotes cumulative and integrated learning.

Grouping at Grades or Levels—Horizontal Organization

Self-contained Classroom This plan in which one teacher provides all or most instruction is the dominant pattern in most elementary shcools. Claimed advantages include flexibility in using time, materials, and teaching strategies, ample time to diagnose needs and get well acquainted with students, opportunities to individualize instruction, integration of instruction within and across subjects, variation in time given to a subject in terms of the child's needs, and benefits to children from working with one teacher. Problems and difficulties include adequacy of teacher preparation in handling new math, new science, and other areas such as art and music, the tendency of teachers to emphasize subjects in which they are most competent, need for children to interact with more than one adult and to get expert instruction in all areas, and breaks in continuity of learning as children move from teacher to teacher in following grades.

Departmentalization Complete departmentalization of instruction with a teacher for each subject is not widely used, although partially and semidepartmentalized plans may be found in some schools, most usually in grades 4, 5, and 6. For example, some schools have special teachers in art, music, and physical education; some have teachers in charge of new math and science programs; the Joplin plan is a departmentalized plan for reading instruction; the Dual Progress plan provides for a half day in a homeroom for social studies and language arts and the other half for departmental instruction in other subjects; some teachers swap subjects to take advantage of special backgrounds which they have. Major advantages are related to use of special competence of teachers, provision of expert instruction in each subject or group of subjects, ability of teachers to keep up to date on new developments in selected areas, provision of special rooms and equipment, and systematic development of sequences of instruction in each area. Difficulties and problems are related to integration of learning across areas, emphasis on subject matter and neglect of the child's whole development, recordkeeping and reporting to parents, and loss of flexibility in varying the emphasis on areas of instruction in terms of children's needs.

Dual Progress Plan As in the Platoon School, Dual Progress is an attempt to get the benefits of both the self-contained classroom and the departmental plan. Children in grade 3 and up spend half the school day with a homeroom teacher who guides learning in social studies, language arts, and health and physical education. The other half of the day is spent in ungraded and departmentalized programs in science, mathematics, art, music, and foreign language (if offered by the school). Progress is graded in the homeroom studies and ungraded in the departmentalized studies, hence the name dual progress. Stated advantages include preparation of children for practices that they will encounter in secondary schools, coordination and counseling of children as in the self-contained classroom, better use of teachers' special backgrounds, children's interaction with several teachers, cumulative instruction over a period of years in departmentalized subjects, and progress of children in accord with their developmental patterns. Difficulties and problems include coordination of the efforts of departmentalized teachers with those of the homeroom teacher, graded progress in some subjects and ungraded in others, and others as noted above under both the self-contained classroom and departmentalization.

Grouping Procedures Heterogeneous grouping is the placing of children in classes without regard to a single factor such as ability or achievement. It is used to form classes at grade levels and subgroups within the classroom. It provides for interaction of students of differing abilities, achievement levels, and other background factors. Homogeneous grouping by ability and achievement is intended to reduce differences in background factors among children. In its extreme form students are grouped by X, Y, Z, or more classes according to data from intelligence tests. It is not widely used now to form classes, but grouping by readiness and achievement is used in classrooms to form subgroups in reading and arithmetic and, at times, in other subjects. Studies indicate that homogeneous grouping of children in classes has no advantage over heterogeneous grouping except for extremely retarded or less able students. Multiage grouping, also referred to as multigrade, interclass, and interage grouping, is the placing of children of different ages in a group. It is intended to promote children's learning from each other, stimulate planning for individual differences, enrich the learning of both older and younger children, and substitute cooperation for competition and rivalry.

Joplin Plan This is a plan for organizing reading instruction. Children are grouped homogeneously in terms of reading achievement without regard to age. Reading classes are scheduled at the same time during the day and children leave their homerooms to work in a class with others at comparable stages of reading development.

Team Teaching This is a plan for using teachers' special competencies and at the same time getting some of the benefits of the self-contained classroom. Basically, team teaching involves the cooperation of two or more teachers in the joint responsibility of providing instruction for a group of students. For example, a team may be made up of three teachers and an aide who have responsibility for eighty-five to ninety students. One teacher is a team leader who coordinates planning, instruction, and evaluation, receiving extra pay for this role. Among the advantages are coordinated planning, individualization through independent study, small-group and large-group activities, orientation of new teachers, interaction of children with several adults, direction of aides, continuing in-service growth, and use of facilities and materials. Problems and difficulties are related to the heavy time requirements for effective planning, maintenance of morale and effective working relationships among members of the team, tendency of some team leaders to spend too much time in coordination and not enough in teaching, use of lectures and other expository methods in large-group situations which can fail to get student involvement, and use of buildings designed for regular class instruction.

Differentiated Staffing This is a plan for assigning specific roles to professionals and paraprofessionals or aides. For example, there may be such assignments as master teacher, resource teacher, reading specialist teacher, social studies specialist teacher, librarian, teacher aide, and student tutor. Assignments are related to background qualifications, formal preparation, experience, and rated competence.

Criteria for Assessing Plans of Organization

A sound approach is to consider plans of school organization in terms of what is best in a particular situation, that is, what is best in terms of goals and objectives, the children, the instructional staff, and available facilities and resources. The following criteria are useful in making decisions about a plan or changes in existing plans:

In Terms of Objectives
Provision of effective conditions for working toward the attainment of major goals of education and achievement of objectives of each area of the curriculum
Flexibility in meeting changing objectives, conditions, and needs
Effects on racial, ethnic, and cultural integration

In Terms of Learning and Instruction
Provision for the improvement of children's learning
Provision for sequential, cumulative, integrative, and scope elements of the curriculum
Provision for security and stability of children, a warm and friendly atmosphere, and total development of the child—intellectual, social, emotional, physical
Provision of opportunities for independent activities, small-group activities, and large-group activities as needed to attain objectives

In Terms of Teaching and Teachers
Facilitation of the teacher's responsibilities for diagnosing children's needs, knowing each child as an individual, and individualizing instruction

Provision of opportunities for teacher-teacher and teacher-pupil planning

Facilitation of the use of effective teaching strategies, instructional media, evaluation of instructional outcomes, and reporting to parents

Feasibility in terms of the background, capabilities, and attitudes of teachers and their willingness and ability to make changes

In Terms of Facilities and Services

Feasibility in relation to available and obtainable facilities, equipment, and instructional resources

Coordination of the efforts of teachers and instructional support services and personnel

THE CLASSROOM ENVIRONMENT

The most crucial elements in the learning environment are to be found in the day-to-day relationships in the classroom and other teaching-learning areas. All the facets of the instructional program are brought together as the teacher and children interact. And it is in this ongoing interaction that the atmosphere for learning is most potent in its impact on children—an atmosphere that should be marked by mutual trust and respect, individual and group concern, security, affection, and belonginess. It should also be marked by a focus on children as individuals so that teacher-child relationships will be personalized as well as individualized.

A Dynamic Setting for Learning

Flexibility, accessibility, and usability are key concepts in providing a dynamic setting for learning. Flexibility in arranging and using work and study spaces and centers, accessibility in terms of direct use by children, and usability of materials and equipment by children in accord with clearly established guidelines are hallmarks of the setting for productive learning. Bulletin boards, chalkboards, display areas, growing things, reading corners, listening stations, centers of interest for science and other areas of the curriculum, reference and supplementary books, equipment, and furniture should be viewed in terms of their uses by both the teacher and the children. Health, safety, and welfare of children are paramount considerations in planning for their use and in establishing standards to guide children's use of them.

Standards are also needed to provide for effective working relationships in the variety of group activities that take place in a dynamic setting for learning. Procedures for the distribution and collection of materials, clearly understood signals for beginning and stopping activities, standards for discussion groups and committees, rules of order for class meetings, rules for fire and disaster drills and for entering and leaving the classroom, suggestions for use of free time, duties of monitors and student tutors, relationships with aides, and rules for quiet-time work periods are helpful in fostering desirable working relationships. The desired outcome is increasing self-discipline and self-control on the part of each child.

Individualized and Personalized Instruction

The richest environments for learning include provisions for both individualized and personalized instruction. Instruction may be individualized in several different ways after needs, capabilities, and achievement of children have been diagnosed (Michaelis, 1972):

Providing individual study of topics, use of materials, use of free time, and use of the library and other resources

Providing individual tutorial by the teacher, a parent, a teacher aide, another pupil, programmed material, or computer

Providing a variety of learning activities in units of instruction, ranging from reading and reporting to constructing objects and role playing

Using a variety of teaching strategies that are compatible with different styles of learning, including discovery, guided discovery, and directed learning strategies

Providing multilevel and multimedia approaches to learning so that each child has usable sources of data related to topics and problems under study

Providing variations in time for individuals and groups so that each child moves at a pace consistent with his rate of learning

Forming and changing groups and subgroups in accord with needs, interests, and capabilities of children

Setting reasonable expectations and standards for evaluation of each child's intellectual, social, emotional, and physical development and learning

Personalization of instruction goes a step beyond to add personal touches to learning. Children's interests, problems, and concerns are considered and used to make instruction more relevant, meaningful, and significant. Special interest is shown in each child as a unique person with a unique cultural background. Special comments, commendations, suggestions, directions, and assistance provided by the teacher reveal to each child that the teacher cares and has the individual's welfare in both mind and heart. In short, the democratic values and beliefs identified earlier are made operational in daily living and learning in the classroom.

Individualization and personalization are carried through as plans are made for the disadvantaged, the less able, the gifted, and other children in need of special forms of education. For the disadvantaged, special attention should be given to active involvement, clear specification of objectives and directions, development of language power and a variety of modes of expression, use of concrete experiences, development of a positive self-concept, and related activities and procedures attuned to their individual backgrounds and needs. For the less able, special attention should be given to all the foregoing plus adjustments to attention spans, ability to concentrate, need for motivation and commendation, avoidance of the attaching of any stigma to special working groups, extension of time, provision of materials on an appropriate level, and other specific provisions for individualizing instruction as noted above. For the gifted special attention should be given to learning activities that challenge their potentialities, round out social and emotional development as well as intellectual and physical development, and extend learning far beyond grades, norms, and other expectancies (Michaelis, 1972).

Several systems of individualized instruction have been developed in recent years.[1] In general, these systems represent attempts to provide units and lessons that have been designed so that students can work on them alone at their own pace. Some are organized around materials available in the school, and others come as fairly complete instructional packages.

Individualization and personalization should also be carried through as various instructional groups and subgroups are formed as outlined in the following section.

Grouping for Instruction

There are several plans for organizing groups for instruction within the classroom and other areas. The following are used in various combinations in different areas of the curriculum.

Whole-group instruction is provided when all students need to be involved in an activity, interaction of differing interests and backgrounds is desired, units are introduced, or other needs common to the group are to be met.

Small-group instruction is provided to meet identified needs of selected children in reading, arithmetic, and other areas. Children are grouped in terms of ability, achievement, specific remedial problems, interests, ability to work together, and skill in such areas as art, music, and physical education.

Learning-station groups may be organized to work at listening posts, reading centers, art centers, and other work stations in or out of the classroom.

Committees are specially designated small groups with a clear objective to accomplish in connection with units of work, construction of needed materials, development of needed plans, or other learning activity.

Divided-day plans, sometimes referred to as staggered day, extended day, or split day, provide for half the class to come and leave an hour before the rest of the class. Divided days are used mainly in early grades to provide small-group and individualized reading instruction.

Special groups are set up at times to meet the needs of the gifted, less able, and handicapped children, and to provide remedial or corrective instruction in reading, arithmetic, or other subjects.

Organizing Small Groups

The organization of small groups is used to provide instruction to children with similar needs. Used widely in reading is the three-group plan which calls for

---

[1] Examples of individualized instructional systems are *IPI· Individually Prescribed Instruction*. Philadelphia: Learning Research and Development, University of Pittsburgh, and Research for Better Schools, Inc.; *Plan: Individually Managed Learning*, New York: Westinghouse Learning Corporation; *IGE: Individually Guided Education* (Unipacs), Denver: Charles F. Kettering Foundation, Institute for Development of Educational Activities (I/D/E/A).

alternation between teacher-guided and independent student activities. Table 6-1 illustrates the pattern of organization (Logan, Logan, and Paterson, 1972).

Sequencing Various Aspects of Group Work

Of particular importance to curriculum developers and instructional planners is the sequencing of various phases of group work to assure cumulative learning on the part of children. In the early grades group work should be guided by simple and brief objectives with a gradual move to longer and more complex objectives in succeeding grades. Gradually decreasing amounts of planning and direction should be provided so that children move away from a heavy emphasis on teacher planning and direction in early grades to increasing amounts of cooperative planning in succeeding grades. Materials should be employed in group work in accordance with capabilities of children. Initially, simple materials and single sources of information should be provided, with the addition of more complex materials and multiple sources of information as children mature and gain experience. Beginning children profit from parallel and partnership activities which become the basis for more involved group activities in later grades. The outcomes of group work are usually shared informally in the early grades, whereas formal reporting is used frequently in later grades. Evaluation of group work in the early grades is done by informal sharing of best ideas and ways in which improvements can be made. Increasing attention is given in later grades to self-evaluation and to formal appraisal in terms of standards for discussion, committee work, and other group endeavors.

Special attention needs to be given to the planning, carrying out, and evaluating of group work in each area of the curriculum. For example, group activities in reading and arithmetic are much more directed than some of the activities provided in art and the social studies. Teaching strategies should be varied in accordance with objectives and the type of related group work that is needed to attain them. The strategies suggested in the following chapter and those included in subsequent chapters on areas of the curriculum should be considered in this context.

Interaction Analysis

A system of interaction analysis has been developed to investigate verbal behavior in the classroom (Amidon and Flanders, 1967). An observer makes a record of teacher talk and student talk in several categories. Teacher talk includes indirect influence with much freedom and interaction; examples are accepting feelings expressed by students, praising and encouraging students, accepting or using students' ideas, and asking questions of students. Teacher talk also includes direct influence with less student freedom and interaction; examples are giving directions, imparting information, and making judgments and criticisms. Student talk is classified in terms of student response to the teacher and student initiation of the talk. Silence or confusion is classified separately.

Table 6-1 Suggested Week's Program, Three-group Plan

Day	Min.	Group 1 (high)	Group 2 (average)	Group 3 (low)
	20	Direct teacher guidance; new material	Work on individual problems, solo-team	Free reading; individual interests
Monday	20	Committee work; planning of book reports	Direct teacher guidance: reading from text	
	20	Free reading	Reaction to story in art, drama, or writing	Direct teacher guidance: new story, guided reading
	20	Free reading; individual interests	Direct teacher guidance: discuss story or answer specific questions	Independent activities, work-study, games
Tuesday	30	Direct teacher guidance: presentation of oral reports, drama	Committee work; individual work	Free reading; work on skills
	10	All-group activity: choral reading, story, dramatizations, etc.		
	25	Reading related to unit of work	Work on individual needs: team, solo reading related to unit of work	Direct teacher guidance: silent-oral reading, work on skills
Wednesday	25	Direct guidance: new story	Reading related to unit of work	Reading related to unit of work
	10	Help the children from different groups who have a common need to practice a specific skill; others continue their activity		
	20	Silent reading and reaction to story	Direct teacher guidance: discussion related to stories; planning of activities	Reading related to stories: help by pupil assistants
Thursday	20	Direct teacher guidance: discussion oral-silent reading, work on skills	Developing activities related to readings (committee work, etc.)	Reading related to stories: help by pupil assistants
	20	Individual guidance on book selection for free reading, for unit reports, etc.; use of library aids		
	40	Free reading	Work on individual needs: team, solo; committee work; reading related to unit, etc.	Direct teacher guidance: discussion; plans for sharing with class
Friday	20	All-group activity: library, dramatizations, storytelling, etc.		

This system of interaction analysis, adaptations of it, and others are useful in helping teachers examine their styles of interaction with students. Results of such an analysis may be used to bring verbal behavior into line with the teacher's view of the kind and quality of interaction that will be most productive in a given situation. As some teachers have frankly stated, the style they desire to project is quite different at times from the style or pattern of interaction identified through analysis.

OPEN-SPACE SCHOOLS

Open-space schools are designed to extend the learning environment and to use it more effectively. Within them may be found a combination of features and procedures discussed in preceding sections. For example, team teaching and differentiated staffing may be used; various instructional groups are formed, ranging from individual and small group to large groups; instructional media are organized in a large center to which children have direct access; some are graded while others are nongraded; and some employ various patterns of multiage or inter-class grouping.

A feature of many open-space schools is the arrangement of classrooms in pods around a library and large multipurpose area. The pods may be designed for early childhood education, primary grades, middle grades, and upper grades or middle school. Within each pod there are classrooms which open directly into a large work center that contains instructional media appropriate to the designated levels of instruction. Children from each pod also have access to the library and multipurpose room. Such an arrangement makes it possible to take advantage of various patterns of organization and grouping. It is also possible to provide differing emphases at different levels, for example, self-contained classroom experiences in combination with increasing amounts of interaction with other groups in early grades and various forms of semidepartmentalization and grouping in middle and upper grades.

But as with any innovation, open-space schools call for detailed planning on the part of the school staff if the advantages they offer are to be obtained. It is relatively easy to continue the same type of instruction provided in traditional schools. The freedom and flexibility available to children and teachers in open-space schools may lead to overstimulation, confusion, and even chaos if plans are not made for optimum use of space, time, and resources. With appropriate planning they can serve as a learning environment that truly extends and opens the education of children.

OTHER EXTENSIONS OF THE LEARNING ENVIRONMENT

Time Extensions The extended school year and extended school day represent time extensions. In considering them, special attention must be given to the kind and quality of learning experiences that are to be provided. Outdoor education in which children live and learn together for a given period of time during the regular school year or during the summer represents an attempt to provide learning experiences that enrich and extend those typically provided in the instructional program. Late afternoon and evening learning activities are illustrative of other attempts to extend the time dimension.

Spatial Extensions The learning environment also may be extended in terms of the spatial dimension, going far beyond the site of the school. As noted below, the full range of community resources should be viewed as media for use in the instructional program. Outdoor education, summer camps, summer facilities provided by labor and industrial groups, and planned travel guided by educational as well as recreational objectives are illustrative of the extension of the spatial dimension of the learning environment.

Alternative Schools For some children and their parents alternative schools represent an extension of the learning environment or at least a major change in it. Such schools take a variety of forms and names including Free Schools, Parent Schools, Black House, La Raza School, Store-Front School, and others noted below under voucher plan.

Voucher Plan The essence of this plan is the issuance of vouchers to parents who can use them to send their children to a school of their choice, either public or private. The receiving school is reimbursed in an amount equal to the current per-student cost in the local school system. The Alum Rock School District in California has used the voucher plan within the school district. Several schools have been designated to offer different programs which range from traditional to a variety of alternative schools and programs, such as Cultural Arts, Daily Living, Enrichment, Nongraded, Individualized Learning, Reading and Communication, Basic Skills, Multicultural, School 2000, Three-R's Plus, and Fine Arts and Creative Expression.

INSTRUCTIONAL MEDIA

A major output of the expansion and refinement of educational technology in recent years has been improvement in the quality and quantity of instructional media. The environment for learning can be both enriched and extended by using the outputs of educational technology which include hardware such as audio-visual equipment and computers and software or courseware such as books and programmed materials along with systems for their use. As with other innovations, new developments in instructional media should not be viewed as panaceas; they are components to be considered along with all the others that go into curriculum development. General guidelines for their use, provision of a variety of types, and criteria and procedures for their selection must be considered if instructional media are to make optimum contributions to the richness of the learning environment.

General Guidelines

The entire school and areas within it should be viewed as an environment or laboratory for learning. The selection, arrangement and rearrangement, and use of materials and equipment to promote learning are basic in the self-contained classroom, the open-space school, and other patterns of organization. Helpful areas and arrangements include learning centers, work stations, and centers of interest that focus on reading, science, art, and other areas of the curriculum, with direct and easy access by children. And multilevel and multimedia approaches to learning should be provided.

All instructional media should be viewed as resources to be used to attain specific objectives of instruction. Books, filmstrips, field trips, data banks, and other media are data sources which students can use in relation to questions, problems, issues, values, and hypotheses that arise in dynamic programs of instruction.

Instructional media should be considered in terms of the level of concreteness or abstractness of experience that is appropriate for the children who are to use them (Dale, 1969). If direct firsthand experience is needed, then weaving, constructing, modeling, and similar activities should be provided with the proper selection of related materials. Field trips, dramatic representation, operating a model, and seeing a demonstration are a move away from direct firsthand experience. On a more abstract level are exhibits, motion pictures, still pictures, and other audio-visual resources. Most abstract of all are books, tables, graphs, and other media presented by means of verbal symbols. All the foregoing are needed but should be selected and used in accord with students' capabilities and instructional objectives.

Instructional media should be selected in terms of criteria directly related to instructional planning. A minimum set of criteria includes objectives to be attained, significance and authenticity of content, fairness and adequacy of treatment of women and ethnic groups, appropriateness to level of development of students, elimination of sex bias and racial and ethnic stereotypes, physical qualities, value of accompanying manuals, and time, effort, and expense involved in utilization.

Instructional media should be utilized in the context of a variety of teaching strategies. In general, readiness for use of a given resource should be developed; use of the resource should be observed and guided as needed; follow-through in related activities should be provided; and teacher and/or group evaluation of the resource should be made. Of utmost importance is the selection and use of media to meet individual differences, as strategies such as those discussed in the next chapter are used to attain various objectives.

Library facilities of several types are essential to the development of a rich instructional program. Children in each classroom or work area should have direct access to library resources, such as the room library in self-contained classrooms and the library resources in the materials center in open-space schools. A large library that serves the entire school opens up opportunities for learning that cannot be obtained in other ways. Access to the varied services of libraries in the community should be capitalized on to the fullest to further enrich and extend learning opportunities.

Instructional media centers should be available to teachers and students. They should provide work spaces, equipment, and materials for the making of needed materials, as well as a variety of resources for immediate use. Both a large center that serves several schools and a center within each school have been found to be helpful in facilitating instruction.

Finally, the entire neighborhood and community should be viewed as a laboratory for learning. Students' experiences in the community and the many different community resources that are readily available should be drawn upon to enrich and extend learning.

Types of Instructional Media

Three main types of media that are generally useful in all areas of the curriculum should be considered. *Printed materials* include textbooks, pamphlets, programmed materials, references, source materials, activity booklets, periodicals, other reading materials, and simulation games. *Audio-visual materials* include sound and film resources such as motion picture and television, realia and models of realia such as costumes and dioramas, pictorial resources such as photographs and sketches, graphic materials such as maps and diagrams, projectors and viewers for handling slides, tapes and other media, and supplies and materials for making charts, slides, maps, and other items. *Community resources* include locally available printed and audio-visual resources plus field trips, persons to interview, service projects, libraries, museums, recreational areas, and the mass media.

Special materials are needed in such areas of the curriculum as art, music, and physical education. These are noted in later chapters.

Computer-assisted instruction and instruction via television are two aspects of instructional technology that merit continuing study and development. They should be viewed as components of a complete program of instruction, not as substitutes for other instructional media.

Criteria and Procedures for Selecting Instructional Media

The use of criteria for selecting instructional media has become standard practice in school systems throughout the country. Criteria are usually prepared by committees and approved by boards of education at the local or state level. Teachers play an important role throughout the selection process and are called upon to analyze materials in terms of such criteria as the following which are adapted from a recently prepared framework for reading (California, 1973).

Factors to consider in selecting reading materials include:

1 Relationships to objectives of reading instruction
2 Provision for continuous progress through all levels of instruction

3 Variety of materials to match individual differences in learning styles, interests, achievement, level of maturity, cultural and language backgrounds, including

Materials that reflect with pride our cultural, racial, ethnic, religious, language, sex and age differences
Materials that recognize multisensory approaches to learning
Materials that provide diagnostic tools and individualized instruction

4 Fidelity of materials to the reading process, including recognition of

The oral base of language
Interrelationships of reading, listening, speaking, and writing
Function of background experiences in reading comprehension
Contributions of linguistics to language mastery
Development of specific reading skills
Development of reading ability in content areas of instruction

5 Quality in terms of writing style, organization, attractiveness, and durability
6 Usefulness and soundness of teacher guide materials

Each of the foregoing may be broken down in greater detail and presented on rating sheets for use in the actual analysis of materials. For example, reading skills may be broken down into such categories as *decoding skills*, including phonetic analysis, structural analysis, and contextual clues, and *comprehension skills*, including literal, inferential, interpretive, and critical. Quantitative ratings may be assigned to each factor, for example, 1 = great extent, 2 = some extent, 3 = no extent, in a set of criteria for use in Indiana (Michaelis and Keach, 1972).

Two basic steps of procedure are usually taken in the selection of instructional media. The first is a preliminary screening to sift out any materials that fail to meet basic criteria. In recent years some materials have been eliminated, for example, because of the manner in which racial, ethnic, other groups, and the sexes have been treated. The second step in the selection process is detailed analysis of screened materials in order to identify those that best meet established criteria.

Keeping Up to Date on Instructional Media

Firsthand examination of new materials at national, state, and regional meetings of professional organizations enables one to keep abreast of new resources for use in reading, language arts, science, and other areas of the curriculum. Professional journals carry regular sections on new materials. References at the end of this chapter, and later chapters on areas of the curriculum, contain listings of producers and a variety of sources of information on instructional media. The following guides, directories, or journals provide fairly comprehensive reviews:

Guides and directories such as *Educator's Purchasing Guide*, North American Publishing Co., Philadelphia; *Learning Directory*, Westinghouse Learning Corporation, New York; *NICEM* (National Information Center for Educational Media), University of Southern California, Los Angeles; *New Educational Materials*, Citation Press, New York; *Audiovisual Market Place*, Bowker Co., New York; catalogs and guides available in local and county school systems and in university and college centers

Journals such as *Booklist, Bulletin of the Center for Children's Books, Grade Teacher, Instructor, Library Journal, Scholastic Teacher, Audiovisual Instruction, Educational Screen and Audiovisual Guide, Educational Products Report*

Guides to free and inexpensive materials such as *Elementary Teachers Guide to Free Curriculum Materials*, Educators Progress Service, Randolph, Wis.; *Free and Inexpensive Learning Materials*, George Peabody College for Teachers, Nashville, Tenn.

Other sources cited in Brown, Lewis, and Harcleroad (1973) at the end of this chapter.

INSTRUCTIONAL SUPPORT SERVICES

Already mentioned in earlier sections of this chapter are basic services and those available through the library and instructional media center. Personnel services available through these two vital service centers should be utilized to improve instruction along with the instructional media which they provide. These services range from direct assistance in utilization of media and preparation of media to assistance in preparing units of study and other guides to instruction.

Of utmost important in terms of quality education, but receiving somewhat decreasing emphasis because of budgetary constraints, is the provision of supervisory services. Both general and special supervisors, coordinators, or instructional assistants are needed. The contribution that they can make to the enrichment of the learning environment in general and the learning of children in particular is of inestimable value.

Other needed services include those related to evaluation, guidance, community relations, research, and provision of special education programs for atypical or exceptional children.

The coordination of the above and the ongoing problems of curriculum revision and development require the provision of leadership whose primary function is the improvement of instruction. Included within the leadership group should be team leaders, principals and vice principals, committee members, curriculum coordinators and/or directors, and assistant superintendents in charge of curriculum and instruction.

FOLLOW-UP ACTIVITIES AND PROJECTS

1 Visit one or more of the following and note the extent to which the criteria for assessing plans of organization are met:
    a A nongraded primary reading program

   b Departmentalized instruction, or team teaching, in a middle school
   c An open-space school
   d An alternative school

2 Select four or five of the suggested ways of meeting individual differences and give an example of how each one may be used in providing insturction in a subject of your choice.

3 Examine a prepackaged system of individualized instruction and note the features that you think are most useful and least useful.

4 Make a plan for organizing small group instruction in arithmetic, reading, or social studies.

5 Visit an instructional media center and note five or six different types of instructional media that you might use in a unit of your choice.

BIBLIOGRAPHY

Amidon, Edmund J., and Ned A. Flanders. *The Role of the Teacher in the Classroom*. Minneapolis: Association for Productive Teaching, 1967. Techniques for observing and analyzing verbal behavior in the classroom.

Blitz, Barbara. *The Open Classroom*. Boston: Allyn and Bacon, 1973. Chapter on classroom organization and room arrangements.

Brown, James W., Richard B. Lewis, and Fred F. Harcleroad. *A V Instruction: Technology, Media, and Methods*. New York: McGraw-Hill, 1973. Detailed treatment of all instructional media and directory of sources of information.

CEDAR Catalog. Portland, Ore.: Commercial Educational Distributing Services, 1974. Listing of products available from research and development centers; sections on early childhood, elementary, careers and teacher education.

Cook, Ruth C., and Ronald C. Doll. *The Elementary School Curriculum*. Boston: Allyn and Bacon, 1973. Chapter on innovations, including organization and grouping.

Dale, Edgar. *Building a Learning Environment*. Bloomington, Ind.: Phi Delta Kappa, 1972. Principles and procedures for improving the learning environment.

_____. *Audio-Visual Methods of Teaching*. (3rd ed.) New York: Holt, 1969. Complete guide to use of instructional materials.

Frazier, Alexander. *Open Schools for Children*. Washington, D.C.: Association for Supervision and Curriculum Development, 1972. Discussion of open space, open structure, and open curriculum.

Gagné, Robert M., and Leslie J. Briggs. *Principles of Instructional Design*. New York: Holt, 1974. Chapter on individualized instruction.

Goodlad, John I., and Harold G. Shane (Eds.) *The Elementary School in the United States*. 72d Yearbook of the National Society for the Study of Education. Chicago: The University of Chicago Press, 1973. Chapters on organizing and staffing the school and prerequisites for improvement of elementary education.

Henrie, Samuel N. (Senior Ed.) *Sourcebook of Elementary Curricula Programs and Projects*, Washington, D.C.: Government Printing Office, 1972. Information on plans for individualized instruction, media, open education, and innovative programs in chapter on general systems and resources.

Howes, Virgil. *Informal Teaching in the Open Classroom*. New York: Macmillan, 1974. Suggestions on the environment, planning, recordkeeping, and role of the teacher.

Hull, Ronald E., "Selecting an Approach to Individualized Education," Phi Delta Kappan, **40**; 169–173, November, 1973. Descriptions of IPI (Individually Prescribed Instruction), IGE (Individually Guided Education), and PLAN (Program for Learning in Accordance with Needs).

Logan, Lillian M., Virgil C. Logan, and Leona Paterson. *Creative Communication: Teaching the Language Arts*. New York: McGraw-Hill, 1972. Chapter on reading instruction.

Michaelis, John U. *Social Studies for Children in a Democracy*. Englewood Cliffs, N.J.: Prentice-Hall, 1972. Chapter on growth characteristics and individual differences.

Michaelis, John U., and Everett T. Keach, Jr. (Eds.) *Teaching Strategies for Elementary School Social Studies*. Itasca, Ill.: Peacock Press, 1972. Chapter on instructional media.

Mirrors for Behavior. Volumes A and B. Philadelphia: Research for Better Schools, 1970. Description of seventy-nine observation systems.

NEA Project on Instruction. *Planning and Organizing for Teaching*. Washington, D.C.: National Education Association, 1963. Suggestions for organizing the curriculum, school, personnel, instructional materials, time, and space.

Olson, David R. (Ed.) *Media and Symbols: The Forms of Expression, Communication and Education*. 73rd Yearbook, National Society for the Study of Education. Chicago: The University of Chicago Press, 1974. Essays on symbol systems, modes of communication, impact of media, and uses of various media.

Overly, Donald R., Jon R. Kinghorn, and Richard L. Preston. *The Middle School: Humanizing Education for Youth*. Worthington, Ohio: Charles A. Jones Publishing Co., 1972. Chapters on team teaching, independent study, differentiated staffing, and teacher aides.

Ragan, William B., and Gene D. Shepherd. *Modern Elementary Curriculum*. (4th Ed.) New York: Holt, 1971. Chapter on forming instructional groups.

Stephens, Lillian S. *The Teacher's Guide to Open Education*. New York: Holt, 1974. Sections on open education, organizing the classroom, and the curriculum.

Van Til, William. (Ed.) *Curriculum: Quest for Relevance*. Boston: Houghton Mifflin, 1974. Readings on criticisms of education, alternative and open schools, and alternative futures.

Wurman, Richard S. (Ed.) *Yellow Pages of Learning Resources*. Cambridge, Mass.: M.I.T., 1972. Guide to community resources with accompanying questions to aid data collection.

Chapter 7

Teaching Strategies

The identification and selection of teaching strategies is a major task of curriculum planners and developers of instructional materials. The task is closely related to other aspects of curriculum planning and frequently is carried out simultaneously or in conjunction with them, for example, as instructional objectives are refined, as instructional media are selected, and as units of instruction are planned. Teaching strategies have been singled out for emphasis in this chapter in order to clarify and present the variety of types that should be considered during the process of curriculum development.

Attention is given first to clarification of discovery, teacher-directed, inductive, and deductive-teaching strategies. Actual examples of concept development strategies are used to illustrate discovery-inductive strategies, discovery-deductive strategies, and other combinations. These examples can readily be adapted for use in units of instruction and specific teaching plans.

The next section includes models which serve as overall teaching strategies within which concept development and other specific strategies may be used. The first model is focused on the development of main ideas in the generalizing mode that was discussed in the chapter on disciplinary foundations. The second model is designed to bring together specific features or characteristics of topics in the integrative mode discussed earlier as noted above. The third model is related to the decision-making mode and can be used as a teaching strategy in all areas of the curriculum, as can the models for generalizing and integrative modes.

Teaching strategies for techniques of inquiry are considered next along with strategies for procedures that are widely used in different areas of the curriculum. Included among the techniques of inquiry are interviews, experiments, and field trips. Included among the basic procedures are demonstrations, role playing, and simulation games. These were selected to give a balanced overview of strategies that differ in emphasis and activity yet have many elements in common.

Teaching strategies that are used to develop cognitive, thinking, or inquiry processes are considered next. Specific examples of the types of questions that teachers may use are included in the teaching strategy for each process of inquiry.

Teaching strategies for the development of skills are considered in the next section. Two examples are given. The first is a teaching strategy that is used in many different developmental programs of reading instruction. The second example is related to the development of psychomotor skills.

The last section is devoted to teaching strategies that may be used to clarify values. Value clarification has been selected for emphasis because of its current emphasis in instructional planning and because the many strategies available are illustrative of desirable approaches to teaching and learning in the affective domain.

Many examples of teaching strategies are presented in later chapters dealing with areas of the curriculum. Some are applications or modifications of those presented in this chapter. Others are different in detail but may be fitted within the types of strategies discussed below. All together they constitute a fairly complete set of strategies to be considered by those charged with curriculum development and instructional planning.

DISCOVERY AND DIRECTED-TEACHING STRATEGIES

In recent years there has been considerable discussion of discovery versus directed-teaching strategies. There has been a great deal of debate about inductive and deductive approaches. Currently there are some who equate discovery and inductive strategies and directed and deductive strategies, and there are many views and definitions of discovery, directed-, inductive-, and deductive-teaching strategies. What is needed is a clarification of distinctions among these terms and related teaching strategies which will be useful in curriculum planning.

Our position is as follows. The discovery versus directed approaches should be placed on a continuum with teacher-directed strategies on one end, discovery strategies on the other, and varying degrees of teacher direction in between.

Most teaching strategies can be placed between the two extremes because of the current emphasis on teacher guidance coupled with increasing recognition of the importance of student involvement and self-direction in learning activities. The inductive versus deductive debate can be resolved by analyzing strategies in terms of their reliance on inductive, deductive, and transductive moves, that is, moving from particular to general, from general to particular, and from particular to particular. When these two views are joined together, it is possible to identify teacher-directed and discovery strategies that move inductively, deductively, or transductively. The following examples are illustrative of those in current use in various instructional materials. Notice that varying amounts of teacher direction are involved in the discovery strategies as well as in the directed strategies. Also notice that it is possible to make discoveries deductively as well as inductively, although inductive strategies are currently being emphasized in many programs.

Discovery-Inductive Strategy

This strategy moves from the particular to the general and is used to guide children to develop a concept by discovering common features and using the common features as a basis for grouping the items. The main steps are the following:

1 Observe and discuss items or data to be used in developing the concept.
   Example: What do you see in this group of objects? (For example, cutout circles and triangles)
2 Identify common features for use in grouping them, noting distinguishing differences.
   Example: How are they alike? How are they different?
3 Decide on a basis for grouping them.
   Example: How might we group them? Why?
4 Label, name, or define each group.
   Example: What is a good name for each group?
5 Have children use the term and find new examples.
   Example: What other examples can we find in these materials?

Discovery-Deductive Strategy

This strategy moves from the general to the particular. A rule or attributes that students have learned, or that the teacher provides, are given so that students can discover applications or new examples. Students proceed deductively from what they know or what is given to find supporting instances as shown in the following example.

1 Review or teach rule or main attributes to be used by students.
   Example: $4 + 1$ and $1 + 4$ both equal 5. Changing the order does not change the sum (commutative property).

2 Have children apply the rule or main attributes.
Example: Let's see if this applies in other cases. Do the examples on the chalkboard.
3 Review the rule of main attributes.
Example: State the rule in your own words. Who can write a general rule on the chalkboard? $(a + b = b + a)$
4 Have students find or do other examples.
Example: Do the examples on page 431.

Directed-Inductive Strategy

In this strategy the teacher directs instruction step by step from the particular to the general, moving from examples or attributes to a generalized meaning of the concept. Notice the expository role of the teacher in the following example of instruction on the concept *value*.

1 Identify examples or critical attributes of the concept to be developed.
Example: Value is the worth or usefulness of something. Here are some objects of great worth: good homes, good health. Here are some ideas we cherish: freedom, justice.
2 Identify nonexamples (nonexemplars) of the concept.
Example: Here are some things of little or no worth or value: worn-out clothes, useless junk. Here are some ideas we do not cherish: undemocratic government, crime, injustice.
3 Have students give examples (exemplars) and nonexamples (nonexemplars) of the concept.
Example: Give examples of objects or activities of worth to you. Give examples of ideas you cherish.
4 State the general meaning of the concept.
Example: We can use the term *value* to mean objects, ideas, and activities that are cherished, prized, or desired.
5 Have students use the term and find other examples and nonexamples.
Example: Use the term in discussion and in reports. Find new examples in the materials we are using.

Directed-Deductive Strategy

In this strategy the teacher starts with the definition of the concept and moves to particular examples of it. The teacher provides direct instruction in all phases except the last one in which students state the definition and give examples of the concept.

1 State the concept to be learned.
Example: Today we are to learn the meaning of *value*.

2 Identify critical attributes of the concept.
   Example: Value is the worth or usefulness of something. We place high value on objects, ideas, and activities that we cherish, prize, or desire.
3 Provide examples to clarify the concept.
   Example: Here are some things we value: good health, freedom, friends, sports, good homes.
4 Present nonexamples to further clarify the concept.
   Example: Here are some things we do not value: worn-out clothes, crime, injustice.
5 Have students state or write a definition and give examples.
   Example: State the meaning of value in your own words. Give examples of things you value and do not value.

Discovery-Transductive Strategy This strategy is useful in creative expression in a variety of forms in which divergent thinking is emphasized. It is also in situations in which children are to associate, relate, or compare words, numbers, patterns, themes, forms, and other items in a variety of ways. The teacher's role is primarily that of facilitator and stimulator. The child's role is that of manipulator and experimenter. Main phases of the strategy are the following.

1 Arrange materials or provide data for students to use.
   Example: Provide clay or other art media for children to use.
   Second example: Provide a list of words such as hot, cold, warm, fiery, icy, fall, winter, spring, red, blue, for children to groups as they wish.
2 Stimulate creative thinking by questions or comments.
   Example: What different things might we create with these materials?
   Second example: In what ways might these words be grouped?
3 Provide time for children to use the materials or process the data.
4 Provide opportunities for children to share, enjoy, and discuss the different outcomes of the activity.

Directed-Transductive Strategy Convergent thinking is emphasized in this strategy which is highly structured in moving children from particular to particular. It is used in teaching specific motor skills, word association skills, map skills, and the like. Main steps are:

1 Direct children's attention to the items to be associated or related.
   Example: Look at the legend on the map. What symbol stands for capitals? Cities? Towns?
2 Provide opportunities for practice.
   Example: Find the symbols for capitals, cities, and towns on this map.
3 Provide assistance to children who need it.
   Example: Arrange for small-group instruction.
4 Provide for application in other situations.
   Example: Notice the symbols on the map in our work for today. What does each one represent?

All the above strategies may be found in recently developed materials with variations in the form in which they are presented. However, the trend is toward increased use of guided discovery and inductive approaches, particularly when new concepts or generalizations are being developed. At the same time there is continued use of directed and deductive approaches. Deduction is typically used to get application of concepts, ideas, or other learning in a variety of situations, Teacher direction is provided in varying amounts to guide learning in profitable directions. This last point should be kept in mind as the strategies presented in the remainder of this chapter are reviewed. Another point to keep in mind is that many different variations may be made in the examples that are presented. No strategy ever emerges in the classroom exactly as it is described in writing.

MODEL STRATEGIES FOR THREE MODES OF INQUIRY

Model for Developing Main Ideas in the Generalizing Mode

The emphasis in this model is on the use of questions and activities that lead to the development of a main idea or generalization. The model has been used extensively in the preparation of teaching units and may be made a part of instruction in all areas of the curriculum. Teacher guidance is provided during all phases of instruction, but there is ample opportunity for divergent thinking within the broad structure of questions and activities.

The first phase of the model includes *openers* which are introductory activities designed to clarify the problem and give direction to subsequent study. The next phase includes a planned sequence of *developmental activities* that focus on the concepts and data needed to move toward the main idea or generalization. The third phase includes *concluding activities* designed to provide for the synthesis of ideas and the stating of the main idea by children in their own words and for evaluation and double-checking of the soundness of the main idea.

The model is illustrated below in the context of a unit on early people, excerpts of which have been adapted from an original teaching unit (Michaelis and Keach, 1972). The main idea to be developed is the following: Discoveries and inventions of early people changed their way of life.

1   Provide an opener to clarify the problem and give direction to learning. *Example:* Have students examine the pictures on page 31 of *Exploring in the Old World.* Have pairs of students select one picture and tell what people would need to know to carry out the depicted activity (for example, use writing, reading, trading). List the responses on the board and have students group them.

2   Provide a sequence of developmental questions and learning activities. *Example:* What inventions were necessary to write, trade, and carry out other activities noted above?

Read one of the sources listed on the chalkboard and find other inventions of early man.

Find as many ways as you can in which the lives of early people were changed by each invention.

What inventions and their effect on early people are shown in the film we are to see today?

3 Provide for concluding activities in which children formulate and check a generalization.

Example: What can we say in general about the inventions and discoveries of early people?

What can we say in general about the effects of these inventions and discoveries on the ways of living of early people?

Model for Bringing Particulars Together in the Integrative Mode

This model may be used to bring together special features of such events, activities, objects, and people as contributions of men and women as they are studied in all areas of the curriculum, health and safety activities, selected masterpieces in art and music, particular habitats, living things, and environmental conditions in science education, authors and literary selections in the language arts, and historical events, places, and cultures in the social studies. Recall that in this mode the emphasis is on specific features of a single item or topic, not on a generalization that has widespread application. Additional examples are various aspects of pedestrian or bicycle safety, unique features of Grofe's *On the Trail,* specific features of air, water, waste, and aesthetic pollution in a given city, main events in the life of an author or composer, main events in the Civil War; the outcomes of inquiry in all these pertain to the specific item under study.

The main phases of the model for the integrative mode are illustrated in the context of a unit on birds in science education. The focus of this part of the study is on the unique features of the Baltimore oriole, a favorite songbird of many children who have observed them.

1 Clarify the specific topic to be investigated.
Example: Several of you have commented on the beautiful song of the Baltimore oriole. Let's find out what is special about this bird.
2 Identify features or elements of the topic to be brought together.
Example: What features should we investigate? How about the concept cluster for studying birds: songs, calls, habits, territory, coloring, body parts—bill, crown, back, tail, breast, throat?
3 Gather and organize data on each feature or element selected for study.
Example: How should we gather data? How about direct observation of orioles in the neighborhood? How about materials in the science corner? How might we divide the search for information?

4 Decide on the form of presentation of findings.
   Example: How shall we present our findings? On a mural? On charts? In a
   booklet? How might we use a tape recorder? What are other possibilities?

Model for the Decision-making Mode

This model-teaching strategy may be used to guide the making of judgments or
decisions about events, activities, actions, and proposals for action that are
studied in all areas of the curriculum. Examples are health, safety, recreational
provisions and proposals, issues and problems related to wild life, plant life, and
other aspects of the environment, uses and abuses of mass media, opportunities
for art and music activities in the community, and various local, state, and national actions, problems, and proposals for change. A critical phase of this mode
is the clarification of values, criteria, standards, or values which students feel
should be used in making the decision or judgment. As in the other modes, sufficient data must be collected so that the decision or judgment is directly related
to the facts in the case.

The main phases of the decision-making mode are illustrated in the context
of a unit on the city environment. The focus is on proposals that have been made
for the provision of recreational areas for public use.

1 Clarify the proposals, issue, or problem.
   Example: Are the three proposals clear? What other facts do we need?
2 Clarify standards or values to be used.
   Example: On what basis should we judge them (extent of use, use by all
   people, city beautification, types of activity, cost, tax loss)? Which standards are most important to you? To others? Why?
3 Collect and organize information related to each standard.
   Example: What are the facts about use, costs? Let's organize the information on a chart so that we can compare each proposal on each standard.
4 Make a judgment or decision, including any suggestions for improvement.
   Example: Which proposal best meets the standards? What changes might
   be made to improve it?

STRATEGIES FOR USING TECHNIQUES OF INQUIRY AND SELECTED TEACHING PROCEDURES

The strategies presented in this section are for use in conjunction with various
techniques of inquiry and teaching procedures that can be used in all areas of
the curriculum. The techniques of inquiry are interviews, experiments, field
trips, and content analysis of reading materials. The procedures selected for
review are demonstrations, role playing, and simulation games.

There are several common elements or phases that may be identified in
teaching strategies for each one. First is the introductory phase in which the use

of the technique or procedure is clarified, objectives are established, interest is aroused, use of related materials is explained, and other preliminaries are handled. The second phase is development in which activities are carried out according to plans made in the introduction. The third phase is the conclusion in which findings are summarized, generalizations are made, or findings are processed in other ways. The fourth phase is evaluation in which both findings are procedures that have been used are appraised by the students, by the students and the teacher, or by the teacher.

Another basic consideration is that of adequate preparation on the part of the teacher prior to the use of the teaching strategies with children. For example, materials that are to be used must be assembled and arranged, the time schedule must be planned, and equipment and classroom furniture should be arranged as needed to provide working spaces for students. In some cases, it may be wise to have a trial run, for example, before a demonstration or an experiment is used with the class.

Interviews

Interviews are especially helpful in getting firsthand information from individuals who have expert knowledge on topics under study. Parents of children in school are possible interviewees as well as experts associated with public and private agencies in the community. Possibilities for using interviews exist in all subjects as needs for fresh data are related to contributions that may be made by artists, musicians, nutritionists, scientists, minority group members, energy and environmental technologists, public officials, or other experts. Preliminary preparation by the teacher includes clarification of objectives to be served by the interview, formulating questions related to the objectives, and identifying the individual(s) to be interviewed.

Introduction Discuss needs for new or additional data; identify individuals to interview; make specific plans, including questions to ask, how to introduce oneself to the interviewee, recording procedures during the interview, and importance of expressing thanks when finished.

Development Have children conduct the interview according to plan; urge children to raise additional questions to clarify points and to get data on unanticipated topics.

Conclusion Have children summarize data and report findings; use data to solve problems and carry out related activities in the unit under study.

Evaluation Have children identify needed improvements in response to such questions as, Which of our questions were answered? How can we improve interviewing procedures? Recording procedures? Reporting procedures?

Experiments

Experiments are used extensively in the science education program and some-what less in health education, art, music, and other areas of the curriculum. To be effective they must be planned and conducted so that children are involved in actually testing an hypothesis, not trying to prove a foregone conclusion by fol-lowing a recipe. Preparation by the teacher includes clarification of the hypoth-esis to be tested, gathering needed equipment and materials, and arranging work-ing spaces for children.

Introduction Clarify hypothesis to be tested and procedures to use; have children explore equipment, demonstrating use as necessary; discuss conditions and procedures, inviting questions from the group; discuss procedures for record-ing data.

Development Have children proceed according to plan; respond to questions and give assistance as needed; be sure children record data.

Conclusion Discuss findings to find out if hypothesis is supported or not; consider needs for more data; state conclusion.

Evaluation Was the hypothesis clear and testable? Were procedures for test-ing the hypothesis adequate? What changes should be made in procedures, equip-ment and materials, and instructions to children?

Field Trips

Field trips are helpful in giving children a firsthand view of people at work, busi-ness and industrial activity, farming and processing of produce, exhibits and collections, plants and animals in natural or man-made settings, environmental problems, and other items and activities related to topics under study. They may be used in any area of the curriculum, ranging from an informal walk in the neighborhood to an extended trip to another community. Preliminary prepara-tion by the teacher includes specification of objectives for the trip, obtaining administrative and parental approval, making travel arrangements, obtaining any needed assistants to help supervise children, making eating and toileting arrange-ments, planning the time-schedule, and informing the guide on the questions to be raised and the maturity and background of the children.

Introduction Clarify objectives with children; identify specific questions to be answered; plan recording and reporting procedures; plan individual and small-group assignments; review standards of behavior, safety precautions, appropriate dress, time schedule.

Development Assist guide as appropriate; have children raise questions; ask additional questions to clarify difficult points; check on children's completing of assignments and recording of information for later sharing; have children raise questions as needed to complete collection of data.

Conclusion Have children summarize data and report findings; develop charts, diagrams, displays, or other materials as appropriate; have children state main ideas or other conclusions; plan and send a letter of thanks.

Evaluation What improvements in procedures do children suggest? What changes are needed to attain initial objectives more adequately? How can ideas be more effectively applied in follow-up activities?

Demonstration

Demonstrations are widely used to teach children how to use equipment and materials, rhythm and other musical instruments, and rulers, compasses, and other items. They are also used to develop skills and concepts such as skipping, waltzing, lifting, candle making, weighing, measuring, graphing, and a host of other activities. Expository demonstrations are designed to impart information directly or to illustrate a skill as children observe. Questing demonstrations are designed to foster discovery of a concept or its application. Preliminary preparation by the teacher includes clarifying objectives, collecting needed materials, deciding who is to do the demonstration—the teacher, a child, a visitor, and planning and practicing the various steps of the demonstration.

Introduction Clarify objectives for children; respond to any questions; be sure each child can see and hear the demonstration.

Development Do each step according to plan; respond to any questions that arise; repeat any steps as needed to clarify understanding; involve children in any steps in which their involvement will clarify understanding.

Conclusion Use a chart or the chalkboard to summarize, or ask children to summarize or demonstrate steps in order; provide for immediate follow-up and application in learning activities.

Evaluation In what ways are children applying what was demonstrated? What aspects need further clarification? To what extent are initial objectives being achieved? What changes should be made if the demonstration is to be done again?

Role-playing Strategy

In role playing children enact situations that arise in daily living, are encountered in units of instruction, or are presented by the teacher. Values may be clarified, insight into the feelings of others may be developed, and practice in decision making may be provided. The main steps in a strategy for role playing are as follows (Shaftel and Shaftel, 1967).

1 Warming up the group (problem confrontation)
2 Selecting the participants in role playing
3 Preparing others to participate as observers
4 Setting the stage
5 Having the role playing or enactment of the situation
6 Discussing and evaluating the enactment
7 Having further enactments to play revised roles, next steps, and so forth.
8 Providing for further discussion and evaluation
9 Having students share experiences and generalize

Simulation Games

Simulation games serve as simplified models of real activities. Roles, rules, and materials restrict players to realistic portrayal of the activity being simulated. Clarifying objectives and relating the game to the unit under study are critical elements to emphasize both during the introduction and the debriefing at the conclusion. The main steps of procedure for any simulation game are the following (Michaelis, 1972):

Introduction Clarify concepts, skills, or other objectives. Describe players' roles, rules, use of materials, and time limits.

During the Game Observe players and handle questions on roles and adherence to rules. Note points to consider in debriefing.

Conclusion Focus debriefing discussion on objectives. Consider any problems and summarize key learnings. Relate learning to the unit under study.

Evaluation How can use of the game to attain objectives be improved? What needs to be done to clarify roles, rules, and use of materials? How can any distortions of reality be corrected?

TEACHING STRATEGIES FOR COGNITIVE, THINKING, OR INQUIRY PROCESSES

A variety of teaching strategies may be used to develop cognitive, thinking, or inquiry processes. Three strategies that have been developed by Taba and refined by her associates for use in the social studies may be used in any subject field in connection with concept development, generalizing, and predicting. The strategies are presented below with focusing questions in the order in which they are recommended for use (Wallen et al., 1969).

Concept Development
(Classifying)

1 What do you see (notice, find, etc.) here?
2 Do any of these items seem to belong together?
3 Why would you group them this way?
4 What would you call these groups?
5 Could some of these belong in more than one group?

Inferring and Generalizing

1 What did you see (notice, read, etc.)?
2 What differences did you notice (with reference to a particular question)?
3 Why do you think this happened? Or, How do you account for these differences?
4 What does this tell you about . . .?

Applying Generalizations
(Predicting)

1 Suppose that a particular event occurred given certain conditions, what would happen? (What would happen if . . . ?)
2 What makes you think that would happen?
3 Can someone give a different idea about what would happen?
4 If that happened, what do you think would happen after that?

Using an analysis of cognitive or inquiry processes in recently published social studies and science materials, Michaelis (1972) developed strategies for thirteen different processes. These strategies may be used in any subject and are designed to be used at all levels of instruction. The order of questioning generally follows that given in the following examples, but it may be varied in terms of children's backgrounds, prior instruction, or emphasis on inductive or deductive approach. Both cognitive and affective dimensions may be involved in any given strategy; this is so because feelings, interests, and values are a part of thinking and inquiry as well as concepts and main ideas. Notice that the three strategies listed above are included in slightly different form.

First-level Processes

The processes at this level are basic to use of the others. Recalling and observing are used by children to marshal the ideas they are to use in a given situation.

Observing involves both direct seeing, touching, and using other senses, and indirect observation by means of films, recordings, books, and other media. Comparing/contrasting, classifying, and defining are used to process information that has been recalled or collected by various methods of observation. Interpreting involves the translating, stating, and explaining the meaning of whatever source of data is being used. Generalizing involves the abstracting of the central or main idea. The teaching strategies for these basic processes are as follows:

Recalling

Is the question (problem) clear?
What clues will help us to recall needed items?
Do examples given thus far make you think of others?

Observing

What do we need to find out?
What sources should we use?
How can we find out? By looking? Listening? Asking? Reading? Other ways?
How might our feelings affect what we observe?
How can we check our findings?

Comparing/Contrasting

What did you see? Hear? Read?
What features did you notice?
How are they alike?
How are they different?

Classifying

What did you see? Hear? Find?
Which ones may be grouped together?
Why can they be grouped this way?
What is a good name for the group?
Can they be grouped in other ways? On what basis?

Defining

What do you mean by _____?
How can we find the meaning?
What is a good way to define it? (By example, demonstration, analogy, synonym or antonym, stating behavior, stating operations?)
Which definition is best in this situation?

Interpreting

What does this show? Contain? Tell?
What does it mean to you?
Can you explain the meaning in your own words?
How can we summarize the most important points?

Generalizing

What did you find?
What common elements are there?
What can we say in general?
Does our generalization hold up as we check other information?

Higher-level Processes

In general, the processes in this group are on a higher cognitive level. They call for use of data that have been processed in one or more ways as noted above. Inferring, hypothesizing, and predicting are interrelated processes which go beyond the interpreting and generalizing that is done with a given body of information. Inferring is reading between the lines or drawing an implication; hypothesizing is the formulating of a proposition that can be tested by gathering additional data; and predicting is the making of an educated guess about what is going to happen, a projection that is based on all the important factors that are related to the prediction. Analyzing and synthesizing are two sides of the coin and are frequently used together, with analyzing as the process of breaking an item down into parts, causes, or reasons, and synthesizing as the putting of parts together. Evaluating may be used along with all the other processes to determine "how well we are doing," and it is used at the end of activities to determine "how well we did and how we can improve." Teaching strategies are as follows:

Inferring

What did you find? Read? See? Hear?
What might have caused that?
Or, how do you think they might have felt?
Or, Why do you think that happened?
What is your reason for saying (or believing) that?

Hypothesizing

What usually happens if ____? Or, What is the usual effect of ____?
Or, How is ____ related to ____? Why do you think so?
What is a fair way to test our hypothesis?
What materials are needed? What conditions should be provided?
Do findings support it? Do we need more data? How should we collect it?

Predicting

What changes (trends, developments) are shown here?
What do you think will happen in the future? Why?
What conditions are necessary for that to happen?
What basis should we use to make a prediction?

What information should we collect?
Should other facts be considered?

Analyzing

How can we break it into parts?
What main parts (types, reasons, causes) should be studied?
What is the meaning of each part? What does each include?
What information do we have on each part?
How are the parts related?

Synthesizing

How can we put the parts together in a new way?
What are the most important items to include?
How should they be organized?
In what form should they be presented?

Evaluating

What is to be appraised? What standards shall we use?
What information do we have (or should get) related to each standard?
How fully is each standard met? If alternatives are to be evaluated, ask:
What are the alternatives? What will be the consequences of each one?
Which alternative best meets the standards?

TEACHING STRATEGIES FOR DEVELOPING SKILLS

Teaching strategies for the development of basic skills in reading, arithmetic, physical education, and other areas of the curriculum are among the most highly refined approaches to instruction. Based on research and study over many years, they have been systematized in developmental programs of instruction. Although there are differences among various strategies for skill development, it is possible to identify several common features. First is the emphasis on preparation, readiness building including development of meaning, and clarification of need for the skill. Second is demonstration or explanation of the skill followed by actual practice on the part of students, practice being recognized as the essential ingredient in skill development. Diagnosis of needs and assistance at the point of need are ongoing activities of the teacher during skill development. Extension and application of the skill are given direct attention so that students will make a transfer to other situations. Finally, evaluation is systematically provided in most programs.

Two examples have been selected to illustrate skill development strategies. The first is used in many programs of developmental reading instruction. The second is used to develop motor skills in physical education, music, and other areas of the curriculum.

Teaching Strategy for Reading

This strategy begins with preparation for reading which serves as an introduction and the establishing of specific objectives for reading the selection. The next phase typically involves silent reading in line with objectives, followed by discussion and sharing of ideas and by oral reading of selected passages, especially in the early grades. Follow-up practice, extension, and evaluation are provided through the use of workbooks or independent activities provided by the teacher. Main steps in the strategy are as follows:

Preparation for Reading Development of readiness and background for the reading selection; presenting vocabulary to be encountered in the selection; building interest; setting purposes for reading; introducing and explaining skills to be developed.

Reading of the Selection Silent reading in line with objectives; individual assistance by the teacher as requested by children; taking notes or completing exercises related to the selection.

Discussion and Sharing Opportunities for children to discuss and share interesting parts, answers to questions, new ideas obtained, how the ideas might be applied, and other objectives set during preparation.

Guided Oral Reading Opportunities for children to read aloud while the teacher observes to note any aspects needing attention; sharing of most interesting passage; emphasis on interpretation of selected parts.

Follow-up Extension, Practice, Evaluation Use of workbook and independent activities prepared by the teacher; practice on vocabulary development, word analysis, reading for main ideas, reading for details, and other skills; related activities in art, individualized practice materials, applications in other areas of the curriculum.

Teaching Strategy for Developing Motor Skills

This strategy may be used for developing psychomotor skills in physical education, music education, or other areas of the curriculum. The strategy involves demonstration plus immediate involvement or participation on the part of children. In fact, at times children themselves may do the demonstrating, beginning with simple aspects and moving to increasingly more complex ones as they develop the skill being emphasized.

The strategy may proceed from part to part (part method), may encompass the entire skill (whole method), or may employ a combination of the part and whole methods. For example, skill in singing a song, or skill in handling a basket-ball, or skill in writing may be approached in such parts as phrases of the song, different passes used in basketball, or the formation of individual letters. Or the approach may be in terms of the whole song, playing basketball, or writing whole words or even sentences. Most experts agree that both part and whole methods should be used, that at times a combination is feasible, and that alert teachers employ all three depending on the background of the children, the complexity of the skill, and objectives guiding immediate instruction.

1 Clarify need for the skill.
   Example: When is it a good idea to use the overhead pass? The bounce pass?
2 Demonstrate the skills, or have a student demonstrate them.
   Example: Watch as I throw an overhead pass. Now, a bounce pass.
3 Provide for immediate practice, observing to note those in need of guid-ance.
   Example: Let's try each kind of pass, the overhead first.
4 Provide individual assistance as needed.
   Example: Have students who are skillful work with others in small groups, take those aside who need help.
5 Provide for immediate use of the skill.
   Example: As we play, let's see how well we can use these two passes.

VALUES ANALYSIS AND CLARIFICATION

Three different approaches to values analysis and clarification are presented in this section to illustrate teaching strategies in the affective domain. The first is a systematic and rational approach that calls for analysis of relevant data in de-tail. The second is designed for identifying values in topics under study. The third approach is useful in clarifying values in a variety of situations.

A Model for Rational Value Analysis

The phases or steps in this model are closely related to those usually included in reflective thinking or problem-solving models that begin with the clarification of the issue or problem, involve the collection and organization of related data, and move to the making and checking of a conclusion (Metcalf, 1971).

Identify and clarify the value question. What is the issue? What is to be judged?

Assemble purported facts. What are the facts? How can we distinguish facts from opinions?

Assess the truth of the purported facts. How can we check the facts? Which are supported by evidence?

Clarify the relevance of facts. Which facts are directly related? Which facts are useful in making a judgment?

Arrive at a tentative value decision. What is a good preliminary judgment? Test the value principle implied in the decision.

Does it apply to new or other cases? Is it consistent with basic values or principles? Does it apply to us as well as to others? What would the consequences be if it were universally adopted?

Identifying Values in Topics under Study

The strategy for identifying values in events may be used in connection with units at all levels of instruction (Taba et al., 1971). The strategy begins with identification of facts and main reasons for the event under study. Students then infer values from the stated reasons. The analysis may be personalized by carrying out the last two steps which call for students to state what they would have done and to infer the values behind positions they have taken.

Clarify the facts about the event. What actually happened? What are the facts?

Identify the main reasons. Why did it happen? What are the main reasons?

Infer values from the reasons. What do the reasons show to be important to them?

Identify what students would have done and the reasons for their positions. What might you have done in the same situation? Why?

Infer students' values from the reasons. What do your reasons show to be important to you?

Value-clarification Strategies

The examples of strategies presented below are based on an approach to values clarification that includes the following processes (Raths et al., 1966):

Choosing: freely, from alternatives, and after thoughtful reflection
Prizing: cherishing, being happy with the choice and willing to affirm it
Acting: doing something, and doing it repeatedly

The teacher's role is one of helping students to clarify values, not to implant values. The teacher should accept students' responses, respect each individual's response and decision to participate or not, encourage honesty and diversity in response, and avoid questions or comments that limit thinking or prevent maintenance of an open atmosphere. The following are illustrative of the teaching strategies based on this approach.

Clarifying-response Strategy In this strategy the teacher responds to comments of students by simply raising such nonjudgmental questions as, Is this something you prize? How did you feel when that happened? Are you glad about that? Did you consider any alternatives? Do you do anything about that? Do you value that?

Value-sheet Strategy A dilemma or problem situation is presented to students in a paragraph or two, or even a single provocative statement. Pictures, cartoons, a recording or other stimuli may also be used to provoke reflection on a value-laden topic. The provocative stimulus is followed by questions that focus on the valuing processes of choosing, prizing, and acting. Students work out their own responses and may or may not share them. Here is an example.

Fairness

True fairness is to do everything one can to treat others equally, even when one's family or friends may not know about it.
What does "fairness" mean to you?
Do you think everyone is fair? If not, why?
Are you proud of your own fairness? All of the time?

Open-ended Statement or Question Strategy Students are asked to respond to incomplete statements or questions that are presented in oral or written form. Students write their responses, and as they are read by the teacher a question may be noted on each paper to stimulate reflection. Some papers may be read anonymously to the class followed by the raising of questions by students on points that they think the author should consider; this is one way of teaching the value clarification process to students. Illustrative statements and questions are the following:

What would you do if you received a gift of $200?
If I could have five wishes, I would . . .
I can hardly wait to be able to . . .
If I had been a scout for the pioneers, I would have . . .
What three things would you do if you were President?

Other Strategies A variety of other strategies based on the Rath's model may be used to help students clarify values related to personal situations or to topics in different areas of the curriculum (Raths et al., 1966; Simon et al., 1972; Harmin et al., 1973). For example:
Value voting may be used by having students raise their hands if they vote yes in response to questions such as, How many of you watch TV more than three hours a day? How many of you think smog devices should not be added to cars during the energy crisis? How many of you think that Custer was right?

Rank order may be used to have students place in order of priority their preference for school subjects, the seasons, summer activities, proposals for school and community improvement, actions taken by public officials.

FOLLOW-UP ACTIVITIES AND PROJECTS

1 In general which of the strategies in the first section do you tend to favor? Discovery-inductive? Discovery-deductive? Directed-inductive? Others? What reasons do you have for your preferences?

2 Select any one of the strategies in the first section and make a short plan of a way in which you might use it to develop a concept with children.

3 Critically review the strategies in each of the remaining sections of this chapter and make a sample teaching plan for each of the following:

a One of the models for the modes of inquiry

b One of strategies for using a technique of inquiry

c Two of the inquiry processes, one of the first-level and one of the higher-level processes

d One of the skill-development strategies

e One of the value-analysis or clarification strategies.

BIBLIOGRAPHY

Croft, Doreen J., and Robert D. Hess. *An Activities Handbook for Teachers of Young Children.* Boston: Houghton Mifflin, 1972. Teaching procedures for a variety of activities in different areas of the curriculum.

Harmin, Merrill, Howard Kirschenbaum, and Sidney B. Simon. *Clarifying Values through Subject Matter.* Minneapolis: Winston Press, 1973. Suggestions on use of clarification strategies in different areas of the curriculum.

Joyce, Bruce, and Marsha Weil. *Models of Teaching.* Englewood Cliffs, N.J.: Prentice-Hall, 1972. Models drawn from four sources: social interaction, information processing, personal, and behavior modification.

Maidment, Robert. *Simulation Games: Design and Execution.* Columbus, Ohio: Charles E. Merrill, 1973. Procedures for creating and using simulation games.

Metcalf, Lawrence E. (Ed.) *Values Education.* 41st Yearbook. Washington, D.C.: National Council for the Social Studies, 1971. A model and strategies for rational analysis of values in topics and issues under study.

Michaelis, John U. *Social Studies for Children in a Democracy.* Englewood Cliffs, N.J.: Prentice-Hall, 1972. Chapter on development of thinking and inquiry processes.

Michaelis, John U., and Everett T. Keach, Jr., (Eds.) *Teaching Strategies for Elementary School Social Studies.* Itasca, Ill.: Peacock Press, 1972. Chapter designs for units.

Morine, Harold, and Greta Morine. *Discovery: A Challenge to Teachers.* Englewood Cliffs, N.J.: Prentice-Hall, 1973. Examples of inductive-, deductive-, and transductive-discovery teaching.

Raths, Louis E., Merrill Harmin, and Sidney B. Simon. *Values and Teaching.* Columbus, Ohio: Charles E. Merrill, 1966. A theory of values clarification and illustrative teaching strategies.

Ryan, Frank L., and Arthur K. Ellis. *Instructional Implications of Inquiry.* Englewood Cliffs, N.J.: Prentice-Hall, 1974. Definitions of inquiry and techniques for guiding inquiry at different levels of instruction.

Shaftel, Fannie, and George Shaftel. *Role Playing for Social Values.* Englewood Cliffs, N.J.: Prentice-Hall, 1967. Examples of role playing at different levels.

Simon, Sydney, B., Leland W. Howe, and Howard Kirschenbaum. *Values Clarification: A Handbook of Practical Strategies for Teachers and Students.* New York: Hart Publishing Co., 1972. Collection of strategies based on Raths' theory.

Taba, Hilda, et al. *Teacher's Handbook for Elementary Social Studies.* (2nd ed.) Menlo Park, Calif.: Addison-Wesley, 1971. Chapters on teaching strategies.

Wallen, Norman E., et al. *Final Report: The Taba Curriculum Development Project in the Social Studies.* Menlo Park, Calif. Addison-Wesley, 1969, Section on teaching strategies.

Chapter 8

Evaluation
and Accountability

Evaluation includes the procedures, techniques, and criteria involved in gathering and processing evidence needed to make decisions and judgments. The decisions and judgments may be related to the curriculum, teaching strategies, instructional media, pupil progress, and other aspects of the educational program. Operationally, effective systems of evaluation are used to clarify goals and objectives, to determine the extent to which objectives have been achieved, to assess alternative approaches to instruction, to identify needed changes in the instructional program, to gather evidence for use in reporting pupil progress, and to interpret the program informally through contacts with parents and formally through accountability systems and other means.

Assessment is carried on at three levels. At the local level are the various procedures and devices that are used by the classroom teacher and the formal measurement program carried on throughout the school district. Assessment at the local level is of utmost importance in terms of curriculum improvement and instructional planning. Many states have testing programs that are given in all school districts with particular emphasis on the measurement of achievement in reading and arithmetic. The growth of accountability systems in recent years has brought an accompanying increase in statewide testing. At the national level is *National Assessment of Educational Progress,* a project of the Education Commission of the States designed to report achievement of selected age groups (nine,- thirteen-, and seventeen-year-olds and adults) on several of the following: reading, literature, writing, science, social studies, citizenship, music, art, mathematics, and vocational education. Their reports include information on educational level of parents, performance of blacks, type of community, regional differences, and male-female differences (National Assessment of Educational Progress).

The focus of this chapter is on evaluation at the local level as a part of curriculum and instructional planning. Attention is directed first to characteristics of an effective program of evaluation, including scope and functions, relationships to objectives and learning activities, an integral part of instruction, diagnostic, formative and summative evaluation, clear objectives, cooperative process, self-evaluation, testing and measurement, variety of techniques, and criteria for instruments and techniques. The next section deals with the making of plans for evaluation and how a table of specifications may be used to guide planning. The third section contains examples of questions and items that may be used to evaluate learning in the cognitive and affective domains. This section also contains examples of charts, checklists, and inventories that may be used to assess affective outcomes. The next section describes accountability systems with specific attention to main characteristics, procedures and roles, various models, detrimental aspects and their avoidance, and possible benefits. The final section is a brief summary of criteria in question form that may be used to evaluate areas of the curriculum. It has been designed to bring together in summary form the major elements discussed in preceding chapters that are useful in appraising all areas of the curriculum.

AN EFFECTIVE PROGRAM OF EVALUATION

Scope and Functions

Evaluation should encompass all phases of the instructional program, ranging from goals and areas of the curriculum to specific aspects of children's intellectual, physical, social, and emotional development. A broad and comprehensive program is needed to improve learning and teaching, improve the curriculum, report pupil progress, provide meaningful interpretation of evidence, judge the merits of alternative approaches to instruction, appraise instructional media, meet individual needs of children, and provide a meaningful accountability system.

Relationships to Objectives and Learning Activities

Evaluation of children's development and learning should be guided by objectives and directly related to learning activities provided in the program of instruction. If the relationships among objectives, learning activities, and evaluation are over-looked, evaluation can easily become a separate or disparate process that contributes little to the improvement of children's learning or the instructional program. The interrelationships are illustrated in Chart 8-1.

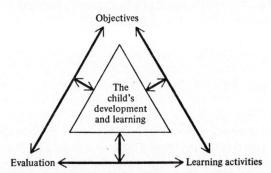

Chart 8-1 Relationships among objectives, learning activities, and evaluation

An Integral Part of Instruction

Evaluation should be viewed as an integral and continuing part of instruction. The ongoing daily evaluation made a part of instruction by the teacher and the individual and group self-evaluation guided by the teacher are of inestimable value. The feedback is useful in adapting instruction and improving learning directly, immediately, and continuously. Objectives can be adjusted to fit the readiness or entry behavior of children for various activities. Teaching strategies can be modified and refined. Individual needs and special interests and aptitudes can be discovered and taken into account as learning activities are planned and carried out. Periodic testing and reporting should contribute to, not detract from, the emphasis on evaluation as a continuing part of instruction.

Diagnostic, Formative, and Summative Evaluation

An effective program of evaluation should include three different but closely interrelated phases (Bloom, Hastings, and Madaus, 1971):

   Diagnostic evaluation prior to instruction to determine the starting point, to identify needed prerequisite skills and causes of learning difficulties, and to place students in learning groups
   Formative evaluation during instruction to obtain ongoing feedback for both the child and teacher on progress and any learning problems

Summative evaluation at the end of a unit or specified time period to assess attainment of initial objectives and to identify other outcomes.

All three types of evaluation are melded in an effective program so that the principle of continuing evaluation is maintained. Some of the same evaluative devices may be used in all three phases. For example, tests, charts, or checklists used during formative and summative evaluation may be used to diagnose needs prior to instruction. Similarly, standardized tests and observation may be used during diagnostic evaluation as well as during summative evaluation to assess children's attainment of particular aspects of instruction.

Clearly Specified Objectives

Objectives of instruction should be kept in sharp focus during all phases of evaluation—objectives that specify observable behavior or performance and products that can be examined as noted in the chapter on goals and objectives. For example, note how the following objectives provide a focus for the appraisal of children's development in the use of processes of inquiry, a neglected area of evaluation in some programs:

Defining Given the word "mayor," the child will define it by stating at least three things a mayor does, drawing upon information obtained during a visit to city hall or to another accurate source.

Interpreting Given a map of cities in our state, the student will identify the three largest ones, using the legend and population chart.

Generalizing After reading a selection in a text, the student will state the main idea in one sentence and support it by citing at least three related facts.

Synthesizing Given a list of fifteen events in the history of our state, the student will construct a time line that shows the events in sequence with correct scale between each event.

A Cooperative Process

Evaluation should be viewed as a cooperative process that involves children, teachers, and parents as well as measurement and other specialists. Teachers must play a central role because of the need to make evaluation a part of ongoing classroom instruction. Within the classroom children should be involved in developing and using standards for appraising and improving individual and group work; they should also be guided to grow in the ability to do self-evaluation. Parents should be involved in goal-setting aspects of the development of accountability systems, in improving systems of reporting pupil progress, and in providing background information that is needed to interpret evaluative evidence. Specialists in evaluation have a leadership and supportive role to play in the development and operation of an effective system of evaluation.

The Importance of Self-evaluation

Self-evaluation by students on an individual and group basis is a key component of an effective program of evaluation. Such goals as learning how to learn and thinking ability call for continuing growth in the ability to make self-appraisals. Charts, checklists, and other devices based on individual and group formulations of standards are needed to facilitate and improve self-evaluation. As children progress in the attainment of conceptual, process, skill, and affective objectives, there should be a corresponding growth in the ability to engage in self-evaluation.

Broader than Testing and Measurement

Evaluation should be viewed broadly to include testing and other means of measurement that are a part of the complete program of appraisal used in making decisions and judgments. Testing should not be equated with evaluation because it is only one method of collecting evidence. Measurement is narrower in meaning than evaluation but broader than testing because it includes the variety of instruments and processes used to collect evidence needed in evaluation.

Standardized achievement tests for reading, mathematics, social studies, and other areas of the curriculum may be used to identify strengths and weaknesses in the instructional program. Analysis of tests for an individual child yields diagnostic information that is helpful in instructional planning. However, various limitations must be kept in mind, such as appropriateness of the norms, and differences between what is measured on the test and what is included in the curriculum. Care should be taken to prevent such misuses of standardized tests as making unjustified comparisons between children, between schools, and between groups and the national norms.

Distinctions should be kept in mind between *norm-referenced* tests which are based on norms developed on a sampling of students and expressed in percentile, grade-equivalent, and other scores, and *criterion-referenced* and *objective-referenced* tests which are based on specified levels of attainment such as 100 percent mastery of addition and subtraction combinations. Increasing use is being made of tests that are tied to specified criteria and objectives in the language arts, mathematics education, and other programs of instruction. It is generally agreed that both have a place in a complete testing program, with norm-referenced tests being used to provide an indication of relative achievement of a given group and criterion-reference tests being used to indicate to extent to which specified levels of attainment have been achieved. Diagnostic, formative, and summative evaluation call for the employment of a variety of tests and other evaluative instruments. The current attention to criterion-referenced measures should be viewed as an addition to a well-rounded program, not a substitute for other useful devices.

Variety of Instruments and Techniques

The evaluation program should include the use of a variety of measurement instruments and techniques. Both subjective-informal techniques and objective-formal techniques are needed. Some of the most widely used techniques are subjective and informal in the sense that teacher judgment is used to determine change in behavior due to instruction, and the techniques are used informally as a part of instruction. Quite helpful in all areas of the curriculum are these subjective-informal techniques: teacher observation, group discussion, group interviews, individual interviews, logs, diaries, checklists, rating sheets, anecdotal records, and examination of children's work.

Objective-formal techniques of evaluation are used at selected points in the program. Included among them are standardized tests that are available for all subjects, teacher-made tests related to units of instruction, rating scales, and inventories of attitudes, self-concept, interests, and values. In recent years most attention has been given to objective-formal measures of cognitive outcomes and minor attention to measures of personal attitudes and values. A primary reason for this change has been the institution of requirements designed to prevent psychological or other harm to children. These requirements usually relate to measures of personal attitudes and beliefs, not to scientific, health, or other attitudes that are considered to be part of the ongoing program of instruction. Guidelines and regulations for the use of formal-objective measures are provided by school districts and should be checked systematically.

A combination of techniques should be used to evaluate various outcomes of instruction as shown in the following summary:

Conceptual objectives tests, samples of work, checklists, observation, interviews

Inquiry objectives tests, observation, checklists, samples of work, charts showing mode and processes, interviews

Skill objectives tests, samples of work, observation, checklists, charts, interviews, discussion, rating devices

Affective objectives discussion, observation, rating devices, inventories, anecdotal records

Criteria for Instruments and Techniques

Measurement instruments and techniques should be selected and developed in terms of several criteria. A first consideration is usefulness of the instrument or device in providing information or evidence needed for evaluation purposes.

There is no place in the program for collecting piles of data that will not be used. Curricular validity should be checked so that all instruments used to assess outcomes of instruction are in fact directly related to what is being taught. Appropriateness in terms of the level of development of the children is an essential criterion, as is practicality in terms of ease of administration and data processing. Other criteria are validity of instruments (measure what they purport to measure) and reliability (consistency and accuracy of measurement).

MAKING PLANS FOR EVALUATION

After clearly specifying objectives, there are several steps or phases that are helpful in making plans for evaluating outcomes of a given instructional program (Bloom, Hastings, Madaus, 1971). A basic step is the preparation of a table of specifications that brings together the behaviors to be developed and the content, units, and learning activities to be used in developing them. Illustrative tables of specifications are presented in the volume cited above for different areas of the curriculum. The example presented in Table 8-1 is an adaptation of one designed to be used in planning for the assessment of outcomes of instruction in the language arts. Notice that cognitive and affective behaviors are identified across the top of the table. These should be stated to conform with those that are being emphasized in a given program of instruction and should be an adequate sampling of them. Down the lefthand side are noted the content and skills to be taught in various components of the language arts program. Specific skills included in listening, speaking, reading, and writing activities should be noted in the appropriate spaces in the lefthand column.

The table of specifications serves as a general guide to the development of test items, charts, checklists, rating scales, and other devices to use in appraising outcomes of instruction. It should be constructed so as to cover objectives of instruction, the full range of assessible behaviors related to the objectives, and a fair sampling of all parts of the instructional program. Frequent reference to such specifications during the process of developing the evaluation program makes it possible to prevent gaps and to give appropriate attention to areas in need of emphasis.

The next phase is the deciding of ways to gather data on the various components in the table of specifications. By working across the table of specifications it is possible to make decisions regarding needed test items, checklists, or other devices. For example, listening skills might be assessed by means of a checklist which contains such standards as watches the speaker, takes notes on important points, raises questions at appropriate times. Or test items might be constructed for the measurement of skills in reading. A rating scale might be used for the appraisal of handwriting skills, and so on. Appropriate notations are made in each cell of the table to indicate progress in designing the evaluation program.

Table 8-1 Table of specifications for the language arts, K to 6

BEHAVIORS

Content Skills Units	Cognitive						Affective			
	Knowledge	Comprehension	Application	Analysis	Synthesis	Evaluation	Receiving	Responding	Valuing	Attitudes
	Terminology Information Concepts	Defining Interpreting Generalizing	Inferring Predicting	Elements Relationships	Creating	Objective Subjective Criteria	Awareness Willingness Attentiveness	Compliance Willingness Satisfaction	Acceptance Preference Commitment	Positive Neutral Negative
Listening a. b. . . .										
Speaking a. b. . . .										
Reading a. b. . . .										
Writing a. b. . . .										

Source: Adapted from Bloom, Hastings, Madaus, 1971.

The next phase is the construction, tryout, and revision of test items, checklists, and other devices. Consideration is given to the development of a pool of test items, charts and checklists of various types, and other devices to use with children of differing backgrounds and capabilities. Attention is also given to scoring systems and possible uses of the devices in the marking, grading, and reporting of progress.

A simplified table of specifications is helpful for the planning of informal evaluation by the teacher. For a given unit of work the conceptual, process, skill, and affective objectives may be noted across the top of the table of specifications. Down the lefthand side may be noted the various sections of the unit. Evaluation devices are then planned or selected to appraise learning in the different sections of the unit and at the end of the unit, with attention to the objectives emphasized in each section.

USING THE TAXONOMIES OF EDUCATIONAL OBJECTIVES

The taxonomies of educational objectives are especially helpful as guides to the preparation of questions, items, and tasks for use in evaluating children's learning (Bloom, 1956; Krathwohl et al., 1964). Many examples of test items related to different categories of the taxonomies are presented in the chapters that deal with different areas of the curriculum in the *Handbook of Formative and Summative Evaluation of Student Learning* (Bloom, Hastings, Madaus, 1971).

Cognitive Domain

Listed below are examples of questions that can be used in informal evaluation and test items that can be used in formal evaluation for each level of the taxonomy. Additional examples are presented in later chapters dealing with areas of the curriculum.

Knowledge Level

What does setting mean when we say setting of the story?
The setting of a story refers to its
a. theme   **b.** style   **c.** location   **d.** main idea

Comprehension Level

Describe in your own words the setting of the story we just read.
The setting of the last story was _____.

Application Level

Today's story is about noise pollution. Where do you think the setting may be?
The setting of a story on noise pollution will probably be in
a. a farm house   **b.** a city   **c.** a village   **d.** any place

Analysis Level

What words in the story does the author use to make us feel how it must be to live in the setting of today's story?

Here is a dittoed copy of the story's setting. Underline each word that is used to make you feel how it must be to live there.

Synthesis Level

Let's create a setting for a story on summer activities. Who can describe a setting for an activity you like?

Write the name of a summer activity you like. Under it write a description of the setting in which you would like to do it next summer.

Evaluation Level

Listen as I read two descriptions of a setting. Which one is more interesting? Why?

Read the two descriptions of a setting on the dittoed sheet. Select the one you find more interesting and list at least three reasons for your choice.

Affective Domain

Below are examples of questions and test items that may be used on the first three levels of the taxonomy, the levels most appropriate for use in elementary schools.

Receiving Level

What did you find interesting in the story?
List three things you found to be interesting in the story.

Responding Level

Why do you think Jim's decision to stay and guard the cabin took courage?
List at least three reasons why you think Jim's decision to stay and guard the cabin took courage.

Valuing Level

What might you have done if you had been in Jim's place in the story? Why?
Write at least two reasons for what you might have done if you had been in Jim's place in the story.

Charts, checklists, inventories, and rating scales may also be developed to reflect different levels of the taxonomy as shown in the following examples.

Listening to Poetry

Yes   No   I am willing to listen to poetry.
Yes   No   I am willing to listen to poetry and discuss it.
Yes   No   I like to listen to poetry and discuss it.

. . .

Interest in Reading

Reads during free time.	Rarely	Sometimes	Frequently
Checks out library books.	Rarely	Sometimes	Frequently
Shares ideas obtained by reading.	Rarely	Sometimes	Frequently

. . .

Participation in Discussion

Pays attention during discussion.	Rarely	Usually	Always
Contributes ideas to discussion.	Rarely	Usually	Always
Helps to evaluate discussion.	Rarely	Usually	Always

. . .

Visiting the Art Museum

Paintings	Like a little	Like	Like a lot
Sculpture	Like a little	Like	Like a lot
Mobiles	Like a little	Like	Like a lot

. . .

Which Would You Like to Learn More About?

People of China	A little	Some	A lot
People of Russia	A little	Some	A lot
People of Mexico	A little	Some	A lot

. . .

ACCOUNTABILITY

Accountability systems have been set up in many states and school systems throughout the country. Curriculum workers and evaluation specialists have been involved with teachers, school administrators, and laymen in setting up systems that meet state regulations. A flood of books, pamphlets, and other materials have been released. Programs of evaluation have been modified to contribute to the operation of different systems, and statewide assessment of students' achievement at specified grades has increased.

Major Characteristics of Accountability

Accountability may be defined as the holding of school systems responsible for educational outcomes, that is, responsible for students' learning. Put another way, it means holding school personnel responsible for consequences of the instructional program. Operationally, this means the identification and removal of undesirable consequences of instruction and revision of the curriculum so that stated objectives are more fully achieved. Objectives must be defined in ways that make measurement and clear reporting or accounting possible. Means must be found to eliminate obstacles or deficiencies that hinder the attaining of specified objectives.

Accountability may be viewed in terms of goals, programs, and/or outcomes of instruction. Major goals in a school district are approved by the board of education, which is held accountable to the public for them. Programs of instruction are designed and carried out under the leadership of school administrative personnel who are accountable to the board of education. Outcomes of instruction are the responsibility of teachers and related instructional personnel who are accountable to school administration personnel.

In some accountability systems each of the above groups—board members, administrators, teachers—may be required to give an accounting in terms of agreed-upon terminal objectives. The following objectives are illustrative of those to which individuals in the different groups may be held:

By April 15 when asked about the goals of education, all board members and school administrators will provide an accurate written statement of the goals adopted by the board of education.

By April 15 each area administrator will submit statements of objectives for beginning reading instruction as defined by teachers in each area.

By April 15 each school principal will provide statements of instructional objectives prepared by teachers in grades 1 through 3 for each level of reading as outlined in the course of study.

By April 15 when shown lowercase letters on a chart 85 percent of the pupils in each grade will identify twenty letters with 100 percent accuracy.

Procedures and Roles

The process of accountability typically includes these procedures. Basic goals of education are prepared by a group made up of school personnel and laymen, approved by the board of education, and broken down into measurable (behavioral) objectives by the professional staff. Assessment is made of the present status of students in relation to objectives and instruction is provided in order to move children toward the attainment of the objectives. Evaluation is made of pupil achievement, and detailed analyses are made of the instructional programs with special attention to ways in which instruction can be improved. In complete accountability systems, designated managers or administrators are responsible for the making of recommendations for improving instruction and for the reporting or accounting of pupil progress to appropriate authorities in the school district.

The school administrative staff plays a key role in adopting or devising an accountability system and in seeing that it is implemented throughout the school district. Beginning with assistance to the board of education in the setting up of procedures to formulate goals, designated administrators coordinate the operation of the system on through all components including final assessment of outcomes of instruction and reporting of findings. Laymen play an important role in the formulation of goals and in helping to clarify effective means of reporting. Teachers and other instructional personnel play a central role in specifying instructional objectives, designing related programs of instruction, and detecting and removing deficiencies or weaknesses in instruction. Measurement specialists and other experts have a role to play in stating objectives in measurable terms,

ACCOUNTABILITY MODEL

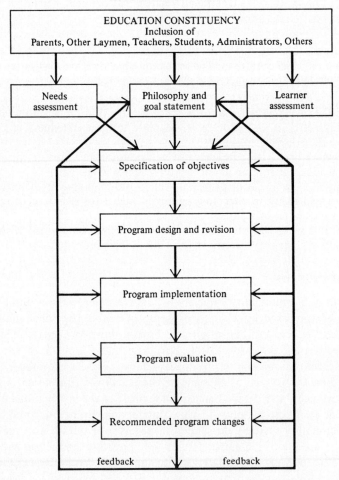

Chart 8-2 Accountability model

planning instruction, diagnosing needs of students, planning corrective instruction, and evaluating outcomes of instruction.

Major components in accountability systems are included in Chart 8-2. The educational constituency includes laymen and school personnel who are involved in stating the school district philosophy and major goals. The statement of specific objectives is related to philosophy and goals, needs assessment, and learner assessment. All the foregoing are related to program design and/or revision. Program implementation includes installation of new programs, in-service education, and ongoing supervision. Program evaluation includes appraisal of the performance of students, teachers and administrators. Feedback from evaluation is used to guide and improve the operation of various components of the system.

The model of accountability proposed by Educational Testing Service for New York City includes these steps (ETS, 1973):

Measure student performance and identify discrepancies in performance.

Diagnose causes of achievement and nonachievement of goals and identify information on causes of discrepancies in performance.

Plan and implement corrective action.

Evaluate corrective action.

Two analyses are made of student achievement: (1) the extent to which minimum standards are achieved in relation to defined objectives and (2) an index of student development that shows progress being made in each school.

PPBS (Planning-Programming-Budgeting System) is used in some school systems in a way that combines or merges instructional accounting and financial or budgetary accounting. The major component processes of PPBS are planning, programming to carry out plans, budgeting to support programs, evaluation of the effectiveness of programs, and decision making related to alternatives and other elements. PPBS may be merged with continuous progress education or other organizational patterns. One system in which PPBS has been merged with continuous progress includes these components: goals; objectives on three levels—general program, program, subprogram; skills; instructional objectives; learning activities; diagnostic tests; performance criteria; learning packages; criterion-referenced tests; and program budget. Cost-effectiveness analysis and decision making related to alternatives and allocation of resources are part of the complete program (Worner, 1973).

Working within state regulations, most school systems work out ways of handling accountability that are acceptable to the board of education, school personnel, and laymen. Some school systems have used plans that shift accountability responsibilities to others. For example, the voucher plan enables parents to make a choice in terms of their goals and preferences by depositing a voucher at the school they select for their children. Performance contracting has been used by a few school systems. Under one plan of performance contracting an external contractor takes charge of instruction and assumes responsibility for meeting goals of education and objectives approved by the board of education.

Under another form of performance contracting, teachers assume the role of instructional managers and are held responsible for the attainment of goals and objectives; additional salary may be made contingent upon the extent to which objectives are achieved.

Detrimental Aspects of Accountability and Their Avoidance

As with any technological innovation in general and systems approach in particular, there are possible detrimental outcomes that are inconsistent with truly humane approaches to teaching and learning. For example, a misapplication of the concept of accountability may lead to loss of professional integrity on the part of the school staff. Such a loss in integrity may be evident in the writing of objectives that are easily attained, preparing items on lower levels of the cognitive domain, and the like. A loss in integrity also may be reflected in a narrow emphasis on measurable aspects of reading and arithmetic, lack of planning for a balanced curriculum, neglect of affective objectives, insidious comparisons of achievement between classes and between schools, scapegoating of teachers, and bending to the demands of pressure groups.

Such detrimental and negative aspects of accountability may be avoided in part by adhering to the following guidelines (Ornstine and Talmage, 1973):

Clarify roles, relationships, and responsibilities of laymen, the board of education, and school personnel. Provide effective channels of communication at all levels.

Check accountability plans and procedures against the school district's philosophy of educaton, changing any features that are inconsistent with it.

Maximize teacher self-evaluation and student self-evaluation, prevent intimidation by pressure groups, and avoid the pitting of teacher against teacher and teacher against students.

Include goals and objectives that go beyond narrowly defined fact and skill objectives; provide adequate time between pre- and post-testing; provide for pilot tryout in selected schools and classrooms before large-scale implementation of accountability; compare a school's performance with data from similar schools if such comparisons serve a useful function and are required; and give consideration to the many different variables involved in learning, ranging from home background and prior educational experiences to learning potential and personal-social characteristics.

Obtain the support of state agency personnel and other available experts in working with laymen, helping the school staff, clarifying measurement problems, minimizing errors of measurement, and other aspects of the system.

Provide appropriate and effective grievance or review procedures for both teachers and administrators so that fairness and justice will prevail and professional integrity will be maintained.

Possible Benefits

There are several benefits that may be obtained if accountability systems are handled in a professional manner. Goals and objectives may be clarified and a better understanding of the basic functions of education may be developed on the part of both laymen and school personnel. A well-balanced statement of goals may be used as a basis for proposing and maintaining a well-planned curriculum and getting adequate support for it. The sharing of good ideas among teachers and other school personnel is possible if effective channels of communication are set up. Strengths and weaknesses in programs of instruction in different areas of the curriculum may be identified and continuing improvement of instruction may be made. An emphasis on self-evaluation and self-improvement may contribute to continuing improvement of instruction. Interaction among and between principals, teachers, and other school personnel can be brought to a high level of effectiveness if a spirit of teamwork and fairplay is emphasized. Children's learning can be facilitated if throughout the entire process their needs, concerns, and well-rounded development are kept in sharp focus.

EVALUATION OF AREAS OF THE CURRICULUM

The last component of our model of the curriculum includes criteria in question form that can be used to evaluate any area of the curriculum. The questions are designed to guide study in depth as well as to appraise different aspects of the curriculum. The outline of questions has been designed to bring together the various components discussed in preceding chapters. Its use may be supplemented by more detailed guides to the evaluation of the curriculum that are presented in the end-of-chapter references.

Foundations

In what ways can the program be improved on:
Historical foundations _____
Philosophical foundations _____
Social foundations _____
Psychological foundations _____
Disciplinary foundations _____

Contributions to Goals of Education

How can contributions to basic goals of education be improved?
Thinking ability _____
Self-realization _____
Human relationships _____
Economic competence _____
Civic responsibility _____
Learning how to learn _____

Objectives of the Area of the Curriculum

How can objectives be made more explicit and useful?
Conceptual objectives _____
Process objectives _____
Skill objectives _____
Affective objectives _____

Organization of the Curriculum

How can the structure of the program be improved in terms of the following?
Scope of breadth _____
Sequence _____
Cumulative learning _____
Integration of learning _____
What improvements are needed in units of instruction?
Unit organization_____
Unit planning _____
What improvements are needed in the following?
Curriculum planning procedures _____
Organizational patterns _____
Clarification of roles _____
Curriculum guides_____

Organization and Extension of the Learning Environment

How can school organization be improved?
Vertical organization _____
Horizontal organization_____
How can the classroom environment be improved?
Individualized and personalized instruction _____
Grouping for instruction _____
Organizing group work _____
Sequencing group work _____
Interaction analysis_____
How can the environment be extended?
Open education_____
Time extension _____
Spatial extension_____
Other ways _____
How can the environment be enriched by means of instructional media?
General guidelines _____
Selection criteria _____
Printed materials _____
Audio-visual resources_____
Community resources _____
Other media and resources _____

How can instructional support services be improved?
Library _____
Media center _____
Supervision _____
Evaluation _____
Other_____

Teaching Strategies

How can the variety and use of teaching strategies be improved?
Discovery, inductive and deductive _____
Teacher directed, inductive and deductive_____
Other _____
Model for the generalizing mode _____
Model for the integrative mode _____
Model for the decision-making mode _____
Strategies for techniques of inquiry _____
Strategies for processes of inquiry _____
Strategies for basic skills _____
Strategies for motor skills _____
Strategies for valuing _____

Evaluation and Accountability

How can the following be improved?
Evaluation of outcomes of instruction _____
The accountability system _____
Evaluation of areas of the curriculum _____

FOLLOW-UP ACTIVITIES AND PROJECTS

1 Investigate the program of evaluation in your locality. How is evaluation conducted in the local school system in terms of:
a Testing program at various grade levels
b Suggested guidelines for use by teachers and others
c Other school systemwide provisions
d Relationships to statewide assessment

2 Examine two or three criterion-referenced or objective-referenced tests that are available in the local school system or nearby college or university library. What level of performance is set in terms of the criterion? Use the example as a model for constructing an eight-to-ten-item test in an area of your choice, using a reference such as those at the end of this chapter as a guide to item writing.

3 Prepare a short table of specifications for use in making plans for evaluating a unit of instruction in an area of your choice. Use the reference by Bloom, Hastings, and Madaus as a guide.

4 Prepare a sample question and a sample item related to each level of the cognitive domain and the first three levels of the affective domain. Use the examples presented in this chapter as guides.

5 Investigate the accountability system in the local system. How is it like and how is it different from the characteristics and models presented in this chapter?

6 Compare the summary outline of questions and topics included in the outline for evaluation of areas of the curriculum with those included in any one of the references cited at the end of this chapter. Indicate any changes you think should be made in our outline.

BIBLIOGRAPHY

Anderson, Scarvia, Samuel Ball, Richard T. Murphy, and Associates. *Encyclopedia of Educational Evaluation*. San Francisco: Jossey-Bass, Inc., 1974. Articles on all phases of evaluation.

Bloom, Benjamin S., J. Thomas Hastings, and George F. Madaus. *Handbook of Formative and Summative Evaluation of Student Learning.* New York: McGraw-Hill, 1971. Principles and detailed suggestions for evaluating learning in various areas of the curriculum.

Bloom, Benjamin S. (Ed.) *Taxonomy of Educational Objectives: Cognitive Domain.* New York: McKay, 1956. Objectives and test items arranged in terms of level of complexity.

Buros, Oscar K. *The Seventh Mental Measurements Yearbook.* Highland Park, N.J.: Gryphon, 1972. Information on tests in this and preceding yearbooks.

Buros, Oscar K. *Tests in Print.* Highland Park, N.J.: Gryphon, 1973. Listing of tests still in print.

Combs, Arthur W. *Educational Accountability: Beyond Behavioral Objectives.* Washington, D.C.: Association for Supervision and Curriculum Development, 1972. Arguments for humanizing accountability and extending it to humanistic goals.

Curtis, William H. *Educational Resources Management System.* Chicago, Ill.: Association of School Business Officials, 1971. An integrated system for planning, programming, budgeting, and evaluating.

Ebel, Robert L. *Essentials of Educational Measurement.* Englewood Cliffs, N.J.: Prentice-Hall, 1972. Suggestions for preparing tests.

ETS Developments. Princeton, N.J.: Educational Testing Service, Summer, 1973. Outline of a model of accountability.

Educational Testing Service. *State Educational Assessment Programs.* Princeton, N.J.: Educational Testing Service, 1973. Descriptions of goals, data collection, and related aspects of assessment programs.

Educational Testing Service. *State Testing Programs.* Princeton, N.J.: Educational Testing Service, 1973. Description of purposes, uses, tests, grades of testing, and related aspects of testing.

Hess, Robert D., and Doreen J. Croft. *Teachers of Young Children.* Boston: Houghton Mifflin, 1972. Chapter on evaluation.

Krathwohl, David R., Benjamin S. Bloom, and Bert Masia. *Taxonomy of Educational Objectives: Affective Domain.* New York: McKay, 1964. Objectives and items arranged in terms of degree of internalization.

Mehrens, William A., and Irvin J. Lehmann. *Measurement and Evaluation in Education and Psychology.* New York: Holt, 1973. Detailed suggestions for preparing test items.

National Assessment of Educational Progress, *NAEP Newsletter.* Denver, Colo.: 700 Lincoln Tower, 1860 Lincoln, 80203. Newsletter available on request.

Ornstein, Allan C. and Harriet Talmage. "The Rhetoric and the Realities of Accountability," *Today's Education,* 62, 70–80, September-October, 1973. Review of issues, models, and guidelines.

Payne, David A. (Ed.) *Curriculum Evaluation.* Boston: Heath, 1974. Readings on curriculum development and project evaluation.

Popham, W. J., et al. *Criterion-Referenced Measurement.* Englewood Cliffs, N.J.: Educational Technology Publications, 1971. Introduction to principles and procedures.

Ragan, William B., and Gene D. Shepherd. *Modern Elementary Curriculum.* (4th ed.) New York: Holt, 1971. Chapter on evaluation and checklist for evaluating the curriculum in Appendix A.

Rippey, Robert M. (Ed.) *Studies in Transactional Evaluation.* Berkeley, Calif.: McCutchan Publishing Corporation, 1973. Observational and other techniques of evaluating programs and practices.

Saylor, J. Galen, and William M. Alexander. *Planning Curriculum for Schools.* New York: Holt, Inc., 1974. Chapter on evaluation of curriculum plans.

TenBrink, Terry D. *Evaluation: A Practical Guide for Teachers.* New York: McGraw-Hill, 1974, Treatment of checklists, rating scales, and other informal devices.

Walberg, Herbert J. (Ed.) *Evaluating Educational Performance.* Berkeley, Calif.: McCutchan Publishing Corporation, 1974. Articles on teacher effectiveness, needs assessment, classroom climates, materials, and other aspects of performance.

Worner, Roger B. *Designing Curriculum for Educational Accountability.* New York: Random House, 1973. Suggestions for merging continuous progress and accountability by means of PPBS.

Worthen, Blaine R., and James R. Sanders. *Educational Evaluation: Theory and Practice.* Worthington, Ohio: Charles A. Jones Publishing Co., 1973. Models, principles, and procedures for conducting evaluation studies.

Part Two

Areas of the Curriculum

Chapter 9

Language Arts

Language is defined as a structured system of arbitrary vocal sounds and symbols used as communication. The language arts are the four modes of communication through human speech: speaking, listening, reading, and writing. These four modes are interrelated in developmental sequence, reciprocity of communication, and relationship to mental processes and behavior.

In developmental sequence, infants first acquire language understanding through listening, and next begin to speak. Later the children recognize and utilize the written representation of oral language, as they learn to read and, soon after, to write. The primacy of use and comprehension of language in its spoken form continues throughout their successive language-learning experiences. They learn to speak by listening and imitating. The extent of their grasp of spoken language affects their ability to acquire skill in recognition, interpretation, and use of language in its graphic form. Throughout life, they are likely to deal with spoken language to a far greater extent than written language. This implies a need for considerable attention to the development and application of listening and speaking skills at every grade level.

Listening and speaking have a reciprocal relationship. In language communication speakers address listeners, and listeners become listeners when they are attentive to speakers. This reciprocal relationship implies the desirability of providing instruction and practice in both skills simultaneously. Reading and writing are reciprocal, although not always simultaneous. One reads what one is writing or what someone else has written.

The language arts are also interrelated in accordance with the children's behavioral and mental processes. Listening and reading are *receptive* forms of communication. Through these means they gain information. Similar comprehension skills are required of them both as a listener and as a reader. These two receptive language arts differ in pace, as the children may set their own pace for reading, but they must listen at the pace set by the speaker. Speaking and writing are the *expressive* modes of language. Both require skill in organizing a meaningful sequence of words and ideas. Speech is the more fluid form of expression, with less structure of formal patterns than written expression, which is more permanent. Instruction in the common elements of the expressive or the receptive form will benefit both language arts in that form.

A child's progress in any language art depends upon his or her growth in the others, because of the many foundational elements, skills, and purposes common to all, and because of the interrelationships outlined above and in the diagram below. Instruction that facilitates development in one language art is likely to benefit the other three and enhance the child's understanding of all aspects of language. Because extensive attention is needed, the language arts are treated in two chapters: this deals with speech, listening skills, written expression, and learning of more than one language; the next with reading and literature.

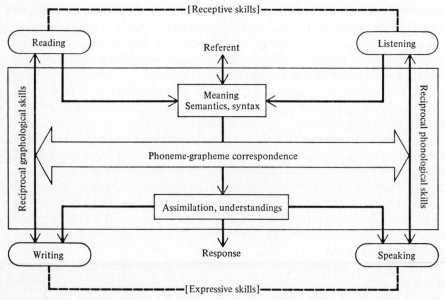

Chart 9-1 A structure of the language arts

As shown in Chart 9-1, receptive language skills and referent objects or ideas provide information and meaning. Assimilation of ideas and understandings leads to response in thought and in expressive language skills. Processes within the rectangle refer to the individual's mental processes in language activity.

CONTRIBUTIONS TO MAJOR GOALS

The language arts make pervasive contributions to the basic educational goals. *Thinking ability* is developed through language, the medium of thought. Vocabulary acquisition is largely a matter of applying labels to concepts or categories. Language enables children to learn about their world. As they develop communication skills, and learn language syntax, they utilize the structure of language to understand and express ideas and to formulate hypotheses, propositions, and so on. *Self-realization* is developed as receptive language skills provide children with information and as they develop expressive use of language that extends beyond social or utilitarian exchanges to various modes of creative expression. *Human relationships* are enhanced as knowledge of one's own culture is acquired in large measure through language. Respect for other cultures is developed through study and use of other languages or differing dialects. Cross-cultural interaction in American society proceeds through acquisition and use of standard English as a means of communication. Standard English is also basic to development of *economic competency,* in addition to later acquisition of technical vocabulary related to different tasks or industries. *Civic responsibility* requires skill in language as one listens to campaign speeches, reads about government, and learns to analyze the connotations of words and writing styles and the language techniques of propaganda. Language learning also involves acquiring ways of clarifying communication between differing individuals or groups. *Learning how to learn* permeates the language arts program as innumerable lifelong learning skills are carried out through use of all the language skills referred to in detail later in this and the following chapter.

OBJECTIVES OF LANGUAGE ARTS PROGRAMS

Language arts programs in elementary and intermediate schools may include learning of reading, writing, listening, and speaking in English and in both English and another language in a bilingual-bicultural program, and may also include learning of English as a second language for non-English speakers, and learning of another language for English-speaking children. The following objectives are applicable to all these types of programs.

Conceptual Objectives

To develop understanding of vocabulary, language concepts, and the structure of language so that children are able to do the following:

State their interpretations of communications in verbal and written form

Express ideas clearly in oral and written form

Interpret and analyze information acquired through mass media

Explain the role of language as a tool of communication and conveyor of culture in his own and other cultures

Use different forms of language structure, different dialects, or different languages in appropriate situations

Inquiry Objectives

To develop skill in using processes of inquiry so that children are able to perform the following:

Distinguish between expressions of fact and of opinion

Express hypotheses, inferences, and generalizations in proper form

Develop criteria statements for evaluation or judgment purposes that are objective and free of ambiguity or subjective connotations

Skills Objectives

To develop skills needed to enable children to do the following:

Locate sources of information

Outline, summarize, take notes, write reports in various formats

Listen with understanding

Speak clearly, pronounce correctly, and use appropriate volume, phrasing, and pitch of voice

Write legibly and correctly

Utilize discussion and debate skills effectively

Write and speak creatively in a variety of forms

Affective Objectives

To demonstrate the values and attitudes of individuals who are able to do the following:

Use language as a creative form of expression in oral or written compositions initiated by the individual

Describe responses to creative use of language in drama, poetry, and literature encountered in the classroom or selected by the individual

Describe and express acceptance of the differences in dialects of English used in their own community and in different regions of the United States

ORGANIZATION OF THE CURRICULUM

The language arts programs of elementary and intermediate schools include enabling the child to understand and communicate in standard English and sometimes in another language as well. The skills involved in this language learning are usually organized for instructional purposes into the categories of oral language (speaking and listening), vocabulary development, grammar and language usage, written expression, handwriting, spelling, and study skills. In addition, attention is being given in more and more new programs to development of skills in visual literacy, which is the recognition and interpretation of visual symbols and objects that convey messages, interpretation and use of nonverbal communication, including body language, and critical analysis of mass media and advertising.

Bilingual-bicultural education is a total program encompassing all areas of the curriculum, but language development is its central component, so this type of program will be given attention in this chapter. As an instructional alternative for children whose first language is not English, some schools teach English as a second language, usually during specific time periods rather than throughout the day. The acronym TESL applies to this approach. In the late 1950s and early 1960s many suggestions were made about the value of foreign-language instruction in elementary schools. Some school systems offer instruction in French, Spanish, German, Italian, or languages of the national backgrounds of community members, but foreign-language instruction has not attained high priority in the crowded schedule of most elementary and intermediate school programs today. A description of foreign language programs and instructional strategies is provided in Chapter 5 of the first edition of this volume (Michaelis et al., 1967).

An examination of current language arts programs indicates that they are characterized by such trends as the following:

Recognition of the interrelationships of the language arts including reading and literature
Greater emphasis on oral language and simultaneous instruction in listening and speaking
Development of skills in thinking, independent learning, and self-evaluation in the context of language-learning experiences
Emphasis on varieties of creative expression for all children
Acceptance of different forms of language usage in different situations

The skills form of organization of language arts programs will be described below, followed by a brief description of bilingual-bicultural programs. But a few words are in order about the "hidden" curriculum in language arts. Because language, verbal and nonverbal, is the medium of interaction between teacher and pupils, and between children, throughout the day, much is learned from the way in which these forms of communication are used. Some examples of this "hidden" curriculum include the following:

The teacher serves as a constant language model for pupils. The teacher's choice of words, use or avoidance of sarcasm, curtness or care in manner of speech, all have an impact on children's feelings, as well as providing examples they imitate in peer communication.

The teacher who corrects the spelling in a child's poem or the grammar of a creative narrative before appreciating the originality of its content is telling the child that correct form is more highly valued than creativity or individuality of expression.

The teacher who deprecates use of nonstandard English or use of the home language in informal or out-of-school situations suggests to children that their adherence to the home culture is "un-American" or that the home culture is "inferior" to some standard "American" form.

Some words have special meanings for children in different age groups or in different cultural groups, and their use by children needs to be understood by teachers whose own cultural background may cause negative reactions to such words and thus barriers between children and teacher.

Teachers need to be aware of the messages they may be conveying inadvertently through facial expression, gestures, and body language that may contradict what they intend to express verbally.

The teacher who remains at the front of the room to instruct is conveying something about the relationship of instructor and learner that differs from the impression conveyed to children by the teacher who moves around the room during instruction and is in proximity to each child at some time.

Skills Organization of the Language Arts Program

Instruction in all the skills areas of the language arts begins in kindergarten and is developed continuously throughout the child's school experience. Although initial instruction in a particular language skill is usually done in an isolated manner to focus attention on the process, the skill becomes a learned behavior when it is applied as soon as possible in many language areas. For example, the learner practices tracing the letter A and sounding it, spending several minutes doing this. Later the child may print the letter in his or her name, label the drawing of an airplane, and recognize the letter in reading *The Cat in the Hat.* Although the various language skills are discussed separately below, the immediate integration of all skills in classroom and nonclassroom applications should be borne in mind.

Since the interrelationship of language and thought is a significant factor in determining the language arts curriculum, a survey of the child's intellectual development related to the language program precedes the following outlines of the scope and sequence of language arts curricula in elementary and intermediate schools.

Intellectual Growth and the Language Arts Program   Infants in the sensory-motor stage form nonverbal associations and concepts and learn language through listening. They begin to communicate through sounds, then through single words which convey more complex meaning ("dog" may mean "I want to pet the dog," or "There's a dog in our yard"), and then through building simple sentences in imitation of adult speech models.

From two to four or five, the crucial years for intellectual development, children become more independent in their exploration of their environment. They seek labels for what they find and answers to many "what" and "why" questions. During these years, in the stage of intellectual development described by Piaget as preoperational, children are learning by direct sensory perception and experience, imitation of others, and trial-and-error efforts. Through accommodation and assimilation, they are learning to use words as symbols to represent reality and experiences. Piaget's descriptions of this stage imply that extensive direct experience should be provided for children because it affords a basis for their individual constructions of mental images and concepts. He points out[1] ways in which infants and young children form mental images and concepts without using language, and emphasizes that thoughts must be constructed by the child for himself before verbal expression of that thought by others can have any meaning for him. The implications for parents and preschool program planners are provision of varied experiences, home and preschool environments with varieties of safe household and "homemade" objects to manipulate, and much discussion with children to enable them to express questions and to acquire and use new words and language patterns. The effect of their thousands of hours of television viewing as a source of impressions and language models needs to be evaluated.

Children entering kindergarten and first grade are generally in the later phase of the preoperational stage. Of course, it should be borne in mind that although chronological ages are used to designate stages of intellectual growth, these are merely approximations. Some children will enter or leave a stage at an earlier or later than "average" age. Any individual may differ in stage of development in different areas of thought (aesthetic, verbal, mathematical, and so forth) at a given age. Five- and six-year-olds are effective in their use of the language spoken at home. Concept development is advanced as children assimilate experiences. They are able to group objects by a single criterion at a time. Perceptually oriented, they describe things as they appear to them. Teachers can provide continuing direct experiences: a rich store of materials, varieties of exploratory and expressive classroom activities, and guided explorations of the expanded environment. There is little effect in formal language instruction at this stage except for brief sessions to develop skills that children can utilize immediately and continuously.

Children from seven to about eleven or twelve are in the stage of concrete operations. They have attained the operations of reversibility, additive composition, associability, and identity, which enable them to begin to use the same words in different ways, to form different types of sentences, to spell, and to compose original ideas in oral and written forms of expression, but all these examples and the many other language skills developed in the elementary school years must have concrete referents for each child. Children in this stage cannot deal with words as complete abstractions. Language relates to reality, to their

---

[1] Eleanor Duckworth, "The Language and Thought of Piaget," in Martha L. King et al. (Eds.), *A Forum for Focus*, NCTE, Urbana, Ill., 1973, pp. 15–31.

continuing discovery through direct experience. Abstractions may be "taught" and the child may repeat them verbally, but attempts at application to a new situation usually fail because no understanding was acquired; the child was not able to perform the necessary intellectual operations without reference to real, or concrete, examples or experiences. Adult language used to introduce concepts not yet constructed in the child's mind has no effect in building concepts. This implies the need for an instructional setting in which language skills are learned in real and purposeful situations. Individual needs for language skills will be perceived by teachers who observe and patiently and attentively listen to children in one-to-one conversations and as they participate in activities that stimulate expression or arouse curiosity and questions. Skills learned should then be applied in daily or frequent use. Continuing direct experience and increasing familiarity with an expanding physical and social environment is needed throughout the elementary school years to form a basis for concepts and language and to serve as referents for understanding of people, places, events, and ideas removed from their direct experience in place and time. Language skills continue to be developed informally and continuously through all school experiences, but more formal or structured learning experiences are added as needed skills become more complex. In early grades children may still need to focus on one criterion for classification or one aspect of a skill at a time. They increase to more elements (cursive writing replaces manuscript print, oral and written sentences become more complex) as children move to later phases of this stage.

The stage of logical thought or formal operations is generally entered in the middle school years. As children develop abstract thinking skills, language becomes a more important vehicle for their learning, for formulation of thought, and for expression. Teachers need to extend vocabulary and knowledge about language structure to provide children with tools for formulating and expressing abstractions and for interpreting at more and more complex levels the communications they receive from all media and personal sources. Although there is comparatively less reliance on direct experience, concrete referents are still needed in some new situations; this continues throughout adult life.

Oral Language Speaking and listening are, of course, the child's first use of language. These skills are utilized throughout the schoolday as a major medium of learning input and expressive output, in formal learning and informal interaction. Oral language practice should be as spontaneous as possible. Language skills are enhanced when children have much opportunity to interact verbally with each other during the day. Expression limited to responses to teacher questions does little for the child's language development. Children need to acquire skills in using oral language in informal conversation, questioning and information seeking, polling and interviewing, discussion, debate, reporting or announcing, giving or receiving directions, giving or listening to formal addresses or lectures, storytelling, poetry recitation, choral speaking, and dramatization from creative dramatics to formal play production. Each type has its own forms of sentence structure, sequencing of expression, syntactic principles, use of voice, and form of listening. Listening skills begin with auditory discrimination of the discrete sounds of the language, then comprehension of the meaning of sounds blended into words in meaningful sequence. Informal listening may involve a lower level of attention to all that is expressed, whereas informational listening involves close attention to all sounds to receive all details. Critical listening involves analysis of what is carefully heard, with response in the form of evaluation or judgment about what is heard. *Auding* is the term usually applied to listening that involves close attention and continuous mental response to what is being heard. At this level, it is an interactive, not a passive or merely receptive, process.

The sequence of skill development in oral language is based on the child's physical and intellectual development and on developing personal and social needs. Of course, individuals will progress through this sequence at different rates.

At the end of grade 2, according to expected levels of language development, the child:

Understands and uses common words
Acquires and uses new action, descriptive, picture, and sensory words
Recognizes rhyming words
Speaks spontaneously, freely, naturally
Has facility in using American intonation
Uses the telephone competently
Begins to pronounce accurately and speak audibly
Begins to contribute to group conversation, discussion
Organizes ideas in sequence to develop a topic or story
Keeps to the subject in speaking and responding
Gives sustained attention for longer periods
Listens to others courteously, attentively, and purposefully
Follows verbal directions
Listens to gain information and form judgments
Begins to distinguish between fact and fantasy

Expected language development at the end of grade 4 includes extension of earlier levels and such additional outcomes as the following. At this time, the child:

Uses qualifying words, similes, metaphors for clarification
Eliminates unnecessary use of "and," "so," "then," or "well" to connect sentences
Develops poise and confidence in speaking
Develops simple standards for use of voice, intonation, and tempo in differing situations
Observe social amenities
Shows increased ability to plan and carry out dramatizations
Uses opening and closing sentences in well-planned reports

Relates what he or she says to contributions of others

Increases the span of attention and speed of perception of ideas when listening

Gains sensitivity to correct and pleasing qualities of speech

Notes how phrases, pauses, and transitional words punctuate speech and aid listening comprehension

Listens to recognize relevant and irrelevant details

Listens to make inferences and to raise questions

Outcomes representative of the level of language development at the end of grade 6 include refinement of all the abilities listed above as well as the following. At this stage, the child:

Is aware of the interest value of variety in vocabulary and uses more vivid words

Expresses thoughts clearly in more complex sentences

Maintains poise in speaking in a variety of situations

Takes an active part in group discussion

Summarizes during and after discussions

Uses transitional phrases

Engages in simple club procedures

Speaks from notes or outlines

Increases span of attention and concentration on content

Uses contextual clues effectively in listening

Compares several broadcasts of news stories

Recognizes some forms of propaganda, bias, and emotional appeal in listening to speakers, radio, television, films

Exercises critical judgment

For a variety of reasons, young children in any socioeconomic or ethnic group may have limited experience in use of language when they are five or six years old. Concern about language deficiency has been a major impetus for preschool programs and compensatory early childhood education and for the Headstart movement. Much attention is given in these programs to development of oral language skills and vocabulary by providing experiences for three-, four-, and five-year-old children that give them impressions and ideas to express verbally and by giving direct instruction in vocabulary and use of language. Sometimes this is done in a formal manner, with all the children in a group repeating the same specific sentence patterns modeled by the teacher or responding in specified ways to particular directions. In other programs, the procedure involves encouragement of individual verbal expression by each child based on his own experiences, observations, or concurrent activities. This language experience, whether formal or informal, is often developed in the context of a reading readiness program, which includes such activities as storytelling, putting pictures into sequence to retell a story, acting out a story or puppet play, and extending children's comprehended and expressive vocabulary through trips, classroom activities with varied games and materials, handling of pets, and viewing of films. Kindergarten and first-grade teachers need to build on children's preschool experiences in order to continue the sequential development of language skills. Children's language growth is limited, and they become bored with school experiences, when they move from preschool programs into kindergarten or first-grade programs that repeat their preschool learnings.

Related Questions and Activities In developing oral language skills, inquiry and thinking skills should be utilized by children, as teachers employ questions at different cognitive levels. In the following examples, the inquiry or cognitive process is indicated in parentheses.

Which of these sounds is different: a, a, i, a (observing, classifying)?
What did Judy mean when she used the word "fantastic" (defining)?
Let's recite one of the poems we enjoyed last week (recalling).
What words did the poet use to express sounds in the woods (analyzing, interpreting)? How are these words or sounds different from city street sounds (comparing, classifying)?
How do we use pauses in our speaking to give meaning to what we say (generalizing)?
What opinions about cleaning up our streets do you think our neighbors will express when we poll them (hypothesizing)?
What are some rules or procedures that will help us to have good discussions (evaluating)?
Tell us your story about a trip to the moon (synthesizing).

Vocabulary Development Although some mental images and processes are nonverbal, most higher level thought proceeds through the medium of language, which provides labels for concepts, words to express relationships of concepts, and a syntax for framing questions and other sentence forms such as statements, hypotheses, and propositions. Therefore, extension of children's vocabulary gives them the content and tools for thought and learning. Language enables them to deal mentally with objects, people, and actions when removed from direct observation of these phenomena in time and place, provides them with a means of communicating their thoughts to others, and enables them to apprehend and assimilate the ideas of others. (Other chapters on mathematics, physical education, and aesthetic education in this book make reference to quantitative, kinesthetic, spatial, visual, and other nonverbal aspects of mental processes.)

Vocabulary development begins with experience. Growing infants begin to perceive objects and people in the context of their total sensations and experiences, begin to make associations, and form categories or concepts, even though they lack any verbal labels for these associations and concepts. As they hear the speech of others and begin to express their own sounds, they find they can use certain sounds to evoke responses from others. As they mature and move around their expanding environment, perceiving more and more, they acquire verbal labels and extend their verbal interaction with others. By the time they are five years old, they have a comprehending vocabulary that may include as many as twenty thousand words. No matter what their cultural or socioeconomic milieu, they are able at that age to comprehend most of the vocabulary needed in their environment and are able to communicate effectively at their level of intellectual and physiological development. Their oral vocabulary, of course, is far less extensive than their comprehending or listening vocabulary; it is limited to the words they need and utilize in their daily experiences within their environment. When they encounter formal schooling, they begin to develop a reading and writing vocabulary which eventually (at about a sixth grade level of reading) will also surpass their oral vocabulary.

Children come to school with an ability to understand and utilize the vocabulary and syntax of the language or dialect spoken in their homes. The teacher's task is to extend their vocabulary in "standard" English to put them in touch with an expanded environment. Through the lingua franca of "standard" English, they communicate with all speakers of English wherever it is spoken, written, or communicated through drama or mass media.

Language is a set of oral and visual symbols used to describe reality and experience. Therefore, experience precedes verbalization as the learning process in vocabulary development. Children need to be provided with direct experiences and encounters with people, objects, situations, and systems in order to expand their knowledge and provide a basis of meaning for words. This involves trips outside the school, explorations within the school, and maximum use of activities, interactions, and materials within the classroom. Vocabulary development based on experience is not a subject taught at a specific time; it is the continuing process of classroom experience throughout each day, and builds on the continuing out-of-school experiences of each individual. This means the teacher must be familiar with the children's environment and exploit it for experience and language development. Their encounters with television and other media should be considered as part of their environment. Teachers also need to be sensitive to the personal responses of children to special words. Listening to their informal classroom speech and peer-group interactions within and outside the classroom, the teacher can discern ways in which children use special words to shock, challenge, or establish themselves as members of a peer group. There may be clues here for starting word analysis but not necessarily for "correction." The teacher should not remove words from the child's arsenal but should focus on the child's acquisition of a fuller expressive vocabulary in the context of explorations of positive feelings, as in small group "magic circle" discussions, for example.

Because vocabulary development is an ongoing, permeating experience, rather than a separate subject, its sequential development must be described in general terms. In the earliest grades, the emphasis is on provision of experience and spontaneous use of language. Children need to be given every opportunity to speak with each other in learning and play activities, in unstructured dramatic play, and in simply planned role playing, puppet plays, or story retelling. The teacher can intervene to provide labels in context. For example, as children construct a fire engine of boxes or blocks, parts of the engine can be labeled, and roles of the participants designated. Then the words can be used in carrying out immediate play activities. Of course, the words would have originally been encountered during a visit to the local fire station. Additional sources of vocabulary are the vast array of stories that can be told or read to children and the wealth of resources provided by learning experiences in mathematics, social studies, science, visual arts, music, and movement education.

In grades 2 and 3, children continue to acquire more specialized vocabulary in each subject area. Dramatics becomes more formal, as do role playing and simulations, requiring more extensive expression, lengthier sentence structure, more sustained ideas. Vicarious experiences can now have meaning, if direct experiences employed in earlier grades are continued and built upon. Books, films, filmstrips, videotapes, and selected after-school television programs can provide sources for vocabulary enrichment. Use of varieties of descriptive words can be developed as children are guided to observe closely, describe, and compare. Use of words extends from oral expression, the major use of language in earlier grades, to reinforcement and application in reading and written expression.

From grades 4 through 8, children can begin to study the structure of words, their origins, changes in meaning over periods of time, and generation of new words, an almost daily occurrence. Creative expression is extended as children gain experience and language power, and words can be analyzed and utilized for connotations and levels of meaning beyond the literal.

Related Questions and Activities   Thinking skills at various levels are involved in developing vocabulary. Following are some examples.

What does "odd" mean? Are there other ways of saying that same idea (defining)? How is each of these similar words a little different in its meaning (interpreting)?

How many words can you think of for food that begin with L (recalling)?

Let's put words in pairs. Think of a word, and ask someone to give a word that has the opposite meaning (comparing, contrasting).

What are some words that are happy words? Scary words? Heavy words (classifying)?

If we know the meaning of "fallacy," what might "infallible" mean (inferring)?

What meaning does "ness" give to words (generalizing)?

What are the parts of this word? What meanings do the prefix, root, and suffix contribute to the total meaning (analyzing)?

What words can you make from the root "term" (synthesizing)?

How do these words for textures help us to see the differences in the animals in this story (evaluating)?

Grammar and Usage   Instruction in grammar in elementary and intermediate grades involves learning the structure and operations of language, classes and functions of words, structure of sentences, and relationships of language units.

"Standard" English, as used in this chapter, does not describe a single, absolutely identified language structure. What is meant by the term are those oral and written structures of English that are used in national mass media, in the literature of United States authors, in newspapers, in business communications, and in other language uses that extend across the nation and involve communication between people of different groups or in different locations. Although written forms of standard English are comparatively uniform nationally, oral forms vary regionally. However, such regional variations do not amount to the degree of difference that would constitute separate forms or dialects.

Instruction in English grammar traditionally used structural models based on Latin forms. Linguistic scholars have changed this approach by providing two grammars that are descriptive of English, as it is actually expressed, primarily according to oral forms, and not in comparison with Latin models. These are structural grammar and generative transformational grammar, presented in detail in references at the end of the chapter. Both grammars emphasize the primacy of the spoken form of English, and both identify model sentence forms which indicate word-order patterns that convey meaning in English.

Structural grammar classifies words into two broad categories: the four open classes—nouns, verbs, adjectives, adverbs—which contain most of the words of the language and several small, closed classes containing a limited number of words—articles, pronouns, connectors, determiners, and so on. Generative transformational grammar has a similar approach, but utilizes a larger number of classifications. Structural grammar describes six or seven basic sentence patterns which, with some modifications, constitute the patterns of meaningful word order for almost all possible sentences in English. A common pattern is that of noun/verb/noun, as in the sentence "The boy threw the ball." Generative transformational grammar identifies similar patterns as kernel sentences, which through specified transformational procedures can generate all other sentence forms. For example, "The boy threw the ball" can become "The ball was thrown by the boy" or "The boys threw the balls" or "Did the boy throw the ball?" or "The short, chubby boy quickly threw the red ball."

New curriculum proposals and materials focus on familiarizing the elementary pupil with kernel sentences which he is to use as models to help him to understand new sentences or utterances and to engage in effective oral and written expression. Children are encouraged to explore the generative possibilities of kernel sentences and to discover for themselves the patterns of word order that convey meaning in English. Emphasis is not on labeling and classifying, but rather on practice and use of correct patterns that will become habitual.

Instruction in usage involves learning the use of acceptable words, phrases, and sentences in given social contexts or situations. Accepted levels or patterns of usage vary from one region or locale to another. The elements and idioms in usage instruction therefore tend to vary from one school situation to another. Usage instruction does *not* involve correction, change, or replacement of any dialect or home language of the child. Rather, it is developed as an additional language that is used in school, in nationwide communication, and in books and media in and out of school.

It is important for the teacher to recognize that dialects are not inferior forms of standard English. Although dialects and the various forms of Black English (referred to in more detail in the next chapter) share much vocabulary with standard English, they are viewed by linguistic scholars as separate language structures with their own complete grammar and rules of usage. Children in communities or ethnic groups speaking dialects, Black English, or foreign languages come to school at the age of five or six with a sufficient knowledge of the grammar of the home or community language to communicate effectively in their environment. They are in no sense "nonverbal," but they may enter school without having had any prior opportunity or need to acquire or use standard English. Any classroom may contain children from several different language backgrounds: those who use a local dialect, those who have moved from other regions of the country, those who speak a form of Black English or a foreign language at home. In each case, the teacher needs to respect children's own language and make clear to them that "school" language is an additional language they will need in situations *other* than those for which their home language is appropriate. To teach standard English effectively, the teacher needs to understand the structure and pronunciations of the child's language and the special problems that may occur in learning a second language (standard English) because of the particular language patterns and pronunciation habits of the home language. The teacher also needs to be able to distinguish between problems related to prior language patterns and an immature level of mastery of standard forms. Although usage instruction involves the learning of specific models and patterns, it does not require complete standardization of expression. There must be room for individual differences in modes of expression in the context of the various social settings in which children use the languages and different forms of usage at their command because language expression is an integral component of personality, and language use is social behavior.

Since the language patterns of children vary more from school to school, or even among members in the same classroom, than the variance from first through sixth grade in a given school, it is virtually impossible to set up a standard sequence of instruction. Identification of language-skill needs and instructional plans must be made by each teacher according to the needs of the particular children in each class.

Children enter kindergarten or first grade with speech patterns that include every part of speech and almost every type of sentence. If their language patterns conform to standard English, they may require little direct instruction beyond that developed in connection with the experiential extension of vocabulary described above, and in the context of development of other language skills outlined below, as grammatical structure and language usage are most effectively learned in the context of oral and written expressive activities. Generally, the early childhood teacher provides experiences for oral expression and intervenes to model appropriate sentence structures. This can be done in informal activities and one-to-one conversations. If specific errors are noted, there can be forms of formal pattern-practice activities for a brief period in the schoolday. When standard English is an additional language form for the young child, more direct instruction by means of practice with sentence patterns would be needed. The teacher must determine the uses of language needed by pupils at particular times, provide brief sessions in which the teacher presents oral models and pupils practice the model, and generate variations of it. The chapter section on teaching strategies provides a model for this. Guidelines for sequence of language needs can be found in some of the current language arts textbooks and teacher's guides.

In grades 2 and 3, reading becomes more extensive and provides models for language structure. Written expression, functional and creative, involves more complex sentences. As needs arise, the teacher continues to develop models with children and gives them opportunities to use the forms in meaningful applications.

From grade 4 to grade 8, children can learn to analyze sentence forms, develop model and generative charts, and evaluate their own oral and written expression. The teacher continues to diagnose individual errors and provides direct instruction as needed. In general, the flow of oral expression should not be interrupted by too many corrections. If children have been taught a correct pattern, then it should be reinforced, but when new errors are noted, they should be noted without interruption and handled through subsequent instruction. The same procedure applies to correction of functional writing. Creative expression is hindered if stress is placed on "errors." After the work has been shared, appreciated, or analyzed in terms of its literary or creative qualities, the teacher can point out any changes based on language structure or usage that would enhance communication of the work to others without reducing or altering its unique or literary characteristics.

Written Expression Written expression is usually divided for instructional purposes into areas of functional and creative writing. Examples of functional writing include notes, outlines, summaries, reports, letters, application forms, lists of directions, recipes, articles, and essays. Examples of creative writing include anecdotes, narratives, descriptions, stories, novels, poems, and plays. Functional writing is employed in expressive situations which are not unique for each writer. Most functional writing employs words at a literal level of meaning, whereas creative writing utilizes words at levels of more subjective connotations. There is, of course, an area between these extremes in which functional forms such as personal letters, articles, and essays involve subjective expression. Creative writing is expressed in literary forms; references to literature in the next chapter have relevance to learning activities in this area.

Functional writing provides children with needed tools of inquiry and communication. Creative writing experiences extend the personal development of each child. Functional forms of written expression should be introduced when needed in meaningful situations. Once mastered, skills are retained and extended if used in learning processes and real communication. Time spent on instruction in functional writing will, of course, depend on the age of children, their level of language mastery, and the form of writing. Creative expression does not spring from "practical" needs and therefore tends to be neglected when time is allotted to language activities. Every effort should be made to provide time for this because there is no way to develop one's creative written expression other than by writing. The teacher provides examples of various forms of creative expression and puts children in touch with stimuli for their expression. Happily, this is easily accomplished in the process of experiential vocabulary and concept development described above and in provision of enriching media and classroom experiences. Functional writing is intended to communicate objectively and should be in standard or technical forms of English. Creative writing should begin in the children's own language. The children themselves should decide when, and if, they want to use standard forms of literary English in their own creative expression. To do otherwise would be antithetical to creativity.

Creative expression is developed in many ways in the total language arts program, and many of these modes will lead into written expression. Creative dramatics can culminate in a written play. Vocabulary exploration can lead to spontaneous poems in various forms. Pictures taken of their environment may stimulate children to arrange them into a story or add to their visual responses with some written commentary. Children producing a film may add their own music and poetry to a sound track.

The sequence of instruction in written expression depends upon the child's level of mental maturity, language mastery, and fund of idea-producing experiences. Kindergarten or first grade children can dictate stories to the teacher or record them on tape. As mastery of reading, handwriting, and spelling increases, they can copy group-composed stories. They may begin to write out their own work in grades 2 and 3, and develop skill in using more complex forms of writing as they mature and progress through intermediate grades.

Expected developmental outcomes in written expression include the following. The child:

After grade 2
Understands such terms as "salutation," "closing," "margin," "indent"
Writes picture stories
Puts ideas into words
Begins to dictate and write ideas in sequence
Begins to be selective as to what is appropriate for inclusion in letters, stories
Understands the need for capitalization in proper names, days, months, holidays, titles, and first word of sentence
Understands the need for punctuation—periods, question marks, commas, apostrophes

Begins to write sentences, short paragraphs, and simple stories independently

After grade 4
Continues to improve previously developed skills
Uses synonyms, action, and descriptive words in place of overworked words
Uses more initiative in selecting a topic and begins to develop ideas around a plot or topic
Recognizes a sequence of action and rearranges ideas in order
States his or her own ideas, reactions, opinions
Writes paragraphs with suitable opening and closing sentences
Shows independence in creative writing

After grade 6
Begins to create mood and imagery through rich vocabulary and figurative language
Develops more complex plot and story design and writes longer compositions
Suits style of writing to interest and comprehension level of intended audience
Senses and creates rhythm in poetry
Increases ability to express ideas clearly, forcefully, concisely
Takes pertinent notes in classroom and individual study
Outlines and summarizes
Begins to use direct quotations
Begins to support factual statements by evidence
Recognizes the purposes of business and social letters and adapts style to these purposes
Uses varieties of increasingly complex sentences
Uses correct paragraphing in writing conversation

Although these descriptions of developmental levels of language ability are stated in terms of grade levels, they do not represent expectations for *all* children at those grade levels. Children enter school at different stages of language maturity and progress at different rates. Therefore, grade-level placement of instruction in written expression varies among school systems, schools, and classes within a school.

Spelling Ability to read and write is a prerequisite to learning to spell. Therefore, instruction in spelling is deferred until the middle or end of the first grade. The children are considered ready to begin spelling when they are able to listen attentively, have developed auditory and visual discrimination, speak clearly, have attained a broad vocabulary suitable to their language level, read a first reader fluently, form letters correctly, and are able to write words from memory.

Spelling instruction begins informally as children need to write particular words. Early experiences often include copying group stories and developing spelling skills as they check to see that they have written the words correctly. Words are suggested for particular grade levels on the basis of their level of complexity and frequency of use in children's expression.

In grades 1 and 2, children may be expected to copy words correctly, learn to use an alphabetical word list and picture dictionary, learn a word-study method, and write spelling words from memory.

In grades 3 and 4, children may be expected to develop a sense of responsibility to spell correctly whatever is written for others to read. They learn proofreading skills; they may keep an individual word list; and they increase their dictionary skills. They apply a word-study method to the learning of new words and are able to draw and apply generalizations as an aid in spelling.

In addition to expanding the skills learned at earlier levels, children in grades 5 and 6 may be expected to increase their power in word-analysis techniques, generalizations, mnemonic devices, and study methods as an aid in spelling words from a basic list and rarer words they may have occasion to use. They are able to proofread accurately, and use a dictionary to understand pronunciation aids, find synonyms, check syllabication, and check doubtful spellings.

Handwriting   Readiness for handwriting instruction depends upon the child's motor coordination, visual acuity, and reading ability. The child in grade 1 is unable to focus on very fine print. His smaller muscles are not well developed. Therefore, his writing experiences utilize manuscript printing, which involves short, simple, unconnected strokes. Early practice at the chalkboard enables the young child to work with easily formed large letter sizes. Later, he uses 1-inch ruled paper, making capital letters and numerals 2 inches high.

At about the time he is in grade 2, he is able to reduce capitals to 1 inch and lowercase letters to half an inch. As his motor coordination and visual acuity improve and his earlier tendency toward farsightedness disappears, he is able to reduce the size of his writing.

Most children are physiologically ready for cursive writing in grade 3. Those who have reading difficulties, however, may need to raise the level of their reading ability before they are ready to read cursive forms.

After the transition to cursive writing, children in grades 4, 5, and 6 may be expected to improve in style, fluency, and speed of writing and to maintain their skills in manuscript printing. As their competency increases, they may be able, in the upper grades, to explore varieties of letter forms for posters, charts, and special purposes.

Structure of Language   The aspects of the total, integrated language arts program described above all contribute to children's knowledge of the structure of the language they are learning. At this point an outline of language structure may be examined in its relationship to the instructional program.

Linguistic scholars outline the structure of language in terms of the basic sound elements, meaning or conceptual elements, and structural principles of the language. This structure is illustrated in Chart 9-2.

Sound elements are the basis of a language, the recognizable sounds that convey meaning when expressed in specific patterns or sequences. Linguists identify between forty-three and forty-six distinct sound elements, or phonemes, in

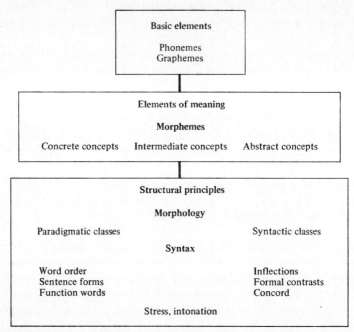

Chart 9-2   A structure of language

English. The twenty-six letters of the alphabet, certain letter combinations, and punctuation marks constitute the graphemes used to represent the phonemes of the English language.

Morphemes are basic elements of meaning in word structure. Roots, affixes, and inflectional changes are classes of morphemes. Morphemes may be described as expressing concepts on a continuum from concrete to abstract. Concrete concepts refer to objects, actions, and qualities and are often expressed by roots of words. More abstract relational concepts may be expressed by affixes, inflectional changes, word sequence, or separate words.

The structural principles of English are the essence of the language (Phenix, 1964, p. 66). These principles pertain to morphology, a classification of words according to their function and structural relationships, and syntax, conventional word patterns, and relationships.

Current morphological classifications are not based on lexigraphic meanings of words, but rather on the basis of their function. Sapir (1921) suggests the division of words into two major classes. The paradigmatic classes include words that change inflectionally or by means of affix alterations, such as nouns (singular or plural), forms of personal pronouns, verbs, and adjectives. Other parts of speech which are not subject to change in form, such as adverbs, prepositions, and conjunctions, fall into syntactic classes on the basis of their use in the organization of word sequence, phrases, and sentences.

Syntax is the structure of word relationships, sets of principles which indicate conventional relationships that convey meaning, in such categories as the following:

Word order: Meaningful sequences of words in phrases or clauses

Sentence patterns: Characteristic patterns of word sequence and varying levels of complexity of each pattern

Function words: Words such as articles and prepositions, having little lexical meaning, which in phrases and sentences serve to indicate relationships between other words

Inflections: Inflectional changes, such as those described in paradigmatic classes of words, which signal changes in word meaning, as in singular or plural nouns or cases of verbs

Formal contrasts: Inflectional or root-affix modifications which alter a root word into differing parts of speech, e.g., friend, friendly, friendless

Concord: Agreement between noun and adjective or subject and predicate

Stress and intonation: Sound patterns which signal meanings for groups of words, such as rising inflection at the end of a question or vocal emphasis on a particular word (e.g., "The *boy* is sick" or "The boy is *sick*")

Chart 9-3 below indicates the ways in which elements of language structure are learned through various aspects of the integrated language arts program. For example, graphemes, phonemes, and morphemes are learned through spelling activities; morphemes are also learned in vocabulary and concept development experiences.

Learning Skills   To meet the goal of learning how to learn, the language arts program develops children's skills in locating and utilizing a variety of sources of information and skills acquisition. These sources include school and public library resources, mass media, government agencies and publications, and the people, artifacts, aesthetic and literary products, institutions, man-made and natural environmental elements that constitute community or cultural resources. Mass media are discussed below. Community and cultural resources are discussed in more detail in Chapter 13.

When children enter kindergarten or first grade, their orientation to the school environment will include visits to the school library or media center, often

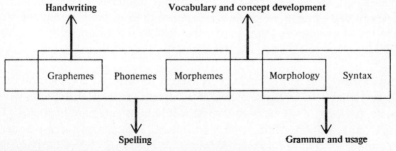

Chart 9-3   Relationships of language structure and instruction

in the context of their social studies program. Follow-up visits for storytelling by the librarian during the year and borrowing of books every month or two for the classroom library corner are fruitful experiences. Social studies programs of first through third grade often include study of the community, with a visit to the public library. Children in these grades can make attractive scrapbooks to bind collections of their creative writing and of their photographs, drawings, maps, and written records of trips, interviews, or other activities. Care in handling of books can be developed from bookmaking experiences. Children should obtain their own public library cards as soon as they are eligible, and they may be encouraged to share books through brief, informal statements about what they enjoyed. Reading instruction includes learning the parts of a book: title, author, illustrator, table of contents, page sequence, and so forth. In second and third grade children can begin to categorize different types of books. The teacher and school librarian can jointly plan and instruct children in locating the books, magazines, picture collections, and other materials available to them. Writing to authors (through their publishers' offices) enhances children's understanding that books are communications between people. Direct contact with people in the community as learning resources occurs as children visit the post office, pet store, nearby farm or factory. Some of these community sources also provide written or pictorial materials for classroom use; of course, the teacher must determine whether the materials are suitable, balanced in viewpoint, one-sided or biased. Use of picture dictionaries provides a beginning for use of reference materials.

Increasing independence in learning skills and more complex subject area needs from fourth through eighth grades provide motivational situations in which children can learn to use dictionaries, encyclopedias, atlases, tape recorders, slide projectors, and the locational tools of the Dewey Decimal System and card catalog. Children in these grades need to tap community, industrial, and government resources beyond their immediate environment. Language skills are applied as they write to paper companies for information on reforestation or to the Government Printing Office for materials on the metric system. They might plan interviews of local or state government personnel regarding transportation or housing plans. Experiences like these will lead back to use of related reference materials in libraries, media centers, museums, local historical societies, and other relevant, available resources. The key to effective development of learning skills at any level is, of course, that children are involved in meaningful investigations that necessitate use of a variety of informational resources. Interest in a worthwhile study and genuine use of newly acquired skills in carrying out the study provide the motivation and application that lead to acquisition of lifelong learning skills.

Mass Media The term "mass media" refers to forms of communication directed or available to an entire community, nation, or the world. Books would, of course, fall into this category, but these will be considered in Chapter 10. This section focuses on the media of television, radio, commercial films, magazines, newspapers, and posters, and their messages, which include both substantive matter (information, entertainment, and opinion) and advertising.

Children's immersion in a mass media and multimedia environment has been well documented (Brown et al., 1973; Grady and Baricevic, 1974; Shane et al., 1971). Children entering kindergarten or first grade may have viewed 4,000 to 6,000 hours of television; by the end of high school they may have viewed up to 20,000 hours, far more than the time spent in school. Of course, children have been observed attending to homework and television programs or transistor radios simultaneously. Films, tapes, and records add to the multimedia environment, in and out of school. Media are not new to schools; stereoptican viewers, lantern slides, radio, films, and educational television were introduced in turn; computers, talking typewriters, rear screen projectors, color organ translators, videotape equipment, and other devices are part of today's available educational technology. Curriculum development includes utilization of these media and equipment as learning materials and also involves helping children to utilize media for their own communication and aesthetic expression and to become intelligent consumers of the information and entertainment conveyed to them by mass media.

Television programs provide models for forms of standard oral English, but listening to models does not automatically change the viewer's speech patterns. Learning and change are the result of deliberate copying of a model through oral practice of pronunciation or language patterns. Programs are available that provide models for different regional patterns or those of ethnic or socioeconomic groups, and these can be analyzed by children in intermediate grades. Drama and films on television, some based on children's literature, augment the classroom study of literature at all grade levels. Use of a television program in school should not be limited to the content alone. Teachers can help children develop lifelong learning skills by having them analyze the ways they use a program and by guiding them to apply their observation skills and follow-up activities to the selection and use of varieties of programs as part of their independent, out-of-school learning.

Analysis of the content of dramatic or informational programs should be part of the language program. Criteria developed at various grade levels for analyzing plot, character, and meaning of stories in the context of the reading program should be applied to analysis of television programs popular with the children. Studies have shown that the favorite programs of elementary school children involve either violent action, comedy, or both (Shane et al., 1971). Teachers need to be familiar with the programs available to their pupils and to guide them in extending the range of programs that would be meaningful to them. Comparisons of news treatment on different channels can be made by intermediate pupils. The propaganda techniques of advertising should be analyzed by using television and radio commercials as well as printed advertisements in newspapers, magazines, and posters, and the overt or hidden advertising in educational materials or informational pamphlets produced by business and industry.

Videotape equipment in schools enables children to make audio-visual records of creative expression, classroom activities, interviews, documentaries about their environment, trips, and other experiences.

Radios can provide music programs on AM or FM stations to supplement the school's record collections and limited number of phonographs. News programs are available throughout the day. Weather conditions can be checked at specified intervals for the science program. Local issues may be discussed on local stations. Evening programs can be taped for classroom use. Children can make tape records of their oral, written, and musical compositions, classroom activities, interviews, sounds of their environment, and so forth.

Commercial films are a form of literature. As part of the language arts program, pupils might attend a suitable film at a movie theater. Classroom discussion should prepare them for the story or musical; follow-up activities such as dramatization, picture or puppet making, and discussion should be carried out to enhance critical enjoyment of the film's visual, musical, and dramatic aspects. Films made by children, while integrated in this program, will be discussed below in the section on visual literacy.

Children in early grades can be introduced to a variety of children's picture magazines. Magazines or newspapers produced for use in early elementary grades can be utilized in reading instruction. As children advance in reading level, critical analysis of newspapers and news magazines should be part of the reading-language arts program, and a variety of magazines should be part of the classroom library.

Posters are a more common means of mass media in China and some European countries than in the United States, but they do tend to be more widely used here in safety, health, or antipollution campaigns, and more extensively during political campaigns. These need to be analyzed for their content as communications. Pupils can utilize this medium for similar purposes at the school and local community level.

Computers are not mass media but constitute the hardware for learning resources used in a variety of school subjects. As their use increases and becomes more sophisticated, pupils in intermediate grades may be introduced to computer language codes. This can enhance their understanding of the nature of communication and the concept of structure in language.

In the incorporation of study and use of mass media in the language arts program, two overlapping basic principles should be observed. The first is that communication skills are a two-way process. Therefore, learning experiences must involve *producing* communication through the various media as well as learning to utilize the communications received through the media. The second is that learning about any communication medium is incomplete unless it is learned through construction as well as consumption. Children learn what reading really is when they write something that others will read; they learn what a map can do by making one, and this facilitates their ability to read maps made by others. The active, productive, creative, synthetic component of use of mass media is as necessary as the analytic, receptive aspect in a complete and effective language arts program.

In the kindergarten and grade 1, children will enjoy videotapes of classroom activities and trips. Although they may not be handling equipment, they can help to plan what is to be taped. Preparation and follow-up activities in the classroom can enhance viewing of selected television programs at home. If the school publishes a "newspaper," their stories, poems, or pictures can be contributed. Tape records can be made of their creative expression, with replays that enable simple evaluation to analyze why the story or dramatization was enjoyable or to make changes.

In grade 2 and grade 3, children should begin to discuss and analyze choices of television programs just as they evaluate choices of books, in terms of what they enjoy and why they find it enjoyable. Specific criteria can be developed over a period of time. Newspapers and magazines produced for young children can be used in the reading program. The teacher can read and display material from local newspapers that would be of interest to them. However, they lack the reading skills to utilize adult news media independently, and therefore they should not be given assignments to "bring in news" that is beyond their level of reading or comprehension. Analysis of advertising can begin as they compare real toys and other products with the ways they are represented in commercials, advertisements, or packages.

In grades 4 to 8, children can refine criteria for analysis of television programs of different types, study ways in which programs may influence people, and write to local stations or national networks to express opinions about programs. Local television and radio stations might be visited to learn about operations and work roles. They can plan and produce videotapes in the same way that they would use films (discussed under visual literacy), but videotapes have the advantage of being erasable, and therefore more easily and economically revised than films. Radio news broadcasts or special programs can be used in the classroom. Differences in presentation of the same news in television, radio, newspapers, and news magazines can be analyzed. Propaganda techniques in commercials, advertisements, and special interest campaigns should be studied at increasing depth in the upper elementary and intermediate grades.

Related Questions and Activities   Analysis and use of media offer extensive opportunity for children to develop creative and critical thinking skills.

What do we mean when we use the terms "enjoy," or "interesting" in discussing a program or film (defining)?

Tell us the story you viewed yesterday (recalling).

What types of programs are shown on television? What are the purposes of each type (classifying)?

What are some similarities and differences in these three news accounts (comparing, analyzing)? What might be some reasons for the differences in facts or emphasis in each version (inferring, hypothesizing)?

Tell us in your own words how Heidi felt about her new home (interpreting).

What is likely to happen as a result of the energy problems presented in the documentary we viewed (predicting)?

What should be included in your documentary on play areas in our neighborhood (synthesizing)?

Visual Literacy The natural environment, man-made environment and objects, works of art, and abstract visual symbols are perceived and noted in differing ways by each individual. The subjective, aesthetic aspect of visual perception is discussed in Chapter 16. At the same time, there may be a comparatively objective message to be derived from whatever is observed. And, of course, there are many ways in which people intentionally use visual means to communicate. These last two aspects of visual perception, or "visual literacy," involve communication skills most effectively developed in relation to the total language arts program. As a thinking process, visual literacy involves the development of skills of visual observation, their reinforcement through other sensory perceptions, and intellectual analysis and use of what has been observed and perceived.

Objectives of visual literacy education include:

Increased knowledge and sensitivity to the natural and man-made environment

Understanding of messages communicated by visual images and symbols at literal and connotative levels

Skill in observing for detail, for a total view or impression, for sequence of images, for relationships within pictures or between parts of films, and so forth

Skill in using visual language and visual media for functional and creative expression

Learning experiences that meet these objectives promote development of verbal language skills. Increased skill in perception of the environment enhances utilization of direct experiences. Analysis of literal, implied, and connotative meanings of the visual component (i.e., film image, drawings, symbols, letter styles) of a verbal communication is necessary for full understanding of the total communication. Use of visual language and media for expression may involve verbal language for planning of the work (film, photo essay, and the like), as a component of the work, or in its translation to a form of oral or written expression.

Visual literacy skills related to perception of the environment can be developed from earliest preschool experiences as children learn directly about their surroundings. In the elementary and intermediate school, this continues to be developed in the context of social studies and science experiences. Skill in use and interpretation of nonverbal symbols used in graphs, maps, flowcharts, and the like, is developed in those curriculum areas as well. Works of visual arts of one's own and other cultures are appreciated and interpreted in the context of art and social studies programs. Nonverbal symbols and symbolic language systems are used extensively in mathematics and music; geometric forms, signs for operations, and musical notation are examples. The visual literacy skills usually, but not exclusively, developed in the context of the language arts program include analysis of visual images in mass media, photographs, advertising and packaging, illustrations, political cartoons, comics, signs, signals, and symbols, and skill in using these forms of expression. Of course, children should be guided to transfer, relate, or apply visual skills developed in one curriculum area to those needed in another.

While photographs and films have comparative objectivity because they are taken directly from the real referents, drawings and illustrations are subjective even when "realistic" in style. In addition to use of the skills of photograph analysis, interpretation now involves analysis of visual art elements and the ways an artist uses them to convey impressions or messages. For example, choice of color can affect the viewer's response. A bright color in clothing may call attention to a person to suggest importance. Harsh colors may provoke negative reactions to that person. Placement of the person in a scene in relation to others may suggest an erroneous view of that person's role in the depicted situation.

At the next level of abstraction in visual communication are cartoons, which intend to distort reality. Cartoons in humorous or "action" comic strips are an extension of illustration techniques, whereas political cartoons use symbols, exaggeration, and stereotypes to convey specific messages.

Interpretation of use of color, size, shape, position, and symbols is used in analysis of visual advertisements and packaging. In addition, television commercials involve movement of elements in an image and sequence of images.

Semipictorial symbols such as those used in international signs for such things as traffic directions, theater exits, or campsites are at a more abstract level. Maps and graphs often use semipictorial symbols. At the most abstract level are such symbols as dots, asterisks, geometric shapes, lines in graphs and contour maps, and the like. The relative sizes of circles on a map, or the distorted height of a line in a graph, can convey a message that differs from the real data the symbolic material purports to represent.

Much use is made of pictures as learning materials in kindergarten and first grade. Observation skills optimize use of photographs and commercial picture sets, as well as increasing perceptions of the environment and aiding analysis of real objects. Children can begin to take pictures with simple cameras; Polaroid cameras give immediate results appropriate for this age level. They can make up stories to describe sequences they construct from sets of pictures, use drawings to express ideas, and make painted glass slides to illustrate stories. In addition to the letter and number symbols they are learning, they need to learn safety symbols and can devise symbols of their own such as yellow circles and blue dots to note sunny and rainy days on the calendar.

Second and third graders extend these activities and begin to apply them to materials depicting other places and times. They can begin to analyze photographs by identifying the photographer's position and camera angle. Before taking their own photographs or making videotapes, they can plan the images to include and put them in sequence. Motion picture film may not be easy to use at this level, but children can scratch designs directly on film, with each child working on a few feet of a group or class film. They should have opportunities to use a variety of media to illustrate their written expression. They might begin to devise symbols to represent themselves, the class or school, holidays, and special events. Television cartoons can be analyzed for visual elements and the way in which both appearances and actions depart from what is possible in the real world. Illustrations should be interpreted and evaluated when books are read and discussed. Other curriculum areas provide many applications for use of symbols in maps, charts, and graphs, and in aesthetic expression.

As children move through grades 4 to 8, the variety of possible activities becomes quite extensive. They are able to learn to handle the film cameras, splicers, and other hardware needed, and can plan more complex sequences of images in photo essays, videotapes, and films, including animated films. These creative efforts should be related to analysis of media; for example, the process of making a live action or animated film enables children to understand and analyze the elements of films others have made. Preparing sound tracks for films develops critical and aesthetic listening skills as effects of sounds are planned or perceived. Videotapes of school and community events can be presented to school audiences. Study of the history of photography and films can be combined with visits to exhibits, books of photographers' works, and viewing of significant films in class or on television, all of which provide many opportunities for vocabulary development and oral or written expression. As children study cultures in other areas or the cultures of periods in the past, analysis should be made of applications of visual literacy in societies with differing levels of language literacy, use of symbols to indicate roles in a society, and differences in styles of visual expression in different cultures or at different times. Analysis should be made of the maps, charts, and graphs in textbooks, newspapers, and other media. More detailed perception can be made of the environment, and its visual impact can be analyzed in terms of the possible effects on people in the environment. Criteria can be developed for analysis of the visual devices of advertising and political cartoons.

Related Questions and Activities   As in use of media, visual literacy activities involve much use of critical and creative thinking skills. The following are only a few examples.

Use these pictures we took to tell about our trip (recalling).

How are Indians and Conquistadors shown in this illustration? What expressions and positions are used? What is the artist telling us about each person? What did the artist do to convey these impressions (analyzing)?

What do you see in this photograph that tells you what kind of community this might be (inferring)?

Why is the mayor, in this political cartoon, shown wearing a Roman toga? What other "imperial" symbols are used? How is the whole cartoon like a metaphor (interpreting)?

What kinds of things will you need to photograph for your slide sequences on needs for open space areas in our neighborhood (classifying, generalizing)?

What is happening in this picture? What must have happened just before? What do you think will happen next? Why (predicting)?

Plan a series of photographs on a subject of your choice (synthesizing).

Body Language and Other Nonverbal Communication Since people communicate extensively and continuously by means of facial expressions, gestures, body movement, and body position, children should learn to interpret these forms and become aware of ways in which they employ body language themselves.

In kindergarten through grade 3, children become aware of their own bodies and their movement potential through rhythmic movement experiences and dance. Both verbal and nonverbal communication are developed as they engage in such activities as imitating animals, or expressing opposite words through body movement or dance; happy-sad, inside-outside, for example. They can collect and analyze pictures showing facial expressions and body positions and begin to interpret body language in the context of visual literacy and mass-media analysis activities.

In grades 4 through 8, children can make more detailed analyses of gestures, positions, and movement, including those characteristic of different cultures, occupations, social classes, or special occasions. Another dimension would be relational situations; for example, use of body language by the same person when interacting with employer, friends, or children. Pantomime, role playing, and formal dramatization provide applications of body language by the children. Dance activities can become more complex and extend to choreography of a group dance that tells a story composed by the class, translates a favorite poem, or expresses a theme or idea. Characteristic gestures and body positions in the dances of other cultures can be compared.

There are, of course, a variety of other forms of communication, and teachers can find many ways of providing activities for children to explore them. For example, children in the earliest grades should learn "safety language," the system of visual and aural symbols of signs, street markings, lights, car horns, garage entrance signals, and sirens to which they need to develop appropriate responses. At all grade levels other sounds and signals in the environment that communicate something can be identified—bells, flares, peddlers' chants, foghorns, and the like. Forms of animal communication are intriguing to study. Children can develop their own systems of sign language or visual codes and study the uses of special forms of communication such as braille, smoke and drum signals, and semaphore.

Bilingual-Bicultural Education Several school systems have developed programs to meet the obstacles to learning encountered by non-English-speaking children who enter schools where all instruction is in English. Such children, particularly when they enter at third-grade level or later, frequently have difficulty in academic areas while they are in the process of learning the new language. A concomitant effect is often less of self-esteem. To overcome these problems, the bilingual-bicultural program provides for initial instruction throughout the schoolday in the children's home language, with English taught as a second language. Vocabulary and language patterns learned in structured lessons are applied in appropriate contexts, and reinforced in other activities, throughout the schoolday. Reading instruction begins in the home language. Initial instruction in reading in English is deferred until reading skills in the home language have been attained and command of oral English is adequate, at criterion levels that may vary from program to program. Children who enter school with sufficient English proficiency may begin to read in English, with instruction in reading the home language deferred, or introduced at about the same time, but this too varies from program to program. As children move through the grades, instruction in other areas is brought to a point where each language is used about 50 percent of the time to ensure practice and proficiency in both.

Major goals of bilingual-bicultural programs include:

Development of competence in English and the home language to a level free of "accent" in either language

Optimum academic achievement

Acculturation in one's ethnic setting as well as in the national context, as opposed to adoption of either one by means of rejection of the other

Development of a positive self-concept and positive ethnic identification through use of the home language, knowledge of the home culture, and increased academic achievement

There are some problems to consider in planning the curriculum for a bilingual-bicultural program. How is the culture of a particular group defined? Are there alternatives or variations in value systems or customs among subgroups within it? What curricular provisions are needed to enable children in a homogeneous ethnic group to interact with, or learn about, people of other ethnic groups? If there are cultural differences in learning styles, should children gradually be introduced to other modes to increase their learning powers? What provisions can be made to meet the needs of children who enter a sequentially planned program in upper grades?

INSTRUCTIONAL MEDIA

An experience-based language arts program utilizes everything available in the environment as a source of learning. In the classroom, media used in all curriculum areas can serve language development. As children discuss plans for an aquarium, transact purchases at the pet store, and keep records of fish growth, they are extending vocabulary and using language, even though the activity may have developed from the science program. Of course, fish stories, poems, and paintings would be stimulated too.

Among the types of instructional media available for specific, preplanned learning activities are the following printed, audio-visual, and community resources.

Language series textbooks: Analyze these for attention to children's oral language forms, encouragement of their creative expression and thinking skills, and activities that meet purposes within their experiences and are in accord with their interests.

Workbooks and programmed materials: These usually call for more convergent responses; use them selectively to meet specific needs in vocabulary development, grammar, spelling, and handwriting.

Children's books about language: Bibliographies of books about words and language entertainingly written to promote children's pleasure in use and exploration of language can be found in language arts teacher-education textbooks such as those in the references at the end of this chapter.

Word blocks or cards: Children use commercially produced blocks with words of one type on each, or teacher-made cards of words, substituting one verb for another, inserting adjectives, and so forth, to generate, expand, or transform sentences.

Printed media: Magazines, newspapers, books, pamphlets, letters, announcements.

Games: Commercial or "homemade," such as Scrabble, word bingo, and the like.

Reference materials: Encyclopedias, dictionaries, almanacs, and the like.

Audio media: Records, tapes, radio, musical instruments and other sound-producing objects, telephones.

Visual media: Photographs, illustrations, art objects, artifacts, signs and symbols, camera and film equipment, materials for use in visual arts expression as listed in Chapter 16, posters, billboards.

Instructional machines: "Talking typewriters" (responsive-environment machines), multimedia carrels, typewriters.

Community resources: Libraries, local television and radio stations, museums, communications personnel to be interviewed.

Media for bilingual-bicultural education include all the above, and in addition:

Books in both languages: Stories from the home culture, textbooks and tradebooks about the home culture and background history, and subject-area textbooks in both languages.

Periodicals: In both languages.

Films in both languages: Films made by children or by community members, commercial films in the home language, films about the culture or country of origin.

Records: Music and poetry of the home culture or country.

Realia: Objects, artifacts, clothing, works of art of the home culture or country.

Mass media: Television and radio programs in the home language.

Community resources: Local museums, food stores and markets meeting cultural needs, community residents interviewed.

ENVIRONMENT FOR LANGUAGE LEARNING

Just as Le Corbusier, a leading architect, defined a house as a machine for living, a classroom may be considered a machine for learning. Teachers and children can make the classroom a language-learning environment; for example:

Activity centers and seating arrangements should be designed to limit sound interference from one area to another so that clear communication can take place in all areas simultaneously.

Spaces can be set up for comfortable recreational reading with a good light source. Shelf or table space should be used for a classroom library and for materials to stimulate written expression; picture files, dictionaries and spelling aids, and the like. Children's own written expression should be placed here too where it is more accessible for reading than when thumbtacked to a bulletin board. Of course, the total floor, storage, and wall space of the classroom would be allotted to provide for activities and materials in all areas of the curriculum.

Children can plan, discuss, and carry out rearrangements of furniture and equipment to meet different learning or recreational purposes in their room. Furniture and space can be used to simulate geographic areas studied and area and measurement problems in mathematics or as a total space for dramatization, rather than limiting action to a small "stage" area.

Children can periodically decorate the room with illustrations, their paintings and sculptures, objects and symbols that relate to a theme or to the months or seasons. Language activities can focus for a few days on words, stories, dramatics, analysis of symbols, and the like, related to the theme or the characteristics and events within the month or season.

Labels can be applied to objects in the room, and parts of the room itself, to develop vocabulary and sight words in primary grades, or in initial stages of second-language learning.

TEACHING STRATEGIES

Although all of the daily experiences in school constitute a setting for language learning and application, this is not accomplished incidentally. Specific experiences need to be provided to ensure development of specific language skills, drawing on language needs in school settings and at the child's developmental levels, and following up with explicit application and reinforcement of language skills throughout the day. Of course there are many occasions when teachers will note an individual's need and help the child with it immediately; learning is often most effectively accomplished this way. But even when working with one child at a time, specific strategies are used. "Teaching strategies," as presented in these chapters, are models of sequences of activities intended to provide children with learning experiences contributing to development of specific understandings, skills, and values. Many different activities and materials may be used in any particular model, depending on objectives and learner characteristics. This chapter and those that follow on each content area of the curriculum outline teaching strategy models as general frameworks. Suggestions for specific activities and materials used in the framework of a particular strategy can be found in "methods" textbooks such as those in end-of-chapter references, in current professional periodicals and publications of professional organizations, and in teacher's guides to elementary and intermediate language arts textbooks.

Language is communication. Therefore, even in open-classroom or other individualized learning settings, realistic language learning involves interaction between children. Of course, some skills are learned in part through such means as individualized spelling lists, spot instruction for needs arising from a particular writing effort, or participation in an individualized reading program. But written expression, when completed, is shared with others; reading comprehension is enhanced when several children who have read the same story or book can share ideas about it. The teaching strategies outlined below are models that may be used with groups of children or, sometimes in a compressed form, with individuals. Some are appropriate for whole-class experiences, particularly those involving oral language. The whole class can also be brought together at that point in a teaching strategy where written or dramatic expression is to be shared or performed. The first strategy, contracting, is a procedure usually used in individualized instruction, but it applies to work undertaken by an interacting group or committee of children as well.

The strategies outlined below may be completed in a single session, or they may extend over several days, depending on objectives, age of children, learning characteristics and rates, and so forth. Within the components of each strategy, teachers will also be utilizing the strategies for cognitive, thinking, and inquiry processes outlined in Chapter 7.

Contracting

Contracting, making an agreement between teacher and child for the child's independent study, can enhance motivation by giving children responsibility for their own learning and by providing for individual differences in needs and interests. This strategy may be used in any form of classroom organization. It provides a tool for individualizing instruction in traditional settings when introduced to a few pupils at a time for a single activity, or to several for a short-term activity, with an increase in number of contracts for each child and in duration of contract when teacher and children are ready. In settings that are already individualized, contracting is not needed for short-term activities or the daily, flexible activity choices made by children. However, some individual and group learning efforts require prior planning and organization because of complexity, need for materials, cooperative efforts of several children, or use of a variety of learning experiences to attain goals. Contracting can provide children with a clear understanding of the purposes, processes, and outcomes of their learning experiences. It offers a means for children to develop skills in setting objectives, analyzing their own learning needs, making choices of activities and materials, planning ways to share learnings, and evaluating their own learning. These skills can then be applied as children engage in other independent learning experiences, without setting up a written or verbal contract.

Contracting Strategy

1 Set objectives. Teacher and pupil discuss and agree on specific learning objectives. In some cases a pretest may be given to determine exact needs. Objectives should be stated in the child's words.

Examples: To learn about dinosaurs
          To improve slant and letter alignment in cursive writing
          To write and film a story about the life of a city squirrel

2 Determine learning activities. Teacher elicits the child's suggestions for activities and materials to use in achieving objectives and evaluating outcomes, adds others that are needed, and helps the child determine sequence and schedule of activities and time for completion.

3 Carry out activities. The child, or group, carries out the agreed-upon activities, which may include independent work combined with participation in group or whole-class activities. Children may contact the teacher for guidance at any time, and the teacher should observe or consult with them to keep abreast of their progress or problems.

4 Evaluate and record. Teacher and child evaluate ongoing processes and outcomes of the experience jointly, using criteria developed in step 2. Records of the outcomes should be made in a teacher's notebook, and examples of the child's work, as well as any tests and checklists, should be kept in a folder throughout the year. Evaluation should be an integral part of all activities in the contract to make adjustments in goals or changes in activities when those originally planned prove inappropriate or inadequate.

Listening Strategies

Two strategies are presented below. Although the activities involved in both are similar, the first focuses on developing a particular listening skill, whereas the second focuses on using listening skills to analyze, interpret, or enjoy oral communication, music, or other sound experiences.

Developing Listening Skills

1 Establish the context or need for the skill.

Examples: Class trip to park—need to listen for bird sounds
          Listening to music as a leisure activity
          Listening to determine a speaker's position on an issue

2 Elicit definition of the skill. Have children suggest what they need to do to meet the identified listening need.

3 Practice the skill. Have children test their suggestions by applying them to a "sample" (i.e., record of bird calls, musical excerpt, statement by the teacher) and evaluating the effectiveness of their listening ability.

4 Identify and apply the skill. Have children revise and retest suggestions if necessary, record their final description of the skill, apply it immediately or next day in the context that necessitated its acquisition (using the second strategy), and increase their skill through its continued use in and out of school.

Using Listening Skills

1 Motivate and focus the experience. Present an excerpt or example of the type of sound the children will be listening to (i.e., music, sounds made by different objects, a recorded drama) and elicit purposes for the experience. This may have already been established if the experience was suggested by the children.

2 Identify appropriate listening skills. Have children identify or briefly review the skill that they have already acquired and are now going to apply.

3 Carry out the experience. Children listen for a period of time suitable to their attention span. If there are many selections to be included, provide for response and discussion at intervals. If the listening experience takes place outside the classroom, such as listening for city sounds on a walk, have children discuss the sound when it is heard and identified.

4 Follow-up or use the experience. Apply the knowledge gained in and out of the class. For example, if the purpose of the experience was to note differences in types of music, children might look for other examples; sounds of the city can be recorded as part of a study of the community; the recorded drama would be analyzed for literary structure and meaning to understand and enjoy a wide range of dramatic forms.

Oral Language Strategies

Many specific oral language skills, such as pronunciation, organization of ideas before speaking, and discussion techniques are developed through a skill-development strategy as outlined under "Learning Skills" later in this section. Strategies for grammar, usage, and written expression also serve for oral expression. One strategy particularly suited to development of vocabulary, intonation, phrasing, pronunciation, clarity of ideas and form in oral sentences, and creativity in oral expression is presented here.

Creative Dramatics Strategy

1 Select the topic. Children should be involved in determining the story or situation they will enact. It may be a favorite story or one of their own or may reproduce a real event. Have children tell the story or sequence of happenings as briefly but clearly as possible.

2 Plan the action. If the whole dramatization is brief, this can be done once. In most cases, the "plot" is divided into parts or scenes, and steps 2 and 3 are repeated for each part, sometimes on succeeding days. Children discuss what each person will do, some things each might say, and how to use floor space and props. This should be very brief, intended only to give a focus and start to the activity; the details develop in step 3.

3 Enact the story or scene. Children act out the story spontaneously, creating the dialogue and movement as they go, within the framework of the review and plans of steps 1 and 2. Enactment of the whole scene should go through without interruption to keep children "in character" and keep up the flow of ideas and expression. Tape the proceeding only if this does not inhibit spontaneity.

4 Evaluate and refine. When the first enactment is completed, participants and observers evaluate to identify speech and movement that were effective and to suggest any changes. The scene is reenacted to try out the suggestions.

5 Perform the drama. Creative dramatics involves no written dialogue or detailed, preplanned directions, and changes with every performance. Two or three "tryouts" should suffice to bring the effort to a level satisfactory to the children without becoming boring. Then the scenes can be put together for one or more complete enactments for the class itself, or a larger audience.

6 Record the drama. Children may want to tape a complete performance, have it photographed or videotaped, or write it out as a play, story, or poem.

Vocabulary Development

Vocabulary is developed informally in many different types of learning experiences throughout the schoolday, as discussed earlier in this chapter. The strategy for creative writing provides one model for a more formal procedure to augment less specific vocabulary-building experiences.

Grammar

Educators and linguists recommend an approach to study of the structure of language that begins with whole sentences and the relationships of words within a sentence, rather than beginning with analysis of isolated parts of speech, or word classes, one at a time.

Strategy for Identifying Word Classes

1 A model sentence is presented (i.e., The girl threw the ball). Lines drawn under the nouns and verb indicate that these are "slots." The noun slot can include the article that precedes it. If adverbs or adjectives are to be inserted, slot lines are drawn between words to leave a blank in the appropriate place. Children should be asked to show where these could be.

2 Substitutions are made. Children suggest different words for a particular slot. Concentration would be on a single word class during initial instruction, with multiple slots used after each class of words has been introduced (i.e., Alice threw the ball. Jack caught the ball. The Indian threw the spear. The silent figure hurled the silvery spear through the air.)

3 Rules or generalizations are formulated. Children express a statement in their own words to identify and label the kinds of words that may be inserted in in a particular slot; they discuss the relationship of words in that slot to others in the sentence and the effect of such words on sentence meaning.

4 Sentence patterns are used in oral and written expressions.

A similar strategy would be used to transform a sentence into variant forms. In step 2, children would be asked to turn the model into a question (Did the girl throw the ball?), say it did not happen (The girl did not throw the ball.), turn it around (The ball was thrown by the girl.), and so forth. Elicit types of sentences in children's words so that they can suggest possible model forms. In step 3 they would label the accepted forms.

Usage

Determine instructional needs by noting the particular errors made by each child. Instruction can be individual, or children who have the same needs can be grouped for initial instruction and practice. Whole-class activities are not usually appropriate as language skills will differ among children. Focus on one type of error, or a few that are closely related, at a time.

Usage Strategy

1 Motivate and clarify need. Present the correct form in a meaningful, interesting context; for example, a speech pattern that will be used in written expression or in creative dramatics.

2 Practice the appropriate form. Have all the children repeat the correct form a few times. Then have each one repeat it in round-robin fashion a few times to make sure each child is able to express the pattern clearly. (For example, "I *have* an apple" to replace "I *gots* an apple.")

3 Reinforce the form. Have children vary the other words in the sentence (Jane has a cat.), respond to pattern questions (What do you have? I have a book.), take turns asking and answering pattern questions and responses, or expand to more complex sentence forms appropriate to the language levels of the particular learners (How many cousins do you have? If Lou has six cookies and Sandy has four, who has more?). Of course, younger children or comparatively slower learners would not move to varying or extended patterns in one session.

4 Use the form. Have children utilize the new form immediately in the context or for the purpose in which it was introduced, and make it an habitual response by providing additional drill practice at various times as needed.

5 Evaluate. Have each child keep a record of the standard forms he has learned and correct mistakes in forms that have been learned as they occur, reteaching if necessary. Game-like tests can be used from time to time, but frequent opportunity to use correct forms in oral and written expression enables children's self-evaluation and reinforces correct usage.

Written Expression

The strategy presented for development of creative writing follows the discovery-transductive model outlined in Chapter 7. The functional writing strategy follows the general outline for skill development in that chapter.

Creative Writing Strategy

1 Motivate and focus the experience. Provide a stimulus for expression; a short film, touching unseen objects with different surface textures, pictures or photographs that depict a mood or people in actions that lead to description or a story, recollection of each one's personal experience in a given situation, and the like.

2 Identify the form or forms to use. The children might have a choice of forms with which they are familiar, or the teacher might present a new form such as a limerick or a concrete poem (in which words are arranged on the page to produce a design or shape representative of, or described by, the words).

3 Elicit examples of expression. If familiar forms are used, have children list some of the types of items to include, the questions to be answered, or examples of descriptive words to use. If examples are generated, limit this to a few to avoid limiting originality as each one begins to write.

4 Children write stories, narratives, poems, or plays. The teacher observes as beginners work to help each one as needed if he encounters difficulties. More advanced writers might work independently. Allow children to write without concern for accuracy of spelling and grammar (of words and structures not yet learned), to avoid inhibiting creative flow of ideas.

5 Share completed work. Have children read each other's work appreciatively and have them discuss the unique or enjoyable aspects of each one.

6 Develop aesthetic criteria. To improve expressive skills and enable each child to formulate his own aesthetic values, have children develop guidelines for writing based on a constructive analysis of what they found to be effective; for example, using words that help you see pictures in your mind, avoiding run-on sentences, and the like.

7 Use the completed work. Since writing is communication, keep the original work, or duplicate it, to be added to the class library. Children will be encouraged to express themselves if they learn that what they write will be read, not thrown in tomorrow's wastebasket.

Vocabulary can be developed through this strategy by using the same type of motivation. A sudden snow, a pet brought to class, a visit to a farm, are other examples that provide an opportunity for children to share words that are used in describing the situation or object, or to discuss meanings of new words introduced by the teacher. This would correspond to step 3 and step 5, as children share the words they suggest. The next step in a vocabulary strategy would be to use the words in oral or written expression.

Functional Writing Strategy

1 Establish the need for writing. Introduction or extension of skills in writing a letter, report, application, and so forth should be developed when there is real need for the skill, immediate or as a foundation for sequential learning needs, that is clear to the children.

2 Elicit a model form. Have them suggest what information should be included and how it should be organized and put in sequence.

3 Practice the skill. Using the agreed-upon elements and form, the children might compose a group or class effort based on the model, or they might go directly to individual work.

4 Evaluate. Have them compare their work with the model and correct as needed.

5 Apply the skill. Use the work as intended in step 1 (sending the letter, preparing reports), and apply it at other times in the school year.

Spelling and Handwriting

Some suggestions for instruction in these tool skills are included in the descriptions of these components of the program in the earlier section on organization of the curriculum. The following strategy can be used to develop handwriting skills and the spelling of phonetically regular words.

Generalizing Strategy

1 Present examples. For handwriting, these would be samples, either the children's or commercial copies, that represent a range from poor to standard legibility. In first grade, some letters may be introduced in isolation, but move to use of whole words and sentences as soon as children are ready. For spelling, these would be words following a particular phonetic rule, such as boat, coat, float.

2 Analyze and compare examples. In handwriting, have children tell which samples are easier to read and the reasons for this. In spelling, have them identify the similarities in letter patterns.

3 State the rule or generalization. Have them turn the reasons for legibility or the common elements in the set of words into a rule to follow in writing or in spelling words with that pattern.

4 Reinforce. Have children practice the handwriting skill immediately. In spelling, have them suggest other words that follow the rule and note exceptions. They can practice spelling the regular words in pairs, taking turns as one child spells and the other listens to correct if necessary.

5 Evaluate. Have children compare their writing with the rules and standards they identified and practice again if needed. Words missed on spelling tests should be restudied after the teacher has ascertained that the child understands the rule that applies.

6 Use what has been learned. Have children adhere to identified handwriting forms or standards (alignment, letter spacing, upper-lower case ratios, and the like) and correct spelling of learned words in subsequent writing.

Learning Skills

This basic strategy provides for skill development in all curriculum areas, involving use of a learning tool. Outlining and note taking follow the similar functional writing strategy.

Skill-development Strategy

1 Establish the need for the skill. Skills should be developed to meet learning needs or interests as they arise and in situations meaningful to the children.

Examples: Using the index in a textbook

                Operating a film projector

2 Explore the learning tool. To focus thinking, have children suggest how the tool might work. Electrical or mechanical equipment should then be demonstrated. In other cases, have them try out and test their suggestions.

Examples: "What are the ways in which you could locate information in this book on Hopi Indian homes?" Children may suggest table of contents, skimming pages, and other ideas. Try them to see how long it takes. Introduce the index, and have them tell what it shows; elicit alphabetical order, subheadings, words followed by page numbers, and other observed features.

                "How do you think this works?" Have children observe components of the machine to suggest their relationships or functions.

3 Demonstrate the skill. If they have suggested the appropriate procedure, have some or all of the children try it out as a demonstration. If the teacher needs to direct this, have children participate as much as possible.

Examples: How might Hopi Indian homes be listed in this index?

                Lee, show us what happens when the lens is turned.

4 Practice the skill. Give each child the opportunity to try out the skill.

Examples: Give, or elicit, items to find in the index and locate in the book. Other books can be used at this point to show variations in headings used in books on the same topics.

                Each child should have a chance to run the machine.

5 Evaluate skill attainment. This might be done by observation during step 4, by analysis of subsequent use of the skill, or by a test.

6 Apply the skill. Have children use the skill immediately in the context established in step 1 and at various times throughout the school year.

Mass Media

Analysis of content in printed mass media is made through strategies of literary analysis outlined in Chapter 10. These strategies also apply to analysis of content of film, television, and radio dramas. The strategy outlined below provides for analysis of documentary films or programs, advertising, and political cartoons.

Media Analysis Strategy

1 Present example to be analyzed. Elicit general responses, and ask each child to write or state very briefly the message that was conveyed to him by the example.

Examples: What was the theme in this documentary?

                What do you think of this product?

                What does this cartoon say about food prices?

2 Analyze message devices. Have children identify elements in the source material that caused them to reach their conclusions.

Examples: What did you see that made you think more housing is needed in this area?

What words gave you that opinion of the product?

How did the artist show the distribution of the consumers's money to stores, processors, and farmers?

3 Set up criteria or guiding questions for evaluation. Refer to the elements identified in step 2 and have children use them to set up criteria or questions for identification and evaluation of message devices.

Examples: What images were selected? What might have been left out? Why? What can we say about this? Why do we want to see all sides of a question? What should we look for in the wording of an ad or commercial?

What can we say about the way cartoonists show the relative sizes of different figures?

4 Apply criteria to other examples. Have each child apply the criteria to a second item and then compare opinions to test the validity and reliability of the criteria. That is, are the criteria appropriate and helpful as guides for evaluating the material, and do they lead to similar judgments about a particular material by all evaluators? (Reliability is not necessary if value judgments are to be made, as these may vary from person to person. In subjective evaluations, criteria might be in the form of questions to raise, rather than as guides to analysis of techniques. For example, "Should advertising use slogans?" rather than "How are slogans used?")

5 Use criteria. Have children apply the criteria or questions to analysis of other materials in and out of school and use them as guides in making their own documentary photo essays or films, in preparing ads for school cake sales, or in using cartoon techniques to express their own views.

Visual Literacy

First experiences with photography and filming may be exploratory. Too much preplanning in the classroom can dampen enthusiasm or create confusion by overwhelming children with directions that seem abstract. When first efforts are produced and children see a need for putting the images in some order, they can utilize the strategy of storyboarding. In their subsequent productions of photo or picture essays, videotapes, or films, they will be able to use storyboarding as a preplanning procedure that helps them to develop a better finished product with an economy of time and film. Preparation of a storyboard enables them to analyze the elements of a film sequence, enhancing their abilities to interpret and evaluate films and television programs they view.

Although children can plan a film based on a story they have read or written, the goals of visual literacy are most adequately met if the storyboard project has a primarily visual focus. Storyboarding involves selecting visual images and determining their sequence, with narration or dialogue added later to accompany the visual images, rather than the other way around. When a story is to be filmed, use a general description of its sequence to set up the visual images, rather than trying to illustrate the story word by word.

To introduce the technique of storyboarding, have each child select an idea or story, and illustrate it with a sequence of several drawings, or pictures cut from magazines. No writing should accompany the pictures. Share the sequences and have other children tell the story or identify the theme they think the picture sequence represents.

Storyboarding Strategy

1 Determine a theme, topic, or story. Children select an idea or theme (faces in the city, anger, flight), a topic (our school, history of our community, why we need a playground), or a story, poem, or drama that can be expressed through visual means.

2 Visualize or select images. Have children think of, and roughly sketch out, the visual images to be included. When enough ideas have been expressed, move to the next step.

3 Make pictures of planned images. In most cases, it is easiest to have children make very simple line drawings to represent images. Older children planning a film might take photographs "on location" as they think through their image selection.

4 Put pictures in sequence. Children arrange and rearrange their pictures to develop a sequence of images. These are posted on a long strip of paper for younger children or in rows on a wall chart in upper grades. The finished sequence provides the guide for filming, videotaping, or the order of photographs, drawings, or magazine pictures in a visual essay.

5 Add directions. (Not for still-picture essays.) Children note camera angle, distance, and other filming directions under each picture in the storyboard. If sound is used, notations for this are also made.

6 Carry out the project. Children use the storyboard as a script for selection of pictures, filming, or videotaping. As a follow-up, they might write out a poem, or just random responses, expressing the idea or theme, a narrative or essay based on the topic, or a version of the story or drama as it turned out after filming.

7 Evaluate. Have children make a constructive evaluation to determine what was effective in the finished work, and what they might do differently, in terms of content, technology, or storyboarding procedures, in their next work.

ORGANIZING FOR INSTRUCTION

In the graded and multigraded vertical classroom organization, most instruction is carried on in groups. Typically, new skills are introduced to the class as a whole or to the appropriate group within the multigraded class. After an initial period of practice, the class or group is further subdivided according to children's needs and rates of learning. Instruction is individualized as the special problems, errors, or interests of children are identified by the teacher. Individualized spelling lists, correction of individual handwriting and usage errors, and freedom of choice in form and topic in creative writing are examples of individualized instruction recommended in courses of study.

In the nongraded and open classroom, some initial instruction can be done with small groups. Then learning proceeds on an individual basis as children progress through sequentially developed skills at their own rates. However, in all three types of classroom organization, some language activities, including most forms of oral communication, are most appropriately conducted with the entire class.

In the self-contained classroom, the teacher will follow instructional patterns in accordance with the type of vertical organization. In a horizontal organization utilizing departmentalization, rare in the elementary school, children may be grouped homogeneously with respect to specific language achievement levels, with a resultant emphasis on group instruction.

When team teaching is utilized, one teacher responsible for instruction in some or all areas of language arts introduces skills in large-group lectures or demonstrations. Individual teachers follow up such lessons in classes or smaller groups. A child may be assigned to different follow-up groups for practice in spelling, handwriting, composition, or dramatics, depending upon his ability or interest without regard to his grade level.

Guidelines for the Teacher

Instructional guidelines provided in curriculum outlines and statements by language educators reflect current emphases on structural and generative linguistic analyses of English, the importance of effective communication, encouragement of creativity in expression, provision for individual differences, and meaningful contexts for language learnings.

General guidelines, applicable to all areas of language arts instruction, include the following suggestions to teachers:

Be conversant with developments in linguistics, understand the structure of language and the primacy of its oral form, and develop language learnings for pupils that are consistent with this understanding.

Recognize the interrelationships of the language arts and relate classroom language activities so that pupils grasp the unity of their varied language experiences and learnings.

Provide varied experiences that simulate children's thinking and provide guidance, through group evaluation and discussion, in the organization of thought, in order to motivate expression and improve the quality of pupils' work.

Teach skills in connection with realistic and purposeful occasions that require their use. Provide meaningful, rather than contrived, occasions and opportunities for language communication.

Recognize the need for language skills in all areas of the curriculum and be consistent in language expectations and skill applications in all activities of the schoolday.

Employ inductive procedures in helping children to develop concepts and derive generalizations.

Group children for instruction in specific skills according to their needs and language levels. Recognize individual differences in rates of learning, and provide individual guidance and correction.

Help children to develop their own suitable standards and guidelines for oral and written expression, and guide them to acquire the skill and habit of evaluating, correcting, improving, and appreciating their own work.

Guidelines in specific language arts instructional areas are extensive. The following represent a selection of current suggestions.

Grammar Utilize descriptive, rather than prescriptive, language teaching based on characteristic contemporary speech and writing. Begin instruction with study and use of entire sentences, and then work down to structural parts, in order to help children to understand the structural relationships of words and phrases. Teach children to use varieties of simple sentences, to vary sentences by substitution of words in appropriate slots, and to expand kernel sentences into more complex and expressive forms.

Usage Recognize that different levels of language usage are appropriate under differing circumstances. Accept nonstandard forms in children's speech that reflect other levels of usage, and build skill in standard usage in addition to other forms. Concentrate corrections on common errors that are unacceptable in standard usage. Be positive in making corrections: motivate pupils to learn correct forms, provide clear examples and instruction, repeat the correct form without the intervening use of incorrect forms, and consistently put correct forms to use.

Spelling Group spelling words which have the same phonetic patterns or which conform to a particular rule in order to enable children to see similarities and to inductively derive generalizations for use in learning new words. Use a natural language sequence in introducing new words: have children listen to words, say them, read them, and then write them. Use individualized spelling lists and encourage independent study in patterns suitable to individual pupils. Incorporate words needed by children in daily classroom activities to supplement words drawn from basic lists.

Handwriting Allow children to write with the hand that is most comfortable. Provide appropriate directions for left-handed pupils. Allow pupils to adopt hand motions and postures that are comfortable if there is no detriment to their writing. Uniform procedures are not appropriate for all. Practice in handwriting should be in meaningful contexts, with words, phrases, and sentences rather than single letters.

Listening and Speaking Recognize that the teacher's own speech patterns greatly influence those of the pupils, and provide appropriate examples of pronunciation and voice modulation. Help children to sense specific purposes for listening. Provide experiences in which they talk and listen to each other. Emphasize the importance of clarity of communication by encouraging careful speaking and listening in all classroom activities.

Written Expression Provide experiences that stimulate imagination, sharpen observation, and provoke children's interest in writing. Help children to set their own reasonable standards for written expression. Encourage expression by minimizing corrections in creative writing. Allow children to explore a variety of expressive forms.

Mass Media and Visual Literacy Utilize experiences in these areas to develop critical and creative thinking skills. Have children keep a record of their own weekly television viewing to note and compare time spent and choice of programs, as a basis for analysis of viewing habits and program content. Encourage them to develop their own criteria and express their own values. Relate analysis of advertising techniques to consumer education. When photography and videotaping skills are introduced, encourage children to utilize them in all curriculum areas.

EVALUATION OF INSTRUCTIONAL OUTCOMES

Evaluation of pupil progress in language skills is characterized by emphasis on the pupil's self-evaluation and by constructive guidance. In all areas of language activities, pupils are encouraged to discuss, analyze, and determine appropriate standards for skill attainment. These standards may be used by the child as a checklist to measure his own progress, or they may form the basis for group evaluation. In other instances, evaluation may be conducted by the teacher alone, by teacher and pupil, or by groups of pupils. In both oral and written expression, there is more emphasis on the *production* of correct forms than on the *correction* of forms. This results in greater integration of continuous evaluation with all phases of instruction, rather than evaluation as a terminating activity for the purpose of reporting achievement levels.

In all areas of language arts instruction, standardized tests and teacher-made checklists and tests are used early in the academic year to evaluate learning needs. Oral language evaluation may involve diagnosis of speech or hearing difficulties. Charts, checklists, and recorded tests are available to enable teachers to detect indications of speech pathology or hearing loss. Minor difficulties may be overcome in classroom learning activities, while more serious problems may be identified for treatment by specialists.

Teacher and pupils may engage in continuous evaluation of speaking skills as these are practiced in all areas of the school program. More detailed and comprehensive evaluation for each pupil may be done by means of checklists, rating scales, teacher-pupil conferences, and tape recordings of pupils' speech. All these techniques lend themselves to cooperative evaluation between teacher and pupils. Listening comprehension may be evaluated in all these ways. In addition, teachers may devise tests based on checklists of listening skills, using oral games that also serve instructional purposes. A few standardized tests are available, but teachers must take into account the fact that responses on these tests involve some reading as well.

Just as pupils devise standards for oral skills in storytelling, discussion, and news reporting, so too they may devise standards for writing letters, announcements, reports, and other forms of functional writing. Specific assignments may be kept in pupil folders for evaluation of progress. Written work in other subject areas is also evaluated in accordance with appropriate standards of written expression skills. In creative writing, evaluation tends to be more subjective and individualized. Certain general questions may be used as guidelines to determine such qualities as originality, appropriate sequence of ideas or events, effective communication of intended meaning, and use of descriptive or colorful words. Evaluation is individualized as each example of creative expression is examined in the light of its author's purposes and is considered in terms of his own level of expressive skill. Folders of work are kept to evaluate individual growth. Intraclass comparison and evaluation may be based on checklists prepared by the class. Some commercial rating scales are available, but are not of recent publication, and are based on limited-time essay tests. Cooperative evaluation of creative expression by teacher and pupil, encouraged in professional publications and recent courses of study, is an integral part of instruction and is considered most effective when the focus is on the quality of the content, rather than form. Teachers are advised to limit corrections and to concentrate instead on the adequate expression of ideas through selection of appropriate content and extension of vocabulary.

Grammar and usage may be evaluated directly through standardized diagnostic or achievement tests, teacher-made tests, essays, or workbook activities. Evaluation of skills in grammar and usage also extends to all of the child's daily language activities in oral and written expression. Spelling achievement is evaluated by means of formal tests, but teacher checklists of spelling study skills, extent of pupils' vocabularies, and awareness of their own needs for correct spelling permit evaluation of the full range of objectives in spelling instruction. Folders of pupils' written expression are kept to determine their progress in the application of spelling and handwriting skills. Handwriting scales are available in chart form to facilitate rating of pupils' work. Using such charts in addition to standard handwriting models enables children to evaluate their progress as their skills improve.

In order to assure evaluation of the full range of appropriate objectives, teachers may utilize objectives in courses of study or other classifications of objectives as guidelines. Examples of the use of certain taxonomies of educational objectives (Bloom, 1956; Krathwohl, Bloom & Masia, 1964) in the evaluation of learning in the language arts include the following.

Cognitive Domain

Knowledge Level Knowledge of the structure of language, including vocabulary development, knowledge of grammatical structure, knowledge of spelling "rules," spelling of specific words, and knowledge of forms for functional writing may be evaluated by means of objective tests. Knowledge of papropriate forms of written expression and of accurate grapheme forms may be evaluated through tests and observation of pupil work. Checklists are used to guide such evaluation as well as the evaluation of pupils' knowledge of rules for effectivesp aeking and attentive listening.

Comprehension Level Pupils' abilities to abstract generalizations about language structure from sets of particular examples may be evaluated by means of standardized and teacher-made tests and observation of children's written work and oral expression. Ability to derive appropriate rules for listening, speaking, and written expression may be determined on the basis of charts developed by the pupils.

Application Level Skill in the use of language knowledge and comprehension is manifested in the pupil's application of knowledge to new communication tasks and situations. In all areas of the language arts program, skill in application is evaluated by observation of pupils' written work, listening habits, and oral expression. The teacher uses checklists and rating scales to guide this observation and may evaluate individual progress by means of anecdotal records.

Analysis Level Pupils' abilities to analyze statements, to determine relevancy and irrelevancy in information or arguments, and to think and listen critically may be evaluated by means of checklists, rating scales, and anecdotal records of pupil behavior. Analysis skills involved in outlining, note-taking, and other forms of functional writing are evaluated by observation of the child's written work. Analysis in creative writing is utilized by the pupil in self-evaluation. This skill is evaluated through teacher observation.

Synthesis Level The child's abilities to produce unique and appropriate efforts in written and oral expression are evaluated by means of direct observation of his work in accordance with guidelines and standards which may be developed cooperatively by pupils and teacher.

Affective Domain

Receiving Level The child's willingness to listen to others and his ability to listen or read with selective attention may be evaluated by teacher observation guided by checklists of appropriate pupil behavior.

Responding Level   The child's willingness to respond orally and in writing and the level of his satisfaction in such response may be evaluated through observation of his behavior and the fluency apparent in his expressive efforts.

Valuing Level   Evidence of the child's value preferences may be found through observation of his behavior, and can be noted by the teacher in anecdotal records in order to evaluate progress over a period of time. In grammar, usage, spelling, and handwriting instruction, the teacher will note the child's acceptance of agreed-upon standards, his preference for alternative standards, and his commitment to various standards as manifested in his adherence to such standards in all areas of his language work. Values related to the child's acceptance of the rights of others to differing opinions, his appreciation of the contributions made by others to class activities, and his interest in the written and oral expression of other children are similarly noted by means of teacher observation, anecdotal records, and attitude or interest questionnaires.

FOLLOW-UP ACTIVITIES AND PROJECTS

1   Outline a plan for the school year, for a specific age or grade level, of experiences to develop creative written expression. Indicate forms children will use (narrative, haiku, etc.), and write out descriptions of lessons and experiences for them in using one of the forms.

2   Plan a sequence of lessons to develop a skill in functional writing, grammar, usage, or learning skills, using strategies suggested in this chapter. Outline ways in which the skill will be applied and extended throughout the school year.

3   Evaluate a language arts curriculum bulletin in terms of the following:
   a   Are objectives appropriate? Clearly defined? Do they include all of language learning and use?
   b   What is the scope of the program?
   c   Is the sequence related to the children's developmental levels?
   d   Does the program emphasize direct experiences and purposeful learning contexts?
   e   Is emphasis given to creative expression?
   f   What teaching strategies are suggested?
   g   What forms of evaluation are used?

4   Examine two or three language arts textbooks at a particular grade level. To what extent does each one meet the objectives of a complete language arts program as presented in this chapter? How does each one develop the components of a complete program as described in this chapter's section on organization of the curriculum? What types of teaching/learning strategies are used?

5   Make your own analyses of a television documentary and two or three commercials, using the strategy in this chapter.

6   If you are working with a primary grade class or early childhood group, make a photo essay or videotape of children's classroom activities using story-

boarding to plan it. If the children are able, have them help. In upper grades, have the children make a photo essay or videotape about their class or the school while you carry out your own project. If you are not working in school, arrange to visit and film or photograph classroom activities. Share with others who have done this your differing selections of images to represent typical, or unusual, classroom experiences.

7 Prepare a sample set of appropriate teacher-evaluate and pupil-evaluation materials covering learning objectives in all areas of the language arts program, at a particular age or grade level. Explain why these evaluation techniques are appropriate.

BIBLIOGRAPHY

Bloom, Benjamin S. (Ed.) *The Taxonomy of Educational Objectives: Cognitive Domain*, New York: McKay, 1956. Classification of objectives and examples of test items.

Brown, James W., Richard B. Lewis, and Fred F. Harcleroad. *AV Instruction: Technology, Media and Methods*. New York: McGraw-Hill, 1973. Guidelines and bibliographies on use of all media including government sources, community resources, realia, free materials. Chapters on audio materials, and attention to visual literacy in chapters on use of pictures, films, television, and photographs.

Croft, Doreen J., and Robert D. Hess. *An Activities Handbook for Teachers of Young Children*. Boston: Houghton Mifflin, 1972. Sections on language activities.

DeStephano, Johanna S., and Sharon E. Fox (Eds.) *Language and the Language Arts*. Boston: Little, Brown, 1974. Articles on linguistics and language arts.

Donoghue, Mildred. *The Child and the English Language Arts*. Dubuque, Iowa: William C. Brown Company Publishers, 1971. Specific teaching suggestions, including chapter on audio-lingual TESL instruction.

Elementary English, March, 1973, **50** (3), Urbana, Ill. National Council of Teachers of English. Entire issue deals with individualizing language instruction.

Eriksson, Marguerite, Ilse Forest, and Ruth Mulhauser. *Foreign Languages in the Elementary School*. Englewood Cliffs, N.J.: Prentice-Hall, 1964. Specific techniques of teaching; sample lessons included.

Finocchiaro, Mary. *Teaching Children Foreign Languages*. New York: McGraw-Hill, 1964. Principles and techniques to use in elementary schools.

Francis, W. Nelson. *The English Language: An Introduction*. New York: Norton, 1965. A reference for the structure of English.

Funk, Hal D., and DeWayne Triplett (Eds.) *Language Arts in the Elementary School: Readings*. Philadelphia: Lippincott, 1972. Articles on all language arts except reading.

Gleason, H. A., Jr. *Linguistics and English Grammar*. New York: Holt, 1965. Evaluations of traditional, structural, and transformational-generative grammar.

Grady, Michael P., and Lawrence J. Baricevic. "Technology, A Creative Use." *Educational Leadership*, February, 1974. **31**:5, 415–417, Discusses use of technology to stimulate creative expression in a school multi-media room.

Greene, Harry A., and Walter T. Petty. *Developing Language Skills in the Elementary Schools*. 4th ed. Boston: Allyn and Bacon, 1974. Chapters on all the language arts.

Henrie, Samuel N. (Senior Ed.) *A Sourcebook of Elementary Curricula Programs and Projects*. Produced by Far West Laboratory. Washington, D.C.: Government Printing Office, 1972. Description of programs, materials, and projects in language arts, visual literacy, foreign language, and bilingual-bicultural education.

Jacobs, Roderick A. "A Short Introduction to Transformational Grammar," *Education*, November, 1965, **86**, 138–141. A concise, useful outline for teachers and curriculum workers.

King, Martha L., Robert Emans, and Patricia J. Cianciolo (Eds.) *The Language Arts in the Elementary School: A Forum for Focus*. Urbana, Ill.: National Council of Teachers of English, 1973. Papers on various aspects of the language arts program, including one on Piaget's views of language and thought.

Krathwohl, David D., Benjamin S. Bloom, and Bertram S. Masia. *Taxonomy of Educational Objectives: Affective Domain*. New York: McKay, 1964. Classification of objectives and sample test items in the area of attitude and value development.

Kuhns, William. *Exploring Television*. Chicago: Loyola University Press, 1971. Text and teacher's guide for critical analysis of commercial television beginning at fifth grade level, with annotated bibliography.

Lado, Robert. *Language Teaching*. New York: McGraw-Hill. 1964. Theory and practice of teaching foreign language based on linguistics.

Laybourne, Kit (Ed.) *Doing the Media: A Portfolio of Activities and Resources*. New York: The Center for Understanding Media, 1972. Specific guidelines and extensive references for using photography, filming, and videotaping in all elementary grades.

Lefevre, Carl A. "A Concise Structural Grammar," *Education*, **86**, 131–137, November, 1965. A brief, useful outline for teachers and curriculum workers.

Marckwardt, Albert H. (Ed.) *Linguistics in School Programs*. 69th Yearbook, Part II. Chicago: National Society for the Study of Education, 1970. Analyses of language and dialects, with applications to classroom instruction.

Michaelis, John U., Ruth H. Grossman, and Lloyd F. Scott, *New Designs for the Elementary School Curriculum*. New York: McGraw-Hill, 1967. Chapter on instruction in foreign language in the elementary school.

Neff, Nancy, and Charles Neff. (compilers) *Aids to Curriculum Planning: English Language Arts K-12*, Urbana, Ill.: National Council of Teachers of English, 1973. Excerpts from curriculum guides on objectives, media, evaluation, and selected language arts.

Olson, David R. (Ed.) *Media and Symbols: The Forms of Expression, Communication, and Education*. 73rd Yearbook, Part I. Chicago: National Society for the Study of Education, 1974. Analysis of media and symbol systems as communication. Chapter XI presents a rationale for visual literacy and use of film in the classroom.

Petty, Walter T., Dorothy C. Petty, and Marjorie F. Becking. *Experiences in Language*. Boston: Allyn and Bacon, 1973. Specific instructional suggestions and references.

Phenix, Philip H. *Realms of Meaning*. New York: McGraw-Hill, 1964. A philosophy of curriculum development. Chapter 5 discusses the structure of language.

Sapir, Edward. *Language*. New York: Harcourt, Brace, 1921. A classic reference for the structure of language.

Shane, Harold G., James Walden, and Ronald Green (Eds.) *Interpreting Language Arts Research for the Teacher*. Washington, D.C.: Association for Supervision and Curriculum Development, 1971. Concise summary of research findings in all areas of the language arts program with extensive list of references.

Smith, E. Brooks, Kenneth S. Goodman, and Robert Meredity. *Language and Thinking in the Elementary School*. New York: Holt, 1970. Interrelationship of language and thinking skills, and guidelines for teaching aspects of language arts. Chapter 6 outlines and relates views of Piaget and Vygotsky. Chapter 10 suggests guidelines for the language arts program.

Smith, James A. *Creative Teaching of the Language Arts in the Elementary School*. Boston: Allyn and Bacon, 1967. Specific instructional suggestions with a focus on creative thinking in all areas of the language arts program.

Spodek, Bernard. *Teaching in the Early Years*. Englewood Cliffs, N.J.: Prentice-Hall, 1972. Chapter on language learning.

Strickland, Ruth G. *The Language Arts in the Elementary School*. Boston: Heath, 1969. Comprehensive treatment of language arts instruction.

Chapter 10

Reading

The act of reading is the process of discovering meaning in written language. Meaning comes from an interaction of the reader's experiential background and language competencies with the written message of an author. It is a complex process that begins with decoding written language and is influenced by the reader's language and experience, attitude and motivation, sensory perception, and comprehension abilities.

Framework in Reading, *1972, p. xi*

Russell identified reading as a thinking process composed of four overlapping stages, shown in Chart 10-1 below: sensation, perception, comprehension, utilization (Russell, 1961, p. 99).

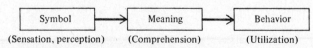

Symbol	Meaning	Behavior
(Sensation, perception)	(Comprehension)	(Utilization)

Chart 10-1 Reading: From symbol recognition to behavior

A comprehensive model of the reading process is thoroughly developed by Ruddell (1974A, pp. 25–46). The model includes all the language arts within a "communication framework." In this model, relationships are indicated among five categories of the communication process. These include oral and written language forms (phonemes, graphemes, morphemes, syntax), aspects of meaning (lexical, syntactic or relational, and nonlinguistic sources of word and sentence meaning), interpretation (integration of meaning at various comprehension-skill levels), memory and feedback (storing of language information among elements in the model), and the category of affective mobilizers (the learner's interests, attitudes, and values) and cognitive strategies (the learner's use of information gathering, hypothesizing, and testing), representing the motivation and goals of the learner.

Reading, according to these views, begins with an "unlearned" response, the visual and mental sensation of graphic symbols. The reader then proceeds to a learned response, association of graphic symbols with specific sounds, an aspect of the reading process often characterized as the "decoding" of graphic symbols into speech.

The oral, or primary, form of language thus decoded serves to stimulate, in the mind of the reader, recall of meanings already possessed, association of ideas or information with known meanings or the reader's experience, or the interpretation and construction of new meanings based on the reader's manipulation of prior concepts and experiences. This comprehension of the meaning of the decoded sounds may be a literal understanding, or extended to higher thought processes and the reader's reaction to what is read in terms of critical analysis, creative interpretation, emotional response, and aesthetic appreciation. Psycholinguistic theories suggest that meaning may be obtained from contextual clues related to the structure of language, even when some words within a passage are not decoded accurately (Goodman, 1973; F. Smith, 1971).

These responses by the reader to the material he reads lead to modifications in thought or behavior which are manifested in his personal and social growth.

The child enters school with an extensive speaking vocabulary, an even more extensive listening vocabulary, a good command of language structure, and some fluency in the use of oral language. The sound symbol that is the spoken word is in itself an abstract representation of reality. The graphic symbol represents a further level of abstraction. Graphic symbols can have little meaning for the child unless there is a concrete or vivid referent for the meaning in his experience and fund of concepts. Therefore, *concept development* must proceed concurrently with reading instruction throughout the elementary grades.

The interrelationships of listening, speaking, reading, and writing, developmentally and instructionally, have been discussed in Chapter 9. Although this chapter focuses on the reading component of the total language arts program, reading instruction and utilization occur throughout the school day, in all activities and content areas. As children gain in vocabulary and concepts through school and personal experiences, as they communicate with peers and adults, as they encounter needs for visual and written materials in content areas, the teacher utilizes these situations to note needs for instruction in particular reading skills, to provide direct reading skill instruction in the context of the situation, or to guide children to apply specific skills learned in "reading lessons" to the needs of the situation.

CONTRIBUTIONS TO MAJOR GOALS

Reading, as a thinking process, is a major contributor to the goal of *thinking ability*, as the reader interacts mentally with the written message to comprehend at literal, inferential, critical, and creative levels. And capable readers have available to them a world of information and ideas, set forth in written forms, to stimulate their own thought and continuing intellectual growth. *Self-realization* is enhanced as skill in reading enables individuals to operate more effectively in educational and work experiences; furthermore, through utilization of both functional and literary materials, individuals learn to develop more completely toward whatever their intellectual, creative, social, or emotional "potential" might be. A direct contribution to the goal of effective *human relationships* may be made by novels, biographies, histories, and current writings that exemplify interpersonal relations or deal with the problems and techniques of past and contemporary human relations issues. Reading opens up avenues of communication between wider ranges of people and enables them to gain knowledge, and, to be hoped, understanding, of others. *Economic competence* is directly furthered as skill is developed in utilizing written material in training for and carrying out occupational tasks, in handling the various technical written material (applications, tax instructions, and the like) in personal situations, and in interpreting advertising as an adroit consumer. Reading as a tool in general learning widens the individual's potential choices for avenues of study and occupation. A literate, informed electorate has always been considered the essential foundation of American democracy; reading instruction has been viewed as a major contributor to the goal of *civic responsibility* since the nation was established. Reading is no less an essential foundation of *learning how to learn* as it is a tool of learning, opening to the learner all the written sources of information and ideas available to him. Reading instruction involves development and application of thinking skills and study skills. Most important, a reading program that helps children to enjoy reading, that motivates them to read, enables them to become lifelong learners.

OBJECTIVES OF THE READING PROGRAM

Although many of the objectives outlined in the previous chapter also contribute to the reading program, the following are important specific goals of the reading component of the program.

Conceptual Objectives

To develop understandings that enable children to do the following:

Acquire an increasing vocabulary and fund of concepts

Interpret literal, connotative, and figurative meanings of words and use of language

Become familiar with various literary forms and styles

Utilize the organizational structure of various forms of functional material

Utilize knowledge of language syntax to derive meaning from written material

Comprehend what is read by identifying main ideas, recognizing supporting details, identifying sequential events, following written directions, interpreting character or motivation, predicting outcomes or effects, and the like

Inquiry Objectives

To develop skill in using processes of inquiry so that children are able to do the following:

Think critically and creatively about what is read, organizing ideas, inferring implicit meanings, evaluating conclusions, and applying ideas to daily life

Distinguish between expressions of fact and opinion

Develop criteria or aesthetic standards for evaluating author bias or objectivity, accuracy of information or reliability of source, and literary merit of written materials

Develop imaginative thinking through encounters with literature

Skills Objectives

To develop skills needed to enable children to do the following:

Utilize a variety of word-attack strategies leading to independence in reading

Read silently with comprehension and appropriate speed

Read effectively for differing purposes, adapting rates of reading to specific purposes

Read orally with appropriate expression and pace

Utilize the structure and organization of written material (table of contents, index, section headings, format, and the like) to maximize information, ideas, or enjoyment gained from the material

Locate various forms of written information, select and evaluate a variety of reference materials, and organize information derived from these sources

Affective Objectives

To foster attitudes and values that enable children to do the following:

Recognize that reading is a thinking process and an active process of communication

Acquire the motivation for permanent interest in functional and recreational reading

Develop refined literary tastes and appreciations

Acquire an appreciation of the ways in which reading can enrich life, extend experiences, and increase their understanding of the world and all its people

ORGANIZATION OF THE CURRICULUM

The reading component of the total language arts program includes development of skills in decoding and comprehension in order to utilize functional and literary written material. Decoding skills are procedures for recognizing sounds and words represented by written symbols. Comprehension skills involve application of thought processes to obtain meaning from what is decoded. Utilization of functional writing includes derivation of information from such sources as newspapers, textbooks, and reference materials, following of written directions, interpretation of written material in vocational tasks, and the like. Literature involves development of interests and tastes for lifelong recreational reading. All these aspects of the reading program depend on continual and concurrent concept and vocabulary development, as discussed in Chapter 9. Some curricula specify instruction in oral reading. This aspect involves learning to read with expression to convey interpreted meaning (not "round-robin" re-reading) and overlaps with oral expression activities discussed in Chapter 9.

The hidden curriculum in reading instruction comes about through practices that affect children's attitudes toward themselves and toward reading. For example:

Children who are organized for an entire year into "group 1," "group 2," and so on for reading, or are seated all day according to reading groups, may learn to view themselves and others in terms of the relative status of each group.

The teacher who smilingly asks, "Did you like this story?" may give children the impression that "yes" is the acceptable response and that classroom success means meeting teacher expectations and avoiding independent opinion. The teacher who asks, "What did you think of this story?" expresses respect for the individual and encourages children to value independence in thinking.

If "readers" are the only books in the classroom, children may learn that the purpose of "doing reading" is to learn to read the reader, with little notion of the many ways they ought to be able to use reading skills. A room with many, varied, readily accessible books and time for independent reading during the day enables children to learn that reading is enjoyable and serves personal, self-directed needs.

Decoding

Word analysis involves the decoding of phoneme-grapheme correspondence and the recognition of whole words. Most reading experts agree that no single word-analysis technique is adequate for all situations because of the phonetic irregularities of English and the differences in children's individual learning styles. When an eclectic approach is used, the several techniques are usually introduced in the following sequence: sight vocabulary, configuration, picture clues, context clues, phonetic analysis, structural analysis, and use of the dictionary.

Many educators recommend that children be taught to recognize some words in their entirety as a first step in learning to read. The graphic pattern of the whole word thus becomes the symbol corresponding to the total sound symbols of the spoken word. Each word is unique; there is no generalization of phoneme-grapheme correspondence from one word to another. The intent of this recommendation is twofold: (1) to provide about fifty to one hundred words, recognized by the child, which can be used as examples for the development of phonetic and structural analysis skills, and (2) to give the child practice in reading whole sentences with understanding sooner than would be possible on the basis of phonetic analysis. The child thus comes to understand reading as a process of deriving meaning, not merely sounds, from graphic symbols. Selection of words for the child's sight vocabulary is largely at each teacher's discretion. Words are usually chosen on the basis of their use in curricular activities, the special interests of the class, high frequency of use in the children's oral vocabulary, and appearance in preprimers and primers to be used by the class.

Some linguistic scholars oppose this approach and instead recommend that reading instruction begin with the learning of the alphabet, grapheme-phoneme correspondence of initial consonant sounds, and the introduction of phonetically regular short-vowel one-syllable words and phonograms. Other linguists maintain that this procedure limits the child's derivation of *meaning* from graphic symbols. They recommend that structural or functional words and some words of high frequency of use in the child's oral vocabulary be introduced as sight words concurrent with instruction in phonetic and structural analysis principles consistent with linguistic principles of the structure of English.

When sight words are used, children are taught to recall and recognize them by means of configuration, picture, and context clues. These techniques involve analysis of length, height, letter shapes, and overall configuration of a printed word; observing and interpreting pictorial illustrations; making inferences beyond the literal content of illustrations; and grasping word meaning on the basis of a word's position in a sentence, the meaning of adjacent words, or the meaning of the total context of the passage.

These context clues are referred to, respectively, as relational or syntactic (grammatical structure as a clue), lexical (denotive or connotative word meanings), and interpretive or organizational (Ruddell 1974a; 1974b; pp. 290-297). Increased attention is being given to direct instruction in the use of context clues at all grade levels because the thinking processes involved are consistent with the definition of reading as a process of deriving *meaning* from written material. F. Smith (1971) provides a thorough exposition and detailed analysis of this view of reading as an inquiry process. A technique for systematic analysis of children's strategies for decoding and deriving meaning that can be used to plan context-clue instruction is provided through miscue analysis (Goodman, 1973; Ruddell, 1974b, pp. 396–405). This technique is discussed further in the section on teaching strategies.

Phonetic analysis is the identification of sounds in printed words. Instruction in this skill, phonics, is the application of phonetic principles to reading and spelling instruction. There is general agreement in most courses of study on the sequence in which principles of phonetic analysis are introduced.

1   Phoneme-grapheme correspondence of initial consonant sounds
2   Consonant digraphs: ch, sh, wh, th, ck, ph
3   Consonant blends: bl, br, cl, dr, str, etc.
4   Short vowel sounds in single syllables, phonograms
5   Final e rule for long vowel sounds
6   Vowel digraphs: au, ai, ay, ee, ie, oa, oe
7   Diphthongs, blended vowels: oi, oy, ow, ou
8   Variant vowel sounds, vowels followed by r, w, ll
9   Sound of soft c and g
10   Silent letters in consonant combinations: kn, ght, mb, lm, lk, gh, wr, gn, ps

While phonetic analysis deals with graphic representations of sound, structural analysis deals with visual observation and word meaning, as children identify the parts of a word which form meaningful units. Words may be grouped into three structural categories: root words with inflectional changes, root words with affixes, and compound words. In addition, polysyllabic words may be separated into their syllabic construction, with phonetic analysis techniques applied to separate syllables. Each specific inflectional change and each use of an affix constitutes a structural analysis principle. There are numerous generalizations regarding syllabication, as well. A few examples are listed below:

I.   *Root words with inflectional changes*
    A.   Endings: ed, ing, s, es, est, er, 's
    B.   Internal changes: man/men, run/ran
II.   *Root words with affixes*
    A.   Definitions of roots: duc = lead, graph = write
    B.   Definitions of prefixes: anti = against, ex = out of, from
    C.   Definitions of suffixes: -ant = being, one who, -ic = like, made of, -less = without
III.   *Compound words*
    A.   Two root words combined: chalkboard, maybe, merry-go-round
    B.   Contractions: can't = cannot, he'd = he had, he would
IV.   *Syllabication*
    A.   There are as many syllables in a word as there are sounded vowels.
    B.   When a consonant occurs between two vowels, the first syllable is usually open and has a long vowel sound (o-bey, ba-by).

Children learn to use the dictionary to check spelling and syllabication; learn word meanings; investigate word derivations, discover synonyms, antonyms, or variant meanings; and determine proper pronunciation. They can begin to use picture dictionaries in the earliest grades after learning alphabetical order. As they explore various dictionaries in later grades, they may be guided to discover such generalizations as the extension of alphabetizing beyond the initial letter of a word, the letters marking the dictionary into thirds or quarters for convenient reference, and the meanings of accent marks, diacritical marks, and the international phonetic alphabet.

Some other approaches to the teaching of beginning reading deal with the problems of word recognition in differing ways. One approach, Words in Color (Aukerman, 1971, pp. 356–367), uses letters in forty-seven different colors and shades in order to identify that number of phonemes in the English language. The color used for a phoneme is constant, regardless of the varying spellings of the sound. After children have learned to associate sounds and colors, they are taught to write and read familiar materials in black and white.

Another approach receiving wide attention employs the Pitman Initial Teaching Alphabet (i/t/a). This augmented alphabet supplies forty-four symbols for a one-to-one correspondence with the distinctive phonemes of English (Aukerman, 1971, pp. 330–344). Children are taught to recognize the sound-symbol relationships, which, unlike the spelling of words in traditional orthography (TO), remain constant. When children have reached a level of independence in reading corresponding to the third-reader level, they begin a transition to traditional orthography. Proponents of the program state that most children taught to read with i/t/a make the transition at the end of the first grade. Because of the regularity of grapheme-phoneme correspondence, teachers using i/t/a have found that the first- and second-grade pupils are more fluent and prolific in their independent written expression than are pupils who learn to read through traditional orthography. However, difficulty with spelling in TO has been noted.

Chart 10-2 Initial teaching alphabet

Comprehension Skills

Comprehension skills may be considered in terms of three categories related to thinking qualities: literal comprehension, critical comprehension, and appreciative comprehension. "Interpretive" comprehension is a term applied to either of the last two categories, since both involve interpretation. These are not mutually exclusive categories; literal comprehension is basic to other levels, and children may utilize all three levels with any given reading material, depending upon their purposes in reading.

Literal comprehension involves the following skills:

1   Understanding the main idea of paragraphs, stories, and other forms of written language
2   Noting details, finding relevant details to answer questions, support viewpoints, or contribute to other comprehension skills
3   Following sequences and predicting outcomes of stories and descriptions
4   Following directions, which involves sequence and details

Critical comprehension involves:

5   Critical evaluation; noting relevancy and irrelevancy, distinguishing between fact and opinion, comparing, evaluating the authenticity of a source of information, determining veracity or bias of materials that are read, evaluating author's viewpoint, purpose, style, and qualifications
6   Seeing implied relationships and hidden meanings; identifying persuasive use of words and propaganda techniques
7   Identifying or inferring cause-effect relationships
8   Interpreting and explaining; summarizing, organizing, synthesizing ideas or information
9   Drawing conclusions, deriving generalizations, and making inferences on the basis of what is read

Appreciative comprehension involves:

10   Noting elements of style in writing, and use of figurative language
11   Obtaining sensory impressions from descriptive writing
12   Sensing mood, feeling, and atmosphere created by elements of writing style
13   Identifying with characters; understanding motivation and relationships in story or narrative
14   Sensing humor, satire, nonsense, and exaggeration and understanding their purpose in what is read
15   Relating ideas and feelings to personal experience
16   Analyzing character, setting, and plot
17   Interpreting and responding to poetic meaning and imagery

Thinking skills involved in literal comprehension are primarily those at the knowledge level of the cognitive taxonomy (Bloom, 1956), with higher levels of thinking and affective responses at all levels (Krathwohl et al., 1964), coming into play at the critical and appreciative levels. Barrett (Robinson, 1968, pp. 19-23) has outlined a five-level taxonomy for reading comprehension incorporating cognitive and affective dimensions: literal comprehension, involving recognition and recall; reorganization, involving analyzing, classifying, organizing, summarizing, and synthesizing; inferential comprehension; evaluation, corresponding to critical comprehension; appreciation, corresponding to appreciative comprehension.

Critical reading is the application of critical comprehension skills; creative reading is the application of appreciative comprehension skills. Beginning readers must devote much attention to grappling with literal comprehension skills during initial stages of their instruction. But the effective teacher will begin development of critical and appreciative comprehension skills suitable to the level of children's mental maturity and the nature of their reading materials concurrently with skills at the literal level. Early training in critical reading is necessary to meet current objectives of education, which place a high value on the child's ability to think.

Reading in the Subject Areas

Use of such functional written materials as letters, reference sources, newspapers, magazines, and advertisements has been discussed in Chapter 9, along with general reference and study skills applicable to all content areas. All the reading comprehension skills listed above are applicable, in varying ways, to reading for meaning in subject area materials. However, additional specific reading instruction is needed in the context of each subject area because of differences in the format, sequence of content, style, vocabulary, syntax, symbols, and types of visual aids found in textbooks in each area. All these materials differ from the structure and content of basal readers and children's literature; reading skills developed with these materials are not automatically transferred to reading in textbooks and reference sources. Above all, in each subject area, relevant concepts must be developed before children can obtain meaning from written material.

Social studies textbooks seem, at first glance, to resemble reading books, but the resemblance is superficial. Stories are read and forgotten as unrelated stories are encountered, but important facts, significant concepts, and major generalizations acquired during earlier readings must be available for recall as the child progresses through the social studies textbook. Sentences are longer and more complex, more information is packed into each sentence, and each paragraph may deal with several complex and imprecise concepts. Both factual and opinionated material may be included, leading to a need for skill in distinguishing fact, opinion, and bias. Reproductions of facsimiles of documents may be included in the text; each of these requires specific comprehension and utilization skills. Unlike other subject areas, social studies courses may have several textbooks, requiring skill in making comparisons of sources and applying other critical comprehension skills. The child will also need to skim for information, locate relevant details, relate main and subordinate ideas, note cause-effect relationships, relate what he reads to his own experiences, be alert to propaganda devices, classify, attain concepts, draw conclusions, formulate generalizations, and make inferences.

Many of these skills also apply to reading in science textbooks. In addition, textbooks and materials in both areas utilize illustrations and diagrams which are essential to understanding. Unlike the social studies book, the science textbook may have several self-contained sections or units, with less book-long continuity of concepts. Like arithmetic, science employs a highly technical vocabulary, involves precise concepts, and requires the reading of various measurement devices. The child needs skill in following a sequence or cluster of relevant details, locating information for problem solving, interpreting cause-effect relationships and correlations, reading for precise information, following directions for research and experiments, and identifying classification patterns.

Arithmetic textbooks have a unique sequence of organization. Topics such as numeration, measurement, subtraction, or multiplication are not dealt with as units, but are developed sequentially throughout the book. The child spends a page or two on one topic, goes on to another, and picks up the next step in the first topic after several other topics have intervened. (Of course, teachers may alter the sequence in their instruction if they deem it necessary.) The child needs to read at a pace that will ensure accuracy of understanding and grasp of all details. He will have to retain facts, concepts, and generalizations related to each topic. The information he encounters is given in quantitative and pictorial symbols which he must translate into words, phrases, or sentences, such as $6 + 4 = 10$ or $50 \div x = 2 \ (x)$. Symbols such as $U, (\ ), \neq$, must be translated into words which have meaning at a conceptual level. Verbal statements of quantitative problems have unique syntactical structures that call for specific skills in determining questions, selecting relevant information, and choosing appropriate processes. In addition, as he is reading, the child often needs to form visual images of what he reads.

Readings in the areas of art and music are similar to those in social studies and science, in that special terms and symbols are used, processes are described, directions are given, and historical or biographical narratives are read.

Literature

The school is often the child's major contact with various forms of literature. This encounter should be designed to provide him with opportunities for enjoyment and creativity; with an extension of his experiences, interests, vocabulary, and understanding; and with an enrichment, through related literature, of learnings in all subject areas.

As the child is introduced to poetry, stories, trade books, plays, and the creative written expression in his own classroom, he learns not merely to recognize, but to use, the different structural forms and elements of literature. He also encounters recurring literary themes and discovers man's use of literary forms to express human feelings and ideas through all ages of recorded history.

Effective teachers provide a classroom atmosphere conducive to the enjoyment of literature. Materials are made available which represent a broad range of reading levels and content as well as a variety of sources and forms. All the language arts come into play as children listen to poems and stories read aloud, recite or dramatize what they hear or read, and discuss what they have heard, read, enacted, and written. They utilize different literary forms in their creative written expression, and, of course, they are provided with time to read.

Professional publications and recent courses of study recommend an emphasis on enjoyment and stimulation of children's creative power by providing a relaxed atmosphere in which children are free to respond in divergent ways. Overanalysis of form and meaning is not encouraged. Instead, children should discover elements of form and express their own interpretations of meaning. Although the literature studied carefully by the entire class may be, in a sense, prescribed in order to contribute to the sequential development of specific concepts, an important goal of literature experiences in the classroom is the development of the child's independence in reading as he is given the opportunity for self-selection of materials and thoughtful, individualized appraisal of what he reads. Recreational reading provides the child with opportunities to apply his reading skills to areas of his own interests and permits a greater degree of individualization of learning.

Increased attention is being given to the need to supplement and enrich children's experiences by introducing literature to children more familiar with films and television. Literature is viewed as more stimulating to development of imagination because readers must draw their own visual images from literary language. Emphasis is on active response in the form of discussion, creative expression, and relation of what is read to their own experiences. This is sometimes extended to bibliotherapy, the use of books, stories, or poems to increase self-understanding, enhance self-concept, or aid social adjustment through the identification or response of the reader to characters, values, or problems in the literary work. This identification can lead to catharsis, the feeling that the reader shares the experiences or ideas about which he or she is reading. This empathetic experience may in turn lead to insights into one's own feelings, changes in values, or solutions to one's own similar problems (Russell, 1970). Although some individual bibliotherapy needs to be handled by specialists in a clinical setting, the classroom teacher will often find opportunities to provide individuals with one of the more realistic children's books available today to help them cope with such concerns as new siblings, awkwardness, or loss of a pet.

Oral Reading

During early instruction, oral reading is used by the teacher to evaluate the child's association of sounds and graphic symbols. At all reading levels, the teacher listens as the child reads in order to determine his ability to see and comprehend words in idea units of meaningful phrases. Direct instruction in the oral reading skills of eye span and vocal phrasing helps the child to read silently in idea units.

Oral reading serves to enhance reading and thinking skills when children select a passage to read aloud in order to answer questions, share information, prove a point, interpret meaning through oral expression, share favorite passages, highlight colorful writing, or entertain others. Children should be helped to formulate standards for oral expression as well as for the listening skills that constitute appropriate responses to the purposes for oral reading.

One of the systems of language structure that provides signals for meaning is intonation: pitch, stress, juncture, and pauses. Children need to learn, as they are learning graphemes formed by letters, that the punctuation graphemes also correspond to sounds and to durations of silence between sounds and that these sounds and silences convey meaning.

Sequence of the Reading Program

Children proceed through a sequence of stages in learning to read, although individuals differ considerably in their rate of progress through each stage and from one stage to another. These stages may be described as readiness, beginning reading, increased growth, and independence.

Children are usually "ready" to learn to read when they have attained an adequate level of skill (as measured by tests, checklists, observation of behavior, discussion) in the following:

Visual discrimination: The ability to differentiate between similar letter forms and word configurations

Auditory discrimination: The ability to perceive and identify differences between similar sounds

Motor skills: Ability to orient body in directions (left, right, up, down, back, forward); ability to copy simple shapes or symbols with chalk, crayon, or pencil

Language skills: Adequate vocabulary in standard or dialect English; ability to express ideas orally in connected sentences; ability to retell a simple story in one's own words, and follow a simple sequence of directions

Cognitive skills: Ability to recall, classify, and order things in a sequence (smallest to largest, day to day, etc.)

Motivation: Ability to pay attention in an activity for five to ten minutes; expression of interest in stories read to the children; examines books available in the classroom; asks for labels for drawings; enjoys dictating stories for teacher or classroom aides to write

Many educators believe that either a mental age between six and seven, or the attainment of what Piaget describes as the stage of concrete operations at about the chronological age of seven, is the level of intellectual development requisite for ability to learn to read. They recommend a program of enriching, firsthand experiences to develop concepts and cognitive growth for children in preschool and kindergarten programs, without formal instruction. Others believe that the skills listed above need not be fully attained, as they can be developed or enhanced through provision of guided experiences or direct instruction. Open classrooms and Montessori schools follow the first view and provide settings in which materials are available and experiences are varied, and individuals are given materials and instruction for reading and writing only when each one expresses overt interest. In other preschool programs, four- or five-year-olds may be given direct drill practice in "school language" or in visual and auditory discrimination skills. A few school systems begin formal reading instruction in kindergarten for some, if not all, children. Most school systems provide something between these alternatives, a "readiness" program in kindergarten and early first grade, which usually includes reading stories to children, encouraging them to compose their own, providing game experiences that develop visual, auditory, motor, and cognitive skills, and providing firsthand experiences as discussed in Chapter 9.

The stage of beginning reading involves initial instruction in decoding and comprehension. Four broad approaches to beginning reading include individualized reading, use of basal textbooks, the language-experience approach, and the multimedia approach.

"Individualized reading" is a term applied to procedures which may vary but which have the following characteristics in common: (1) availability in the classroom of numerous trade books, library books, magazines, and other materials in a wide range of reading levels and topics; (2) the teacher's observation, encouragement, and guidance of self-selection of books by pupils; (3) children's progression from one book to another at their own pace; (4) development and evaluation of comprehension primarily through individual pupil-teacher conferences.

The basal approach uses a series of graded textbooks with a selection of increasingly longer, more complex stories and a sequential development of vocabulary, word analysis, and comprehension skills. Initial instruction usually includes development of sight vocabulary, but some texts developed with the participation of linguists use a vocabulary limited to words that conform to regular sound-symbol relationships. Concomitant attempts are being made to write primary-grade stories in the manner of children's natural speech patterns to facilitate comprehension. There is a trend toward inclusion of excerpts of works of children's literature in order to improve literary quality and acquaint the child with the best of classic and recent poems, stories, and essays. Several recent basal series include multiethnic content, stories of integrated groups of people in urban settings. The purpose of these books is to overcome the difficulties in comprehension that the disadvantaged urban child may encounter when he must read stories unrelated to his sociocultural environment. Attention is also being given to avoidance of stereotypes in male and female roles.

A third type of program is based on the assumption that children can more easily read material that they have written. The "experience" program in the primary grades usually begins with provision for enriching curricular and co-curricular experiences of the pupils. Children are then guided to record their personal and group experiences in their own words. These charts constitute the children's major reading material, but discussion and related activities lead to reading of related trade books.

A similar program for slow readers in the upper elementary grades utilizes creative writing and retelling stories to a greater extent than it does personal experience. It is referred to as the "multimedia approach" because it uses films, records, dramatizations, and other media to stimulate intensive discussion of topics of interest, to generate creative ideas, or to present a story to be retold in the pupils' own words. The resultant reports, discussion summaries, or stories are duplicated and read by the group or class. The experience and multimedia approaches actually go beyond reading instruction; they are strategies for the simultaneous development of skills in all the language arts. This approach provides children who are in the beginning stage of reading at an upper- or middle-school level with materials, content, and teaching/learning experiences appropriate to their developmental and interest levels.

Each approach has particular advantages and limitations, and children differ in the ways they learn most effectively. Rather than adopting one approach exactly as it is described or defined, teachers can modify a basic approach to meet specific needs and overcome limitations. For example, some instruction in word analysis or comprehension can be done in small groups within an individualized program. Basal reading instruction can be supplemented with individual selection of tradebooks and use of experience stories to suit content to individual interests. Language-experience approaches can incorporate some use of basal books, or the suggestions in the teacher's manual, to develop specific comprehension skills. In addition, a variety of instructional materials can be used within any of these approaches. Commercially produced programs provide guided workbooks, programmed instructional materials, or charts and manipulative materials for development of phonetic analysis. Machines like the "talking typewriter" (or Edison Responsive Environment), a computer-based typewriter with sound tape and visual screen, can be used for individualized practice with word analysis, spelling, and sentence formation.

During the stage of increased growth in reading, children extend their use of a variety of word recognition techniques and begin to use dictionaries for word meaning, spelling, and pronunciation. Vocabulary is expanded, comprehension skills are advanced, and greater use of reading is made in subject areas. Independent selection of reading material for information and recreational reading begins.

Children have reached the stage of independence in reading when they are able to locate and utilize a variety of materials, read with understanding in the subject areas, are aware of varied purposes for reading, and have developed skills of critical evaluation of material read. Their reading interests are extended and literary tastes or values are refined, and they begin to use reading as a tool in problem solving. All these skills, of course, continue to be developed into adult life.

Related Questions and Activities Thinking skills at all levels are developed and applied as children learn to read. Some examples follow:

Have several children each retell part of a story in sequence. (recalling)

What are the meanings of the words "wise," "clever," "smart," "shrewd," and "crafty?" How are these meanings alike, and how do they differ? (comparing, defining)

What other words begin with this sound? (classifying)

Have groups of children act out scenes from favorite stories. (interpreting)

What problems do (the story characters) face? What do you think they will do next? Why? (predicting, hypothesizing)

What can we say about the sound of vowels in these words that end with a silent e? (generalizing)

What character traits did the leading characters in these four stories have in common? How were these traits related to the course of action each one followed? (generalizing)

ORGANIZING FOR INSTRUCTION

Various forms of school-wide organization have been described in Chapter 6. In the Joplin and dual-progress plans, reading instruction takes place at a specific time, with all children in a school, or in a group of classes, moving to different locations for instruction in ability or achievement-level groups. Instruction may be further individualized within groups. However, this form of organization limits integration of reading instruction with other aspects of language arts and with development of reading skills in content areas.

In some schools, children are assigned to self-contained classes within a grade level on the basis of reading achievement, usually assessed by a single norm-referenced standardized test. This form of organization, "homogeneous grouping," does little to reduce intraclass differences because reading abilities vary at any given achievement level, and variations in other abilities, in achievement levels, and in learning styles may not be reduced. Research shows little or no difference in reading achievement between homogeneously and heterogeneously grouped classes, and many educators suggest that homogeneous grouping limits social interaction between children of different achievement levels and has an undesirable effect on self-concept at all levels.

In ungraded and multigraded self-contained classes, use is made of individualized and small-group instruction, often in combination. Whole-class instruction in *reading skills* is not effective in meeting individual differences even in homogeneously grouped graded classes. Of course, there are many occasions when reading enjoyment and comprehension are furthered by means of such whole-class activities as trips, dramatics, storytelling, films, and the like. Small-group instruction within a classroom is a means of reducing some learning differences if such organization is flexible, rather than permanently fixed for the school year. Children grouped by ability or achievement level should be able to move into other or newly formed groups when their learning levels change. An alternative is the group formed on the basis of a common need discerned by the teacher and disbanded when that learning objective has been attained. To supplement both of these organizations, children of differing achievement levels can work together in groups for such activities as planning a book fair, preparing a puppet show, or sharing opinions of books in an area of common interest.

Individualized reading has been described earlier in this chapter. Open classrooms based on the British infant school model use a similar but somewhat more informal approach. In an individualized program, children usually spend a certain amount of time in specific reading activities each day and confer with the teacher at regularly scheduled intervals. In an open classroom program, a child might not be expected to engage in what may be designated as specific reading activities every day, as other projects or activities may occupy a full day or so, and the teacher might work with a child at any time for brief instruction, consultation, or evaluation. In both of these forms of organization, the teacher selects or makes available a variety of books and materials and is responsible for continuous curriculum making for each child in terms of guidance in selection of books and the content and procedures of each instructional interaction with that child. A more formal, commercially produced program, "Individually Prescribed Instruction," provides multimedia materials and specific, preplanned lesson activities or exercises. The teacher assigns a lesson to a child, who follows the directions in the lesson assignment by selecting the specified work sheets and other materials, carrying out independently, and evaluating, alone or with the teacher, the completed work. On the basis of this evaluation, the teacher then assigns the appropriate lesson for the next day. In all these forms of individualized instruction, children are also brought together from time to time in interest, activity, or learning-need groups, or for appropriate whole-class experiences.

INSTRUCTIONAL MEDIA

All the media listed in Chapter 9 apply, of course, to the development of reading in the total language arts program. Additional media and resources for reading instruction include the following.

Printed Media

Basal textbook series, with workbooks, and sometimes additional manipulative, printed, or audio-visual materials
Content area textbooks and related printed and visual materials

Tradebooks (children's literature and poetry)

Newspapers, periodicals

Programmed instruction books

Comprehension skills workbooks and kits (McCall-Crabbs, Gates-Peardon, Reader's Digest Skill Builders, SRA Reading Laboratories, Random House Pacesetters, etc.)

Tests: diagnostic, achievement, informal

Activity cards, flash cards, charts of letter-sound correspondence

Charts for experience stories, word lists, etc.

Audio-visual Media

Tape recorder for use by children and use of commercial programmed tapes for phonics practice

Instructional machines; tachistoscope for focus on words or rate of reading, computer-assisted typewriter terminals

Films and filmstrips, including those made by children

Picture sets, photographic essays, children's pictures

Television and radio programs

Community Resources

School library or media center and librarians

Community library and museum facilities and personnel

Children's book clubs

Environmental material; familiar product packages, store signs, street signs and traffic signs, posters, signs on trucks and buses, etc.

Storytellers; community residents who can tell about events of earlier days, or know stories from other regions or other countries

TEACHING STRATEGIES

The teaching strategies outlined below are general models. Within the framework of each model, a variety of activities and materials may be used. Suggestions for these may be found in "methods" textbooks such as those in the references at the end of this chapter, in current professional publications and periodicals, and in teacher's guides for basal readers.

Guided Reading

This strategy is usually used with basal readers, but it is applicable to the reading of newspaper or periodical articles or pupil-written materials. Although the stories and selections in basal readers follow a sequence, any material that is not suited to learners in a particular class may be omitted. Teachers should also be flexible in using workbooks and make differing assignments in their use for each child according to his or her learning needs.

1 Determining objectives. The specific understandings, reading skills, and/or attitudes to be developed in the lesson should be determined on the basis of

the particular learning needs of the children, rather than just those objectives in the teacher's guide. Select reading material that is suitable for these objectives, of course, rather than using the basal textbook as an unalterable curriculum.

2 Providing background. Briefly discuss the setting or some aspect of the content of the story or article. If these elements are unfamiliar to the children, provide pictures, objects, or other appropriate materials to give them a reference as concrete as possible.

3 Introducing vocabulary. Some unfamiliar words may be identified during background discussion. Present them visually in the context of sentences that form a brief "story" to emphasize word meaning and use of context clues. Have children apply word-recognition skills to decoding of new words and ask them for their own sentences using these words.

4 Setting purposes for reading. Refer to illustrations, title, the background discussion, or the new words to elicit children's anticipation of the content of the story or article. Use their responses to formulate questions to guide reading, adding any other questions necessary. These questions should be written out, so children can refer to them from time to time as they read.

5 Silent reading. Children read the entire story or article, when this is within their skill and comprehension levels. If the teacher is not using this time to work with other groups or individuals, the children should be observed to note whether any are pointing, vocalizing, or squinting as they read. There is no reason to have them re-read the entire selection aloud unless it is a poem or lends itself to dramatization, in which cases development of expressive oral reading skills would be a purpose of the lesson.

6 Discussion. Begin with open-ended questions to elicit responses to the material. Then have children answer the questions raised in step 4.

7 Building or extending skills. Use earlier questions or additional ones in a comprehension-skills strategy such as the one outlined later in this section. Workbook pages or other materials might be used to provide practice and reinforcement.

8 Evaluating. Teachers and pupils should jointly assess attainment of skills or comprehension based on each one's oral responses and any written work related to the lesson.

9 Extending comprehension or interests. Provide opportunities for a variety of follow-up activities in other curriculum areas; constructing models of places in stories, locating them on maps and globes, dramatizing or illustrating, writing one's own poem or story related to the form or content of the reading selection, reading other books or stories, and the like.

Using Experience Charts

This strategy, a basic procedure in a language-experience or multimedia approach, is useful in any instructional program. The experience used to stimulate a story, poem, narrative, or description might be a trip, the first snow, new pets, a favorite television program, a film, an experiment, a simulation or role-playing activity in social studies, and the like. Upper- and intermediate-grade children at beginning or early reading levels can also utilize many content area experiences as they write an historical account based on a filmstrip, prepare a list of guidelines for effective discussion, or storyboard a photographic essay.

The underlying principle of experience charts is that children can read materials they dictate in their own words and can comprehend the material because it is drawn from their own experiences or interests. To introduce new sight vocabulary, or new words for development of phonetic analysis skills, the teacher provides, or has children recall, an experience that will include the use of such words.

Charts should be developed with small groups to provide each child with opportunities to participate. Experience stories can be shared with other groups. The development of group-composed stories can be used as a preliminary step in encouraging individual oral and written composition.

Steps 1 through 4 or 5 might be done on one day, the remainder the next day.

1 Providing or recalling the stimulus. Have pupils discuss the experience briefly enough to maintain interest but long enough for all to participate.

2 Eliciting statements. Ask children for a title to guide relevant contributions to the composition. Write out the children's sentences on the chalkboard or large sheets of paper, using the children's words and syntax. (However, words should be spelled in standard English form, even if pronounced in variant ways.) Use questions or clues to elicit new words for sight vocabulary or word analysis. Call attention to these words if they arise in the discussion in step 1.

3 Organizing the composition. Have pupils put the statements in sequence. In upper grades, statements might be grouped to form paragraphs. Use manuscript print to transcribe the sentences to a chart.

4 Reading the chart. Have children take turns reading the chart. Younger children might each read a sentence, while older ones might read a paragraph. Avoid pointing to each word to prevent reading word by word.

5 Building word-recognition skills. Have children point out the new words introduced. Have each one write a word on the chalkboard, and have all of them write the new words on individual chalkboards or notebook word lists.

6 Extending word-recognition skills. On the following day, have children review the new words and point out the word recognition skills they use. If new words were introduced to develop a particular sound-letter correspondence or form of analysis, provide or elicit additional examples.

7 Reinforcing reading skills. Have children re-read the chart, and match a sentence copied onto a strip of oaktag with the corresponding sentence on the chart. Do the same with words that are new or need review.

8 Extending learning. Provide a variety of follow-up activities for individuals or small groups; reading easy tradebooks on related topics, illustrating the chart, writing individual stories, and the like. Keep the chart on display for a while. It may be added to a large "book" of class stories or duplicated for individual folders.

Individualized Reading Conference

This strategy, used in an individualized approach, can also be used to provide some individual attention from time to time in other types of programs.

1   Developing comprehension skills. Ask the child for opinions about the story or book he or she has read. After the child has responded to open-ended questions, use questions at different levels of the cognitive taxonomy to develop literal, critical, and appreciative comprehension skills.

2   Developing word-recognition skills. Have the child read a few passages from the story or book. Note any miscues and determine whether to provide instruction during the conference, plan a reading strategy lesson at another time, or wait a few days to identify and group several children needing the same instruction.

3   Extending learning. Determine next steps and related activities with the child. The teacher should have a notebook for each one, keeping a record of the child's reading selections, noting word analysis needs, and utilizing a checklist of comprehension skills. The teacher may find that the child needs guidance in broadening the range of selected readings. Provision for practice in comprehension skills might be made through commercially produced skills-development booklets or selected workbook exercises. Develop literary analysis through a variety of activities. For example, the child could make a diorama showing the setting of the story or book, a series of pictures showing important actions in the development of the plot, or a written description of the main character. Periodically, children could interest each other in these selections by displaying the dioramas, posting the pictures in random order to raise questions about the story, or duplicating the descriptions in a class newspaper.

Reading in Subject Areas

Three factors need to be considered when subject area textbooks are read. First, children must have an understanding of the concepts in the text based on other, and more concrete, learning experiences if material that is read is to be meaningful. For example, a number problem cannot be read with comprehension if the child does not understand the computational processes it calls for; a passage on electrical circuits means little if the child has not made a model circuit; a chapter on the revolution includes concepts such as independence, liberty, and representation which may be developed in role-playing activities or discussion. Concept development, of course, proceeds through such strategies as those outlined in Chapters 11 through 17.

A second factor is the structure of the subject area textbook as a learning tool. The skill-development strategy outlined in Chapter 9 can be used to enable children to analyze the elements or features of a textbook; the organization (chapters, units, sections), headings and subheadings, glossary, index, graphs, diagrams, maps, illustrations, and so forth. This analysis, and application through use of the organizational structure or a particular learning-aid feature, could take several sessions, after an initial, unguided exploration of the book by each child. Specific learning aids used in the book can be analyzed as they are encountered or needed.

The third factor is the difference in use of language when compared with "readers" and children's literature. Much more attention needs to be given to the exact meaning of key words in a sentence, and the rate of reading is usually slower than that used for recreational reading. Length of passages or number of pages to be read at any one time would usually need to be much shorter than the amount of "story" or other recreational material the child could read.

When all of these factors have been taken into account, children can be taught to read the textbook using a strategy such as the following.

1 Developing vocabulary. Most of the unfamiliar words relevant to a particular topic are related to concepts, and their meaning should be developed in the context of other preliminary experiences. Where possible, essential "new" words would appear on children's picture titles, in experience charts, on maps or collections of objects, on classroom models or diagrams, and so forth. Review any words in the material that may be difficult to decode, and have children apply the word-analysis skills appropriate to their reading level. Beginning readers can utilize sight vocabulary skills to recognize words that have become familiar and important to them through direct and interesting experiences. More advanced readers can apply syllabication and structural analysis skills. If a key word, representing a new concept or process, is defined or explained clearly in the book, guide their reading of that part of the text after their initial survey of the material to be read.

2 Setting purposes for reading. Through background discussion or reference to other learning experiences relevant to the topic, guide the children to raise questions that will aid them in gaining information from the material to be read.

3 Reading silently. Have children read all the specified portion of the material as a survey to get an idea of what is included, how the material is organized, or how various parts are related. Then have them re-read carefully, to meet the purposes or answer the questions set in step 2.

4 Using the reading material. Have children respond to these questions, and to additional questions at literal and critical comprehension levels. Such comprehension skills as reading for details, noting or inferring cause and effect, interpreting, inferring, classifying, analyzing, hypothesizing, predicting, and generalizing are essential for learning in the subject areas. Transfer of these skills from reading of literary material is not automatic because of differences in vocabulary, concept load, and syntax. Therefore, much attention should be given to this phase of the subject-area reading strategy. To guide interpretation of word problems in mathematics, have children analyze sentence structure and identify key words as clues to directions for appropriate mathematical operations.

5 Following up or reinforcing learning. Have children record information gained and relate this to information on the topic obtained from other sources or learning experiences. Children might add data to retrieval charts or maps, prepare diagrams or models, use the information to guide role playing or simulation, and the like.

Literature Strategies

Provision of numerous books in a classroom library and time for recreational reading help to encourage children to read for enjoyment and personal interests. However, many may read at a superficial or literal level. Lessons in literary analysis are needed to enable children to increase their awareness of a varied and extended use of language and of such literary elements as characterization, plot development, and setting, to enhance their enjoyment of a variety of forms of literature and enable them to develop their own criteria and tastes.

The first strategy outlined below provides a framework for analysis of a particular work of literature as well as for comparison of two or more works. The second is a strategy that applies literary analysis to development of children's oral and written expression.

Literary Analysis

1 Presenting the selections. Read the story, poem, or passages aloud, show a film or filmstrip relating to the selection, or refer to selections with which the children are familiar. Encourage children to express their responses without using any structured questions. Avoid *asking* whether or not they liked a selection, but accept responses that express their evaluations whether negative or positive.

2 Analyzing the selections. If a single story, book, poem, or play is to be analyzed, have children identify such elements as the following (although not necessarily all elements in one session, or in the analysis of one particular selection):

Theme Common personal experiences (growing up, family living, attaining a goal, etc.) or universal values (friendship, freedom, courage, honesty, etc.)

Form Types of poems, biography and autobiography, drama, legend and myth, short story, novel (true to life and fantasy)

Plot Sequence, important points (introduction, development, turning point, climax, conclusion), possible alternatives

Character Characteristics of main characters, relation or interaction of characters, motivation of characters, feelings of empathy with particular characters, symbolism or representation by characters (as in myths and legends)

Setting Location in time and place, how setting affects or relates to theme, plot, or characters, how setting is described (descriptive narrative, "color," details)

Use of language Connotations of words, use of similes and metaphors, sentence form (active, passive, etc.)

If two or more selections are to be compared, begin by asking what they have in common. Then guide children to make comparisons of relevant elements (theme, setting, etc.).

3 Expressing personal responses. Have children tell what they might think or do in the setting of the selection, what action they might take if they were in the place of a particular character, or what similarities or contrasts they find between situations in the selection and their own experiences.

4 Applying analytic skills. Have children summarize their analytic or personal observations and apply them in analysis and discussion of other selections they have read. As their understanding of various literary elements develops, guide them to apply this to their own written expression or creative dramatics. From time to time some children might write something as an extension of the selection studied; their own poem on the same theme, their own story using characters from the selection, and so forth. Individualize application activities to meet differences in interests and abilities. "Formal" book reports using elements and criteria developed by the children as a framework for analysis can be used from time to time for application and evaluation of skills, but should not be used for every book read. Informal means such as group discussions and bulletin board displays can also be used to enable children to share or recommend what they have read.

A language arts program organized around children's literature is "A Curriculum for English" (Olson, 1967), developed at the University of Nebraska. It is designed to identify the concepts and generalizations which describe the classifications, structures, and themes of literary works and to develop these understandings at increasingly complex levels through the grades. The spiral development of the curriculum carries forward nine classification strands from first to sixth grade: folktales, fanciful stories, animal stories, adventure stories, myths, fables, stories of other lands and people, historical fiction, and biography. The concepts developed in these grades are intended to provide a basis for the study of more formal, analytical units in junior and senior high school: units on the epic, tragedy, the idea of a play, and so on.

The overall strategy of the project is the presentation of selected works, in oral or written form, as sources of enjoyment to be discussed informally and to which children may respond in creative ways. Although each unit contains a literary analysis for the teacher's background, the children are not expected to analyze the works in adult terms. Rather, the stories are intended to provide a fund of examples upon which children may draw for inductive discovery of patterns and classifications in literary forms. The unit is then extended to provide for study of language structure, and development of oral and written expression.

A basic strategy for presentation of a specific work involves the following procedures:

Preparing The teacher familiarizes herself with the story, poem, or book and any relevant background information. If she plans to read aloud or recite, she practices in order to convey style, mood, meaning. If children are to present the work, they too should be adequately prepared.

Responding Children express their responses in oral and written form. Although they do not engage in formal analysis, they may outline sequences with pictures or act out a story. Such responses add activities at the levels of application and synthesis, in contrast to the analytical strategy outlined previously.

Composing The form, patterns, or theme of the work may be used as a model or stimulus for the children's own written or oral compositions. As an aid to concept formation, visual models or pictures are utilized—symbolic figures and objects which represent thematic elements such as the monster, the hero, the secure home, rather than the characters of a specific work.

Additional readings The teacher guides each child in the selection of related readings appropriate to his individual requirements.

Evaluating Evaluation of each child's written or oral responses is individualized and positive. Attention is given to one or two important areas of improvement, without correction of every detail. This is not to say that some errors are ignored; rather, some change is made in the composition, while other corrections are made in the form of separate activities or language lessons.

Developing Comprehension Skills

This strategy for developing comprehension skills can be used in the contexts of all the strategies outlined above.

1 Preparing for reading. Before the children begin to read the selection, help them to set purposes or raise questions that involve specific comprehension skills.

2 Questioning for comprehension. Use questions relevant to the specific comprehension skills to be developed in a particular lesson, at literal, critical, and appreciative levels. Use questions at the literal level as needed to establish a base for extended comprehension at the other levels. When working with a group, elicit responses to each question from several children, and pose a sufficient number of questions for each skill to ensure that all of the children have the opportunity to think and respond.

3 Reinforcing skills. If needed, use comprehension-skills workbooks or write questions for teacher-selected passages to provide additional practice in noting details, predicting outcomes, inferring cause and effect, and the like.

4 Applying skills. Have children use the comprehension skill in another context. For example:

Inferring Ask children to tell something they "know" about the story or about a character, even though it is not stated in the material read.

Distinguishing fact and opinion Have each child write or tell a fact about something, and then his or her opinion related to the fact or to the situation from which the fact is drawn.

Detecting persuasive use of words Have children compose an advertisement or brief argument using persuasive words. Have them identify these words in each other's work.

Developing Phonetic-Analysis Skills

In most reading programs, teachers find it useful to develop some sight vocabulary to provide early reading experiences and examples to be used for later teaching of word-analysis skills. In the strategy outlined below, words familiar to the children and recognized by sight should be used in steps 1 and 2.

1 Distinguishing sounds. Pronounce three or four words with the same initial consonant, vowel, or ending sound. Have children identify and repeat the sound. Do the same with another similar sound or one made by similar letters. For example, initial consonants b and p might be presented together because the sounds are similar, or b and d might be compared because they are similar in visual form and some children have difficulty distinguishing them. Long and short sounds of the same vowel can be compared and contrasted, or two sets of symbols for the same sound, as in coat and vote, or the same symbol for two different sounds, as in circle and cake.

2 Relating sounds to letter symbols. Print the words on a chart or chalkboard, with the common letter or letter combination of the words in alignment. Have children identify what they see that is the same in all the words and what is different, and have them point out the letters that represent the sound. Then do the same for the contrasting sound.

3 Generalizing. Have pupils suggest other words that use the sounds. Focus on one sound first, then the other. At the earliest levels of instruction, if a child offers a "wrong" word, have the child listen again to earlier words to compare and distinguish the "wrong" sound. At more advanced levels, write the word so that the child can see how it differs. Show objects or pictures of things that use the sound and symbol to help children think of applicable words. Then have them state in their own words the "rule" about the sound-symbol correspondence.

4 Applying the skill. Have the children practice writing the letter or letters, and have them identify letters representing the sound in the words they suggested.

5 Evaluating the skill. Provide exercises for recognition of words using the sound-symbol correspondences of the lesson. For example, have them circle the word in a group of three that has the sound of the word pronounced by the teacher.

Using Context Clues

Children need direct instruction to optimize their skills in using context clues for word recognition. The context may be a sentence, a paragraph, or an entire story, chapter, or section of a subject-area book. Types of context clues include illustrations, sentence meaning or meaning of adjacent words, or sentence structure and class of adjacent words.

1 Introducing the skill. Present a sentence within the children's decoding and comprehension levels, with a word missing at the end. Have them suggest what it could be. When several acceptable alternatives have been suggested, have children explain why each one is suitable. Do the same with a few more sentences, with some of the missing words in earlier positions in the sentence.

2 Identifying the skill. Ask children to explain how they were able to figure out the probable missing words, and list responses on a chart or chalkboard for reference. Ask for other ways that they could verify their choice, or determine which of several alternatives is correct. Present an illustrated paragraph with several sentences in which a word is missing, except for the first letter. Have each child supply a missing word and identify the elements he or she used as clues: illustration, explanations in previous sentences, main idea of paragraph, sentence structure, sound-symbol relationship (the word begins with the sound of the letter indicated), the fact that the word "makes sense" in the sentence, and so forth.

3 Reinforcing the skill. Have children practice the skill through such exercises as identifying unfamiliar synonyms in meaningful sentences, comparing different meanings of the same word (as in "time *ran* out," "the mouse *ran* down," "we *ran* a cake sale for the school"), or making up "mystery stories" for each other with key sentences in which a word is missing.

4 Applying and evaluating the skill. Have children utilize context clues in silent and oral reading.

Miscue Analysis

A "miscue" is an oral response by a reader that differs from the actual written symbol. The reader may express the wrong sound for a letter or syllable, substitute a different word, add or omit a word, or leave off a word ending. A miscue is not necessarily considered an error. For example, a mispronunciation, or omission of word endings, may be the result of application of sound patterns in the child's home dialect or language. A substituted word may be a more familiar synonym that does not alter the meaning of the sentence. In these cases, the child is reading with understanding and may need no correction.

Miscue analysis is an approach used for assessment of the *types* of miscues made by a child and for the planning of individualized lessons to enable that child to develop needed, specific "reading strategy" skills. The miscue-analysis approach emphasizes enabling the reader to derive meaning from written material.

To assess miscue patterns, the teacher has the child read aloud, without prior silent reading, an entire story or self-contained selection that is somewhat difficult for that child, above his or her instructional level. However, content and concept load should be within the reader's experience, not dealing with anything remote or unfamiliar. The material should be long enough to generate at least twenty-five miscues. As the child reads, the teacher notes, on a copy of the material, the types of decoding miscues made. A tape recording of the reading enables the teacher to review later and note any miscues not "caught" the first time.

After this, the child re-reads the story silently and then is asked to retell it in his or her own words. The teacher asks open-ended questions to elicit responses in any areas of the material omitted by the child, but without using any wording that would supply information or clues to a specific answer. This enables the teacher to assess comprehension.

When the teacher has determined the types of miscues made by a particular child, materials can be selected, or written by the teacher, to provide instruction and practice in the reading strategy needed for each type. For example, a child might substitute "trial" for "trail." The teacher would determine, from other miscues the child made, whether the confusion was due to word-analysis error or to inability to use context clues. If the former, words using ai and ia would be presented in two lists for comparison, identified by the child, and then read in sentences or paragraphs. To develop a strategy for using context clues, the teacher might write three paragraph-length stories, one using "trail" in as many sentences as possible, one using "trial," and one using both. The child would practice association of word meaning and context by reading the first two paragraphs, and analyzing with the teacher the types of context clues that indicate why the specified word is correct. The child then applies the strategy he or she has learned to the third paragraph.

More detailed descriptions of miscue-analysis procedures are found in Goodman (1973) and Ruddell (1974a, pp. 531–544; 1974b, pp. 396–405).

Reading and Dialect or Foreign Language

Children who speak another language or a nonstandard dialect at home may encounter some difficulties in decoding standard English because of differences in the set of sounds and of sound-symbol correspondences, used in the two dialects or languages. Difficulties in comprehension may arise because of differences in syntactic structures. It is important for teachers to know the kinds of difficulties children may encounter because of the phonemic and syntactic structure of their particular home dialect or language to plan instruction to meet their different learning needs. For example, speakers of a black English dialect may omit some final consonants, pronouncing "four" as "foe," or omit words such as the present tense of "to be," as in "She going home." Spanish-speaking children may pronounce b and v alike because they represent the same sound in Spanish, or place adjectives and adverbs before nouns and verbs in an English sentence as in Spanish syntax. Chinese-speaking children may have difficulty with sounds represented by "th," as these are not used in Chinese dialects, or omit articles or prepositions in an English sentence, using Chinese syntax. Newly arrived children speaking languages of Asian countries may encounter further initial difficulties because of the greater differences between graphemes, direction of writing, and vocabulary than children speaking romance languages will experience between their home language and English.

Children speaking a black English dialect have an understanding of standard English. The differences between standard English dialects and other American dialects are primarily a matter of syntax and pronunciation, more than of vocabulary. Some educators recommend that dialect-speaking children should be taught to read with standard English materials. Others suggest that differences in syntax and vocabulary may pose comprehension difficulties for beginning readers and recommend a language-experience approach in which vocabulary and syntax of experience stories are recorded as expressed by the children, but with words spelled as in standard English. A few educators have carried this concern further by recommending the use of reading materials with parallel stories written in standard and black English, using content drawn from the background of black American children (Baratz and Shuy, 1969; Henrie, 1972, pp. 326–328). This approach is based in part on the assumption that some dialect-speaking children may be slowed down in their reading rate because they need to translate written material into the dialect syntax. This process might also make it difficult for them to complete a time-limited test other-wise within their comprehension. Other educators, and some black community members in various school districts, object to the use of such material because it might retard the child's access to instruction in, and use of, standard English.

Members of a bilingual-bicultural community may also have differing views of language and reading instruction. In communities where bilingualism is desired, reading instruction may begin in the child's home language, unless the child is more fluent in English. Reading instruction in the second lan-guage begins when the teacher judges the child's oral fluency adequate for the level of materials to be used. In communities where parents prefer to stress learning of English, oral language development precedes initiation of reading instruction. Among the few materials available that are specifically designed for bilingual learners (Henrie, 1972, pp. 320–321, 324–325) are the Miami Linguistic Readers for Spanish-speaking children and the Peabody Rebus materials, which utilize a rebus or picture symbol in place of a word. Later the spelled word is introduced with the rebus superimposed, and finally the rebus is omitted.

References at the end of this chapter (Baratz and Shuy, 1969; Cullinan, 1974, pp. 87–108; Ruddell, 1974a, pp. 263–291) are among the sources for specific guidelines in reading instruction for children speaking a dialect or foreign language.

GUIDELINES FOR THE TEACHER

Many guidelines have been explicitly stated and implied in the preceding section. Additional guidelines found in curriculum outlines and professional publications include the following suggestions:

Utilize a variety of approaches to reading instruction. No single method has been shown to be the best solution to the full range of reading problems in any school system or even within one class. Select the techniques and materials best suited to the varying needs of different groups or of individual learners.

Use flexible grouping. Organize children in different groups for specific skill instruction, common interests, or special activities. Provide opportunities for children to work in groups that cut across reading levels. Evaluate progress continuously, and regroup children whenever their needs change.

Provide a variety of reading materials in the classroom. Try to obtain materials on diverse topics, and at reading levels below, at, and a year or two above the range of the pupils' reading levels. Encourage children to cross grade or reading levels in their use of these materials.

Recognize individual differences and involve every child in every lesson. Encourage the participation of each pupil and ask questions that are geared to specific kinds and levels of comprehension.

EVALUATION OF INSTRUCTIONAL OUTCOMES

Reading involves much more than a unitary skill. Indeed, the term "reading" applies to a broad complex of behaviors including, among others, word-recognition skills, comprehension, reference, and thinking skills, tastes, attitudes, and interests. Acquisition of this complex of behaviors is a highly individualized process and varies both in rate and level of attainment among children in the same grade or age group. Therefore, evaluation of pupil progress in reading must extend to all aspects of reading instruction and must be individualized. Although specific programs and instructional techniques vary, the following guidelines (Artley, 1965) are applicable to all programs of reading instruction.

Evaluation of the individual pupil's reading achievement should be made in relation to his capacity for achievement. This guideline involves such determinations as the following:

1 How does the individual's current reading achievement compare with measures of his or her intelligence?

2 How does his performance compare with that of other children of the same age?

3 What level of material is he able to read independently, at what level does he require instructional help, and at what level does he reach the point of reading frustration?

4 What is the rate and consistency of his progress in all areas of reading behavior?

Questions 1 and 2 are assessed by means of a variety of techniques. Standardized achievement tests given early in the school year provide one measurement scale, but such tests are too limited in scope to be suitable as the sole form of measurement. Further dimensions of achievement and ability are gained by means of diagnostic tests and the use of cumulative records of a child's reading experiences. Forms for such records are provided in many school systems as new reading programs are implemented.

Question 3 refers to the child's independent reading level, defined as the level at which he recognizes 99 percent of the words and comprehends at least 90 percent of what he reads; the level at which he profits from instruction, defined as recognition of 95 percent of the words and about 75 percent comprehension; and the frustration level, defined as 70 percent word recognition and about 50 percent comprehension (Betts, 1957). This question, as well as the first two questions, is determined by means of individualized informal textbook tests, miscue analysis, teacher-made tests, and observation of the child's reading performance in a broad range of classroom activities. This type of observation, guided by checklists, also enables the teacher to assess question 4.

Evaluation of pupil progress must be continuous. More effective instruction is possible when evaluation of pupils' difficulties and achievement levels is continuous and is thoroughly integrated with individualized instruction.

Self-evaluation should be encouraged. Because learning to read is an individualized process, the pupil gains independence in learning when he is taught, through teacher-pupil conferences or class discussions resulting in cooperatively prepared criteria, to recognize and evaluate his own difficulties and accomplishments.

Evaluation must be directly related to all the objectives of the instructional program and should assess the pupil's growth both in and through reading. The classroom teacher may accomplish this by enumerating the objectives of the reading program, such as those discussed in this chapter, and determining appropriate evaluative instruments and techniques for each objective. If the stated objectives are limited, taxonomies of objectives may be used, as in the examples that follow (Bloom, 1956; Krathwohl et al., 1964).

Cognitive Domain

Knowledge Level Basic language knowledge, concept and vocabulary development, knowledge of word-recognition techniques, and knowledge of criteria or procedures for oral reading, study skills, and reading in subject areas. These and other examples of language knowledge may be evaluated by means of standardized and teacher-made tests, observation of pupil performance, and workbook assignments.

Comprehension Level Literal and critical comprehension as described on page 232, above. The specific skills therein outlined may be evaluated by means of teacher-made tests, both formal and informal, oral questions and classroom discussions, informal textbook tests, teacher-pupil conferences to discuss pupils' records of individualized reading, workbook activities, pupil reports, and anecdotal records to evaluate growth in comprehension skills.

Application Level The child's use of his word knowledge, word-recognition skills, comprehension skills, study skills, and oral reading skills in his encounters with new reading materials in the developmental program, in subject-area reading, and in recreational reading. Teacher observation of the child's performance in varieties of reading situations is an appropriate technique and may be structured by means of checklists, rating scales, skills inventories, and anecdotal records. Informal classroom questions, teacher-pupil conferences, workbook assignments, and children's reports add to the dimensions of evaluation at the level of application.

Analysis Level The child's application of critical thinking to his reading experiences, involving skills of critical comprehension as outlined on page 232, above. Analytical skills may be evaluated by means of teacher-made tests, reports by pupils, and teacher-pupil conferences.

Synthesis Level The child's creative interpretation of reading content and his utilization of his readings in the formulation of his own thinking or creative expression. Skills of appreciative comprehension, outlined on page 232, fall within this level and may be evaluated by teacher observation, checklists, rating scales, anecdotal records, pupil compositions and reports, classroom discussions, and teacher-pupil conferences.

Evaluation Level In reading instruction, skills at the levels of comprehension, analysis, and synthesis, developed from the earliest grades, are utilized in combination by children in the upper elementary reading levels as more highly developed skills of evaluation of the content, purposes, and literary techniques of reading materials. Such evaluative skills may be observed and rated in a similar manner to the related skills at other levels.

Affective Domain

Receiving Level At the reading-readiness stage, the child's attention to what is read to him and his attentiveness and interest in beginning reading instruction. An effective evaluative technique is teacher observation, guided by check lists, rating scales, anecdotal records, and cumulative record cards.

Responding Level Evidence of the child's interest and satisfaction in reading. In addition to the techniques utilized at the receiving level, evaluation at both the responding and valuing levels may be conducted by means of pupil records of individual reading, reports and compositions, classroom discussion, questionnaires, and pupils' responses to incomplete projective statements.

Valuing Level Evidences of the child's regard for reading, his valuing of reading activities, development of scope and depth of interests in reading, valuing of critical appraisal of reading material, care of books, use of libraries, and further reading at home. In addition to techniques outlined above, attitudes, interests, and values may be evaluated with interest inventories, and in teacher-parent conferences.

Organizing Level The child's development of sets of values, criteria, attitudes, and tastes in regard to reading. Pupil-teacher conferences, class discussion, and pupils' reports provide evaluative information at this level.

Characterization Level The child's assimilation of reading experiences into his total growth and development; his use of reading to extend his experiences and enhance his understanding of the world in which he lives. This level of behavior transcents identifiable subject lines and requires assessment techniques relevant to the child's total outlook and behavior, primarily through anecdotal records and case study procedures.

FOLLOW-UP ACTIVITIES AND PROJECTS

1 Examine the curriculum bulletin for reading in your school district and compare it with two or three others from the campus or district curriculum library. What objectives are included? How is reading defined? What instructional guidelines are given? How is reading related to the other language arts? What evaluation procedures are used?

2 Plan a reading program (for about a two-month duration) for one child or for a small group. Identify diagnostic techniques for determining each one's reading instructional level and specific learning needs. Specify objectives, determine materials to be used, and outline specific teaching/learning experiences. Explain why all of these are appropriate for the child or individuals in the group.

3 Examine and compare books at a particular reading level from three or four current basal series in terms of the following:

    Content of material: Language style (related to children's language)
                                  Types of stories, poems
                                  Topics of selections in the book

    Instructional procedures: Rate and amount of vocabulary introduction
                                  Provision for comprehension skills
                                  Strategies in teacher's guide

    Illustrations and format

4 Survey teachers in your school to determine the approaches to reading used with other classes and groups, and describe the total program in your school. What prior reading-instruction experiences did your class have? What are the probable experiences they will encounter during the next academic year? How does this relate to your own instructional program?

5 Visit the children's section of your local library to determine ways in which your class can use the facilities. Select four or five books suitable for children in your class and evaluate them on the basis of criteria suggested by Arbuthnot (1964), Huck and Kuhn (1968), or J. S. Smith (1967). Obtain the children's responses to these books. Analyze reasons for differences in opinion among the children or between you and the children.

6 Analyze your school's community as a reading resource. For example, what could the children write about their area in preparing their own "book" for use in instructional or recreational reading? Are there unusual or special geographic features or structures? What aspects of local history could be investigated and recorded? Other sources might include local legends or stories told by members of different ethnic groups. What reading material suitable for your children might be included in newspapers or other locally produced publications?

BIBLIOGRAPHY

Arbuthnot, May Hill. *Children and Books.* Chicago: Scott, Foresman, 1964. A standard reference on children's literature, with annotated bibliography of selected books for children.

Artley, A. Sterl. "Evaluation of Reading." *Instructor,* March, 74:89, 110, 1965, Outline of evaluation techniques.

Aukerman, Robert C. *Approaches to Beginning Reading*. New York: Wiley, 1971. Descriptions and analyses of over one hundred programs and materials systems used in beginning reading instruction.

Baratz, Joan C., and Roger W. Shuy. (Eds.) *Teaching Black Children to Read*. Washington, D.C.: Center for Applied Linguistics, 1969. Guidelines for instruction in reading.

Betts, Emmett A. *Foundations of Reading Instruction*. New York: American Book, 1957. Evaluation guidelines which continue to be utilized.

Bloom, Benjamin S. (Ed.) *The Taxonomy of Educational Objectives: Cognitive Domain*. New York: McKay, 1956. Classification of objectives and examples of test items.

Burron, Arnold, and Amos L. Claybaugh. *Using Reading to Teach Subject Matter*. Columbus, Ohio: Charles E. Merrill Publishing Co., 1974. Principles and techniques for improving reading in content subjects.

Chall, Jeanne. *Learning to Read: The Great Debate*. New York: McGraw-Hill, 1967. Critical analysis of findings and implications of research in reading instruction, and analysis of the most widely used basic and supplementary beginning reading programs.

Cullinan, Bernice E. (Ed.) *Black Dialects and Reading*. Urbana, Ill.: National Council of Teachers of English, 1974. Issues involved in teaching black children to read standard English, with guides for diagnosis of children's language and instructional strategies for teaching oral language and reading.

Dallman, Martha, R. L. Rouch, L. Y. C. Chang, and John DeBoer. *The Teaching of Reading*. New York: Holt, 1974. Comprehensive treatment of all aspects of the reading program.

Dillard, J. L. *Black English: Its History and Usage in the United States*. New York: Vintage Books, Random House, 1972. Analyses of variations of black English with some educational implications.

Durkin, Dolores. *Teaching Them to Read*. 2d ed. Boston: Allyn and Bacon, 1974. Detailed discussion of various aspects of reading instruction.

Elementary English, Vol. 50, No. 3, March, 1973. Urbana, Ill.: National Council of Teachers of English. Articles on individualizing reading instruction.

Framework in Reading. Sacramento, Calif.: California State Board of Education, 1973. Objectives, outline, and evaluation procedures for a complete reading program, with attention to needs of readers speaking Spanish, Chinese, and black English dialects.

Fries, Charles C. *Linguistics and Reading*. New York: Holt, 1963. A linguistic scholar's discussion of the reading process.

Fry, Edward. *Reading Instruction for Classroom and Clinic*. New York: McGraw-Hill, 1972. Specific teaching strategies for phonics and comprehension instruction, detailed guidelines for testing, annotated lists of tests, and instructional materials.

Goodman, Kenneth S. (Ed.) *The Psycholinguistic Nature of the Reading Process*. Detroit: Wayne State University Press, 1973. Discusses reading as a thinking process, with attention to the importance of the reader's language ability, physiology, and experiential background related to obtaining meaning from written materials.

_____. (Ed.) *Miscue Analysis.* Urbana, Ill.: National Council of Teachers of English, 1973. Articles on techniques and applications of miscue analysis in reading instruction.

Hafner, Lawrence E. (Ed.) *Improving Reading in Middle and Secondary Schools.* New York: Macmillan, 1974. Articles on developmental reading instruction and reading in different subjects.

Harris, Larry A., and Carl B. Smith. *Reading Instruction through Diagnostic Teaching.* New York: Holt, 1972. Suggestions for diagnosing, planning, and teaching various aspects of reading, and developing library and study skills, with an emphasis on individualizing instruction.

Herber, Harold L. *Teaching Reading in Content Areas.* Englewood Cliffs, N.J.: Prentice-Hall, 1970. Guidelines for instruction.

Henrie, Samuel. (Senior Ed.) *A Sourcebook of Elementary Curricula Programs and Projects.* Produced by Far West Laboratory. Washington, D.C.: Government Printing Office, 1972. Descriptions of programs and materials for reading instruction through eighth grade.

Huck, Charlotte S., and Doris Young Kuhn. *Children's Literature in the Elementary School.* New York: Holt, 1968. Guidelines for analysis and selection of children's literature, and specific teaching strategies.

Karlin, Robert. *Teaching Elementary Reading: Principles and Strategies.* New York, Harcourt, Brace, Jovanovich, 1971. Comprehensive treatment of reading instruction with a focus on an eclectic approach and the meeting of individual needs.

Krathwohl, David R., Benjamin S. Bloom, and Bertram S. Masia. *Taxonomy of Educational Objectives: Affective Domain.* New York: McKay, 1964. A classification of objectives and sample test items in the area of attitude and value development.

Lee, Dorris M., and R. V. Allen. *Learning to Read through Experience.* New York: Appleton-Century-Crofts, 1966. Description of reading instruction based on children's own experiences and written expression.

Lefevre, Carl A. *Linguistics and the Teaching of Reading.* New York: McGraw-Hill, 1964. A linguistic scholar's approach to reading instruction.

Neff, Nancy, and Charles Neff (Compilers) *Aids to Curriculum Planning: English Language Arts K-12.* Urbana, Ill.: National Council of Teachers of English, 1973. Excerpts from curriculum guides on objectives, evaluation, and instruction in reading and literature, and criteria for writing curriculum guides.

Olson, Paul A. *A Curriculum Study Center in English.* (Final Report CRP-H-001). Washington, D.C.: Office of Education, Bureau of Research, 1967. Rationale and description of the Nebraska literature-based curriculum.

Robinson, Helen M. (Ed.) *Innovation and Change in Reading Instruction.* 67th Yearbook. Chicago: National Society for the Study of Education, 1968. Chapters on directions in instruction at readiness, beginning reading, and upper elementary levels.

Ruddell, Robert B. *Reading-Language Instruction: Innovative Practices.* Englewood Cliffs, N.J.: Prentice-Hall, 1974. Detailed and comprehensive treatment integrating reading instruction and language arts instruction. Chapter 2 provides a useful model of the reading process.

_____. (Ed.) *Accountability and Reading Instruction: Critical Issues.* Urbana, Ill.: National Council of Teachers of English, 1973. Critique of limitations of reading tests, and analysis of possible uses and limitations of behavioral objectives and performance contracting in reading instruction.

_____ et al. (Eds.) *Resources in Reading-Language Instruction.* Englewood Cliffs, N.J.: Prentice-Hall, 1974. Collection of articles on all aspects of reading and language arts instruction.

Russell, David H. *Children Learn to Read.* Boston: Ginn, 1961. Principles and procedures in reading instruction with attention to thinking processes.

_____. *The Dynamics of Reading.* Robert B. Ruddell (Ed.) Waltham, Mass.: Ginn-Blaisdell, 1970. Discusses literature in the classroom program in terms of psychological needs, bibliotherapy, and personal responses of children, with instructional suggestions and guidelines.

Sanders, Norris M. *Classroom Questions.* New York: Harper & Row, 1966. Examples of questions for comprehension skills related to the Bloom cognitive taxonomy.

Shane, Harold G., James Walden, and Ronald Green (Eds.) *Interpreting Language Arts Research for the Teacher.* Washington, D.C.: Association for Supervision and Curriculum Development, 1971. Reviews of research on teaching of reading and literature.

Smith, E. Brooks, Kenneth S. Goodman, and Robert Meredith. *Language and Thinking in the Elementary School.* New York: Holt, 1970. Chapters on reading instruction, literature, and teaching strategies that emphasize thinking processes.

Smith, Frank. *Understanding Reading.* New York: Holt, 1971. Detailed psycholinguistic analysis of the reading process and implications for instruction, with annotated references.

Smith, James A. *Creative Teaching of Reading and Literature.* Boston: Allyn and Bacon, 1967. Specific suggestions for instruction with attention to problem-solving and creative thinking, and use of the language-experience approach.

Smith, James Steel. *A Critical Approach to Children's Literature.* New York: McGraw-Hill, 1967. Emphasis on literary aspects of children's literature with guides for literary analysis and attention to children's interaction with good literature.

Spodek, Bernard. *Teaching in the Early Years.* Englewood Cliffs, N.J.: Prentice-Hall, 1972. Chapter on beginning reading.

Mathematics Education

Mathematics is composed of quantitative concepts and generalizations, their properties and relationships, and modes of logical reasoning that have widespread applicability. Like man's verbal language, mathematics consists of arbitrary symbolic forms with rules of construction and interpretation. It is organized into logical systems that enable man to think about, utilize, and communicate with a high degree of precision quantitative ideas and the relationships among them.

In recognition of these characteristics, curriculum planners have transformed the arithmetic program into a program of elementary school mathematics. The change of designation gives recognition to the changes in content and approach which have characterized the reform of this curriculum area. The program for children is part of a continuum of mathematics which extends from early number identification to complex abstraction. Furthermore, the term "mathematics" gives support to the view that the separation of material into various compartments, such as grade levels, or into particular specializations, such as algebra, fractions, and percentages, should be done only for instructional convenience. The modern elementary school mathematics program accents the relationships among mathematical ideas and promotes the continuous development of mathematical thinking.

Contributions to Basic Goals

Mathematics education contributes to major goals of education in several ways. *Thinking ability* is enhanced as children learn to employ logical processes in pure and applied mathematics; order concepts of number, operation, and relation into useful problem-solving tools; develop systems of proof; and use number concepts in and out of school. *Self-realization* is developed as children learn the language and procedures of mathematics and put them to use in situations of vital personal and social concern. Contributions are made to *human relationships* as children discover uses of mathematics in conservation, homemaking, transportation and other basic human activities. *Economic competence* and *civic responsibility* call for innumerable applications of mathematics in connection with consumer and civic activities. *Learning how to learn* is enriched as children develop basic mathematic concepts and skills needed for lifelong learning. Other contributions may be noted in the statement of illustrative objectives in the next section.

OBJECTIVES OF MATHEMATICS EDUCATION

At the turn of the century, objectives of mathematics instruction in the elementary school centered upon the development of computational skill. In the 1920s and 1930s, goals shifted to a focus on practical application and everyday mathematical usage. These objectives have not been cast aside in current practice, but they have been placed in a more balanced perspective. Educational scholars today are cognizant of cultural and technological changes which have created needs for greater understanding of mathematics concepts and reasoning on the part of an increasing proportion of the population. In addition, the future is expected to bring new and changing requirements for mathematics skills. Many educators and mathematicians suggest that needs for current understanding as well as for future learnings are most effectively met when the pupil is able to perceive and understand structure in mathematics: concepts, relationships, principles, and modes of mathematical reasoning. Recent courses of study tend to give emphasis to the following objectives.

Conceptual Objectives

To develop understanding of mathematical concepts and principles so that the child is able to identify, recognize, describe, and demonstrate the use of the following:

The real numbers including special attention to whole numbers, integers, and rational numbers

The fundamental operations and relations involving these numbers, algebraic formulations

Computational algorithms for addition, multiplication, subtraction, and division

Basic tools and procedures such as mathematical sentences, approximation, axiomatic methods, cartesian graphing, mathematical logic

Geometric concepts on euclidian and noneuclidian geometries, simple geometric and algebraic proof

Principles of measurement, applied mathematics, probability

PROCESS OBJECTIVES

To develop competence in using cognitive or inquiry processes so that the child is able to do the following:

Demonstrate how strategies and tactics of problem solving may be applied to solve different types of mathematical problems

Demonstrate in mathematical activities how classifying, defining, analyzing, predicting, and other processes may be used

Demonstrate how a model or graph can be used to analyze a quantitative problem and interpret the result

Skill Objectives

To develop the skills needed to work effectively in different strands of the mathematics education program so that the child is able to do the following:

Develop and solve mathematical statements involving equalities and inequalities

Immediately call into use the basic combinations for addition, subtraction, multiplication, and division involving whole numbers

Perform necessary computations in the four operations on integers and other rational numbers with accuracy and flexibility

AFFECTIVE OBJECTIVES

To foster an appreciation for mathematics so that the child is able to do the following:

Recognize and appreciate the importance and value of mathematics as an area of study and enjoy creative mathematics

Understand the value of mathematics as a functional tool in our modern industrialized world

Observe the many ways in which mathematics is a part of our cultural heritage and observe its use as a language of discourse for the expression and recording of quantitative ideas

Gain personal fulfillment and pleasure from the learning and use of modern mathematics

ORGANIZATION OF THE CURRICULUM

The scope and sequence of currently recommended elementary mathematics programs are constructed on the basis of the following assumptions:

The elementary mathematics program should be viewed as a segment of a structure of mathematical concepts which may be interrelated at every instructional level.

Fundamental mathematical generalizations should be developed sequentially over a period of time in a spiral program that treats each topic at intervals of increasingly complex forms.

Mathematical concepts are most effectively learned if their presentation is carefully adapted to known characteristics of children's learning at various cognitive developmental stages.

Mathematical content is the overriding consideration in the organization of the elementary mathematics curriculum. Although the development of individual programs is responsive to value trends, content guidelines ultimately serve to structure the program or serve in its defense. For example, in one period the program outlines will clearly emphasize the structure of the discipline of mathematics, reflecting current thinking in the selection and ordering of content with minimal consideration to details of presentation. At another time, attention will center upon process dimensions, and therefore the nature of mathematical experiences and the presentation of material will be key considerations. Still another phase may give priority rating to children's learning characteristics, and programs will be organized and presented so as to best adapt to the most promising theories regarding human learning. Yet regardless of which of these value orientations is dominant at a particular time, a mathematics program will be judged not only according to affective and process criteria but also according to its strands of content.

Thus, the most prominent organizational feature of an elementary mathematics program is its content. The program usually is organized around content strands to ensure comprehensive treatment of individual topics and to stress topics of paramount importance. There is near unanimity in modern programs regarding the content strands to be covered in the elementary grades. Furthermore, despite the illusion that the so-called mathematics revolution of the 1950s and 1960s replaced some old school mathematics with entirely new mathematics, the basic content dimensions of elementary school mathematics have remained relatively unchanged over the past one hundred years. To be certain, there have been some shifts in instruction levels and changes in nomenclature, but the conceptual core of the program has remained fairly stable.

Organization by Strands

Most elementary programs are organized around strands that include fundamental mathematical concepts and concept clusters. Within the concept strands, individual concepts usually serve as the focus for separate lessons and activities. Units or modules of work may be viewed as groups of such activities. Within such units or modules, concepts are selected and treated in clusters to illuminate the interdependence of mathematical ideas and to promote efficiency in learning.

The following are so fundamental that curriculum planners should include attention to them at various levels in instruction:

Sets Collection, elements, one-to-one correspondence, pairing, matching or equivalent, equal, serial ordering, proper, improper, finite, infinite, empty or null, subset, operation, intersection, union, disjoint, complement, cartesian product

Numbers Property of set, cardinality, ordinality, counting, betweenness, natural, zero, whole, integers, rational, irrational, real, positive, negative, prime, composite, factors, multiples, numeration, patterns, density, equality, inequalities, ordered pairs, equivalence class

Operations Addition, multiplication, subtraction, division, basic facts, inverses, sentences, interactions, algorithms, role of computing, flexibility, compensation, identity, commutation, association, distribution, closure, binary and unary, nondecimal bases

Problem Solving Estimation, prediction, approximation, strategy, analysis, induction, deduction, generalization, representation, models, probabilities, error, interpretation, definitions

Logic Inference, deductions, statements, assumptions, connectives, quantifiers, negation, conjunction, disjunction, conditional, biconditional, class inclusion, seriation, truth, proof

Applications Synthesis, analysis, graphing, models, probabilities, physical sciences, social sciences, representation, computation, direct usage, tables, percent

Functions and Graphs Ordered pairs, functional relationship, continuous variables, graphs in one, two, and three dimensions, coordinates, axis, slope, intercepts, interpolation, extrapolation, interpretation, linear, quadratic, exponential

Measurement Comparison, units, dimensions, arbitrary and standard units, likeness, number, scale, calibration, precision, accuracy, error, relative error, absolute error, approximate numbers, significant digits, metric system, conversions

Geometry Classification, point, line, segment, plane, region, three-dimensional space, ray, arc, end point, vertex, intersection, union, polygon, parallel, perpendicular, bi-section, similarity, congruence, metric, nonmetric

Statistics and Probability   Prediction, probability, chance, distribution, average, mean, median, mode, variance, standard deviation, correlation, graphing, models, sampling

Primitive Number Theory   Factors, multiples, primes, composites, least common multiple, greatest common factor, tests for divisibility, relations

Relations   Pairing, ordered pairs, ratio, percent, plane of number lines, mapping pairs on a plane, cartesian system, graphing, slope, intercept, interpolation, extrapolation, equations for straight lines, functional relationships, equivalence relations

In recent years there has been a tendency to consolidate concept clusters into fewer and fewer major strands. For example, the concepts in the clusters above are all included under the following headings:

Applications and problem solving
Arithmetic, numbers, and operations
Geometry
Measurement
Probability and statistics
Relations and functions
Logical thinking

Within concept clusters are subclusters of concepts. For example, numeration includes concepts of grouping, the decimal characteristic, notation, positional systems, nondecimal bases; subtraction includes concepts of separation, comparing, compensation, equal additions, decomposition, complements; and prism includes concepts of regions, faces, edges, vertex. Concepts within these subclusters are interrelated until the clustering process results in the formulation of generalizations. Viable relationships are exposed through carefully selected strategies, questions, and activities. The following questions and activities are illustrative.

Illustrative Questions and Activities

Sets   Find a set of bottlecaps *equivalent* to the set of pencils (defining, interpreting). Arrange this set with nine members into *equivalent subsets* (analyzing). Join these two *disjoint* sets. Give the *number* (synthesizing). What is the last member in the *set of whole numbers* (analyzing)? Which term, "and" or "or," belongs with *intersection* (analyzing)?

Numbers   Give the *counting* numbers from one to one hundred (defining). How many tens in eighty-five (interpreting, analyzing)? Are these numbers *equal* (analyzing)? Find the *standard name* for $(6 + 4) \times 2$ (synthesizing). In the set of *whole numbers,* find the number *greater than* $24 - 13$ and *less than*

4 + 3 + 6 (interpreting, analyzing). Which of the following are not *prime factors* of 48 (interpreting, analyzing)? Use the repeated-subtraction *algorithm* in these computations (defining, interpreting).

Operations Is addition or multiplication better for the following: 27 + 27 + 27 + 27 + 27 (interpreting)? What is the *inverse operation* for *subtraction* (defining)? Find the ratios and express them in the form a/b (analysis). Find the standard names for these rational numbers (analyzing). Is the set of integers closed with respect to multiplication (defining, interpreting)? Use the associative property to simplify and solve the following example: 32 × 125 (synthesizing).

Sequence of Concepts and Processes

There is considerable agreement on the sequencing of concepts according to instructional levels. The following may be used as a model for the scope and sequence of mathematics topics in grades kindergarten through 8.

Preschool and Kindergarten Children engage in manipulative and nonformal activities designed to focus attention on classification, sets of objects, properties of objects and sets (color, form, size), and relationships—larger, smaller. They learn the natural numbers 1 through 9. They use numbers in various activities stressing cardinal and ordinal meanings, number relationships (greater than, less than, equal), and some intuitive preoperations (joining disjoint sets, separating sets).

Levels 1 and 2 Children become involved with more formal aspects of mathematics. They learn to use written forms (sentences) to express mathematical relationships. They use formal operations, principally addition and subtraction and their corresponding algorithms. The principles of our positional notation system are taught so as to deepen understanding and increase flexibility with computation. Axiomatic properties (commutation, association, identity) are approached as laborsaving aids in computational exercises. If . . . then reasoning is begun; simple data collection and probabalistic inference are introduced as number patterns are stressed. Basic nonmetric geometric concepts are treated (point, line, plane), and intuitive study of simple polygons is begun. Principles of measurement are stressed (principally involving linear and area measurement) employing arbitrary as well as standard metric and English measurement units. Emphasis is placed upon understanding whole numbers 0 through 100 and upon habituation of the basic combinations for addition and subtraction.

Levels 3 and 4 Problem solving and applications are extended so that children are effectively responding to questions involving quantitative considerations. Whole-number operations are expanded to include multiplication and division, and the complexities of equations and algorithm forms are increased.

The distributive property is taught, and the habituation of multiplication-division combinations is emphasized. Problems involving measurement and graphing (cartesian plane) are more frequently encountered and simple functional relationships are explored. Nonmetric and metric geometry are extended to include formal analysis of polygons, study of angles, and simple constructions. Rational numbers are introduced, principally through concrete identification modes focused upon part of unit and part of collection concepts.

Levels 5 and 6 As power with mathematics is extended, children encounter more complex uses of whole numbers. However, considerable attention is given the rational numbers, including the four operations and their algorithms, and negative integers are encountered. Applications from the physical and social sciences are taught including elementary statistics (mean, median, range, normal distribution), probabilities expressed in the form a/b, and the representation of linear relationships in equation form. Nonmetric geometry focuses upon similarity and congruence, extending to consideration of irregular polygons and symmetry, and metric geometry includes the study of prisms and circles. Decimal fraction notation is introduced, and computations involving fractions expressed through positional notation is begun. Prime numbers and prime factors receive considerable attention. Of course, relationships expressed as ratios are introduced and thoroughly explored, including percentage applications. Prime composite numbers receive treatment also.

Levels 7 and 8 Consolidation and extension characterize these levels. Students extend their uses of integers and rational numbers through increasing complexity and rigor. Number systems are defined and axiomatic properties are formalized. Challenging applications of mathematics to the physical and social sciences are encountered, including simulation, statistical analysis, projection, estimating probabilities of ordered and independent events. Notation is extended to include exponents and scientific notation. Metric geometry includes the derivation and use of formulas, including the Pythagorean theorem, for analysis of two- and three-dimensional forms, and transformational analysis is encountered. Linear functions are studied and patterns are analyzed including finite and infinite series and equivalence classes. Topics from number theory are explored, stressing patterns and functional usage.

It may be noted that the measurement strand has included metric units at all levels as a part of the treatment of underlying principles of measurement. Recently, some elementary school programs have undergone major revision to include emphasis upon the standard units in metric scale, but in most cases they were programs emphasizing superficialities rather than principles of measurement. When the measurement strand is properly developed, metric units are as natural as arbitrary units or standard English units (and somewhat easier for children to learn and use).

Beneath the overriding content guidelines which structure the elementary mathematics program, there is clear recognition that topics and activities must be in consonance with child development characteristics at all levels. The work of Piaget as discussed in the chapter on psychological foundations has had a great impact on the design of modern programs. Another influence beginning to have an impact is the emerging theory of imagery learning. This theory challenges the belief that all human learning proceeds through verbal mediation. Human thought (and hence learning) may proceed through the transmission and storage of images which are not translated into symbolics or verbal associations. This emerging theory, like Piaget's theory, also would tend to cause reexamination of curriculum organizations and teaching methodologies which predominantly emphasize abstract mathematics without regard for concrete embodiments and applications.

INSTRUCTIONAL MEDIA

Although it is possible to restrict the presentation of mathematics concepts to abstract symbolics and paper and pencil activities, there is a growing awareness of a need to bring mathematics concepts into the range of young children's sense experiences. Drill procedures which emphasize repetitions of the same stimuli are coming under increasing challenge. Experience procedures which emphasize the nonrepetitive use of a wide variety of stimuli are looked upon with greater favor. The prescribed use of concrete referents and manipulative materials is increasingly prominent in program formulations. In addition to the variety of real objects commonly found in elementary classrooms, there are a number of materials designed especially to impinge mathematical concepts on the senses of young children. Among the most useful of those appearing in recent years, and adaptable to use across the elementary sequence, are the following:

Number Blocks or Strips

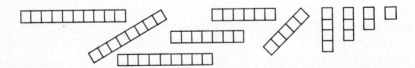

These blocks or strips may be viewed as intact collections of square units for each of the first nine or ten natural numbers. Their most frequent and effective use is associated with early identification and manipulation of these numbers, although they also are effectively used in later work with algorithms, introduction to rational numbers, linear measurement, and area measurement. The strips usually are 1 centimeter to 2 centimeters in width and vary in length by multiples of the width dimension from one through nine or ten.

Multibase Blocks

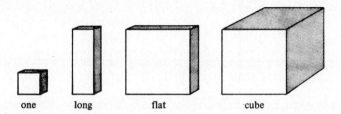

one   long   flat   cube

These "blocks" are constructed of wood and plastic, and most follow a rough model of point, line, plane, space dimensionality. They are designed to make concrete the mathematical basis for our positional-notation system with special attention to the increase of power of an arbitrarily chosen base number as one proceeds to the left through natural number positions. Since the total set of blocks includes nondecimal bases as well as ten, it is suitable for introduction to positional notation, algorithms, some work with rational numbers, and elementary algebra.

Number Balance

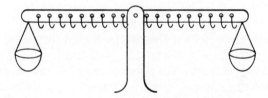

The balance can be used to illustrate number relations and serves equalities and inequalities equally effectively. The model illustrated here may be used in several ways along two pathways. First, the pans suspended at the end of the beams may be used in a simple balance relationship to solve for unknowns, that is, two disguised packages of washers ($2x$) plus three washers may be balanced by seventeen washers in the other pan, with the children's goal to solve for x. Second, the calibrated intervals from the fulcrum may be used. Two washers hung on the hook at 3 may be balanced by how many washers hung on the hook at 2? The balance may be used for all operations involving early whole numbers, axiomatic properties, rational numbers, some geometry, and some physical measurement.

Pegboard

Pegboards are prepared commercially in various forms. Essentially, they are merely wood or plastic sheets of arbitrary dimension with punched holes into which pegs may be placed. Of course the pegs may be placed so as to serve as

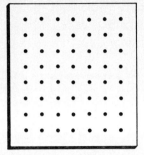

vertices of various polygons, and various geometric concepts may be illustrated or approached concretely merely by connecting the pegs with yarn or rubber bands. Similarly, if the pegs are viewed as locaters of points in a cartesian system, graphing and functional relationships may be shown. The pegboard may be used in teaching whole number operations, number relations, fractions, metric and nonmetric geometry, and coordinate geometry.

TEACHING STRATEGIES

There are many different ideas about how best to teach mathematical concepts and generalizations to children. Some of these ideas are revealed in total curriculum approaches, which may be viewed as macroteaching strategies. Others are seen in approaches to individual lessons or short sequences of lessons. These may be regarded as microteaching strategies.

At the present time, quite different approaches to instruction are found among the macrostrategies in elementary mathematics. Process-oriented and child-development-oriented programs place a premium on the nature of children's mathematical encounter, and rigid content hierarchies commonly are abandoned. Popular among such programs are the so-called laboratory programs which range from relatively unstructured experiences in a richly furnished environment of manipulative materials, games, puzzles, and audio-visual media to the more disciplined task-card approach in laboratory learning. In the former type, children freely choose laboratory activities on the basis of interest and/or need. It is expected that as knowledge grows, interests ultimately will be enlarged to include all necessary and worthwhile mathematics topics. In the task-card programs, children may choose or are assigned various tasks in the laboratory setting, the completion of which assures encounter with certain mathematical concepts. Most programs of this type are found to be quite motivational, at least at the beginning. Most commonly stressed disadvantages are their relatively uncontrolled, poorly articulated coverage of mathematical content, and their failure to help children to develop needed concepts in depth.

Another trend producing some programs of different appearance is the trend toward complete individualization of mathematics instruction. A typical procedure is to have children work through the required mathematics material at their own pace. Each child submits written exercises when completed for teacher evaluation. If the written work does not meet some prescribed standard, a similar activity is assigned from the same or another source. In such programs the teacher serves principally as an evaluator and remediation instructor.

Other individualized programs are created from new cloth and are organized in an hierarchical structure of mathematics skills. For example, the operation addition is reduced to sequenced steps of increasing difficulty, usually related to algorithms and computational procedures. Each of these steps is the subject of a single worksheet. The child proceeds through the worksheets and hence the steps in order, taking written tests at fixed intervals to demonstrate command of the skills under instruction.

Programmed printed materials and computer-assisted instruction serve the same purposes, but they offer some advantages over the programs described above. With branched rather than linear programming, it is possible to extend the individualization concept to bypass many small steps where such skipping is warranted by student achievement. Similarly enriched reinforcement is easily undertaken when evidence suggests that the student has only partial grasp of concepts under attention. The computer has no equal when it comes to handling the bookkeeping and record-storing chores associated with teaching.

Unfortunately, at this time, structured programs which are fully individualized have dealt almost exclusively with the mechanical routines of mathematics. They have used drill and repetition as the most profitable avenues for human learning. Apparently, they have been unable to offer the range of presentation which characterizes good teaching and only rarely have they departed from response mechanisms of the paper-and-pencil variety. On the other hand, unstructured programs which are fully individualized may avoid these limitations, but critics claim that they fail to offer children a sufficient encounter with the orderly and systematic progression of mathematical ideas.

A promising approach on the horizon may be named the applied-experience approach that incorporates the better features of other approaches. Mathematics concepts are encountered in problem-solving situations involving concrete, real-world objects. This is contrasted with programs which first introduce mathematics concepts in abstract form, then later have lessons on applications. In the applied experience programs, individualization may be achieved through variable pacing or enrichment, but usually the teacher is involved in some prepared teaching, not merely as evaluation and remediation source. The concrete, real-world orientation offers much of the motivation and sense-impingement features that characterize laboratory programs, yet it holds to a structured content organization for the progressive and orderly expansion of mathematical knowledge. Likewise, these programs seem to be well adapted to contemporary learning theory and knowledge of child development characteristics. They lend themselves to either textbook, task-card, or computer-assisted presentation.

Beyond these macrostrategies are the day-to-day strategies that program framers and teachers use to make the mathematics program a lively, interesting, and absorbing adventure—the microstrategies. Over the past decade a powerful influence on the microstrategy has been the idea of discovery.

Discovery Strategies

In a sense, discovery methods in school mathematics follow two paths, which may be called deductive and inductive. In deductive discovery, children are urged to perceive relationships and patterns in particular constructions which permit them to generalize and supply missing parts of a construction. Although no formal imposition of logical methods is made, the children's success is related generally to their scheme of logical analysis. Deductive discovery strategies vary considerably, but numerical data often are presented in tabular or graphic form, and children are led to observe the relationship between the entries in the table or the configuration of the graph and some independent phenomenon. Then the children are asked, on the basis of their analysis, to supply the parts of the table or graph that have been omitted. The accuracy of their entries provides an immediate evaluation of the extent to which their observations of number patterns have been complete and the extent to which the general pattern has served to suggest specific examples. An example for the intermediate grades follows. The rules are the following:

1 Multiply each number in the shaded row by the number at the top of each column. Add the products. This sum must be the same as the number in the circle on the left.

2 Fill in the unshaded row with numbers, following 1, so that the sum of these numbers is as small as possible.

	64	16	4	1
(88)	1		5	4
(88)				

The general properties of our positional notation system using a base of four are given in the example. The child will use this generalized model as a basis for the regrouping necessary to develop a base four numeral in its final form.

Inductive discovery depends upon the child's creation of mathematical ideas that build upon one another and proceed to some generalizations. "Guided inductive discovery" is a more accurate expression because of the remote likelihood that children will simply create systems of new mathematical ideas without assistance from the teacher. Guided inductive discovery may be illustrated by the following example:

```
91  92  93  94  95  96  97  98  99  100
81  82  83  84  85  86  87  88  89  90
71  72  73  74  75  76  77  78  79  80
61  62  63  64  65  66  67  68  69  70
```

51	52	53	54	55	56	57	58	59	60
41	42	43	44	45	46	47	48	49	50
31	32	33	34	35	36	37	38	39	40
21	22	23	24	25	26	27	28	29	30
11	12	13	14	15	16	17	18	19	20
1	2	3	4	5	6	7	8	9	10

With only an introduction of the above 10 X 10 arrangement of the first one hundred natural numbers and an arrow, a group of children may proceed to develop a primitive mathematical system. Although details will vary, 4↑ usually means begin at four and move up one location in the table. Therefore 4↑ = 14. Similarly, 13→→ = 15 and 86↗↓ = 87. The scheme may be developed so that children see → and ← or ↑→ and ↙ as inverses. They may develop equations such as 13 →↑ = 36 ↙←, or they may merely observe that the order of appearance of the same arrows does not affect the value represented. Depending upon the group of children and under proper guidance, some sophisticated mathematics may be developed. In any event, the emphasis upon detection of patterns or generalizations and upon the development of skill in observation and analysis is the same as with the deductive mode. In this case the child operates without a preexisting model of generalization.

In both deductive and inductive modes children are participating in a study of mathematics through means that depart significantly from the mechanical computational mode still prominent in too many classrooms. They are more likely to enjoy their study and they are infinitely more susceptible to learning and appreciating the logical nature of mathematics.

The aspect of guiding the discovery of generalizations is clearly revealed in other sorts of examples focused more directly on specific field properties. For example, a common teaching strategy is to have the learner critically examine what has been done by imaginary children elsewhere. Ruth's and Jerry's lists of identities are given as follows:

Ruth's list	Jerry's list
$3 \times \square = \square \times 3$	$\square \times (\triangle + 3) = (\square \times \triangle) + (\square \times 3)$
$4 \times \square = \square \times 4$	$\square \times (\triangle + 5) = (\square \times \triangle) + (\square \times 5)$
$1960 \times \square = \square \times 1960$	$\square \times (\triangle + 2) = (\square \times \triangle) + (\square \times 2)$
$1{,}000{,}000 \times \square = \square \times 1{,}000{,}000$	

Then the children are asked whether they can shorten the lists or whether they can contribute to some organization of a list. The hope is that the general identities for commutation with respect to multiplication and for distribution of multiplication over addition will be developed.

The motivational aspect of the discovery orientation is exploited to create interest in activities which otherwise may be drudgery. For example, note the practice with specific addition; basic facts are necessary to solve the mystery in this example, yet the children do not face the sterile abstract repetitive model. The task is: Mark an X on the door that has only nines behind it.

7 + 2	6 + 3	5 + 4
3 + 6	8 + 1	2 + 7
0 + 9	9 + 0	6 + 3
5 + 4 ●	4 + 5 ●	1 + 8 ●
1 + 8	1 + 7	9 + 0
3 + 5	6 + 4	8 + 1
2 + 7	3 + 6	7 + 2

Likewise, note the underlying discovery model in this early lesson on the subtraction algorithm. Children are to discover the weight of each of the various-shaped objects. In this pursuit the subtraction algorithm is a necessary tool.

A Model Strategy

The teaching or microstrategies above may be seen to play a role in a systematic development of concepts. The latter two examples fit what has been called the "fixing of skills" step in the concept-development model of teaching strategies. This model assumes that instructional activities for particular concepts will follow a step by step-by-step development such as that in the following widely used model shown in Table 11-1 (Marks et al., 1970, page 45).

Other Strategies

On the other hand, teaching strategies for single lessons may be selected principally to offer variety and motivate learning, with some sensitive adaptation to particular learning tasks. For example, strategies may be chosen on the basis of the amount of child and teacher involvement. The following continuum will illustrate this idea.

Trial and error	Follow the model	Work together	Pooling ideas	Discuss with teacher	Answer teacher questions	Listen and follow

With the *trial and error* strategy, each child works independently, finding his own way without *any* help from the teacher. Using *follow the model*, the child is given a model to follow by the teacher, but works on his or her own without further teacher involvement. In *work together*, the lesson would involve children working in pairs or small groups collaboratively with minimal teacher assistance. *Pooling ideas* lessons involve the children's exploration and ideas following group discussion procedures with the teacher presiding. *Discuss with teacher* means that the teacher takes a more active role in limiting discussion topics and ensuring that focus is upon preselected concepts and skills. In *answer teacher* lessons, the teacher leads the activity by direct interaction with groups or individuals. *Listen and follow* suggests complete domination of the lesson by the

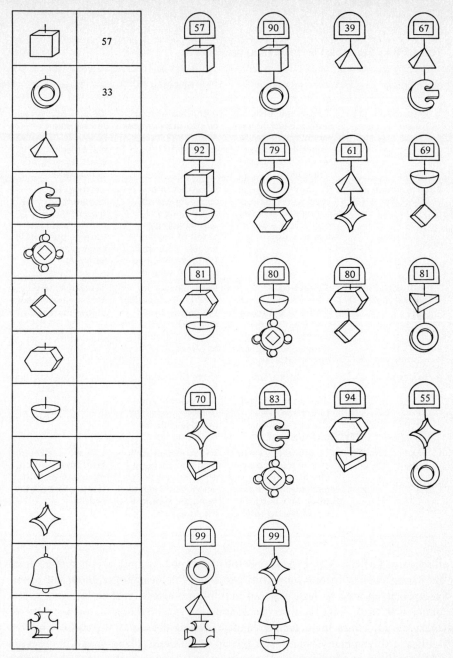

teacher, usually imposing a step-by-step procedure for children to follow. In modern classrooms, one should find a range of such strategies with emphasis upon the left of the scale.

Other organizations of teaching strategies may be arranged on a continuum of discovery application, that is, from no discovery to complete open-ended

Table 11-1 Flowchart of the Learning Sequence

Step	Purpose	Activities	Materials
1. Preparation	To provide readiness: both subject matter— including prerequisite skills, vocabulary, and concepts— and interest	A checkup—formal or informal—on prerequisite skills and vocabulary	Tests, if necessary, teacher-made or commercial. Models, real objects, and other learning aids as necessary
2. Exploration and discovery	To lead the pupil to develop the concept (or operation) as a solution to a problem situation	Presentation of a stimulating problem situation requiring improvisation of the process, concept (or operation) as a means of solution	Learning aids as needed to provide the setting. Materials as required for manipulation in exploratory activities
3. Abstraction and organization	To develop an understanding of the nature of the operation (or concept) and the interrelationship with other operations	Development of generalizations about the operation (or concept) and its interrelationships to others	Textbooks and semisymbolic manipulative materials
4. Fixing skills	To make manipulation of the operation automatic and to provide overlearning to assure retention	Memorization of facts, organization and memorization of tables, repetitive practice with the operation	Textbooks, practice materials, tests
5. Application	To promote transfer of training by developing ability to recognize the typical situation calling for use of the operation (or concept)	Experience in application to a variety of situations, with emphasis on identifying the appropriate situations	Life and simulated problem situations, models, visual aids, textbooks, bulletin boards

discovery format. Yet others may be developed around a concrete-abstract sequence, ranging from purely concrete lessons involving no symbolics or paper-and-pencil activity to lessons requiring nothing except abstraction and paper-and-pencil work. Ideally, whether considering macrostrategies, microstrategies, or broad guidelines for organizing and presenting the school programs in mathematics, a three-phase development should be followed. These phases in order are (1) development of imagery, (2) employment of symbolism, and (3) generation of systems. This means that the program should be organized and taught so as to ensure first that children's imagery for mathematics concepts is clear and reliably based in sound perceptual experience. When concepts are well developed at this level, symbolism is introduced to represent them. In turn, concepts are further explored, related, and seasoned through symbolics. Finally, structured systems of mathematics concepts may be studied and/or created based upon fully matured mathematical concepts. For example, within the subclusters on multiplication and distribution, imagery may be developed at the level of basic facts through use of realistic arrays. Imagery for 4 X 9 may be built through known combinations 4 X 4 and 4 X 5 using concrete array models.

```
. . . .     . . . . .
. . . .     . . . . .
. . . .     . . . . .
. . . .     . . . . .
```

Simply combining the two arrays to form the 4 X 9 array helps build imagery for the new basic fact. Many experiences of this sort build imagery for the distributive property. With the concept at hand the employment of symbolism consists of 4 X 4 = 16; 4 X 5 = 20; 4 X 9 = 36, modified to (4 X 4)+ (4 X 5) = 4 X 9 = 36, and such other symbolic representation as may be appropriate to needs. The generation of the systems stage involves the use of the generalization (a + b) X c = (a X c) + (b X c) as a field property in the analysis of an axiomatic system. Properly applied, the phases help organize teaching for planned conceptual growth and help structure the mathematics curriculum from early to later years.

GUIDELINES FOR THE TEACHER

Young children's mathematics learning is enhanced by presentations which impinge directly upon children's senses. Concrete referents (real objects or pictures) are vital components in the chain of experiences for young children's mathematics concept learning. Later learning is dependent upon the imagery developed through concrete embodiments.

Varied experience methodology is more beneficial to productive learning than repetitive-drill methods. Excepting the few cases where an habituated response is the instructional goal, drill serves no useful function in mathematics learning. Analytic and thoughtful responses are not encouraged through extensive stimulus-response repetitions. Instead, approaching mathematical ideas from many directions and through various media best serves the goal of functional understanding.

Concepts should be encountered through applications, not merely practiced through them. Situations which require the use of mathematics should be used for presentation, elaboration, reinforcement, and evaluation of mathematics concepts whenever possible. There is no valid basis in school mathematics for separating applied mathematics from pure mathematics. Problem solving, puzzles, mysteries, simulations, and other applications should permeate the mathematics program at all levels.

Abstract symbolics and axiomatic systems are dependent upon well-formed concepts. Advances into symbolic modes and systems analysis should not be encouraged until there is assurance that children have a solid grasp of the underlying concepts upon which such abstract work depends.

Children should be offered as much opportunity as possible to learn mathematics through discovery approaches. Although it is not a reasonable expectation that children will come to a full understanding of all important mathematics generalizations through open discovery, a guided discovery approach is favored over a strict expository approach. Such an approach encourages careful observation, thorough exploration, flexible thinking, comparisons, and discernment of patterns, all of which are important in mathematics learning.

Highly verbal materials and approaches should be avoided. To the extent possible, children's mathematics learning should not be dependent upon other learned skills or knowledge. Of course, mathematics should not be isolated from other subjects, but, at the same time, disabilities in skill subjects such as reading should not be interpreted as poor performance in mathematics. The principle of "learning by doing" is clearly demonstrated in mathematics learning and direct, purposeful child involvement is amply rewarded.

Computation should be viewed as a mathematical tool rather than as a central mathematical concept or generalization. Programs which centrally focus on computation distort the nature of mathematics and generally fail to provide fully for the children's development of mathematical understanding or process skills. Computation serves mathematics and problem solving, not the reverse of this.

Individualization procedures should involve many presentation variables, not merely pacing. Most so-called individualized programs merely permit different children to proceed through materials at their own pace. True individualization adjusts presentation to individual learning styles, interests, attitudes, and backgrounds, and demands active, insightful, and well-planned teaching.

Learning outcomes should be under continual evaluation. The extent to which instructional objectives have been achieved should be monitored continually by the teacher. Evidence in terms of performance criteria should be systematically gathered, carefully recorded, and thoroughly analyzed.

EVALUATION OF OUTCOMES OF INSTRUCTION

The definitive nature of mathematics has lent itself over the years to precise objective evaluation of facts. It has been possible to measure the student's facility with mathematical material or the effectiveness of an arithmetic program through either pure computational exercises or "word" problems. The evaluation of learning has been, in its simplest terms, the percentage of problems to which correct responses have been assigned. Though such appraisals were regarded as adequate in the past (when in truth they were not), there is general agreement on their insufficiency today. They fail to give proper recognition to the new dimensions of the modern program, even though they continue to play a role in the total evaluation package.

Increased attention is being given to evaluation schemes which measure the entire field of conceptual outcomes while also treating some aspects of instruction beyond the cognitive domain. Such evaluation dictates not only the development of a vast array of new and different objective tests but also the creation of appraisal tools which may be neither objective nor tests. As interest continues in the development of evaluation which is properly adapted to the goals of newer programs, there is likely to be an evolution of evaluation procedures and techniques which parallels the evolution of the "modern" elementary school mathematics program.

A comprehensive plan of evaluation includes the use of direct observation and a variety of instruments to assess the attainment of objectives. Significantly, in recent years there has been an increasing tendency to evaluate instructional outcomes in terms of children's overt behaviors with respect to precisely stated objectives for programs, modules, and lessons. Accordingly, precise statements of behavioral objectives have been required. Such behavioral objectives serve to guide teacher observations as well as to prescribe the content and often the nature of tests. The effect of this total movement, in general, has been positive with respect to evaluation in mathematics. It has directed some long-overdue attention to this important aspect of good instruction. It also has drawn some proper criticism. First, it has been observed that a single narrow behavioral objective for a lesson fails to recognize that any good mathematics lesson includes several objectives. For example, a new concept may be introduced while another is being maintained, and motivated interest is being established for the later introduction of a new concept. This criticism has much merit, because the multiple-objective mathematics lesson is clearly in the direction of better teaching. Another criticism leveled at current practice with respect to behavioral objectives is that they seem to have an inordinate focus upon computation and mechanical manipulations of mathematics while all too frequently ignoring substantive conceptual underpinnings. An examination of lists of such objectives today offers convincing evidence that this criticism also has merit. The lists, in total, describe a bad program by any modern standard. However, it cannot be denied that clear statements of instructional objectives and clear evidence regarding children's performance with respect to these objectives are virtually necessary in good mathematics instruction. Perhaps the evolution of the trend toward behavioral objectives and accountability eventually will produce the sort of enlightened, comprehensive evaluation system which school mathematics requires.

Two prominent considerations in evaluating conceptual outcomes are *recall* and *transfer*. The following examples will serve as examples of the types of items which may be used for each consideration in terms of a specific behavioral objective.

Objective: The student will add two and three one-digit numbers with sums $\leqslant$ 20.
(recall)   Write sentences and add these numbers

    a   7, 8
    b   9, 7
    c   2, 4, 7
    d   6, 5, 6

(transfer)

A
B
C
D
E

Find the length of each chain
- Chains AC together are the same length as DE together.
- Chains B and E are the same length.
- Chain A is 4 feet shorter than Chain E.
- Chain D is 4 feet shorter than chain C.
- Chains B and D are the same length.
- Chains DE together are 20 feet long.

Using Taxonomies of Objectives

The taxonomies of educational objectives may be used to plan questions and items for use in assessing both cognitive and affective outcomes of instruction (Bloom, 1956; Krathwohl, Bloom, and Masia, 1964). An example of a question and a test item is given in the following outline, which includes each level of the cognitive and affective taxonomy.

Cognitive Domain

Knowledge Level Who can define and give an example of the associative property? Put an X by the one of the following expressions which represents the associative property.

_____ 4 + 0   = 4 = 0 + 4
_____ (3 + 2) + 4 = 3 + (2 + 4)
_____ (4 + 2) X 6 = (4 X 6) + (2 X 6)
_____ 16 + 9 + 11 = 11 + 16 + 9

Comprehension Level Does the commutative property deal with manner of grouping elements, order of elements, or size of elements? Express the commutative property in equation form.

Application Level If Gordy has more bottle caps than Sally, and Sally has more bottle caps than Susie, who has more bottle caps, Gordy or Susie?

Use the transitive property to put the Jones children in proper order with respect to their ages.

Analysis Level   If $3 \times (2 \times 5)$ = 30
                    and $(3 \times 2) \times 5$ = 30
                    then $3 \times (2 \times 5)$ = $? \times (? \times ?)$

Analyze the line graph and predict the coordinates for its extension.

Synthesis Level How many ways are there to divide common fractions? See if you can find a way that no one else uses. Devise a plan to show the relationship between the number of even prime numbers and odd prime numbers.

Evaluation Level Is the solution to problem A correct? Is it the best one for solving the problem? Check the steps which were followed in bisecting angle B to see if they were the best steps we could use.

Affective Domain

Receiving Level Did everyone contribute some good ideas to our discussion of multiplying fractions? Give two cases where if we have not listened to someone's idea our understanding of multiplying fractions would not be so complete.

Responding Level Which way of dividing whole numbers do you like best? Make an outline of the good features of your choice.

Valuing Level How does arithmetic help people to live better lives? Name a few jobs that cannot be done if we do not know arithmetic.

FOLLOW-UP ACTIVITIES AND PROJECTS

1 Examine a fully individualized elementary mathematics program with respect to the following features:
   a Extent of concrete, imagery-building presentations
   b Amount of computation
   c Nature of diagnostic evaluations
   d Kind of individualization beyond flexible pacing
   e Nature and extent of recordkeeping
   f Role of the classroom teacher
2 Look over the teacher's editions for a current series of mathematics textbooks for grades K through 6. Do they contain these features? If so, how are they treated?
   a Concrete presentations for all concept introductions in children's text as well as in teacher presentation
   b Concept introductions through applications
   c Lesson objectives stated in behavioral terms
   d Integrated content, spiral approach
   e Motivational practice exercises
   f Computation as a tool in problem solving
   g Discovery orientation
   h Provision for individual differences
3 Make a list of at least ten features that you feel must be included in a good elementary school mathematics program; then rank order the features in terms of importance. Defend your choices and your ranking.

4 Plan a sequence of lessons for teaching a particular concept through the hierarchy (a) development of imagery, (b) employment of symbolism, and (c) generation of systems.

5 Briefly outline a plan for having children understand (a) subtraction in grade 2 or (b) ratio in grade 6.

6 Select and name some specific teaching strategies you will use in teaching mathematics at a grade level of your choice. Arrange the strategies in a structured organization if possible.

BIBLIOGRAPHY

Biggs, E. R. and J. R. MacLean. *Freedom to Learn: An Active Learning Approach to Mathematics.* Don Mills, Ontario: Addison-Wesley, 1969. A theoretical and practical manual for establishing an activity-oriented mathematics program in any elementary school.

Bloom, Benjamin S. (Ed.) *Taxonomy of Educational Objectives: Cognitive Domain.* New York: McKay, 1956. A classification of educational objectives into a hierarchy of complexity.

Cambridge Conference on School Mathematics, *Goals for the Correlation of Elementary Science and Mathematics.* New York: Houghton Mifflin, 1969. Contains proposals and arguments for infusing applications into elementary school mathematics and in particular for thoroughly integrating instruction in mathematics and the natural sciences.

Copeland, R. W. *How Children Learn Mathematics: Teaching Implications of Piaget's Research.* (2d Ed.) New York: Macmillan, 1974. Detailed consideration of children's mathematics learning based upon the formulations of Jean Piaget.

D'Augustine, C. H. *Multiple Methods of Teaching Mathematics in the Elementary School.* (2d Ed.) New York: Harper and Row, 1973. Presents a wide variety of methods, techniques, and vehicles for presenting elementary mathematical concepts to children.

Evans, E. C. *Contemporary Influences in Early Childhood Education.* New York: Holt, 1971. Discusses the theoretical and functional sources of current movements in education for young children.

Forbes, J. E., and R. E. Eicholz. *Mathematics for Elementary Teachers.* Menlo Park, Calif.: Addison-Wesley, 1971. A presentation of mathematical content designed to familiarize elementary school teachers with mathematical concepts underlying the modern elementary program.

Krathwohl, David R., Benjamin S. Bloom, and Bertram S. Masia. *Taxonomy of Educational Objectives: Affective Domain.* New York: McKay, 1964. A classification of objectives according to degree of internalization.

Lamon, W. A. (Ed.) *Learning and the Nature of Mathematics.* Chicago: Science Research Associates, 1972. A collection of articles by prominent mathematicians and mathematics educators on aspects of learning in this field.

Marks, J. L., D. R. Purdy, and L. B. Kinney. *Teaching Elementary School Mathematics for Understanding.* (3d Ed.) New York: McGraw-Hill, 1970. A comprehensive treatment of instructional method and organization for the elementary school mathematics teacher.

May, L. J. *Teaching Mathematics in the Elementary School.* (2d Ed.) New York: Macmillan, 1974. Teaching suggestions for the range of concepts included in the elementary mathematics program; emphasis upon concrete presentations.

Piaget, J. *The Child's Conception of Number.* New York: Humanities Press, 1952. The observations of the renowned psychologist-logician on children's patterned development of number knowledge.

Riedesel, C. A. *Guiding Discovery in Elementary School Mathematics.* (2d Ed.) Englewood Cliffs, N.J.: Prentice-Hall, Inc., 1974. A useful reference for teaching methodology in either standard or performance-based elementary mathematics programs.

Schminke, C. W., N. Maertens, and W. Arnold. *Teaching the Child Mathematics.* Hinsdale, Illinois: Dryden Press, 1973. A reference textbook on organizing and teaching mathematics in the modern elementary school with attention to learning theory, learning hierarchies, and teaching strategies.

Chapter 12

Science Education

The natural sciences represent man's continuing search for understanding of the universe in which he lives. In essence, the activities of science may be described as quests for patterns and generalizations that are useful in explaining, predicting, and controlling natural phenomena. Nonliving phenomena are studied through physical sciences such as physics and chemistry. Living phenomena are studied through life sciences such as botany, zoology, and physiology. Within the physical sciences are special groupings of disciplines, such as the earth sciences which include geology and meterology. Within the life sciences are interdisciplines or specializations that cut across disciplines, such as biochemistry and biology. In these and other disciplines in the broad domain of science a central goal is to increase man's reliable knowledge of the natural world.

Scholarly study in the natural sciences is marked by free and open inquiry, theory building, precise definition of terms, formulation of testable hypotheses, objective collection of data, replication of findings, public review of findings, and a continuing search for better explanations. Beyond the natural (often called basic) sciences are the applied sciences, particularly the several branches of engineering.

Since the basic natural sciences are the fountainhead of knowledge for the applied sciences, their importance to the technological progress of civilization is well established. Similarly, their crucial importance to the preservation of a planet earth which is capable of supporting and nurturing life forms is unquestioned. There has been concern not only that the natural sciences be given a role in the school curriculum that is commensurate with their contributions to our lives, but also that the approach to scientific study in the schools reflect the nature of scientific study in both natural and applied science. The concern has been especially evident within the past ten years, reflecting a maturing awareness of the ecological dependency of life forms, the finite limits of the earth and its resources, and the crucial importance of the products of science in the present and future of humanity.

CONTRIBUTION TO BASIC GOALS

Science education is rich in contribution to major educational goals. *Thinking ability* is developed as children learn to satisfy their curiosities about the universe through systematic inquiry and logical inductive analysis and as they develop useful, factual explanations for intuitive and nonintuitive phenomena. *Self-realization* stems from the profound sense of achievement which children derive from ability to gain knowledge about the objects and events of the natural world and from their uses of the knowledge itself. Children learn about responsible *human relationships* as they work together in the common enterprise of scientific inquiry, as they consider the separate contributions to knowledge from a vast number of persons and approaches, and as they weigh the potential uses of scientific knowledge for the betterment or the detriment of mankind. Contributions to *economic competence* may be found in children's consideration of the technological developments deriving from scientific knowledge, particularly consumer products, and their effect upon the cost and standard of living. *Civic responsibility* is made clearer to children as they recognize the importance of direct participation in the decision-making processes and understand science's dependency upon the individual investigative contributions of many individuals and groups. *Learning how to learn* is enhanced as children continuously increase their skills in scientific inquiry and in problem solving.

OBJECTIVES OF INSTRUCTION

The reform movement in science education over the last decade has been characterized by a shift in emphasis and, to some extent, a restatement of the purposes of science education. In the past, emphasis was placed on the "facts" of science and on technological applications. Currently, emphasis is given to the study of science qua science, and content and process are intertwined. A central goal is to develop scientific literacy based on the direct study of the natural world. Systematic descriptions and explanations of natural phenomena are desired outcomes but they are to be associated directly with useful inquiry methods. Sometimes generalizations developed in the instructional program may be related to technological development, and their social significance also is considered. However, facts and social significance do not overwhelm the characteristics of natural science. Rather, the focus is on the nature of investigative science and embedded inquiry processes so that students will move progressively toward the attainment of science objectives which are consistent with the nature of science. Such objectives as the following characterize the modern program.

Conceptual Objectives

To develop an awareness and understanding of scientific concepts, principles, and generalizations so that the child is able to do the following:

Classify objects of the natural world into orderly arrangements according to known and observed characteristics

Explain the continual changes in the natural world and cite evidences of processes of change

Identify common examples of the change of state of matter and explain the composition of matter in terms of particles which are in constant motion

Explain common examples of energy transfers based on the knowledge that energy exists in a variety of convertible forms

Describe the condition of ecological balance and its importance to various life forms including *Homo sapiens*

Explain fundamental differences between living and nonliving forms, and describe characteristics of simple and more complex life forms

Process Objectives

To develop a functional competency with the procedures of scientific inquiry so that the child is able to do the following:

Observe and classify natural phenomena with care and objectivity

Form and test hypotheses relating to counter-intuitive observations and discrepant events

Make predictions and generalizations about objects and events of the natural world

Develop creative designs for solving problems, answering questions, and testing hypotheses through experimentation, field study, use of references, and other means of investigation

Skill Objectives

To develop a functional competency with the tools of science so that the child is able to do the following:

Use common laboratory apparatus in scientific investigation

Measure and record scientific phenomena with precision and understanding

Employ appropriate quantitative methods to record and interpret data derived from scientific investigation

Accurately report the results of scientific investigation orally and in writing

Affective Objectives

To develop a view of science which helps the child to do the following:

Recognize that learning and satisfying curiosity about the natural world is a fundamental human inclination

Recognize the social relevancy and applications of scientific knowledge and put inquiry processes to use in everyday living

Demonstrate a growing awareness of and sensitivity to environmental problems and ways in which they may be handled

Describe relationship between the quality of human life, other living things, and the environment

Although there is considerable general agreement about the objectives of a modern school science program, organizations for statements of objectives differ markedly from program to program. For example, instead of the process, content, skill, and affective categories, objectives may be classified as follows: (1) science knowledge, (2) rational thinking processes, (3) manipulative and communication skills, and (4) scientific attitudes. Note, however, that the difference between the two forms is more superficial than real. They are essentially equivalent.

ORGANIZATION OF THE CURRICULUM

Organizing a school science program designed to achieve the foregoing objectives may follow a variety of approaches. First, it may be organized in terms of content and/or process hierarchies drawn directly from the separate disciplines of physics, chemistry, astronomy, biology, physiology, and geology. Or it may be organized around interrelated areas of science study such as living things, matter and energy, the earth, and the universe. A third pattern for organizing a complete program may use themes that are emphasized throughout the natural sciences—classification and order, variety and pattern, continuity and change, and interaction and interdependence. Increasingly, organizational outlines are developed around processes generalizable to all branches of science, such as classification, observation, measurement, inference, and prediction. Still another plan of organization may use broad conceptual schemes drawn from the natural sciences; for example, energy may be transformed, but it cannot be created or destroyed *or* for every action there is an equal and opposite reaction.

There is some merit to each of the foregoing organizational emphases for an elementary school science program. Likewise, there is merit in some existing eclectic combinations of organizational plans where these emphases are employed.

For example, emphasis may be given to processes of science within carefully defined and isolated content strands, or themes may be stressed as generalizations to be derived from a systematic process-oriented curriculum.

A prominent movement in science education over the past few years has been the increasing emphasis upon processes of science. There is general agreement today that process and content are inextricably bound together in a good science program but the balance of attention has shifted in favor of process for three reasons: (1) the sterile treatment of science as facts to be learned fails to reveal the nature of science and fails to keep abreast of burgeoning knowledge, (2) unless the process dimension receives systematic attention in an activity-oriented environment, children's learning is inhibited and their natural tendency to inquire is stifled, (3) in earlier programs the content emphasis was so disproportionate that a proper mix of content and process could be achieved only through geometric expansion of the process dimension. Thus, elementary science programs organized around the inquiry processes of science are becoming more abundant and process considerations are becoming more important in programs organized around content headings.

Process Organization

A singularly influential and classic model for process organization (AAAS, *Science: A Process Approach*, 1965) is designed around eight basic and five integrated processes. Instructional sequences are designed to bring children to increasingly greater proficiency in each of the processes. Science content is viewed as the medium for inquiry, while the inquiry processes are regarded as essential ingredients of all science, regardless of content. Expected terminal behaviors are explicitly stated for each category. Activities within the categories are selected to provide children with the necessary experience for reaching these behaviors. The following are illustrative.

Classification The desired terminal behavior is competence in making multistage classifications which may then be used to identify and describe independent objects. Experiences are suggested for classifying objects according to such properties as texture, color, hardness, shape, size, and other special characteristics. Single-stage classifications are followed by two-stage and multistage classifications, as shown in the following illustrative sequence: Name objects in a collection of shells or leaves; name several properties, that is, color, texture, shape; make and explain a single-stage classification; make a two-stage classification; use a color code to classify the objects; make a multistage classification.

Inference The desired terminal behaviors include competence in drawing more than one inference from a set of data, demonstrating that inferences can be tested by further observation, and demonstrating that an inference can be tested by applying known tests of the properties of objects under study. Special attention is given to distinguishing between observations and inferences and between the observer and what is observed. The following sequence is illustrative: Induce inference that plants use water; demonstrate a way to measure the water used by a plant; induce inference that water drawn through plants is transferred to the atmosphere; infer and use the concept of evaporation; test inferences regarding the water usage of plants through additional observations.

Communication The desired terminal behavior is competence in describing an experiment so that an individual who has not seen it can carry it out. Experiences clearly describing objects and events are followed by recording tools such as charting and graphing as shown in the following example: Identify and name events that can be quantified, such as five bounces of a ball; make a chart for recording the frequencies of several observed events; make a bar graph to show the relative frequencies, record and graph measured variables, describe measured changes in speed, temperature, and other properties; make a prediction on the basis of recorded measures; make a graph to show the prediction; record and graph experimental data so that replication is possible.

Measurement Desired terminal behaviors include competence in quantifying physical variables through direct and indirect measurement, in measuring the magnitude and direction of variation in an illusion, and in explaining that differences exist in perceptions of the dimensions (length, weight, area, volume, rate of evaporation, rate of change) of the physical world. The following sequence is illustrative: Distinguish and relate properties of objects by using such terms as "heavier" and "lighter"; identify relative weight by lifting; use a balance to distinguish heavier from lighter objects; order objects according to relative weight using a spring scale; select and assign arbitrary and standard units to weight measurement; explain effects of gravitation and inertia; use weight measurement to describe, order, and classify various objects.

Numbers The desired terminal behavior is competence in naming rational numbers "greater than one as a product of ten and a rational number between one and ten." The intention is to develop those number concepts needed for the descriptive, quantitative aspects of science. The following sequence is illustrative: Identify and use cardinal numbers; identify and use ordinal numbers; arrange the integers (positive and negative) on a geometric continuum; perform basic operations in the field of rational numbers; express numbers exponentially; use scientific notation for numbers derived from science inquiry.

Observation The desired terminal behavior is competence in observing natural phenomena and in translating observations into records useful to others. Attention is given to both oral and written descriptions of objects and events in terms of measureable variables such as length, area, volume, weight, time, and temperature. The hierarchy begins with observing and describing single objects or events and moves to the describing of relationships between variables as shown in the following example: Describe objects according to color, texture, relative size, and other properties; distinguish and describe differences in temperature; identify and name factors in weather variability such as temperature, moisture, air pressure, air movement, land forms; describe weather; distinguish between adequate and inadequate descriptions of observations; describe selected items so that others can identify them, including plants and animals; describe relationships between objects and behaviors.

Space/Time The desired terminal behaviors include competence in ordering objects according to position or rate of change and in finding the rate of change or the position of an object. Measurement of location in time intervals and distance are given attention as shown in the following example: Distinguish various angles according to size; identify and name angular and compass directions; use angular measures to designate changes in position; describe relationships to observer position using angles and distance; relate speed and time of arrival of moving objects; describe and quantify speed of objects; use a rule to find speed of objects; order objects in terms of their speeds.

Prediction The desired terminal behavior is competence in making and testing predictions involving two measurable quantities. Various tasks are included such as organizing data, graphing data, interpreting line graphs, and understanding functional relationships between measured variables. The following example is illustrative of a sequence that involves graphs: Use a cartesian section to graph some measurements; analyze a graph to determine the pattern of relationships (increasing, decreasing, stable); use a graph to predict a continuation of a trend (extrapolation); predict independent events using a graph (interpolation); recognize the value of making predictions from several observations; conduct an experiment to test predictions.

Building upon the background of experience in the early levels the program for intermediate- and upper-elementary levels focuses upon the five integrative processes more directly involved in systematic science investigation. These processes follow:

Formulating Hypotheses Children draw upon earlier work with inferences and prediction and learn to frame testable hypotheses regarding predicted behaviors or relationships. They learn to seek generalizable information over limited information. For example, they are encouraged to state an hypothesis about the behavior of plants rather than about the behavior of lilies, when to do so is appropriate. They learn to develop hypotheses that lend themselves to testing and to state them in very specific, clear language. They also learn to modify statements of hypotheses that can not readily be tested or are unclear and ambiguous. They are encouraged to use graphs, pictures, and models as aids in presenting hypotheses.

Defining Operationally Activities underlying this process help children refine their skill in defining. They learn to distinguish operational from non-operational definitions. They are expected to apply two criteria in framing operational definitions: (1) the definition must include an action—what is to be done—and (2) the definition must include observation—what is to be observed. For example, an experimental procedure may be defined as follows: "I will plant the six bean seeds—two in the sandy soil, two in the clay soil, and two in the regular soil. Then I will take care of them the same way and see which will grow better."

Controlling Variables Earlier experiences in observation and measurement are drawn together as well as skills in inference and prediction in the sequence of activities on controlling variables. Children are taught to observe events and interactions carefully and to infer certain cause and effect relationships, then suggest tests for these inferences under controlled situations. For example, the question of liquid movement in various materials is considered. The children may infer that the nature of the material affects the movement of the liquid. In analyzing what properties of the materials affect the behavior of the liquids, the separate properties are isolated for independent testing.

Interpreting Data The various forms for presenting and clarifying data are extended and refined. Children learn to reason from data. They extend their abilities to perform numerical analyses that bring out otherwise obscure findings. Predominantly, data are obtained through the children's direct observation. In other cases, data are supplied for special analysis by the children. For example, the children may be given a series of measurements representing experimental trials. They are asked to prepare a table for recording and organizing the data and then asked to construct a histogram for purposes of clarification. They make predictions about new trials and suggest hypotheses which may explain patterns observed in the data.

Experimenting This process includes all other processes in some form. Absolute proficiency and complete independence with experimental methodology are not expected in elementary grades, but increasing sophistication is sought in each of the underlying processes: observing, constructing questions for investigation, predicting, constructing hypotheses, identifying variables, stating operational definitions, controlling variables, drawing inferences and organizing data, interpreting data, modifying hypotheses, summarizing and reporting findings.

ILLUSTRATIVE QUESTIONS AND ACTIVITIES

The broad range of scientific processes which serve as organizational components of process-oriented curricula and which may receive some measure of attention even in content-oriented curricula may be more clearly revealed through some illustrative questions and activities. The processes included here are not confined to those listed for the model program above, but represent processes given attention in a large assortment of process-oriented programs.

"What do you notice when this drop of acid is added to the solution?" (observing) "How can we ask about the plant's growth so we can find out?" (framing questions for investigation) "What do you think will happen when we slow down the wheel? Why?" (predicting) "Is 'Plants need sunlight to live' more clear than 'If we put the bean and pansy plants in the closet and make it real dark they will die'?" (framing hypotheses) "Perhaps the little boat was too heavy. What else may have caused it to sink?" (identifying variables) "In your experiment what are you going to do with the ice? What will you be looking for?" (stating operational definitions) You decided to keep the water temperature at 70°F and use only one gram of salt. Why? (controlling variables) There is only water in the compartment where we put the ice. What can we guess about the temperature? (drawing inference) Make a graph using the measurement numbers you put in your table. Find the line of best fit. (collecting and organizing data) What does your graph tell us about the amount of water dripping from the faucet every minute? (interpreting data) Your experiment showed us that the longer candle did not burn longer. What did you say about the candle's thickness? Should we try a new experiment? (modifying hypotheses) Julie wants to study bees also. Write the story of your experiment so that she can use the result or check your work. (summarizing and reporting findings)

Content Organization

Historically, content structures have served as organizing bases for science programs at all levels. Today, some programs maintain discrete content boundaries, and other programmatic features are subsumed under content headings. Although content strands labeled physics, chemistry, biology, zoology, botony, biochemistry, geology, and physiology are rarely seen in elementary school programs, topics drawn from these disciplines may be found as principal organizational components. For example, some programs are developed around such content strands as *Animals and Their Surroundings, The Human Body, Living Plants, Meteorology and Our Changing Environment, The Earth's Changing Surface, Our Solar System, Matter and Energy, Magnetism and Electricity, Machines, Heat and Its Actions, Sound and Sound Transmission, Light and Its Behavior.*

Today there is a growing acceptance of the notion that content-centered elementary science programs should focus upon what may be called conceptual schemes or systems rather than upon narrowly defined topics such as those above. Such conceptual schemes are seen as deriving from the "great ideas" or pervasive principles of science. These major structures are then broken down into subgeneralizations, concept clusters, and concepts. Usually a spiral approach is used; concepts are reencountered throughout the elementary levels, each time at a higher plane of understanding. Concepts within a conceptual system are arranged in sequences that take account of children's cognitive developmental characteristics as well as the logical development of the "great idea." Among important conceptual schemes are such major themes as the nondestructibility of matter, the transformation of energy, the replication of life forms through heredity, and a statistical, probabilistic view of the universe. Within each of these major themes there are major generalizations as illustrated in Table 12-1.

Major generalizations are subdivided into clusters and discrete concepts. The internal structure of the conceptual scheme "Energy is neither created nor destroyed; it can only be transformed from one type to another" is illustrated in Chart 12-1.

The scope of the broad conceptual schemes composing a modern, conceptually oriented science program is illustrated by the following (Science Framework for California Public Schools: 1970):

A Most events in nature occur in a predictable way, understandable in terms of a cause-and-effect relationship; natural laws are universal and demonstrable throughout time and space.

B Frames of reference for size, position, time, and motion in space are relative, not absolute.

C Matter is composed of particles which are in constant motion.

D Energy exists in a variety of convertible forms.

E Matter and energy are manifestations of a single entity; their sum in a closed system is constant.

F Through classification systems, scientists bring order and unity to apparently dissimilar and diverse natural phenomena.

    1 Matter is organized into units which can be classified into organizational levels.

    2 Living things are highly organized systems of matter and energy.

    3 Structure and function are often interdependent.

G Units of matter interact.

    1 The bases of all interactions are electromagnetic, gravitational, and nuclear forces whose fields extend beyond the vicinity of their origins.

    2 Interdependence and interaction with the environment are universal relationships.

    3 Interaction and reorganization of units of matter are always associated with changes in energy.

A very significant content focus in newer program outlines is that of ecology and/or environmental education. The interdependencies of life forms, the effect of environmental decay, the human population explosion, and the depletion of natural resources are being awarded increasing attention, consistent with their crucial importance today and in the future.

Table 12-1 Major Themes and Major Generalizations

Major themes	Major generalizations
Matter	
1 All objects are made of matter and although this matter can be altered or transformed, sometimes into energy, it cannot be created or destroyed.	**1.1** Matter is any substance that occupies space and has weight. **1.2** Matter has several physical states—solid, liquid, or gas determined by the degree of molecular activity. **1.3** Matter is considered over a wide spectrum of sizes from subatomic particles to the immensely large phenomena such as galaxies and universes. **1.4** Matter may be living or nonliving.
Energy	
2 All activity, living or nonliving, involves energy. This energy can change form, but it cannot be created or be destroyed.	**2.1** Energy is the ability for doing work. (Anything that "happens requires energy.) **2.2** Energy is derived primarily from four sources: gravity, electricity, magnetism, and nuclear activity. **2.3** Some convenient designations for available energy are heat, sound, light, electrical, chemical, atomic, and muscular energy. **2.4** Energy can be changed from one form to another.
Interaction	
3 There is a continuous inter-action of energy and matter (or of materials), both living and non-living.	**3.1** Energy is involved in all interactions of nonliving matter. **3.2** Gravity affects the position and movement of molecular, terrestrial, and celestial objects. **3.3** Living organisms are dependent directly or indirectly on solar (nuclear) energy. **3.4** Living organisms require certain environmental conditions to exist, and these environmental factors usually limit the abundance and distribution of the organism.
Change	
4 Most materials of the universe and of the organisms found on the earth experience aging, changing, or evolving processes.	**4.1** The surface of the earth is continually changing. **4.2** Prehistoric organisms and earth strata give evidence of an evolutionary change. **4.3** There is evidence of continuity and change in the development of living organisms. **4.4** Our celestial universe seems to be constantly changing. **4.5** A state of balance or equilibrium occurs between any two opposing forces or influences.

Source: Santa Clara County, California, 1964.

Dual Emphasis

The dichotomy of process and content is relatively artificial when applied to curriculum practice. Regardless of whether content or process guidelines serve to organize a science program, both ultimately are included in its implementation. Thus, relative emphasis upon content or process determines a curriculum

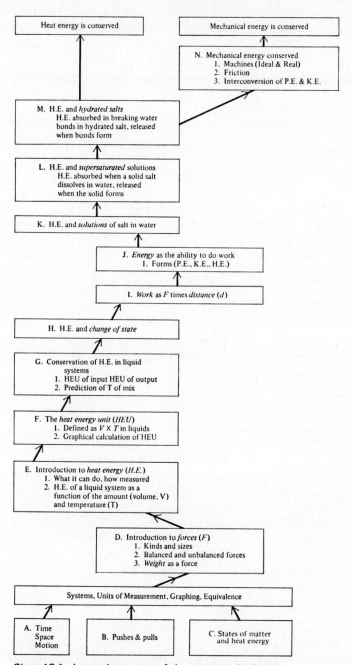

Chart 12-1 Internal structure of the conceptual scheme.
(*Source:* Conceptually Oriented Program in Elementary Science, New York University, 1974.)

organization rather than presence of absence of one or the other. Some organizational structures stress relative balance of these two important components. For example, the conceptual schemes organization within the physical and life sciences is obvious in the following organization. At the same time, process dimensions have been very influential in organizing the program as shown in Chart 12-2.

Life Sciences		Physical Sciences	
Conceptual system	*concept*	*Conceptual system*	*concept*
ORGANISMS	organism birth death habitat food web	MATERIAL OBJECTS	clusters object property material serial ordering change
LIFE CYCLES	detritus growth development life cycle genetic identity biotic potential generation plant and animal metamorphosis	INTERACTION AND SYSTEMS	evidence interaction evidence of interaction systems interaction-at-a-distance
		SUBSYSTEMS AND VARIABLES	subsystem evaporation histogram
POPULATIONS	population food chain food web optimum range		solution variable
		RELATIVE POSITION AND MOTION	reference object relative position relative motion
ENVIRONMENTS	environment environmental factor range optimum range		polar coordinates rectangular coordinates
		ENERGY SOURCES	energy transfer energy chain energy source
COMMUNITIES	photosynthesis community food transfer producers consumers		energy receiver
		MODELS: ELECTRIC AND MAGNETIC INTERACTIONS	scientific model magnetic field electricity
ECOSYSTEMS	consumers decomposers raw materials ecosystem water cycle food-mineral cycle oxygen-carbon dioxide cycle pollutant		

Chart 12-2
Source: Science Curriculum Improvement Study

A paramount objective of the program is to build a broad scientific conceptaul structure so that the learner's present and later interactions with the natural world may be properly assimilated. At the same time the selection and articulation of topics provide the learner with new ways to perceive and study his natural environment. Concepts within each unit (conceptual system) unfold in a sequential way, but the unfolding process is something more than progressing through a logical hierarchy of concepts. The cognitive developmental mappings of Jean Piaget have served to guide the deployment of student activities so as to build inquiry processes gradually as children become ready for them. Likewise, conceptual treatment is adapted to this developmental plan.

A different sort of balance may be achieved when content is chosen because it is especially suitable for inducing process development. One such program (Elementary Science Study, ESI, 1973) uses a large number of well-chosen units to permit learners a choice of subject matter. Hence it has no content sequence per se. While the units are chosen because they offer fertile ground for children's independent investigation and still promote a continuous development of investigative skills, the program also has no prescribed process sequence. It is held that as children interact with the well-selected instructional materials, they will acquire strategies for handling observations and they also will assimilate important science concepts. Children are provided with interesting materials in the form of kits and are urged to manipulate, observe, and follow their own curiosities. Written prescriptions and teacher directions are kept at a bare minimum. In this way, responsibility for learning is shifted directly to the children, and they are stimulated to develop their own questions and means for gaining and interpreting information. The guidelines for organization are thus vested principally in child motivation with balanced attention devoted to process and content objectives. Some examples of units offered in this individualized-type program are the following:

Life sciences	Physical sciences
Behavior of mealworms	Kitchen physics
Peas and particles	Mirror cards
Changes	Rocks and charts
Euglena	Batteries and bulbs
Bones	Gases and airs
Microgardening	Pendulums
Growing seeds	Melting ice cubes
Small things	Mystery powders
Earthworms	Light and shadows
Eggs and tadpoles	Primary balancing
Brine shrimp	Spinning tables
Activity wheels	Colored solutions
Budding twigs	Slips and slides
Crayfish	Baloons
Pond water	Sink and float

As may be appreciated from these well-known program examples, the wide divergence of elementary school science programs permits no clear generalization with respect to organizational structure. Unlike other curriculum areas, there are no widely accepted models from which minor departures are made. Other than the conceptual schemes that most programs include along with content from the basic sciences and inquiry processes, there are no pervasive guidelines to elementary science curriculum organization. Expectedly, the range of program models is nearly infinite.

Similarly, the sequencing of content and/or processes from early to later grades follows no consensus guidelines. Nearly all topics within the range of young children's comprehension may be found at nearly all levels. Nearly all inquiry processes, except refined independent experimentation, may be found at nearly all levels. However, there does exist a general rule that the approach to the content and the depth of penetration is conditioned by child development knowledge. Programs vary considerably in their accommodation to this principle. As indicated earlier, attention to processes may be sequenced as in the following distribution in Table 12-3.

Similarly, within each process, behaviors may be sequenced. Each sequence begins with first-level behaviors and moves to terminal behavior as shown in the example of classifying presented in Chart 12-4. An advantage of arranging such hierarchies of behaviors is that a child's vertical position can be determined, and instruction can be planned to provide for continuing progress to higher levels. It is assumed that the attainment of behaviors on each higher level depends on development of the behaviors listed at the preceding level.

	Grades							
Processes	*K*	*1*	*2*	*3*	*4*	*5*	*6*	*Total*
Observing	10	5	3	4				22
Space/Time relations	6	6	3	3		1		19
Classifying	3	3	2	3	2			13
Using numbers	2	3	4	3	3	2		17
Communicating	1	4	3	4	1			13
Measuring	2	5	6	2	3			18
Inferring			3	4	2			9
Predicting			2	3	1	1		7
Defining operationally					2	3	4	9
Controlling variables					7	5	3	15
Interpreting data					3	11	5	19
Formulating hypotheses					1	3	3	7
Formulating models					1	1	6	8
Experimenting					1	1	6	8

Chart 12-3 Sequencing
Source: AAAS. *Science: A Process Approach*, 1965.

Classifying

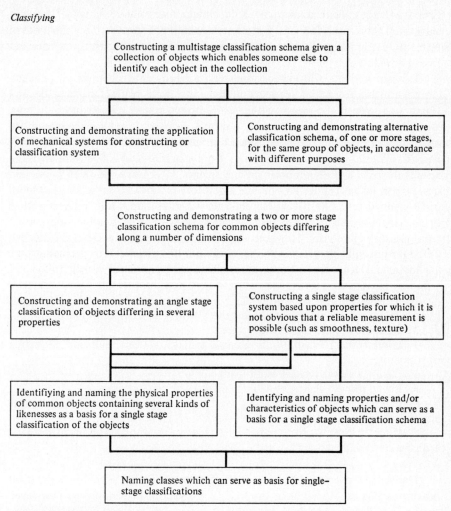

Chart 12-4 Classifying

INSTRUCTIONAL MEDIA

Science education is unique in the elementary school curriculum in demand for instructional materials. In some sense all the real objects of the natural world may be considered materials of school science. Such constraints as finances, space, special equipment, and staff narrow the range of choice. Beyond this the characteristics of young children at the various elementary levels (physical dexterity, caution, ability to abstract) further delimit the selection of objects suitable for study. However, the activity-oriented curriculum with its process objectives demands a broad assortment of material for study and appropriate laboratory equipment to support independent investigative activity. It is not surprising, therefore, that lists of necessary equipment for sustaining the modern elementary science program usually include between two hundred and fifty and five hundred items.

To help mitigate the expense and physical problems accompanying the accumulation and storage of necessary equipment, various planes have been devised for sharing science equipment within and between several schools or classrooms. Where it is not possible to maintain a special, fully equipped science laboratory at the school site or to equip each classroom unit fully, a kit containing the most needed materials may be transported from classroom to classroom. In some school districts a well-equipped mobile science laboratory has been developed using a van or bus frame. This mobile laboratory is moved from school to school on a planned schedule. Grouping children within a school into interest groups or sequencing material usage over longer periods of time provides some relief from multiple purchases. However, there is no escaping the fact that the modern elementary science program is neither easily nor inexpensively maintained.

In general, it is agreed that a good science program must have the following:

1 A wide range of measuring devices (thermometers, barometers, balances, hydrometers, galvanometers, rulers, breakers) with emphasis upon metric units
2 Microscopes and related equipment
3 Tools (construction tools, pumps, pulleys, motors, scissors, dissecting instruments)
4 Chemicals and related equipment
5 Living things (plants, small animals, fish, simple life forms)
6 Laboratory facilities (running water, gas supply for heat, small pressure chambers)
7 Miscellaneous — (dry cells, bulbs, lenses, thermostats, bunson burners, acquaria, terraria)

The science program has been at the forefront of what probably is the most notable recent development in the field of instructional technology. This development has been called the creation of "instructional systems." It is a phenomenon which grew out of the realization that the classroom teacher simply had neither the time nor skill to bring together the large number and variety of materials needed in the modern science program. Without logistical assistance for the teacher, program objectives could not be accomplished. Thus, the instructional system approach began as a concession to the realities of teaching. In simplest terms, it involves nothing more than a "kit" of instructional materials which serves a single science activity or a sequence of such activities. A kit may include materials needed by one child, a group of children (usually five or six), or a class (usually thirty children), depending upon instructional recommendations. The kit may contain all necessary experimental materials needed by children for a delimited activity including objects under study, measuring instruments and other equipment and supplies prescribed in the instructional plan.

It also may include instructional sheets, work sheets, tests, and other printed materials for children, and a printed instructional guide for the teacher. Finally, it may include augmentation materials such as audio tapes, film loops, prepared models, and projection materials. The only necessary materials not included in the kit are the materials common to all schools or easily and inexpensively obtainable. It is apparent why this integrated approach has been called a multi-media or systems approach. Chart 12-5, an excerpt from an activity in a modern program, will reveal its scope.

The idea of the multimedia system has developed and flourished to meet the special needs of modern science education, but it has been transplanted to other curriculum areas.

Obviously, the single textbook approach to science education is becoming obsolete. The demands of contemporary science teaching ensure an increasing adoption of the systems or multimedia approach. Beyond this there is an increasing tendency to extend science instruction well beyond classroom boundaries. For example, with the increasing importance of ecology and environmental education as topics of study in elementary school science, "outdoor laboratories" have become more common. These laboratories vary considerably in character, ranging from a small plot of ground on the school playground to nature areas of considerable size. In all cases they are designed to offer children the opportunity to know and appreciate an unspoiled natural environment and to study life science phenomena first hand. Current recommendations favor the incorporation

RELATED MATERIALS

Listed below are the materials required to conduct this exercise.

Some items cannot be supplied at all or are not supplied by Xerox in the Standard Kit. These are designated as *NS*. Note, however, that many items so designated are supplied in the Comprehensive Kit. A separate list of these items is included with the comprehensive materials.

It should be noted that some supplied items are expended in the course of this exercise. These expendable items are designated as *EXP*.

Items too large for the Exercise Drawer will be found in the Teacher Drawer and are designated as *TD*.

Bean seeds, 100 (EXP)
Flowerpots, 2 (EXP)
Vermiculite, 1 package (TD, EXP)
Geranium plant, 1 (NS)
Celery stalks, 30 (NS)
Dishpan, 1 (NS)
Single-edge razor blade, 1 (NS)
Red food coloring, 1 bottle (EXP)
Plastic cups, 30 (EXP)
Large pail, 1 (NS)

Leafy shoots of willow, pine, privet, sycamore, cotton-wood, tomato, or geranium, 10, approximately 35 cm long (NS)
Flexible plastic tubing, 8 pieces
Masking tape, 1 roll (NS)
Cardboard, 10 pieces, 25 × 50 cm or larger (NS)
Modeling or florist clay (NS)
3-decimeter metric rules, 10 (found in Exercise "i" drawer)
Graph paper, 2-mm squares printed in green ink, 100 sheets (TD, EXP)
Plastic bags, 8 (EXP)
White petroleum jelly, 1 tube (NS)
100X microscope or a microprojector, 1 (NS)
Microscope slides, 6 (NS)
Cover slips for slides, 6 (NS)
Potted plants, 2, 15 to 20 cm high (NS)
Illustrations (as in Figure 4), 1 copy
Graph (as in Figure 5), 1 copy

Chart 12-5 Multimedia Approach
   Source: AAAS. Science: A Process Approach, Part D, Loss of Water From Plants.

of such study areas into all elementary school sites or within reasonable access to all schools, particularly those in heavily populated urban centers where needs may be greatest.

TEACHING STRATEGIES

The most common teaching strategies in elementary school science are those which serve as models for scientific inquiry. The same processes listed as program objectives and with which the children are to become increasingly familiar are used to fashion teaching. The underlying theory behind the use of such strategies may be expressed by the age-old maxim that children "learn by doing." Thus, the teaching strategy which opens the inquiry field but which leaves children free to question, explore, and investigate is the preferred strategy in the modern science program.

Apparent in teaching strategies built upon scientific inquiry is the important factor of discovery. Implicit in such a process orientation is the idea that one learns about his natural world largely through the satisfaction of curiosity about observed phenomena and discovery of new wonders in the natural world. Such curiosity satisfaction is accomplished through systematic inquiry and what has been called inductive discovery. Learning through discovery modes has been found to produce at least as much factual knowledge as expository modes. Importantly, discovery produces much greater retention of content and process generalizations and, hence, more useful knowledge.

It is generally conceded that open-ended discovery is neither sufficiently efficient nor controlled to satisfy the demands of a developmental science program for young children. Instead, what has come to be known as the guided-discovery strategy is predominant in school science. Since this strategy is preferentially used, the range and number of other teaching strategies have been narrowed in this field.

In guided discovery the teacher may help to focus observations, prompt discussion, prepare appropriate clarifying demonstrations, instruct in the use of equipment, and, in general, serve as the organizing agent for the activity. However, teacher actions are carefully restrained so as only to facilitate student inquiry and student discovery. Following such guidance, the children are brought to higher and higher levels of skill in the use of investigative processes, through active involvement, not through mechanistic performance.

Strategy-guiding Experimentation

The following part of a lesson sequence shows how such processes as observation, exploration, demonstration, prediction, suggestion of experimental procedures, experimentation, recording data analysis, and drawing conclusions may be developed through a guided-discovery orientation based on these processes. The purpose of this particular experiment is to find out how the size of the opening in bottle caps is related to the time needed to empty a bottle of water. Suggested procedures are as follows:

1 Distribute bottles and caps to the students. Permit *exploration* of them so that they will learn to fill and empty the bottles and will notice the different sizes of the openings in the caps.

2 *Demonstrate* the filling and emptying of the bottles. Ask the students to *predict* how size of opening will affect the time it takes to empty a bottle. Ask the students to *suggest procedures* that may be used to find out.

3 Have each team of students proceed with the *experiment,* keeping time records *and recording data.*

4 Have the children discuss and *analyze* the findings of different teams. Let them explore reasons why minor differences in findings were noted (errors in counting, errors in writing).

5 Consider *conclusions* regarding the size of the opening and the time needed to empty the bottle.

This experiment may be followed by others which emphasize the same sequence of steps or others which are based on the same model but which place emphasis upon other steps. In a comprehensive use of guided-discovery strategies special emphasis is selectively given to observing, questioning, predicting, designing experiments to test predictions, and collecting and analyzing data. Rigid steps of procedure are not suggested. Rather, students wrestle with questions and propose answers on their own level. The teacher's role is simply to help students conduct their own experiments. Important elements in the teaching strategy may be considered preparation steps. For example, planning so that there is adequate time for the children's exploration and manipulation of equipment, and class interactions to sharpen predictions and collection and analysis of data, are important aspects of the teaching strategy. In this atmosphere, children inevitably will raise questions, plan procedures, conduct the experiment with minimum guidance, make their own observations, and draw their own conclusions.

From time to time it is important to involve the children in a capstone experiment which will unify subjective findings and reinforce major scientific goals. Such experiments which serve to unify and corroborate the discoveries are necessarily direct and often more prescriptive than the flexible and open development of experiments identified with children's fact finding. The following experiment is illustrative:

After the children have studied aspects of animal coloration through a carefully designed series of subjective experiences, it is expected that they are aware that (1) the color blending of an animal and its background reduces the conspicuousness of the animal and that (2) concealing coloration bears a relationship to survival in a predatory environment. Leading children in the development of an experiment to unify and substantiate the bases for this awareness is a part of the strategy for a lesson which may include the following recommended procedures:

1 Discussion and summary of previous experiences
2 Planning and preparation for the experiment
3 Carrying out the experiment
4 Recording the data
5 Discussion and agreement on results
6 Recording of results
7 Discussion of experimentation involving animals
8 Revisiting the experimental site (to confirm experimental results)

The chosen experiment must be a good model for the adaptation of the experimental mode to the group enterprise. In this case, it involves all children in the imaginative role of birds preying upon caterpillars. Each child (bird) has a "crop" into which caterpillars are placed and later counted. The "caterpillars" are half-toothpicks, some with concealing coloration and some with contrasting coloration. For example, if a lawn is available, five hundred half-toothpicks are colored green to match the lawn and five hundred are uncolored. The experiment is conducted by having the children (birds) search for the toothpicks (caterpillars) for a given short period (one to two minutes). The caterpillars are placed in receptables (crops), which are emptied upon return to the classroom. Graphs are constructed which show the distribution of "eaten" camouflaged and uncamouflaged "caterpillars." The result of the experiment is convincing demonstration of the role of adaptive coloration in animal survival. It reinforces and corroborates the summary results of earlier experiments. It also provides a model of experimentation which may be generalized for individual scientific inquiry. Significantly, the experiment provides a field-study experience in the life sciences which enriches the study in a manner not possible within the confines of a schoolbuilding.

Explore, Invent, Discover

Under the umbrella of guided-discovery there are various models or substrategies adapted to particular programs or particular needs. For example, one popular program suggests a three step approach (SCIS, 1974). The steps may be summarized as follows: (1) preliminary *exploration* to introduce a new experience, (2) *invention* of concepts to interpret the experience, and (3) *discovery* or application of the concepts in new situations. Before a new concept is introduced, children are provided opportunities to explore familiar objects in a way that creates a problem they cannot handle adequately. This is followed by the introduction of a concept that may be used to interpret the experience. The concept is introduced through activities which involve the child. A verbal label is usually associated with the concept so that communication can follow. The discovery phase is encountered as children use the concept to predict and interpret new events.

The three phases of exploration, invention, and discovery may be illustrated by the following examples drawn from the unit on systems:

Exploration In the first lessons in the unit children select objects, such as a battery, wire, paper clips, string, and scissors and paper, and use them in an experiment. Each child records the objects that were selected and used. Children make arrangements of parquetry blocks and record the blocks in the arrangements.

Invention In the next set of lessons the teacher uses blocks to demonstrate a system and the word "system" is used to describe it. Other systems are demonstrated and the term "system" is used to describe them and is written on the chalkboard. Children are asked to identify objects in each system.

Discovery In the remaining lessons children use the systems concept to observe and analyze other systems. Objects are arranged and used in a system; records are made of each system; and objects in pictured systems are identified and discussed. Systems in the classroom, such as bookshelves, scissors and paper, and the clock, are discovered and discussed. Systems are isolated from their environment and discussed. The concept is extended by identifying and discussing systems found out of school, such as cars, toys, and sports equipment. A general model for guiding discovery experiences includes the steps shown in Chart 12-6. Within each category inductive modes are followed and subdiscoveries are encouraged. Discovery activities that may be included under each category are as follows:

1 *Focusing experiences* help the children discover connections between a new concept or generalization and their prior experience. Example: Have children consider the movement of various objects on an inclined plane and their experience riding a bicycle down a hill.

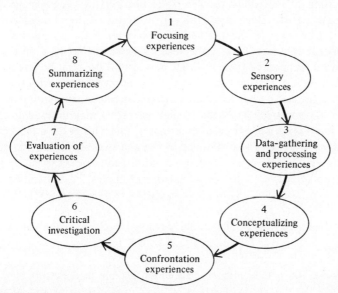

Chart 12-6 Guided-discovery model
   Source: Science Framework for California Public Schools, 1970.

2 Sensory experiences help children to discover particular features of materials under study. Example: Have children feel the surface of rocks with eyes closed and tell what they notice.

3 *Data gathering and processing experiences* enables students to discover new information about objects and events. Example: Have children count and record the number of times their heart beats per minute before and after exercise.

4 *Conceptualizing experiences* assist students to discover the conceptual ties between new ideas and existing ideas. Example: Have children examine the coloration patterns of various animals and consider possible reasons.

5 *Confrontation experiences* help children discover the unexpected, the discrepant event, the divergent behavior. Example: Have children consider why only the can that was sealed collapsed when all cans were cooled together.

6 *Critical investigation* enables the student to confirm his hypotheses and depend upon his observations. Example: Help children seal several heated cans and confirm that all will collapse if cooled.

7 *Evaluation of experience* helps children to discover any errors in their perceptions and understanding. Example: Have children measure and record what is actually a "snail's pace."

8 *Summarizing experience* enables children to make applications and to discover gaps in knowledge. Example: Have children design a water wheel.

Strategies for Demonstrations

Demonstrations are common in science programs and may be conducted for a variety of purposes ranging from showing how to use equipment to performing an experiment. Sometimes the demonstration constitutes the major strategy of a particular activity. Such strategies vary in terms of the immediate purpose and the point of view of the teacher. For example, if the purpose is to test a specific concept or principle and the teacher believes that it is wise to use a straightforward approach, then a direct demonstration may be provided in a preplanned sequence. On the other hand, if the purpose is to perform an experiment and the teacher wishes to involve the students to a maximum degree, then a more flexible and open approach to demonstration may be used so that students can raise questions, suggest hypotheses, and engage in other phases of the learning experience. The difference in the approaches may be characterized by referring to one as a telling demonstration and the other as a questing demonstration (Gega, 1970). The following examples are illustrative of each approach.

Telling Demonstrations The straightforward teaching of the cause of night and day might proceed as follows in a telling demonstration:

1 A globe and a lightbulb are placed on a table in the front of the classroom in which the shades are drawn.

2 The students are asked to observe carefully to find out about (discover) the cause of night and day.

3 The place where the students live may be shown by the teacher or indicated by a student.

4 The lighted bulb is held at a distance from the globe which makes it possible for the students to see the light and dark hemispheres. The students are asked to tell where it is day and night.

5 The globe is turned slowly and the students are asked to observe the change from day to night.

6 Students are asked to make a conclusion regarding the cause of day and night. Further demonstration may be provided as needed.

Questing Demonstrations Here the strategy is designed to involve students more actively in the learning experience. For example, if the purpose is to guide students to discover the cause of night and day, using the same materials as noted above, the steps of procedure might be as follows:

1 The teacher introduces the problem by a discussion of the question: Why do we have night and day?

2 The students suggest possible reasons or causes.

3 The teacher asks for suggestions regarding ways in which the globe and lightbulb might be used to show the cause of day and night.

4 The students' proposals are considered and tried out. For example, one student may rotate the globe while another holds the lighted bulb. In another demonstration, a student may hold the globe while another walks around it with the lighted bulb.

5 The different demonstrations are discussed and students attempt to bring concepts learned earlier to bear upon the question: Which demonstration is the better explanation?

6 Students are asked to generalize about the cause of night and day or to search for further information if they are unable to do so.

The trend is clearly toward the use of questing demonstrations. However, there are times when telling demonstrations are suggested, particularly in teaching the use of equipment, in clarifying a concept or principle, in posing a problem, and in clinching an idea that is to be used in subsequent activities. In all demonstrations, whether telling or questing, it is recommended that plans be made ahead of time in light of objectives, equipment be checked to make sure it works, a trial run be conducted, pacing be keyed to capabilities of the students, students be involved to the extent that is feasible in light of objectives, and motivation for further study be secured even if the demonstration does not materialize according to the plan.

Questioning Strategies

Regardless of the underlying model for the inductive, guided-discovery strategy, a crucially important ingredient is questioning. Teacher's and children's questions are central to both open-ended guidance and discovery. Therefore, it is to be expected that questioning strategies have received considerable attention. With the realization that children's total inquiry skills could be enhanced through improving their skill in asking questions, studies were made of children's questions. Some guidelines emerged: (1) children should be encouraged to ask many more questions (rather than perpetually answering them), (2) they should be taught to ask directed (specific, precise) questions, (3) they should be given more time (teacher wait time) to develop or respond to questions, and (4) child-child questioning should have equal standing with child-teacher or teacher-child questioning.

Children's questions may be classified according to purpose. A comprehensive strategy elicits questions in all categories.

Verification Questions In the early part of inquiry sessions children should ask questions which permit them to verify the contents of the system under study. For example, "Is that water in the beaker?"

Evidence Questions As inquiry proceeds, children should ask questions about behaviors, actions, and relationships. For example, "What was the growth for the first week compared to the growth for the second week?"

Analytical Questions These are questions which children should ask to help identify important variables, define conditions for behaviors, and identify assumptions. For example, "How might air pressure have something to do with the water staying at this level?"

Empirical Questions During the experimental phase of inquiry children may adjust the experiment mentally and try to predict outcomes. They should ask questions about addition, elimination, or substitution of parts of the system. For example, "If we took out the middle wire, how might the heat of the element change?"

Implication Questions Children should ask questions to determine the relationships among variables. For example, "If we let the water continue to run out of the tank how will the rate of flow change?"

Stimulating children to raise questions as well as to give answers is most commonly undertaken through teacher questioning. The following categories for teacher's questions have been distinguished as components of the questioning strategy.

Questions for Problem Identification Designed to encourage children to identify a problem, that is, "Did you notice anything unusual when the object sank?"

Questions Seeking Information, Facts, Observations, Data Intended to prompt children to reveal prior knowledge, present data or tell what they observed, that is, "Can you remind us of what we know about the plant's need for water?"

Questions to Clarify Experimental Procedures and Design   To encourage children to tell what they did to set up and carry out an experiment. "From the beginning, what did you do to answer your question about whether the mouse can see colors?"

Questions to Clarify Inference and Empirical Relations   Intended to induce children to use evidence as a basis for stating relationships between variables. "If the ice melted, what do you know about the temperature of the surrounding air?"

Questions for Interpretation and Explanation   To prompt children to put together a sequence of ideas in explaining a system or comparing systems. "What will cause the pendulum to move more slowly? Will it ever stop?"

Questions of Application   To encourage children to interpret new experiences or envision uses of concepts already gained. "After our study of machines, what would you use to lift a piano?"

Often the give and take of questioning sessions is enlarged into group discussion sessions called colloquia in which questioning plays an important role.

The Colloquium

The colloquium is a freewheeling exchange of ideas based on common experiences (Lansdown, Blackwood, and Brandweing, 1971). A primary purpose is to get children to think freely, express their own reactions, and raise questions. Divergent ideas are considered, and convergent thinking in terms of arriving at a predetermined conclusion is avoided.

An effective colloquium is marked by a pooling of ideas of data gained from a set of activities so that they may be viewed from various points of view. Children have an opportunity to share what each has discovered in an atmosphere of openness and acceptance. Discrepant events may be suggested by the students. Different ways of testing solutions or hypotheses may be suggested. New questions may be raised and used to guide further inquiry.

The teacher's role in a colloquium is largely one of encouraging free and open expression of ideas. Of critical importance is the selection of a proper moment for convening a colloquium because it is essential that participants have some common experiences as a basis for sharing discoveries. Once the timing has been determined, the teacher's role is to encourage participation by others, provide security and maintain a climate of mutual respect, help students clarify ideas, identify discrepant events, arrange for recording of key ideas, identify questions for further study, and identify follow-up activities. Questioning rather than telling serves as the principal medium for accomplishing these ends.

In summary, the guided-discovery strategy and incumbent questioning sub-strategies are characteristic of the modern school science program. This is not to indicate that there is no use of expository strategies or other defined strategies for special purposes and in special cases, but the support for the inductive discovery strategy is very widespread at this time. Proponents argue that other strategies do not suit so completely the objectives of science education and the nature of science. They argue that both process and content objectives are best served through this strategy because the object of discovery is some concept, generalization, or relationship—a content objective. The systematic, scientific means through which discovery is achieved is, by definition, a basic process objective.

GUIDELINES FOR THE TEACHER

As indicated, the primary role of the teacher in science education is to guide children's inquiry. The strategies and substrategies noted in the preceding section are illustrative of how this role may be carried out. The inductive approach in which students are confronted with problems, discrepant events, and questions and use a variety of techniques to handle them has a dominant place in new programs of instruction. Basic guidelines for the teacher may be summarized as follows:

Intertwine content and processes as appropriate to further inquiry. Both are essential to inquiry and both are a part of science. Examples given earlier amply demonstrate the interdependencies of these two features of modern programs. Data and concepts must be coupled with processes of science as students investigate the variety of topics and problems in science education. Help students to discover that observation, hypothesis formulation, experimentation, prediction, and other processes call for the creative use of information and concepts and that sound generalizations are based on verified data. Conversely, help students discover that facts and concepts take on dynamic meaning when derived through independent investigation.

Use models of inquiry and problem solving flexibly. Models that include such phases of inquiry as encountering problems, raising questions, formulating hypotheses, gathering and verifying data, interpreting data, and drawing conclusions are very valuable and should be viewed as general guidelines to inquiry. However, they should not always be followed routinely. The creative and intuitive flashes of insight that occur in inquiry are highly personal and cannot always be disciplined into a series of steps. A flexible approach makes it possible to spark creativity by drawing useful ideas from a model while at the same time assuring attention to all necessary processes.

Keep attention focused on key concepts, conceptual schemes, and generalizations around which content can be organized. The vast storehouse of content in the natural sciences makes it imperative that a critical selection of "organizers" be made. Students need concepts and principles to organize their ideas about the natural world. Helping students to cluster subconcepts around key concepts is a means of assuring steady growth toward the comprehension of the big ideas, the principles, the generalizations that have greatest value. Introducing concepts at the propitious moment when students need them to sharpen and organize thinking is a part of the art of teaching that may be improved by drawing suggestions from guides, diagnosing individual progress, and using questioning substrategies as indicated in the preceding section. Premature pressure on students to generalize should be avoided. Generalizations must be based on adequate data and a clear grasp of the concepts that are used to make them. Each child develops his own generalizations and the process of generalizing is aided by a planned sequence of instruction. Clues as to when to focus on generalizing can be obtained from students themselves as they interpret data, share ideas in discussion, and consider needs for further information.

Gear the instructional program to the capabilities of the students. Encourage individual enterprise and provide group activities and colloquia that spark contributions from each student. Provide opportunities for students to suggest and carry out different approaches to the investigation of problems. Avoid the imposition of abstract terminology, adultlike recordkeeping, and other activities that smack of an artificial view of science. A guiding principle is to maximize each student's opportunity to investigate questions and problems to the best of his ability in a sequence of experiences that lead to continuing growth.

Formulate questions and make comments that promote active inquiry on the part of students. Questions and comments should stimulate a continuing search for better answers rather than "the right answer." Such questions as, What do you think? How can we find out? What techniques should we use to gather data? What materials do we need? Which idea is most useful? How can we test the value of these ideas? How can we improve the statement of the problem? How can this be clarified? are illustrative of those which keep responsibility for inquiry on the shoulders of students. Similarly, comments such as the following help to promote inquiry: Explain it in your own words. Describe it as you saw it. Tell us what your idea is. Show us how it should be used. A guiding principle is to be supportive of each student but neutral with reference to his ideas.

Provide for the use of a variety of techniques to investigate questions and problems. Data-gathering techniques of various sorts are necessary in inductive science. Such techniques as seeking reference materials, taking field trips, studying collections, seeing exhibits, observing models, using audio-visual materials, and seeing demontsrations should be selected and used as appropriate. Inquiry is a comprehensive venture. Existing knowledge and new ideas may be uncovered in various ways.

Provide opportunities for summary considerations of processes of inquiry. Students can grow in their understanding of inquiry processes if at appropriate times the teacher will provide for discussion and evaluation sessions in which questions such as the following are considered. What are theories? Where do we get them? How are they used? What other means can we use to gather data?

What does it mean to know something? How can we make decisions about causes? How many ways can data be used to explain something? How can theories be used to explain something? What are scientific laws? How do we get them? What is the difference between data and laws?

Arrange for the use of a variety of instructional media as needed to investigate questions and problems. A guiding question is: What equipment and materials are essential for this activity? The answer will vary in terms of purposes, approaches, classroom organization, and capabilities of students. Instructional systems including science kits, or prepackaged units including study materials, measuring instruments, supplies, film loops and other audio-visual materials, textbooks and library materials for reference, worksheets, tests, models, and suggestions for possible study trips in the community should be considered. The selection of materials for a given situation should be arranged for students' use so that independent investigation on their part is maximized. When appropriate, children themselves should have a hand in selecting materials needed to pursue a given topic or problem. After all, equipment and materials are a part of the inquiry process, and the desired outcome is growth in the ability to handle all aspects of inquiry.

Maintain a classroom atmosphere that is consistent with the spirit characteristic of scientific approaches to knowing. Attitudes and values are an important part of the scientific enterprise. Of key importance are longing to know and to understand, questioning of all things, searching for data and their meaning, seeking verification, respecting logical operations, considering premises, and considering consequences. By studying a classroom in which values such as these are paramount, students will grow in affective as well as cognitive dimensions of scientific literacy.

EVALUATION OF OUTCOMES OF INSTRUCTION

The evaluation of learning outcomes in elementary school science is beset with difficulties similar to those found in other curriculum areas. The factual material of science lends itself to the group written test, and factual knowledge remains an accepted product of successful instruction. However, many dimensions of the modern program including the important process dimension are not adequately appraised by the fact-oriented group-written test. Some attempts have been made to provide group tests for the appraisal of approach and process, but little success has been noted. At the high school level, some success has been achieved with the use of group written tests which do not call for outlines of fact but rather present new and unfamiliar situations for analysis. In this test situation, knowledge of science material and familiarity with the processes of science are purportedly revealed as the student seeks for understanding of the unfamiliar situation.

In newer elementary school programs, recognition is given the fact that if the objectives of instruction are placed in behavioral terms, the evaluations of learning must have a major behavioral component. Such behavior may be observed or appraised in a hierarchy of learning stages or steps. It also may be differentiated into tasks which relate to scientific processes such as naming, recognizing, identifying, classifying, distinguishing, describing, and ordering. Above all, it must be observable in children's work in science.

The range of evaluation has been extended through the use of self-evaluation guides for children's use, behavioral checklists to be completed by children, attitude and interest surveys, informal surveys of time allocations and other devices. Some characteristic approaches to evaluation in elementary school may be noted in the examples which follow.

Completion of Tasks

Direct assessment of instructional outcomes may be obtained by having students complete tasks that require application of what has been included in teaching episodes. Tasks for use in assessing process outcomes have been outlined in detail in a current project (AAAS. *Science: A Process Approach*, 1965). Two examples are:

Classification Have students place the following into groups according to any scheme they choose: several plastic knives, forks, and spoons of differing sizes and assorted colors. Note the basis for classification on the chalkboard: size, color, set, such as knife, fork, and spoon, or multiple basis, such as a set of the same size and color. Ask if they can think of other ways to group them (all knives, all knives of same color, all knives of same color and size). Record the different suggestions that are made.

Predicting Divide the class into two equal groups and have the students in each group list their three favorite flavors of ice cream. Have the students summarize the information obtained from one group and make a bar graph of the findings. Ask individuals in the class to make predictions of what will be found when the second group's list is summarized. List predictions on the chalkboard. Summarize and graph the second group's listings and compare findings with predictions. Have different children tell how they made their predictions.

Using Checklists

A variety of outcomes may be assessed by using checklists which include statements or questions designed to focus attention on specific behaviors, attitudes, interests, and skills. The following examples are illustrative.

Anecdotal Evaluation

Increasingly, the evaluation of children's progress in school science is regarded as an inquiry task of the teacher to parallel the inquiry tasks in which the children are engaged. Viewed in this light some of the separate science processes

Table 12-2 Checklists for Assessment of Instructional Outcomes

Making predictions	Making classifications	Measuring length
___Collects data in an organized way ___Makes a graph to order data ___States prediction based on data ___Devises test for predictions ___Changes prediction on basis of new data or new organization	___Carefully observes physical characteristics ___Classifies by single characteristic such as color or length ___Classifies by two characteristics such as color and length or color and use ___Classifies by several characteristics such as color, use, and size ___Changes classification system as purposes change	___Notes differences in linear dimension ___Makes intuitive comparisons using terms such as longer and shorter ___Identifies equal and unequal lengths through indirect methods ___Compares objects using some arbitrary unit Use numbers ___Uses standard English and metric units ___Structures and orders measurement data ___Allows for measurement error in computation

such as observation, prediction, data collection, and data analysis have become a part of the teacher's repetoire of evaluation aids. While the analog is imperfect, it has served to surface an individualized, anecdotal sort of evaluation which many teachers find useful. In essence, the teacher observes carefully, using recording media where possible (experiment reports, taped discussions, written summaries). All evidence of children's performance, objective and subjective, is gathered. An important source of input is informal self-evaluation by the children. Most often, this information is obtained through the age-old teaching technique of, "How could we have done this better?" Based upon the accumulation of data, periodic observations on the performance of each child are recorded in anecdotal form. An example is Johnny Smith.

Rating	titration experiment	crystal growing	plant growth	plant reproduction	evaporation	photosynthesis	sun's rays
Intense interest							
Active interest							
Some interest							
Little interest							
No interest							

Chart 12-7 Checklist for Individual or Class Interests Appraising Interest in Different Experiments

October 8: Johnny has begun his work with saturated solutions. He seems to have difficulty in measuring the separate amounts of salt and water. He and I agree that he needs some practice with using the balance. I asked why he was weighing the water and he said that was what Bill had done so it must be right! The tape of the group's last session indicates that he is relying too much on Bill's judgment and Bill's leads.

October 21: Johnny is moving along nicely. He was excited to find that the amount of salt after evaporation was 22 grams, the amount he had dissolved in the hot water on his last try. His measurement skills are growing and he seems to be on top of evaporation even though he is not clear about the nature of saturated solutions as yet. I note that he needs some help with putting data into tables and looking for patterns in the numbers. I noted in the last written report that Bill was asking Johnny for a bit of help.

The combination of anecdoted evaluations and checklists of some form apparently provide the most useful and comprehensive evaluations of modern school science, but they are not useful unless used continuously and systematically. Some teachers find the combination expensive in terms of time. Note the potential usefulness of the checklist for processes in Chart 12-8, if also accompanied by anecdotal records. The entries in the checklist are numerical according to the following code:

0 — not observed today
1 — use of process not apparent
2 — uses process ineffectively at this level
3 — uses process effectively at this level
4 — understands and improves upon process for this level

CHECKLIST — PROCESS GROWTH

NAME: Johnny Smith Record	Observation	Classification	Measurement	Communication	Quantification	Hypothesis	Identifying variables	Controlling variables	Recording data	Interpreting data	Prediction	Creating models
1	3	0	2	0	0	0	1	0	2	0	0	0
2	3	2	2	2	1	0	0	0	2	1	1	0
3	3	2	2	0	2	0	1	0	2	1	2	0
4	3	3	3	2	2	1	1	0	2	1	2	0
5	3	3	3	3	2	1	2	0	2	2	2	0
6												
7												
8												
9												
10												

Chart 12-8 Checklist—Process Growth

USING THE TAXONOMIES OF OBJECTIVES

Appraising instructional outcomes in science may be structured and systematized through use of taxonomies of educational objectives. Classroom questions and performance tasks may be patterned to the various levels of the taxonomies to provide a comprehensive evaluation program. The following examples include a question and an item for each level in the cognitive and affective domains (Bloom, 1956).

Cognitive Domain

Knowledge Level What is Newton's third law? Put a circle around that chemical expression in the following list which represents carbon dioxide:

Comprehension Level What concepts should be clustered together in the key concept "life cycle"? Underline each of the following that is a part of the life cycle. . . .

Application Level Why did Ann fall out of the front of the wagon when the wagon hit the board and stopped? Write 0 before each statement that is an observation. Write 1 before each statement that is an interference.

___ There are drops of water on the steps.
___ It must have rained last night.
___ There is water on the lawn.
___ Dew formed on the surface of uncovered objects.
___ Someone may have watered the yard this morning.

Analysis Level Why did crystals develop when solution A was evaporated, whereas the evaporation of solution B produced no crystals? List all the reasons you can for explaining why the polar bear is white.

Synthesis Level How can we test the hypotheses that have been proposed? From our many experiments with growing plants make a summary chart showing those things which are necessary in order for plants to grow.

Evaluation Level Is our explanation for the behavior of mercury correct? Are there other possible explanations? List the strengths and the weaknesses of our experiment on evaporation of water.

Affective Domain

Receiving Level Were we careful to consider everyone's ideas in designing our experiment? Let us design an experiment that will bring together the ideas of committee A and committee B.

Responding Level Which experiment can we do in the classroom? List on a sheet of paper any suggestions you may have for committee A to make their experiment as effective as possible.

Valuing Level Why is science important to all people in our world today? Tell why we must be careful to gather all the information we can before we draw conclusions.

FOLLOW-UP ACTIVITIES AND PROJECTS

1 Select a modern science program organized around content headings. Examine it with respect to the following features. Extent to which:

    a Children are actively involved
    b Guided discovery is used
    c Scientific processes are named and defined
    d A wide variety of materials is used
    e Major scientific themes are exposed
    f Quantitative methods are used
    g Children are free to follow their own interests

2 Select a modern science program organized around process headings. Examine it with respect to the following features. Extent to which:

    a Children rely on textbook or other printed materials
    b Instructional systems are used
    c Questioning strategies are incorporated
    d Processes are sequenced
    e Content is prescribed and organized
    f There is assessment of children's growth in process skills
    g Children are free to follow their own interests

3 Discuss process without content and content without process as possible variations in elementary school science programs.
4 Discuss the viability of expository strategies in elementary school science.
5 List a series of questions you will use in a guided-discovery approach to a science topic of your choice.
6 Construct a checklist for assessing children's attitudes about process-oriented science activities.
7 Examine a current textbook series for elementary science. List its strength and weaknesses, then determine if you would use it in your teaching. Defend your decision.
8 Write a lesson plan for an introductory science activity at a grade level of your choice. Identify five of its most important features with respect to children's learning of inquiry skills.

BIBLIOGRAPHY

AAAS, Commission of Science Education. *Science: A Process Approach.* (3d Experimental Ed.) Washington, D.C.: American Association for the Advancement of Science, 1965. Hierarchies of processes charted in an evaluation model and its applications; suggestions for teaching exercises designed to develop processes of science in fourteen booklets; background information in commentary for teachers.

Anastasion, Clifford J. *Teachers, Children and Things: Materials–Centered Science.* Toronto: Holt, 1971. Practical outline of philosophy and methodology of a modern elementary science program.

Bloom, Benjamin S. (Ed.) *Taxonomy of Educational Objectives: Cognitive Domain.* New York: McKay, 1956. Sample behavioral statements and test items arranged on six levels of complexity.

Blough, G. O. and J. Schwartz. *Elementary School Science.* (5th Ed.) New York: Holt, 1974. An updated standard reference for elementary school science program organization and teaching.

California. *Science Framework for California Public Schools–Kindergarten–Grades One Through Twelve.* Sacramento State Department of Education, 1970. A sample framework for the modern science program.

Conceptually Oriented Program in Elementary Science. New York: New York University, 1974. Science curriculum for elementary schools centered in five conceptual schemes in science organized into laboratory style sequences developing major and supporting concepts.

Educational Services, Inc. *Elementary Science Study.* New York: McGraw-Hill, 1966. Self-contained units in science dealing with various subject matter, apparatus, level of complexity, and style of presentation designed to acquaint elementary school children with the nature and significant concepts of science through an unstructured, open-ended approach.

Friedl, Alfred E. *Teaching Science to Children: The Inquiry Approach Applied.* New York: Random House, 1972. Teaching suggestions for a process-oriented science program, built around discrepant events and intuitive processes.

Gega, Peter C. *Science in Elementary Education.* (2d Ed.) New York: Wiley, 1970. A thorough treatment of the components of teaching in a modern elementary science program.

George, K. D., M. A. Dietz, and E. C. Abraham. *Science Investigations for Elementary School Teachers.* Lexington, Mass.: Heath, 1974. Helps teachers with inquiry oriented science teaching by exposing them to a learn by doing method.

George, K. D., M. A. Dietz, E. C. Abraham, and M. A. Nelson. *Elementary School Science.* Lexington, Mass.: D. C. Heath and Co., 1974. Objectives, procedures, and evaluation.

George, K. D., M. A. Dietz, E. C. Abraham, and M. A. Nelson. *Elementary School Science, Why and How.* Lexington, Mass.: Heath, 1974. A sourcebook for teachers on understanding and teaching the modern elementary science program.

Henrie, Samual N. (Senior Ed.) *Sourcebook of Elementary Curricula Programs and Projects.* Washington, D.C.: Government Printing Office, 1972. Chapter on science and chapter on environmental education and ecology.

Hurd, P. D., and J. J. Gallagher. *New Directions in Elementary Science Teaching.* Belmont, California: Wadsworth, 1968. A summary of new developments and new programs in elementary school science.

Krathwohl, D. R., B. S. Bloom, and B. S. Masia. *Taxonomy of Educational Objectives: Affective Domain.* New York: McKay, 1964. A classification of affective objectives according to degree of internalization.

Lansdown, B., P. E. Blackwood, and P. F. Brandwein. *Teaching Elementary Science Through Investigation and Colloquium.* 1971. Theory and practice in modern elementary science in a comprehensive, useful presentation.

Piaget, Jean. *The Construction of Reality in the Child.* New York: Basic Books, 1954. The noted psychologist-logician's theoretical formulations regarding children's perceptions and cognitive development.

Piltz, Albert, and Robert B. Sund. *Creative Teaching of Science in the Elementary School.* Boston: Allyn and Bacon, Inc., 1974. Techniques and activities for different aspects of science education.

Rowe, Mary B. *Teaching Science as Continuous Inquiry.* New York: McGraw-Hill, 1973. A guide to process-oriented science teaching, including practical examples.

Science Curriculum Improvement Study, Berkeley, Calif.: University of California, 1972. An ungraded, sequential physical and life science program for elementary grades, designed to illuminate basic science concepts through a Piaget-oriented, child-involvement approach.

Washton, Nathan S. *Teaching Science in Elementary and Middle Schools.* New York: McKay, 1974. Science teaching from content organization, methodology and concepts.

Chapter 13

Social Studies

The social studies program is focused on the interaction of people with each other and with their human and natural environment. Included are those aspects of human activities believed to be of greatest value for the general education of students. Of key importance are relationships among people, between people and institutions, between people and the environment, and between people and values. Content on human relationships is drawn from the social sciences and from the humanities as well as from experiences of students and current affairs. Attention is given to issues and problems in both the present and past as our own and other cultures are studied. The program also includes modes and methods of inquiry from the scientific side, the humanities side, and the policy/ evaluative side of disciplines that deal with human interaction. All the foregoing are brought together into a program that makes vital contributions to the goals of education as shown in the following section (Michaelis, 1972).

CONTRIBUTIONS TO MAJOR GOALS

The social studies make many contributions to basic goals because of the diversity of learning activities that tap problem-solving, critical, and creative thinking. *Thinking ability* is developed as children use concepts to guide study that calls for interpreting, generalizing, analyzing, and other processes; it is further extended as they check hypotheses, develop generalizations, evaluate proposals, and discover the importance of such attitudes as openmindedness, respect for the views of others, and regard for freedom of expression. *Self-realization* is promoted as children learn about roles in the family, as they, in school, develop other concepts and social skills related to personal activities, and as they discover the importance of positive attitudes and values as a part of one's self-concept. *Human relationships* are of central importance in the social studies, including relationships among people and groups, and between people and institutions, between people and value systems, and between people and the environment. *Economic competence* is developed through activities that focus on skills and attitudes of good workmanship, the world of work and career awareness, economic concepts such as division of labor, producer and consumer, and economic opportunities in a free society. Innumerable opportunities are provided to develop *civic responsibility,* ranging from responsibilities in home, school, and community activities to those in national and international settings. Many contributions are made to *learning how to learn* as children develop strategies and attitudes through individual and group study that are useful in lifelong learning.

Additional contributions to major goals of education may be noted in the statement of objectives of the social studies that follows.

OBJECTIVES OF THE SOCIAL STUDIES

Key social studies objectives are illustrated below under four main headings that are widely used in current programs. *Inquiry* objectives have been separated from *skill* objectives to highlight the current emphasis being given to them. *Conceptual* objectives have long been stressed, whereas *affective* objectives have been given increased attention in recent years with special emphasis on value-clarification strategies.

Conceptual Objectives

To develop understanding of information, concepts, and main ideas so that students are able to identify and describe the following:

Functions of social institutions and roles of individuals and groups in diverse cultural settings at home and abroad in both the past and present

Influences of values, traditions, technological developments, education, and other aspects of culture on individual and group behavior

Social, economic, political, geographical, and historical aspects of topics and events under study

Inquiry Objectives

To develop skill in using processes, methods, and modes of inquiry so that students are able to do the following:

Demonstrate through actual use such processes as comparing, classifying, generalizing, inferring, analyzing, synthesizing, evaluating

Make plans for investigating topics and problems, collecting data, organizing and processing data, deriving conclusions, and assessing outcomes and procedures of inquiry

State generalizations based on studies in the analytic mode, describe particular events and places based on studies in the integrative mode, and state consequences of alternatives based on studies in the decision-making mode

Skill Objectives

To develop new skills and refine basic skills, including the ability to perform the following:

Locate, gather, appraise, summarize, and report information

Interpret and make maps, graphs, tables, time lines, and other graphic materials as needed in both individual and group activities

Demonstrate how a variety of data sources, ranging from printed and audio-visual materials to community resources, may be used to further inquiry

Work as a member of groups, participating in decision making, carrying out plans, adhering to group standards, and evaluating individual and group efforts

Affective Objectives

To demonstrate in individual and group work the values and attitudes of individuals who do the following:

Are openminded, responsible, cooperative, curious, creative, and show concern for others and respect for duly constituted authority

Value democratic beliefs such as civil rights, human dignity, general welfare, cooperative action, use of intelligence to solve problems, human freedom, contributions of others, diversity among ethnic groups, and recognize the place of moral and spiritual values in human affairs

Use valuing strategies to clarify value-laden topics in social studies units and in individual and group problems of personal or local concern

Have self-respect, and show respect for others without regard to race, creed, sex, social and economic status, and national origin

ORGANIZATION OF THE CURRICULUM

Several considerations are vital in organizing the social studies curriculum. The breadth or scope of the program should adequately sample major areas of human activity; include ethnic, environmental, and other studies of critical importance; be balanced in terms of disciplinary emphasis, cultures, and areas selected for study; and be related to problems, events, and issues of importance in daily living. The sequence of topics and units in the program should be related to developmental stages and characteristics of children; provide for the progressive development of concepts, generalizations, skills, processes, and affective objectives; and permit adaptations and modifications at various levels so that individual differences can be met and important contemporary affairs can be given attention.

A new trend is to plan the K-12 curriculum so that adequate attention is given to three types of studies that emphasize three different modes or styles of inquiry (Michaelis, 1972). One type of study, on the social science side of the social studies, is designed to develop generalizations or main ideas of broad applicability. A topic or problem is studied in depth in several different settings to make a generalization. For example, role of mothers, services provided by cities, production of wheat, the energy shortage, and similar topics are investigated in several different settings, data are organized and interpreted, and generalizations are made. All programs include this type of study which involves a scientific-analytic mode of inquiry.

A second type of study, on the humanities side of the social studies, is designed to develop understanding and appreciation of the unique and special features of people, places, and events. For example, such topics as Our Neighborhood, How Our Community Developed, History of Our State, Contributions of Martin Luther King, The Civil War, and Life in Mexico have special features that need to be brought together to provide a comprehensive view. This type of study involves an integrative-comprehensive mode of inquiry in which relevant elements, not a single topic, are brought together to give a distinctive flavor to the person, event, or place. Emphasis is given to synthesizing a variety of information in a single setting, not to the analyzing of a single topic in depth in several different settings.

A third type of study is designed to develop competence in making decisions on proposals or judgments about events and activities. For example, issues and problems represented in the following questions call for decision-making and judgmental skills and concepts: How can we improve our floor map of the area around our school? How should our city curb water pollution? Which proposal for urban renewal is best? Which ways of conserving energy should be adopted? What should the United Nations do about this problem? The policy-evaluative mode of inquiry in this type of study emphasizes clarification of values, setting of standards, and the appraisal of alternatives in terms of standards.

These three modes of study may be a part of a single unit as well as a special emphasis throughout the K-12 program. For example, in a unit on Our Community the scientific-analytic mode may be used to find out if other communities provide such basic services as education, transportation, recreation, and the like. After investigating other communities, a generalization may be made. The integrative-comprehensive mode may be used as children study the development or history of their community, giving attention to changes in education, transportation, and other aspects of community life so that they get a comprehensive yet distinctive view. And the policy-evaluative mode may be used as children weigh alternatives regarding such issues and problems as urban renewal, safety, pollution, and the like.

Sequence of Topics and Units

The themes, units, and topics in the social studies vary from school district to school district except in states where a mandated curriculum exists. Yet there are many similarities that can be identified. In the early grades may be found studies of family life, the school, neighborhood and community life, transportation, farms, and other aspects of the immediate environment. In grades 4 through 6 attention is given to studies of our state, geographic regions throughout the world, life in early and modern America, regions of the United States, Canada, Latin America, world cultures, and Western and Eastern Hemisphere. In grades 7 and 8 may be found studies of world cultures, Eastern or Western Hemisphere, our state, U.S. history, local/state/federal government, and the Constitution. In grades 9 through 12 are courses in world geography, world history, U.S. history and government, economics, sociology, Asian studies, Afro-American studies, and a variety of other courses. At all levels attention is given to ethnic studies, contributions of individuals and groups, contemporary affairs, the environment, career education, current issues and problems, and holidays and special events.

To identify the sequence of topics and units in a particular school system, it is necessary to examine the course of study. As this is done, special attention should be given to relationships between units within grades and between grades. The reader is urged to check the guide for the school system in which she or he resides. As the following illustrative example from the New York City guide is examined, note the theme identified for each grade level and the sequence of units within each grade level. How might such topics as ethnic studies, career education, and contemporary affairs be developed in the context of various units at each grade level?

The New York City program begins in prekindergarten and extends through grade XII.[1] Unnecessary repetition of content has been eliminated, there is flexibility in themes and case studies, and teachers are advised to adapt to neighborhood needs. Themes and topics are:

Prekindergarten. Orientation to the World We Live In: Developing Individuality and Self-Respect, Relating to People, Responsibilities, Future Rewards, People and Places Nearby and Far Away, Special Days

---

[1] *Course of Study*, New York City Schools, 1970–71.

Kindergarten. Home and School Environment: Together in the Classroom and School and Its Environment, How the Family Meets its Needs, Needs Met by People Far Away, Adapting to Change, Special Days

Grade I. Living and Working in the Community: People Live in Groups, Workers Supply Needs, Government Services, Communities Are Interdependent, Community Changes, Special Days

Grade II. City Communities Around the World: New York City and Suburbs, Other U.S. Cities, World Cities, Communication and Transportation Bring People Closer Together, Special Days and Customs

Grade III. Cultures Around the World: Comparative Studies of How People Live in Tropical Rainforests, Deserts, Grasslands, Northern Forests, and Mountain Regions, Man's Inventiveness, Good Citizenship

Grade IV. American People and Leaders, and How the U.S. Began and Grew: How People Discovered and Explored America, Settled and Developed the Colonies, Established the U.S., Developed Our Nation (to 1900), and Have Been Developing a Great Society (since 1900)

Grade V. Our World – Geographic and Economic Studies: How People of the United States and Canada Use Their Geography, How Latin Americans Use Technology, New Economic Relationships in Europe, How the People of Asia or Africa (select one) Use Their Geography

Grade VI. Our World–Early Civilizations: How We Learn about the Past, How Man Developed, Western Civilization, (two of the following) How Civilization Developed in India, China, Pre-Columbian America, Africa

Grade VII. American History: Why People Moved to the New World (1492-1775), Permanent Settlements (1607-1775), How the Thirteen Colonies Became a Nation (1660-1789), Changing Political Climate (1783-1890), Response to Twentieth-Century Needs (1890 to the present)

Grade VIII. Urban Growth: New York Metropolitan Area, Urbanization in New York State, Urbanization at Home and Abroad, Changing Federalism in Urban America

Grades IX-XII. World Studies: Eastern Civilization in IX, Western Civilization in X, a two-year sequence; American Studies in XI, Economics in XIIa, one elective course in XIIb.

Plans also must be made to include attention to new developments such as career education, environmental education, and future education. For example, *career education* may be made a part of the social studies as children investigate workers included in different units of instruction. Career awareness may be developed as various community workers are studied in the primary grades, the contributions of various workers to the development of our states and nation are explored in the middle grades, and workers around the world are investigated in units in the upper grades (Bottoms, 1973; Wernick, 1973). *Environmental education* may be made a part of regular units with special attention to such concepts as ecosystem, food chain, resources, interdependence, balance, land use, conservation, pollution, and quality of life. Examples of units that focus directly on the environment are Forest Conservation, Urban Environment, Air Pollution, Water Pollution, and Our Environment (Michaelis, 1972; Sale, 1972). *Future education* may be included in regular or special units with emphasis on glimpses of the future as reported by experts, projecting technological, population, and other trends, making predictions, clarifying values related to the future, and analyzing the consequences of actions and proposals for the future (Toffler, 1970).

Conceptual Structure

Concepts and concept clusters from history and the social sciences are put to use in units of study at all levels of instruction. For example, in units on the family, school, and neighborhood in the early grades use is made of such concepts as role of members of the family, role of workers in school and in the neighborhood, producers of goods, producers of services, and the acquisition of food, shelter, and clothing. In units on community living and living in urban centers wide use is made of such concepts as transportation, communication, conservation, education, government, recreation, environment, meeting basic needs, interaction with other communities, industry, business, inner city, suburb, urban renewal, and city problems.

In middle and upper grades as state studies, regional studies, culture studies, growth of our country, and other units are taught, use is made of the preceding concepts which are brought to higher levels of development. In addition, other concepts are introduced and concept clusters such as the following are used to guide study and organize data:

Resources   People, animal life, vegetation, minerals, soils, water
Settlement patterns   Isolated, village, town, suburb, city, metropolis, megalopolis
State history   Indians, explorers, settlers, first towns, transportation, communication, business, schools, government, industry, agriculture, labor, recreation
Factors of production   Land, labor, capital, management, government
Economic processes   Production, exchange, distribution, consumption
Processes of government   Legislative, executive, judicial
Civil liberties   Freedom of thought, speech, worship, petition, association
Some culture universals   Language, marriage, child training, religion, funeral rites, property, art, moral code, toolmaking
Basic institutions   Family, education, economics, religion, government

A Model for Regional Studies   Concept clusters may be brought together to form a model for regional and other studies. The example that follows has been adapted from recently prepared guides to show how clusters of concepts can be used to guide the study of any region or to make comparative studies of two or more regions.

The setting — physical features

Location: Latitude and longitude, relative — site, situation, in relation to other places, time and distance from own location

Spatial features: Area (size), shape, length and width, boundaries — natural and political

Major landforms: Plains, hills, plateaus, mountains; pattern of distribution

Water features: Underground waters, rivers, lakes, seas, oceans, bays, straits, coastlines and shorelines

Climate: Temperature — range, average, growing season; precipitation — average, seasonal amounts, causative factors

Resource base: Soils, water, vegetation, animal life, minerals

The people — human activities

Population: Number, growth rate, origins, migrations, racial characteristics, distribution, settlement patterns, areas of concentration, central city, other key cities

Economic activities: Agriculture, industries, trade, transportation, communication, relation to other areas

Political processes: Ideological base, political processes, form of government, decision making, administrative units, relations with other nations

Sociocultural features: Links to other cultures; dominant social values; social control; social stratification — classes, castes, minorities, rigidity-fluidity; social institutions — the family, education, religion; social and cultural change; language; art; music; architecture; health and sanitation; other features

Key problems and future plans: Economic development, population growth, health, standard of living, nationalism, social and political tensions, relations with other nations, urbanization, others

An outline such as this can be used flexibly as a model to study a variety of regions, ranging from local areas to international groupings of nations. Topics of greatest importance can be highlighted as a given area is studied. Relationships among topics can be emphasized and topics can be combined as desired to show links between them, for example, problems and future plans can be made a part of preceding topics, economic and political activities can be intertwined. Beginning with a few selected topics in early grades, others can be added in subsequent grades to round out regional studies.

Recently developed programs are based on key concepts and concept clusters. (See the reference by Henrie, 1972 for a detailed list.) For example, *Man, A Course of Study* is designed around the following key questions and concepts:[2]

What is *human* about human beings? How did they get that way? How can they be made more so?

Language: Acquisition, signs, symbols, voice-ear system, phonemes, syntax, language, and thought

[2] Cambridge, Mass.: Education Development Center, 1970.

Tool making: Uses of tools, extensions of human capacities, tools and evolution

Social organization: Roles, reciprocity, exchange, family, kinship, contrast between human and primate organization

Child rearing: Long childhood, skill development, childhood as shaper of adulthood

World view: Urge to explain, myth, art, legend, using symbols, hunting, and gathering

The Field Social Studies Program includes attention to concepts, clusters of concepts, and generalizations, such as the following:[3]

Roles: Family, school, community, state, nation, other lands

Interaction: Cooperation, competition, conflict, assimilation, accommodation

Interdependence: Economic specialization has led to increasing interdependence

Social control: Societies need a system of social control in order to survive.

Our Working World includes attention to such economic concepts and concept clusters as:[4]

Specialization: Division of labor, geographical, occupational, technological

Economic values: Growth, stability, security, freedom, justice

The market: Goods, services, spending, saving, income, supply, demand

Special attention is given to the spiral development of key concepts and related generalizations. Planning for spiral development is done by identifying specific grade level applications. This may be illustrated by noting, first, examples of how a single concept is used at different levels and, second, the growth of generalizations from level to level. The concept *interdependence* is useful as an example because it is stressed in all social studies programs. The following questions illustrate how it may be developed from level to level.

Prekindergarten–K: How can we help each other? How can we help each other at home? What are some things adults do for us in school? At home?

Grades 1-2: How do we depend on each other in school? At home? In the neighborhood? In our community?

Grades 3-4: How do people in cities depend on each other? On farmers? On people who produce things in other places? How do people in different regions depend on each other? Why is interdependence increasing?

Grades 5-8: In what ways were people interdependent in Colonial Times? How has interdependence increased? Why has interdependence increased more rapidly throughout the world in more recent times?

---

[3] Menlo Park, Calif.: Addison-Wesley, 1972.
[4] Chicago, Ill.: Science Research Associates, 1970.

The following generalizations built around interdependence further illustrate how meaning is extended and deepened as children progress through the social studies program:

Members of the family depend on each other, as do people in neighborhoods and communities.

People depend on producers of food, shelter and clothing, and on producers of services, who in turn depend on others for goods and services.

People in cities around the world depend on each other and on workers who live outside of cities.

People in the United States and Canada are interdependent in a large number of economic activities.

The interdependence of people in North and South America has increased greatly because of technological developments.

Interdependence is characteristic of life in cultures around the world.

Related Questions and Activities Concepts such as those presented above may be used to formulate inquiry-conceptual questions for use in each unit of study. In the following examples, concepts are italicized and the inquiry or cognitive process is in parenthesis.

What *services* are provided by the workers we just saw in the film (recalling)?

Look at these pictures and find the *natural resources* that are shown (observing).

Tell what the word *judge* means by stating four things a judge does (defining).

After the reading is completed, group the different *governmental activities* that are mentioned under these three headings: *legislative, executive, judicial* (classifying).

What *landforms* are shown on this map of the United States (interpreting)?

What is the main idea that can be drawn from the report on *pollution* (generalizing)?

First find the *resources* that are shown on this map. Then state the *products* that you believe they can make (inferring).

What *products* do you think people in *industrialized* countries usually produce when they have these *resources* (hypothesizing)?

Given the present rate of oil *depletion*, how long do you think it will be before existing supplies are exhausted (predicting)?

Which of the statements on the chalkboard include incidents that involve one or more of these *civil liberties: freedom of thought, speech, worship* (analyzing).

Prepare an outline or written report that brings together the reasons for *conserving natural resources* (synthesizing).

Which of the proposals for urban renewal is best in terms of the *environmental* concerns expressed by the select committee on urban problems (evaluating)?

Variety of Learning Activities   Each unit of study should include a variety of learning activities to meet individual needs of children and to attain objectives of the unit. Language activities such as reading, writing, telling, discussing, and questioning help to develop basic skills as well as serving as means of gathering and evaluating data and expressing ideas. Such doing activities as participating in study trips, constructing objects, processing materials, expressing thoughts and feelings through art, and engaging in music activities add dimensions to meaning that can be obtained in no other way. Dramatic activities, ranging from dramatic play and role playing, to simulation and dramatization of historic events, give zest to learning. Also helpful are mapmaking, chartmaking, graphing, designing tables, drawing cartoons, and the constructing of models that highlight topics under study. Of special importance are creative activities such as story writing, poetry writing, drawing and painting, modeling, and composing in which children express in fresh and original ways thoughts and feelings related to units under study.

Criteria for Selecting Units   Decisions about units to include in the curriculum are made in terms of such criteria as the following:

In what ways can contributions be made to attainment of social studies objectives?
___ Conceptual objectives   ___ Process objectives   ___ Skill objectives
___ Affective objectives
What opportunities exist to provide for the use of three modes of study?
___ Single topic to develop generalizations   ___ Single setting to get a comprehensive
     and unique view   ___ Evaluative mode to assess alternatives
Can adequate instructional resources be obtained?
___ To meet individual differences among students   ___ To provide rich learning exper-
     iences   ___ To meet critical needs such as ethnic and environmental studies
How can adaptations be made to meet local conditions?
___ Special school or neighborhood needs   ___ Significant problems   ___ Staff
     capabilities

Similar criteria are used by teachers as they select units from those suggested in the social studies framework or guide. Special attention is given to the selection of units directly related to educational needs of children, to adaptations that can be made in terms of local conditions, and to availability of instructional materials.

INSTRUCTIONAL MEDIA

A variety of instructional materials may be found in a well-rounded social studies program. Along with basic textbooks and supplementary books, library books, documents, diaries, facsimilies of historical documents such as the Constitution and Declaration of Independence, are used paperbacks, juvenile and adult newspapers and magazines, pamphlets, brochures, and other free and inexpensive materials. In middle and upper grades such reference materials as almanacs, anthologies, atlases, directories, encyclopedias, yearbooks, and *Who's Who* volumes are widely used.

Opportunities abound to draw upon community resources, including individuals to interview, places to go on study trips, observation of construction projects, museums, arts and crafts centers, and resource persons who can come to school. Also available are multimedia kits that contain sets of pictures, filmstrips, recordings, charts and other resources directly related to different units of study, as well as the full range of audio-visual resources.

Among the special resources needed for a good program are maps and globes that are designed for use at different levels of instruction. Simplified maps and globes are needed for the early grades while more advanced ones are needed in later grades for units that deal with states, our country, Canada, Latin American, Europe, Africa, and Asia. Of special value in teaching map and globe skills are charts of map terms which show different land and water bodies, outline maps, map skill projects that can be related to individual needs, and map projectuals.

Other resources that are needed to round out the supply of media include games, and materials for construction projects, for the processing of wool and flax and various types of food, and for craft and art projects related to cultures under study. Graphic materials such as posters, cartoons, charts, time lines, tables, and graphs are used in many units. Resources from other areas of the curriculum, particularly art and music, are drawn upon as needed.

TEACHING STRATEGIES

The full range of teaching strategies, from expository to discovery, may be found in the social studies. The current emphasis on inquiry and valuing is highlighted in several of the examples presented below. The first examples are illustrative of models of inquiry that can be used in any unit of instruction. The second set of examples are illustrative of strategies that can be used to attain specific objectives such as concept development, inquiry process and skill development, and value clarification.

Models of Inquiry as General Teaching Strategies

Problem-solving Model The most widely used model of inquiry is based on steps of problem solving that may be used in variable, not lock-step, order depending on the problem and experience of students. The main procedures in this basic strategy are (Michaelis, 1972) the following:

1 Clarifying and defining questions and problems. (*Example:* What was our community like in early times? Who were the first settlers?)
2 Recalling information and hypothesizing. (*Example:* What old buildings have you seen? What other things do you know about early times in our community? Who do you think the early settlers were? When did the first railroad come in?)
3 Group discussion/planning of next steps. (*Example:* Where can we find

ideas related to our questions? What people might be interviewed? What questions might committees investigate?)

4 Interpreting and classifying information. (*Example:* How can we use data from these maps, stories, and pictures? How should we group the data to answer our questions?)

5 Further processing of information as needed. (*Example:* Can the data be broken down (analyzed) into periods? Could ideas be brought together (synthesized) in a time line? What conclusions can we make?)

6 Evaluating procedures and outcomes. (*Example:* Do our conclusions square with the facts? What parts of our study need improving? How might improvements be made in gathering and organizing data?)

Decision-making Model This model may be used as a part of problem solving with an emphasis on assessments of alternatives and consequences of alternatives, or it may be used as outlined below provided adequate information is collected and processed as noted above in the problem-solving model.

1 Define the issue or problem. (*Example:* Why is waste disposal a pollution problem in our city? What are the facts? What are the main issues?)

2 Clarify goals and values and put them in order of priority. (*Example:* What objectives have been identified? Which are most and least important? What values are most important?)

3 Consider alternative ways of achieving objectives. (*Example:* What proposals have been made? How are they related to objectives?)

4 Examine consequences of alternatives, choosing the best one in terms of values and objectives. (*Example:* What will happen if alternative A is chosen? Alternative B? What values lie behind the choice of each alternative? Which one best meets the objectives and values?)

Model for Development of Main Ideas The emphasis in this model is on the provision of instruction to develop a main idea or generalization. Students are guided by a sequence of focusing questions and related learning activities that begins with *openers* in which the problem is clarified, issues are defined, related ideas are recalled by students, and interest is aroused in much the same way as noted above in the first two phases of the problem-solving model. Next, *developmental* learning activities are provided so that students can gather and organize the data needed to formulate the main idea. Third, *concluding* activities are provided to synthesize ideas and to formulate and check generalizations. The model is presented below and illustrated in the context of a unit on the Dairy Farm in which the main idea is, *Land, labor, and capital are needed to produce goods.*

1 Provide an opener to clarify the problem and arouse interest. (*Example:* How many have been to a dairy farm? What was it like? What does a person need to run a dairy farm? List responses and have children group those which go together — tools and equipment, workers, land.)

2 Provide a sequence of learning activities to develop the main idea.

(*Example:* Show filmstrips on dairy farms, identifying equipment, workers, land use. Read stories and interpret photographs to gather data. Visit a dairy farm to gather data.)

3 Provide concluding activities so that students can formulate generalizations. (*Example:* Make an illustrated scrapbook to show what is needed to operate a dairy farm. Arrange picture displays to show how capital (equipment), workers, and land are needed. Have students state in their own words what is needed to operate a dairy farm.)

Included in all the models noted above are a variety of specific teaching strategies that may be used to develop concepts, inquiry processes, skills, and value-clarification techniques. Examples of each of these are presented in the sections that follow.

A Strategy for Techniques of Inquiry

Involved in the models of inquiry noted above are specific techniques of inquiry such as interviewing, making and interpreting models, analyzing source materials such as letters and diaries, and making and interpreting maps. The strategy below may be used with any technique of inquiry. It begins with defining the problem and setting questions or hypotheses to guide data collection. This is followed by planning steps of procedure, collecting and classifying data, noting needs for additional data, and making and testing conclusions along with evaluation of the procedures.

1 Define the problem and use questions or hypotheses to guide data collection.
>   *Example:* What is meant by contributions of minority groups?
>   What contributions have they made in our community?

2 Plan steps of procedure to be used.
>   *Example:* The following procedures may be used to *interview* local people.
>   (a) Introduce yourself. (b) State the purpose of the interview. (c) Ask questions in order. (d) Listen carefully to answers. (e) Take notes on hard points. (f) Ask further questions on special points. (g) Express thanks when finished (Michaelis, 1972).

3 Classify the information under each question or hypothesis.
>   *Example:* What information can be used to answer the first question? Second?

4 Note needs for additional information to fill gaps.
>   *Example:* What additional information do we need? How can we get it?

5 Make and test conclusions and evaluate procedures.
>   *Example:* What can we conclude about minority contributions?
>   What difficulties were encountered in interviewing?
>   What improvements can be made in our procedures?

Note that the strategy above is similar to the problem-solving model except that the focus is on the use of a single technique to gather data. It is both fruitful and easy to use the strategy as an integral part of any of the models noted above.

Concept Development Strategies

Discovery-Inductive Model This strategy is used to guide students to discover common features that may be used to group items and to label or define them. Main procedures are:

1 Observe and discuss items to be grouped and labeled.
   Example: What items are shown in these pictures?
2 Identify common features for use in grouping them, noting distinguishing differences.
   Example: How are they alike? Different?
3 Decide on a basis for grouping the items.
   Example: Which ones can be grouped together? Why?
4 Label, name, or define the group.
   Example: What is a good name for them?
5 Have students use the term and find new examples in materials being used.
   Example: What examples can we find in these materials; How can we use the term in discussion, reports, etc.?

Expository-Inductive Strategy This strategy is similar to the one above in that the teacher directs instruction from the particular to the general, moving from attributes to a generalized meaning of the concept.

1 Identify critical attributes of the concept to be developed.
   Example: Here are some objects of great worth: good homes, good health. Here are some ideas we cherish: freedom, justice.
2 Identify nonexamples of the attributes of the concept.
   Example: Here are some things of little or no worth: worn-out clothes, useless junk. Here are some ideas we do not cherish: undemocratic government, injustice.
3 Have students give examples and nonexamples of the concept.
   Example: Give examples of objects of worth to you. Give examples of ideas you cherish.
4 State the general meaning of the concept.
   Example: We can use the term *value* to mean objects and ideas that are cherished, prized, or desired.
5 Have students use the term and find new examples and nonexamples.
   Example: Use the term value in discussion and in reports. Find new examples in the materials we are using.

In both of the above may be noted certain features of concept-development strategies. The intention is to develop a generalized meaning that students can put to use. Attention is given to relevant and irrelevant attributes. Both examples (exemplars) and nonexamples (nonexemplars) are included in instruction, and students are expected to use the concept name or label and to find examples and nonexamples.

The strategies may be mixed or used in a variety of combinations. For example, a teacher may begin with the discovery model by having students identify items that are to be classified and then shift to an expository stance and provide a definition and label. This may be followed by having students (or the teacher) give new examples and nonexamples.

A Strategy for Using Inquiry Processes

The strategy below is illustrative of one that may be used to develop competence in using inquiry or thinking processes. The example is drawn from a unit on Pollution in Our Community. The inquiry or thinking process is *analyzing* which begins with identifying ways to break the problem into parts. This is followed by classifying data under each part and stating a conclusion based on the analysis. Similar strategies for other processes are reported by Michaelis (1972).

1 Identify ways to break the problem into parts.
   Example: What are the main parts (types, causes, reasons, groups)?
   What are the main types of pollution in our city?
2 Define each part clearly.
   Example: What is the meaning of each part? What does it include?
   What is air pollution? Waste pollution? Noise pollution?
3 Organize data related to each part.
   Example: What information do we have on each part? What information do we have on each type of pollution?
4 State explanation or conclusion based on the analysis.
   Example: What does our analysis show? What can we conclude?
   What can we conclude about each type of pollution?

Similar strategies may be developed for other processes by keeping focusing questions in mind. Notice the order in which the following are given for three processes that are used extensively in the social studies.

Generalizing What did you find? What common elements did you find? What can we say in general? Does our generalization check with the data?
Hypothesizing What usually happens if ____ ? Why does that usually happen? How can we state our idea so that it can be tested? What is a good way to test our hypothesis? Do the findings support it? Do we need more data?
Synthesizing How can we bring together the main findings on this topic? What are the most important items? How should the parts be organized? What form (map, report) should we use?

A Skill-Development Strategy

The skill-development strategy presented below may be used to develop map and globe, time and chronology, and other skills in the social studies. The strategy begins with preparation that includes clarification of the need for the skill, development of related concepts, and review of related skills and concepts. This is followed by development of the skill through actual use and by further refinement and extension of the skill.

    1 Preparation for developing the skill: Build interest, clarify need for skill, relate to past experience, introduce skill, develop related concepts.
        Example: To improve skill in using the legend to interpret maps, have students recall the importance of always checking the legend. Review map symbols for capital, boundaries, and so on, that have been used in prior lessons. Review basic steps: Find legend; check meaning of symbols; find symbols on the map. Introduce new symbols for copper, coal, and other resources, clarifying the meaning of each resource as needed.
    2 Development of the skill: Provide for immediate application of the skill.
        Example: Ask students to turn to the map in their textbooks which shows mineral resources in New England. Direct attention to the legend, focusing attention on the symbols for mineral resources. Ask children to identify resources in each of the New England states.
    3 Provision for practice and further refinement and extension of the skill:
        Example: Ask students to compare mineral resources in New England and western states. Have students add mineral resources to an outline map of the United States.

A Simulation Strategy

Simulation situations and games are scaled-down models of real-life situations, problems, or activities. The players assume realistic roles and make decisions according to specified rules, or within the limitations of a particular role or position. Simulation activities can produce student involvement, develop and extend concepts, clarify key aspects of life situations, and develop the abilities to weigh alternatives and make decisions.

The following strategy may be used for simulation experiences and games.

    1 Set goals with students and review relevant information.
        Example: What must you do to win in this game? What do you need to know if you are a mother in a Japanese family?
    2 Plan briefly for carrying out the activity.
        Example: Review game rules, time limits, and handling of pieces, cards, or related materials. Where in the classroom will each family have its "home"? How much space will each group need?
    3 Carry out the simulation activities or play the game.
        Example: As students play a game or simulate a life situation, the

teacher should observe to note whether each participant understands his or her role and whether accurate concepts are
expressed through students' actions or statements during the
activity.
4 Debrief to express understandings and evaluate effectiveness of the activity.
   Example: What happened during the game? What did you think of as
   you played it? What would you need to do to win next time?
   How did this game help us to understand how a bill is passed
   in Congress? How did you feel as a brother in this family?
   What made you feel that way? In what ways was your role
   like that in your own family? In what ways was it different?
   Why?
5 Learning can sometimes be extended by repeating the game or simulation
with changes suggested by students during debriefing and evaluation, or with
reversal of roles.

Clarifying Values in Events

The strategy for clarifying values in events may be used in connection with units
at all levels of instruction (Taba et al., 1971). The strategy begins with identification of facts and main reasons for the event. Students then infer values from
the stated reasons. Next, students state what they would have done, give
reasons for their answers, and infer what the reasons reveal about their own
values.

1 Clarify the facts about the event.
   Example: What facts are known? What happened at the Boston Tea
             Party?
2 Identify the main reasons.
   Example: Why did it happen? What were the main reasons?
3 Infer values from the reasons.
   Example: What do the reasons show was important to them?
4 Identify what students would have done.
   Example: What might you have done in the same situation? Why?
5 Infer students' values from the reasons.
   Example: What do your reasons show to be important to you?

Other Value-clarification Strategies

A large number of other valuing strategies may be adapted for use in the social
studies. The following have been selected from around ninety strategies
included in the cited references. The procedure for adapting them is simply to
provide directions to students that focus attention on people and events in the
social studies.

Clarifying Responses Nondirective questions may be used in response to
comments of students to help them clarify values (Raths et al., 1966). The

questions may be used in two ways: to clarify students' values and to infer values held by others. The following questions are designed to help students clarify their own values: Is this something you prize? Are you glad about that? Did you consider alternatives? The foregoing questions can readily be changed to help students infer values held by others: Was that something he prized? Was he glad about that? Did they consider alternatives?

Value Sheets   A value-laden statement, or a paragraph or two, or a cartoon or photograph may be presented to the class. Questions are raised to get students to indicate alternatives they might choose, what they prize, and what they might do.

Role Playing   Value-laden events may be used as the basis for role playing followed by discussion of values (Shaftel & Shaftel, 1967). The main steps in this strategy are warm-up in which the situation is presented; selection of participants; preparation of audience to observe; setting the stage; role playing; discussion and evaluation; further enactment of certain parts, revised roles, alternatives; further discussion; sharing of experiences and generalizing about the experience.

Rank Order   Students are asked to rank three or four items or alternatives in rank order in terms of importance, preference, need, priority, or order in which they should be done (Simons et al., 1972). Values are clarified through follow-up discussion of the ranking.

A Model for Value Analysis   A model has been proposed which is based on rational analysis of situations and is similar to the problem-solving, decision-making model (Metcalf, 1971). The procedure is as follows:

1   Identify and clarify the value question.
    Example: Should thermonuclear generating plants be built now? What are the issues? Problems? Proposals?
2   Gather and organize the facts.
    Example: What are the facts? Which statements are facts? Which statements are evaluative assertions? List negative and positive facts and arguments.
3   Assess the truth of facts.
    Example: What is the evidence? On what do authorities agree? Disagree?
4   Clarify the relevance of facts.
    Example: How should the facts be weighted? Which are most important? Least important? Why?
5   Arrive at a tentative value decision.
    Example: Plants should be built to meet energy needs, but with the utmost care.
6   Test the value principle implied in the decision.
    Example: What value(s) lie behind the decision? Applicable to new cases? Subsumable under basic values? Possible consequences?

GUIDELINES FOR THE TEACHER

The teacher has an inquiry-oriented role to play in new programs of social sciences education. The strategies noted above are illustrative of key aspects of the teacher's role. To be sure, teaching styles vary greatly and most teachers employ a combination of strategies and approaches ranging from inductive and discovery methods to straightforward development of key concepts and main ideas. In spite of variations in style and use of various strategies, the following guidelines appear to be in the forefront in new projects and curricula.

Keep attention focused on concepts, themes, and main ideas around which content can be organized. Avoid fact gathering and isolated learning of unrelated details. Guide students to organize and classify information within periods or regions or around themes and concepts. Various modes of organizing data may be used in each unit of study to help students develop an ever-growing understanding of key concepts and ideas in the social studies program.

Give special attention to concept clusters as guides to study and original inquiry. Use them to organize information, make comparisons, and formulate generalizations. For example, the cluster "major landforms: plains, hills, plateaus, and mountains" can be used to formulate questions, gather data, compare countries, and make generalizations as the United States, India, China, Japan, and other countries are studied. The cluster "factors in production: land, labor, capital, and entrepreneurship (know-how)" may be used as economic problems are studied in the community, state, nation, and other lands. Students themselves should discover concept clusters and link them to others in cognitive maps that are a part of their grasp of the underlying structure of the social sciences.

Plan and use teaching strategies that are consistent with the modes of inquiry used in history and the social sciences. For example, economists and other scholars typically associate rather precise meanings with concepts, and the meanings may vary widely from popular usage. Historians and geographers may organize data into various periods and regions. Sociologists, anthropologists, and economists tend to use concepts and concept clusters as organizing centers. Historians tend to deal primarily with themes and generalizations related to particular events, while social scientists deal primarily with generalizations that cut across societies and cultures.

Provide opportunities for students to use a variety of models and techniques of inquiry. Help students grow in the ability to select models and techniques that are most useful in different situations. Although primary attention may be given to critical reading and analysis of source materials, provide for the study of pictorial, graphic, and other resources. Go beyond the analysis of content as prepared by others and presented in textbooks, films, and other media to original content production based on interviews, direct observation of activities, field trips, simulation, and other techniques.

Use questions formulated in terms of inquiry processes to guide study. Bear in mind that questions are needed on the recalling and observing levels to assure adequate foundations of understanding. Proceed to interpreting, generalizing, and higher levels in a sequence and at a pace that suits the capabilities of students in the class. Help students learn to formulate questions in terms of processes so that they will become increasingly independent learners.

Develop the basic study skills that are essential to a high level of learning. Basic skills of importance in social studies and in other subjects include locating, organizing, and evaluating information, reading, listening, observing, communicating in oral and written form, interpreting pictures, charts, graphs, and tables, and working with others. Skills which should be developed in social sciences education include reading social sciences material, applying thinking processes to social issues and problems, interpreting maps and globes, and understanding time and chronology. The foregoing skills are put to many uses as models, methods, and processes of inquiry are employed in the social studies.

Provide for continuous evaluation through a variety of procedures, by both teacher and students. Gather data through observation, discussion, appraisal of students' work, testing, and review of previous records. Each individual's progress should be studied, with special attention paid to clues for use in planning and directing learning. Student self-evaluation should be encouraged to stimulate individual learning and self-understanding.

EVALUATION OF INSTRUCTIONAL OUTCOMES

Teacher observation of children's use of concepts, processes, and skills, and their expression of attitudes, values, and interests is one of the most effective evaluation techniques used in the social studies. Observation may be sharpened by the use of charts and checklists developed by the teacher or cooperatively developed by children and the teacher. The following examples are illustrative:

Evaluating the Use of Concepts ___ Which children use them accurately in discussion? ___ In oral and written reports? ___ Which children look out for shifts in meaning? ___ Check the meaning of new terms? ___ Which children need instruction on the foregoing?

Evaluating the Use of Processes Process of Generalizing: ___ Which students identify the facts? ___ Find what is common in the facts? ___ State the central idea? ___ Check the idea against the facts? ___ State the main idea and supporting details? ___ Which students need instruction on the foregoing?

Evaluating the Use of Skills Map Interpretation Skills: ___ Which students orient maps correctly? ___ Which students interpret directions correctly? ___ Which students consistently check the legend? ___ Which students need instruction?

Evaluating the Expression of Attitudes, Values, Interests Which children demonstrate respect for views of others in discussions? ___ Which children make positive comments about activities of people in other cultures? __ Which children recognize and state contributions of minority groups? __ Which children show interest in role playing? __ Which children need help on the foregoing?

All the above can easily be turned into charts for students to use in self-evaluation, another basic technique of great value in the social studies. For example, the items related to the process of generalizing may be restated as follows for student use: __ Which facts are most important? __ What can be stated in general? __ Does my general idea check with the facts? __ Can I state the main idea and give supporting details? The others can be adapted in a similar fashion (see Michaelis, 1972, for other examples).

A variety of other informal means of evaluation also may be used in the social studies. Group discussions, small-group interviews, and individual interviews may be used to appraise outcomes of instruction. For example, children's ability to use a concept in interpreting a picture may be assessed by showing a picture of people building a house and asking, How does this picture show *division of labor?* As a second example, children's interests in various aspects of other cultures under study may be appraised by raising such questions as: What have you found to be most interesting? Least interesting? Most different? How about their food? Housing? Clothing? Sports? Arts and crafts? Still other informal devices may be used in the social studies. Logs of units, diaries of activities, scrapbooks made by students, collections made by students, and samples of children's work may be examined to determine progress that has been made, difficulties that have been encountered, and individual needs that call for instruction. A guiding principle in this type of informal evaluation is to make appraisal an ongoing and natural part of instruction.

Using the Taxonomies to Improve Evaluation

The taxonomies of educational objectives (Bloom, 1956: Krathwohl, Bloom, & Masia, 1964) are helpful guides to the planning of questions and items for use in evaluation. Questions on different levels may be used in interviews, discussions, and other situations to assess outcomes of instruction. Test items may be prepared and developed to fit units of study. The following examples are illustrative of questions and items on the various levels of the taxonomies.

Cognitive Domain

Knowledge Level What are the major landforms? Draw a line under each of the following that is a major landform: plains, cliffs, plateaus, hills, valleys, mountains.

Comprehension Level Can you explain the meaning of nuclear family? A nuclear family includes Parents and their children Parents only Parents, children, and cousins All people related to the parents.

Application Level How can we use the concept cluster "major landforms" to compare our country and Brazil? Read the paragraphs below and use the concept cluster "major landforms" to find the landforms common to both Brazil and our country. (Provide paragraphs that present data on landforms in both countries.)

Analysis Level Why has Japan become a leading industrial nation even though she is not richly endowed with natural resources? Analyze Japan's productive capacity in terms of the concept cluster "factors of production: resources, labor, capital, and management."

Synthesis Level What shall we include in our reports on Japan? Formulate original hypotheses about production possibilities in Japan after you have studied the tables and charts on the chalkboard. (Provide tables and charts on factors of production.)

Evaluation Level How can we improve our reports on Japan's arts and crafts? Which of the following are most important in improving our discussions? Clarifying the topic   Speaking clearly   Taking turns   Preparing ahead of time Making a good summary

Affective Domain

Receiving (Attending) Level Did you notice any instances in which we did not listen to the views of others? List three ways you can show respect for the views of others.

Responding Level: What parts of the story of the fishing village were most interesting? Make a check by each of the following that you enjoy doing in class:

_____ Reading stories about people in Japan
_____ Discussing stories with others
_____ Finding out about the author
_____ Telling about the author

Valuing Level Did you feel that you should do something to help the fisherman's family? Tell about it. Make a check by each of the following that you try to do to understand Japanese ways of life:

_____ Think of what I would do if I lived there
_____ Find the reasons why they eat and dress as they do
_____ Try to understand why their holidays are important to them
_____ Find out why they do other things the way they do

FOLLOW-UP ACTIVITIES AND PROJECTS

1 Examine a course of study for the social studies and note the following:

   a Objectives of the social studies. How are they alike and different from those presented in this chapter?
   b What are the main themes and units for elementary grades? What suggestions are given for prekindergarten and kindergarten? What changes do you think should be made in the sequence of units?
   c What teaching strategies, instructional media, and learning activities are recommended? Which ones suggested in this chapter might be added?
   d What suggestions are given for the evaluation of children's learning?

2 Write three or four questions based on concepts and concept clusters presented in this chapter. Note the inquiry process that is emphasized in each one.
3 Devise one question and one test item on each level of the taxonomy of the cognitive domain. Use the examples presented in this chapter as models.
4 Select any two of the teaching strategies presented in this chapter and make a brief plan showing how you might use it in a unit of your choice.
5 Note two or three examples of ways in which one of the following might be included in a unit of your choice: career education, environmental education, future education.

BIBLIOGRAPHY

Banks, James A., and Ambrose A. Clegg, Jr. *Teaching Strategies for the Social Studies.* Reading, Mass.: Addison-Wesley, 1973. Complete treatment of social studies instruction.
Bottoms, James E., et al. (Eds.) *Career Education Resource Guide.* Morristown, N.J.: General Learning Corporation, 1973. Activities, materials, and procedures for K-12 programs.
Carpenter, Helen. (Ed.) *Skill Development in the Social Studies.* 33d Yearbook. Washington, D.C.: National Council for the Social Studies, 1963. Basic reference on social studies skills.
Fraser, Dorothy M. (Ed.) *Social Studies Curriculum Development.* 38th Yearbook. Washington, D.C.: National Council for the Social Studies, 1969. Guidelines for organizing the curriculum.
Grossman, Ruth H., and John U. Michaelis. *Schools, Families, Neighborhoods; Working, Playing, Learning; People, Places, Products.* Menlo Park, Calif.: Addison-Wesley, 1972. Teachers' editions include examples of inquiry-conceptual questions.
Joyce, Bruce R. *New Strategies for Social Education.* Chicago: Science Research Associates, 1972. Complete treatment of social studies instruction.
Hess, Robert D., and Doreen J. Croft. *Teachers of Young Children.* Boston: Houghton Mifflin, 1972. Chapter on social concepts and behavior.
Henrie, Samuel N. (Senior Ed.) *Sourcebook of Elementary Curricula Programs and Projects.* Washington, D.C.: Government Printing Office, 1972. Chapters on social studies, affective education and personal development, and ethnic education and intergroup relations.

Jarolimek, John. *Social Studies in Elementary Education.* New York: Macmillan, 1971. Complete treatment of social studies instruction.

Jarolimek, John, and Huber M. Walsh (Eds.) *Readings for Social Studies in Elementary Education.* New York: Macmillan, 1974. Selections on all phases of instruction.

Lee, John R. *Teaching Social Studies in Elementary Schools.* New York: Free Press, 1974, Chapters on games, role playing, and case studies.

Michaelis, John U. *Social Studies for Children in a Democracy.* Englewood Cliffs, N.J.: Prentice-Hall, 1972. Complete treatment of social studies instruction.

Michaelis, John U., and Everett T. Keach, Jr. (Eds.) *Teaching Strategies for Elementary School Social Studies.* Itasca, Ill.: Peacock Press, 1972. Selections on all phases of instruction.

Michaelis, John U. *Teaching Units in the Social Sciences.* Chicago, Rand McNally, 1966. Three paperback booklets, one each for grades, K-2, 3-4, 5-6.

Marien, Michael, and Warren L. Ziegler. (Eds.) *The Potential of Educational Futures.* Worthington, Ohio: Charles A. Jones Publishing Co., 1972. Essays on educational futures, modes of viewing the future, planning and teaching in terms of the future.

Sale, Larry L. *Environmental Education in the Elementary School.* New York: Holt, 1972. Guiding principles and activities.

"Social Studies in Alternative Schools," *Social Education,* **38,** 236–255, March, 1974. Articles on instruction in different types of schools.

Spodek, Bernard. *Teaching in the Early Years.* Englewood Cliffs, N.J.: Prentice-Hall, 1972. Chapter on social studies for young children.

Thomas, R. Murray, and Dale L. Brubaker. *Decisions in Teaching Elementary Social Studies.* Belmont, Calif.: Wadsworth, 1971. Approaches to the solution of instructional issues and problems.

——————. *Teaching Elementary Social Studies: Readings.* Belmont, Calif.: Wadsworth, 1972. Attention to social issues and problems, disciplines, instruction, and evaluation.

Toffler, Alvin. (Ed.) *Learning for Tomorrow: The Role of the Future in Education.* New York: Random House, 1974. Articles on education for the future.

Wernick, Walter. *Teaching for Career Development in the Elementary School.* Worthington, Ohio: Charles A. Jones Publishing Co., 1973. Activities for various subjects and levels.

Chapter 14

Health Education

Health and physical education are core components of a complete school health program. Health education includes instruction designed to help students learn those aspects of healthful and safe living that are essential to the attainment of a high level of personal and community well-being. Physical education includes instruction designed to promote students' well-being through physical activities as shown in the following chapter. Both health and physical education are related to and coordinated with school health services and healthful school living, two other components of a complete school health program.

The four components of school health programs are shown in Chart 14-1. The four main components are coordinated so that learning in health and physical education, use of health services, and maintenance of healthful school living are maximized. In addition, the four components are related to national, state, and community health programs that include services available from various public and private agencies. Many different foundation disciplines are drawn upon to improve all phases of the program.

Good health has been defined by the World Health Organization of the United Nations as "a state of complete physical, mental, and social well-being

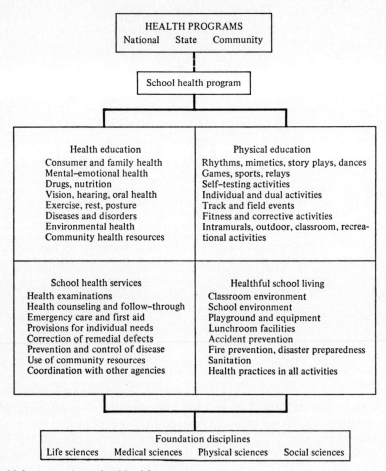

Chart 14-1 A complete school health program.

and not merely the absence of disease and infirmity." Good health involves the capacity, or inner strength, to meet a variety of conditions and situations. It is based not only on normal functioning of the body, but also on an understanding of elements of healthful living, positive attitudes, personal and social values, adjustment to environmental conditions, and social/emotional/mental health.

CONTRIBUTIONS TO BASIC GOALS

Health education makes many contributions to major goals. *Thinking ability* may be sharpened as students consider health problems, use critical thinking skills to assess proposals for health care and improvement, and use classifying, generalizing, hypothesizing, and other inquiry processes to investigate topics and issues. *Self-realization* is enhanced as students develop and maintain high levels of physical, social, emotional, and mental well-being. *Human relationships* are facilitated in an environment in which personal and community health are maintained at high levels. *Economic competence* depends on a broad program of healthful living involving the individual, coworkers, and the community. *Civic responsibility* can reach a high level if one's physical, mental, social, and emotional well-being provide the capacity and inner strength that are needed to discharge personal and social responsibilities. And *learning how to learn* takes on special significance as students develop the competencies needed for lifelong learning of ways to develop, maintain, and improve healthful living. Additional and more specific contributions may be noted in the illustrative objectives that follow.

OBJECTIVES OF HEALTH EDUCATION

Conceptual Objectives

To develop understanding of information, concepts, and generalizations about healthful living so that students are able to identify and describe the following:

Needs for rest, sleep, exercise, cleanliness, grooming, recreation, a balanced diet, health habits, immunization, care of one's body

Drug use and misuse, environmental health problems, consumer health, family health

The structure and functioning of the body, prevention and control of disease, essentials of safe living and accident prevention

Individual and group responsibilities in family, school, and community health, individual differences in health needs, variations of ways of maintaining good health

Inquiry Objectives

To develop competence in using processes, methods, and modes of inquiry so students are able to do the following:

Demonstrate through use such processes as interpreting, inferring, generalizing, and evaluating in units focused on health instruction

Make plans for investigating health and safety problems, using such methods of inquiry as taking field trips, interviewing, reading, experimenting

Skill Objectives

To develop the skills involved in sound health habits and to apply language and other skills to the study of health problems so that students are able to perform the following:

Describe sound habits of rest, grooming, bodily care, exercise, selection and care of clothing, disease prevention and control, proper use of drugs, eating

Demonstrate effective ways of working with others, maintaining mental health, preventing accidents, taking safety precautions, using services of health specialists and agencies, observing laws and regulations

Demonstrate how printed materials, community resources, and audio-visual materials may be used as sources of data in the study of health topics and problems

AFFECTIVE OBJECTIVES

To demonstrate in individual and group work the values, interests, and attitudes of individuals who

Have an interest in and desire to practice sound health and safety habits, promote the health and safety of others, utilize health services, and provide a healthful environment

Express appreciation of the contributions of health workers and the function of the home, school, and health agencies in promoting well-rounded well-being

Use strategies to clarify values involved in making decisions on proposals and practices related to healthful well-being

ORGANIZATION OF THE CURRICULUM

A continuing trend in health education is to structure the curriculum around generalizations and concepts related to major areas of content. Units of instruction are planned within each area of content to develop key concepts and main ideas that are contributory to the attainment of major generalizations. This approach may be illustrated by taking examples from a state program that includes the ten areas of content noted below (California, 1970). Key concepts have been included under each area to indicate the instructional emphasis.

Consumer Health Need for effort, time, money; costliness of failure to maintain health; use of scientific knowledge to make decisions; avoidance of self-diagnosis, self-treatment, quackery, and faddism

Mental-emotional Health Factors influencing mental health; need to understand oneself and others; handling stress; impact of maladjustive behavior; help available for maladjustive behavior

Drug Use and Misuse Benefits of proper use; factors in misuse; effects of tobacco, alcohol, drugs; individual and group responsibility for preventing misuse

Family Health Interactive influences of family members; factors determining masculinity and femininity; factors in successful marriage; understandings related to roles of males and females; planning to improve family health

Oral Health, Vision, Hearing Effects of neglect; prevention and treatment; using services

Nutrition Importance in daily activities; basic human requirements for certain nutrients; varying amounts for individuals; food processing and preparation in relation to nutritional value and safety; weight control; dietary fads and misconceptions

Exercise, Rest, Posture Physical fitness as one component of total health; balance in exercise and rest; posture and appearance and bodily function

Diseases and Disorders Occurrence and distribution as affected by heredity and environment; personal and economic effects; variation in prevention and control

Environmental Health Hazards Environmental influences on health; changes in health hazards; potential for accidents; accident care; responsibilities for maintaining a healthful and safe environment

Community Health Resources Benefits of health resources; shared responsibilities of the individual and community agencies; need for international teamwork; variety of opportunities for health careers.

Major generalizations are listed under each of the above areas of content. The generalizations serve as overall guides to the planning of instruction at different grade levels. They are used to generate related subgeneralizations or main ideas that can be used to plan units of study. The following are examples of generalizations for two areas of content that have been given increased emphasis in recent years.

Drug Use and Misuse

When used properly, drugs are beneficial to mankind.

Many factors influence the misuse of drugs.

Tobacco is harmful; alcohol and drugs, if misused, are harmful to the individual and society.

Individuals and groups need to accept responsibility for preventing the misuse of drugs.

Environmental Health Hazards

An individual's environment, including aesthetic characteristics, influences his total health.

There are ever-changing health hazards in the environment.

The potential for accidents exists everywhere in the environment.

Individuals should be prepared to act effectively in case of accidents.

Maintaining a healthful and safe environment is the responsibility of the individual, the family, and society.

Generalizations such as those above are used to generate related main ideas or subgeneralizations and to identify related content. This is done at different levels of instruction. For example, the following main idea for primary grades is related to the first generalization under "Drug Use and Misuse": Some commonly used substances can be harmful if misused. Related content includes cola drinks, coffee, aspirin, and other commonly used substances. The following examples further illustrate this approach. They are presented by levels of instruction and include specific objectives to show how unit and lesson planning may be given a sharp focus.

Drug Use and Misuse

Primary Level

Main idea: Some commonly used substances can be harmful if misused.
Objective: The child identifies substances that can be harmful.
Content: Cola drinks, tea, coffee, alcohol, aspirin, diet pills, other medicines

Intermediate Level

Main idea: Individuals react differently to the chemicals in drugs.
Objective: The child describes differences in individuals and their reactions.
Content: Body size, sensitivity, metabolism

Junior High

Main idea: Drugs may cause harmful effects that are immediate and long-range.
Objective: The student identifies potential harmful effects of drugs.
Content: Effects from tobacco (cancer, etc.), effects from drugs (hallucinations, etc.)

Environmental Health Hazards

Primary Level

Main idea: Children and adults have responsibilities for a healthful and safe environment.
Objective: The child describes responsibilities for maintaining the environment.

Content: Picking up litter; putting belongings away; not playing with matches, medicines, and poisons; reporting unsafe conditions

Intermediate Level

Main idea: Healthful and safe recreational areas enhance the environment.
Objective: The child states examples of how recreational areas can be kept safe.
Content: Keeping lakes and streams clean; preventing fires; maintaining campsites

Junior High

Main idea: Community control activities protect the health and safety of individuals.
Objective: The student describes community activities.
Content: Control of air, water, and soil pollution; noise reduction; pesticide control

The one major health education project, *School Health Education Study,** used the concepts growing, developing, interacting, and decision making as the basis for formulating generalizations to be used as organizing strands. Examples of the generalizations, referred to as organizing concepts by the developers, are as follows: (Henrie, 1972)

Growth and development influence and are influenced by the structure and functioning of the individual.
Utilization of health information, products, and services is guided by values and perceptions.
The family serves to perpetuate mankind and to fulfill many health needs.

The examples above are illustrative of a planning procedure that has long been used in curriculum development. The main steps in this approach are as follows: (1) Identify major areas of content to be included in the area of curriculum under study. (2) List major generalizations under each area of content, obtaining the assistance of experts as needed. (3) List related sub-generalizations for each major generalization, designing them for emphasis at different grade levels so that a sequence is evolved that leads to the development of the major generalization. (4) Identify related content that is needed to develop each subgeneralization at different grade levels.

Sequential Development of Concepts

Sequential development of concepts is handled in two important ways. The first provides for continuing instruction from grade to grade on each of the major topics that serve as strands for defining the structure of the program. The second provides for a cycling of units of study in different grades so that students have recurring encounters with key concepts on succeedingly higher levels of complexity.

School Health Education Study, 3M Co., St. Paul, Minn.

Level-to-level Sequencing

The following examples show how there is a buildup from level to level for three selected topics:

Body Functions and Structure. In the early grades attention is given to the senses of sight, hearing, touch, and taste, functions of the teeth, need for activity, rest, relaxation, and exercise, height and weight differences, and the contributions of foods. In grades 2 and 3 new material is introduced on the senses, teeth, body needs, height and weight gains, nerves, the heart and other organs, and the functions of muscles and bones. In grades 4 through 6 instruction includes deeper studies of the foregoing plus the nervous system, the digestive system, function of glands, and the effects of tobacco, alcohol, and narcotics.

Food and Nutrition. In the early grades attention is given to needs for milk and fruit juices, an adequate breakfast, foods for lunch, between-meal snacks, importance of a pleasant atmosphere for eating, development of a taste for variety, and cleanliness. In grades 2 and 3 material is introduced on the nutritive value of dairy products and margarine, protein in the diet, balanced meals, food preparation, elimination, and basic food groups. Building on the foregoing, the program in later grades includes food production and preservation, nutrients in an adequate diet, digestion, effects of emotions, balanced diets, and weight control.

Mental Health. In the early grades attention is given to taking turns, sharing, being kind, adjusting to disappointments, learning consideration for others, discussing feelings with others, using simple courtesies, and controlling oneself. The foregoing are continued in grades 2 and 3, and attention is given to growth in friendliness, courtesy, kindliness, concern for others, adjusting to unfortunate happenings, accepting responsibility, welcoming newcomers, controlling anger and other feelings, admitting mistakes, releasing feelings through art and other activities, accepting handicapped individuals, facing difficulties, and talking problems over with others. With a focus on individual differences, attention in later grades is given to reasons behind behavior, expression of emotions, personal and social needs, peer-group relationships, relationships between physical condition and feelings, effects of feelings on body processes, facing reality, respecting oneself and others, and solving problems.

Cycling of Units of Study

It is common practice to cycle units of study at different grade levels. The underlying theory is that deeper understandings, skills, and appreciations will be developed as children encounter topics and problems in greater depth. Incidental instruction is given to topics that are not singled out for unit emphasis in a particular grade; this is done to maintain continuity of learning. In prekindergarten and kindergarten programs primary emphasis is given to healthful living throughout the school day and to the development of appropriate health habits, although mini-units may be included in the kindergarten program. Here are some examples of the cycling of units:

Consumer health   Units in grades 2, 4, 6, 8
Mental health   Units in grades 1, 3, 5, 7
Drug use and misuse   Units in grades 3, 5, 7, 8
Family health   Units in grades 1, 2, 4, 6
Oral health   Units in grades 1, 3, 4, 6, 8
Nutrition   Units in grades 1, 3, 5, 7
Exercise, rest, posture   Units in grades 2, 4, 6, 8
Disease and disorders   Units in grades 3, 5, 7
Environmental health   Units in grades 1, 2, 3, 5, 7
Community health services   Units in grades 3, 5, 8

Not shown above are the parts of units of study in other subjects that focus on various aspects of health. For example, units on the family, community living, and living in our state typically include aspects of healthful living. Many units in science education deal directly with several of the areas of content noted above. This fact must be kept in mind as the cycling of health units is planned. Several examples of how health education is made a part of other subjects are presented in a later section of this chapter.

Concepts, Concept Clusters, Related Questions

The health education program abounds with basic concepts and concept clusters. In addition to the concepts already noted above under areas of content are others that are widely used in different units of study. The following concept clusters are of special importance at all levels of instruction:

Physical needs: Food, water, rest, sleep, activity, protection from disease, care of the body
Social-emotional needs: Acceptance, belonging, security, love, growing independence, intellectual stimulation, success, sense of worth, faith
Basic food groups: Meat, fish, poultry, eggs; cooked and raw vegetables and fruits; milk, cheese, butter, margarines; bread and cereals
Food nutrients: Proteins, fats, carbohydrates, vitamins, minerals
Disease prevention and control: Rest, food, cleanliness, immunization, examination, precautions, care during illness, preventing causes of disease, use of medicines and drugs
Social-emotional health: Self-respect, respect for others, acceptance of reality, self and group discipline, social skills and standards, being a leader and follower, individual and group problem solving, release of tensions through activity
Growth and development: Individual differences, importance of diet, activity, and sleep, relationships with others, functioning of body systems of

circulation, respiration, and elimination, body changes, effects of tobacco, alcohol, and narcotics

Community health: Local conditions and problems; local, state, and national agencies; safety and health practices; contributions of leaders; careers

Independent and group study in health education may be improved by using concepts and concept clusters to formulate questions and plan activities. The following examples of inquiry-conceptual questions and activities are illustrative. The inquiry process is identified in parenthesis after each question or activity.

What *food nutrients* does everyone need (recalling)?

How might we design a picture chart to show the *basic food groups* (synthesizing)?

What usually happens when the skin of an apple is broken? Will it decay faster or slower than an apple whose skin is not broken (hypothesizing)?

Read to find out what the writer of this article believes to be the main reasons for *drug abuse* (interpreting)?

Based on ideas presented in the film and readings on *disease control* in the community, state a principle related to the responsibilities of individuals (generalizing).

Given the soil conditions described in the reading for today, what can we say about the *vitamin* and *mineral* content of foods grown there (inferring)?

Study these two menus and give reasons why you think one is better than the other in terms of *basic food groups* and *nutrients* (evaluating).

Study the two lists of words on the chalkboard. Organize them into two groups by listing them under the following headings: *physical needs* and *social-emotional needs* (classifying).

Make a chart that shows the main activities of local, state, and national health agencies in the area of drug abuse education (synthesizing).

INSTRUCTIONAL MEDIA

In addition to films, recordings, trade books, and other media widely used by effective teachers in all subject areas, the following materials are useful in health and safety education:

Models Use of commercial biological models or models made by the teacher or children to illustrate concepts or principles and to demonstrate processes

Advertisements of Health-related Products Application of critical thinking skills to the analysis and evaluation of advertising claims, using such principles of good health as criteria and drawing upon a variety of sources of information

Charts and Records Use of health record forms, height-weight charts, dietary records, and diaries as continuing records kept by children along with those kept by the teacher and/or school nurse

TEACHING STRATEGIES

Many of the strategies used in science and social sciences education are also used in health education. In fact, such units as "How Our Bodies Work" and "Vital Organs" may be taught in either the science or the health education program. And such units as "Safety in the Community" and "Health Workers and Services" may be taught as part of the social sciences or health education program. The strategies and techniques presented in preceding chapters, therefore, should be viewed as applicable to health instruction. In this section are presented examples that show specific applications to units and topics in health education.

Experiments

The experimental model is a useful strategy because children can discover key ideas for themselves as they engage in firsthand observation of phenomena under controlled conditions. Defining the problem or question clearly, stating hypotheses, outlining procedures, observing critically, organizing and interpreting data, and formulating and checking conclusions are key ingredients in effective experiments. The following are illustrative of experiments included in health instruction:

Growth of Bacteria Prepare three cultures; use sterile dishes and seal them. In the first, place fingernail dirt on a moistened piece of bread; in the second, place dirty water; and in the third, place sterile water. Use a magnifying glass to observe growth of bacteria daily for three days.

Need for Refrigeration Cover two sterile glasses in which milk has been poured. Place one in the refrigerator and the other on a nearby shelf. Observe and compare changes during the week.

Food Decay Select two apples as near alike as can be found. Make a break in the skin of one and leave the other intact. Observe and compare the decay process over a period of several days.

Effects of Washing Sprinkle salt on the hands of selected children who have washed their hands. Have each child wipe his hands with paper towels and then determine if he can taste salt by touching the tip of his tongue to his hand. Next, have the children wash their hands, dry them, and determine if they can still taste the salt.

Effects of Contamination Rub a piece of boiled potato with dirty hands, and another piece with washed hands. Place the pieces of potato in two sterile jars. Put lids on and observe the difference.

Demonstrations

Demonstrations are useful in concept development, application of principles, clarification of appropriate behavior, motivation of learning, and initiation of units. The following are illustrative of demonstrations that may be conducted by the teacher or selected students:

Cleanliness and Grooming Demonstrate washing and drying of hands, cleaning of fingernails, the use of a handkerchief or tissue to blow the nose, how ordinary soap disperses oil more effectively in warm water than in cold.

Community Health and Safety. Demonstrate proper way to use drinking fountains, cross at intersections, get on and off buses, dispose of paper and other litter, care for pets.

Care of the Eyes Show proper ways to sit while reading, carry objects that might be injurious, remove objects from the eye, control lighting by means of shades, use a magnifying glass, participate in vision screening tests.

Problem Solving

The problem-solving model is used extensively in health instruction because it is an effective means of dealing with concerns of students and with many topics in the program of instruction. As in other areas of the curriculum, problem solving in health education includes recognizing and defining a problem, gathering and interpreting data, and formulating and applying conclusions. Illustrative problems are the following:

What foods should be eaten to promote healthful growth?
What are sound ways of preparing and preserving foods?
What steps can be taken to minimize tooth decay?
How can the spread of disease be kept under control?
How can we obtain the use of community health services?
What should we do to promote good relations with others?

Field Study

Field trips and surveys may be used to observe health and safety practices, to gather data on problems, to see demonstrations, and to confer with health service workers. They may be conducted in the school, home, neighborhood, or broader community. The skills involved in planning, observing, interviewing, note-taking, mapping, evaluating, and other activities are applied to health questions and problems. Study trips may be taken to such places as the school nurse's office, cafeteria, food market, dairy farm, water purification plant, and health department. Surveys may be made of such problems and topics as safety hazards, eating habits, safe street crossings, types of food eaten, types of illness, and daily amount of exercise.

Developing Generalizations

Generalizations may be developed through direct instruction that begins with an introduction or opener, proceeds through a series of developmental activities, and concludes with experiences in which students formulate a generalization. For example, the generalization "The human body needs foods containing vitamins, minerals, proteins, fats, and carbohydrates" may be developed as shown in the following abbreviated outline:

Opener Discuss what is meant by a balanced diet, using pictures of food arranged on the bulletin board. Have the students recall ideas they have about food elements all of us need. List their responses on the chalkboard.

Development Begin by showing a filmstrip or having the group read a section in their health books that presents information on basic food elements. Discuss the functions of vitamins. Make a summary of foods that are rich in different vitamins. Continue in the same manner with minerals, proteins, and other food elements. Organize the information on a chart that shows the relationship between foods and vital nutrients. Plan shopping lists and menus that include foods with essential nutrients. Have individuals investigate and report on rickets and other diseases that result from poor diets. Conduct an experiment to show the effects of rich and poor soil on the growth of plants.

Conclusion Have students summarize the main idea in their own words. Have a group make a mural or individuals make posters which illustrate the generalization. Provide for application by having students keep records of foods they eat.

Developing Safety Behaviors

The importance of safety education as an essential part of the health education program cannot be overemphasized. Accidents are the primary cause of death and permanent injury to children of elementary school age. The instructional program should be designed to develop both attitudes and behaviors conducive to safe living. Children in the elementary school should be helped to develop an awareness that daily activities involve some dangers, a desire to be attentive to such dangers and to take adequate precautions, a sense of responsibility for one's own safety, a commitment to the value of safety procedures, and the organization of a value system related to safety of oneself and others in all situations. Specific behaviors consistent with safety in particular situations must be taught and reviewed and practiced consistently so that they may become habitual.

Strategies for the development of understandings and attitudes leading to habitual safety behavior utilize techniques similar to those described on the preceding pages. Steps in a safety development strategy might include a problem-focused, attitude-encouragement clarification of specific behaviors, practice of behaviors, and evaluation, as described below. Problem situations of concern in the elementary school include such examples as pedestrian safety, safe places to play, use of specific tools, safety in sports activities, kite safety, rules for safe public transportation, and, of course, many others.

Focus   The specific situation to be considered may be brought to the attention of the class by pupils or by the teacher as the result of a particular incident or as part of the systematic program of safety instruction. Attention is focused on the situation by means of verbal description by children or teacher, use of role playing for reenactment of an incident or presentation of a story, or through vicarious examples in films, storybooks, records, or newspaper articles.

Understandings and Attitudes   After the problem situation has been described, children should be guided to recognize the potential dangers in the situation and to understand and accept the need to identify appropriate safety procedures. These understandings and attitudes may be developed through discussion directed by the teacher's questions, with reference to the focus situation and to experiences of the children in similar activities.

Clarification of Behaviors   Using a progression of questions, such as those based on taxonomies of cognitive and affective objectives as outlined in the preceding section, teacher and pupils can discuss ways of meeting the safety hazards they have identified. Demonstrations may be used to test suggested procedures or to teach those already proved. As agreement is reached on specific behaviors or on the total sequence of procedures, these should be recorded on charts such as those shown in Chart 14-2. This process enables children to develop favorable attitudes and a sense of self-responsibility as they work out their own safety rules or analyze and understand reasonable rules set by others.

Practice of Behaviors   Use of safety procedures begins with classroom enactment by some pupils during the previous instructional step. Whenever possible, the entire class should have the opportunity to immediately enact the procedure in a simulated situation in order to clinch behavior changes, instead of terminating the lesson at the level of verbalization. The behaviors should then be habituated through repeated practice in real situations.

Evaluation   As procedures are developed or analyzed in the preceding steps, children engage in evaluation of their efficacy. Charts drawn up during safety lessons should be kept for future reference and review. Some lists of safety procedures related to school, playground, and classroom activities may be permanently posted in an appropriate location. For example, rules for use of tools should be posted where the tools are stored. The teacher should observe children's behavior to ascertain the extent to which each student has developed the attitudes and habits that promote continuous and consistent adherence to safety procedures. Children should engage in continuing self-evaluation of behavior and group evaluation as needs arise. Chart 14-2 illustrates points to keep in mind during evaluation.

GUIDELINES FOR THE TEACHER

The teacher may play a variety of roles in health education ranging from director of systematic experiences that develop attitudes and habits of safety essential to group welfare to arranger of situations in which students discover for themselves key ideas from basic sciences. The multiple instructional approaches recommended by experts in health education clearly indicate that many similarities exist between teaching strategies in this area and those employed in science education and in social sciences education. What is unique about health instruction is the focus on personal and group aspects of healthful living. Strategies are selected, adapted, and devised to guide the attainment of objectives related to a broad concept of good health. The following guidelines are recommended by health education specialists.

Safety to and from school	Safety on a bus
1. Cross streets only in cross walks.	1. Wait on the curb until the bus door opens.
2. Walk across streets.	2. Go straight to your seat so others can get on.
3. Obey the traffic patrol.	3. Remain seated at all times.
4. When possible, use a corner where there is a signal.	4. Keep arms and head inside.
5. Watch for cars backing out of driveways.	5. Do not disturb the driver.
6. Leave dogs and other animals alone.	6. Watch your step when getting off.
7. Do not accept rides with strangers.	7. Be careful in crossing the street before boarding and after leaving the bus.
8. Walk on the left side of the road facing traffic if there is no sidewalk.	

Passing safely	Using doors safely
1. Watch where you are going.	1. Use the knob to open.
2. Always walk, never run.	2. Open slowly so as not to hit anyone passing by.
3. Watch out for opening doors.	3. Keep hands away from the opening on both sides.
4. Look out for others.	4. Watch out for others when closing the door.
	5. Take turns in passing through the doorway.

Safe fire and disaster drills	A safe playground
1. Act quickly and quietly when the alarm is sounded.	1. Walk to the area assigned to you.
2. Walk quietly without talking.	2. Keep hands off others.
3. Go to the place assigned to your class.	3. Use playground equipment correctly.
4. If in the toilet at the time of the alarm, join the nearest line going out.	4. Walk around the play areas of others.
5. Be alert for direction from the teacher.	5. Keep equipment and other objects out of play areas.
	6. Look out for others.
	7. Report accidents to the teacher.

Chart 14-2 Examples of safety procedure charts.

Provide systematic health education instruction that is viewed as an integral part of the total school health program. Administrators, teachers, school nutritionists, and custodians provide and maintain conditions for healthful school living. The teacher is particularly responsible for safe arrangement of classroom furniture, safe condition of classroom equipment, and attention to adequate lighting and healthful ventilation in the room. In some schools, specialists are available for physical education, but in others this may be the teacher's responsibility. In either case, there are times when the teacher will need to conduct games, exercise, dances, or rhythmic activities in the classroom. School health services are provided by medical specialists, but the classroom teacher's daily observation of the children is an important part of this aspect of the health program. A major area of the total program is the development of cognitive and affective objectives related to health and safety. No staff member is so well equipped and so well placed as the classroom teacher for the provision of systematic and continual health instruction designed to develop understandings, positive attitudes, and specific behaviors conducive to the child's safe and healthful living. Several health education experts suggest that provision of two periods each week in the primary grades and three periods each week in grades 4 through 6 helps to ensure systematic and meaningful learnings in health and safety.

Utilize every possible opportunity for incidental health and safety instruction. No other area of study is so close to the child's personal needs or so permeating in his total experience as is the subject matter of health education, for it is concerned with the child himself. Therefore, systematic health and safety instruction must be supplemented by instruction that meets the needs identified as children raise questions or recognize problems, take health examinations, encounter safety hazards, or exhibit any behavior that seems to be detrimental to the health or safety of the individual or group. Meaningful incidental instruction may also be initiated by current events or by questions arising from studies in other subject areas.

Try to integrate health instruction with the child's daily activities and home conditions. The teacher can provide more adequate and relevant instruction if some knowledge can be obtained about home conditions related to the child's diet, schedule of activities, sleep, health habits, etc. The teacher may gather needed information from school records, home visits, interviews with parents, or questionnaires sent to the home. The teacher should make it possible for parents to be aware of the ongoing health program in the school, and whenever necessary, work with parents to plan appropriate schedules, activities, or conditions for the child's healthful living at home. The teacher should observe the clothing worn by pupils to ascertain that shoes are comfortable, glasses fit properly, and clothing is adequate and appropriate for the weather.

Observe children carefully for symptoms of illness or referral to health specialists. The classroom teacher is sometimes responsible for testing pupils for visual and auditory acuity. Even when specialists handle these tests, the teacher should be alert, throughout the school day, to any indications of visual and auditory difficulties evidenced in a pupil's behavior. As the person who sees the child for several hours every school day, the teacher provides for the health of individuals as well as the entire class by careful observation of each child in order to detect symptoms ranging from generally poor health to the beginnings of serious illness or disability. Checklists are available which direct the teacher's attention to specific signs and symptoms in regard to general appearance, behavior, eyes, ears, and nose and throat. Examples of symptoms in these areas are as follows:

General Pale complexion, overweight, tires easily, poor posture
Behavior Nervousness, undue restlessness, excessive use of lavatory
Eyes Squinting, frequent headaches, inflamed eyes, crusted lids
Ears Dullness and inattention, watches speaker intently, discharge from ears
Nose and throat Persistent mouth breathing, frequent colds or sore throat

Measurement of pupils' weight and height is often conducted in the classroom and can readily be incorporated in other subject area studies.

Make health and safety instruction a part of learning experiences in other subject areas. Judiciously planned activities can augment health learnings and provide realistic, meaningful applications for subject area understandings and skills. A few examples are:

Language arts Writing reports; applying study skills to the gathering and processing of data in health and safety studies
Reading Using health education materials of high personal interest to motivate reading; using health and safety charts developed by the children as materials in an experience-based reading program
Foreign language Learning words for parts of the body; learning names of foods in clusters based on nutritional groups; noting the health implications in practice dialogues dealing with meals, bedtime, and family activities
Social studies Community, national, and international health services; health and safety responsibilities related to responsible citizenship; health practices in other times and places
Science Biological studies; contributions of life sciences and medical sciences to health understandings; conducting health experiments
Mathematics Recording height and weight measurements; using measurements and other health statistics in mathematical operations
Music Expressing health or safety ideas and catchphrases as chants or as songs composed by the children
Art Application of design principles to posters promoting important ideas about health and safety

EVALUATION OF INSTRUCTIONAL OUTCOMES

As indicated in the preceding sections, teacher observation of pupil behavior is an important aspect of continuous evaluation in health and safety education.

Observation of behavior may be guided by checklists and recorded in anecdotal records. Information about the health history of children taken from cumulative record cards can be useful in planning individualized learning experiences and assessing long-term changes in health attitudes and behaviors. Teacher-pupil interviews, paper-and-pencil tests, questionnaires, interest inventories, and samples of pupil's reports and other work are examples of evaluative tools.

Cognitive Domain

In addition to checklists for behaviors conducive to safe and healthful living, cognitive outcomes may be assessed with questions and tasks such as the following:

Knowledge Level Factual information related to principles of health and safety procedures
Why is it wise to include milk in our daily diet? What procedure do we follow in a fire drill?

Comprehension Level Interpretation of learnings in relation to one's own health and safety; expression of understandings in nonverbal forms
Explain in your own words the reasons why good posture is important to your health. Design a poster to show other children how to be safe on the playground.

Application Level Use of health principles in the child's daily life; adherence to safety regulations
Keep a record of the foods you eat for an entire week. List everything you do when you want to go across a street.

Analysis Level Understanding of the relationships between various health principles; ability to detect relevant and irrelevant information in statements about health and safety; understanding of relationships in safety rules
How does the amount of sleep you get at night affect your work in school?
Which sequence of procedures (of three or four alternative sets) would be most effective for our daily dismissals?

Synthesis Level The pupil's own organization of ideas related to good health and safety procedures
How can we help the first-graders to follow safety rules in and around the school? Write a short story that illustrates an important health idea.

Evaluation Level Application of criteria for safety and health to one's own habits; self-appraisal in regard to adherence to health and safety habits
I get eight hours of sleep at night ＿＿＿ (always, often, sometimes, never).
How effective and fair are our rules for the use of playground equipment?

Affective Domain

Affective outcomes may be assessed by means of checklists, attitude inventories, and interviews with children and their parents. Illustrative questions and items are:

Receiving Level Awareness of the difference between good and poor health; willingness to learn health and safety principles

What does "good health" mean to you? What reasons can you think of for rules of behavior on the playground.

Responding Level Satisfaction in development of health habits; voluntary participation in learning activities

Do you wear boots or rubbers in wet weather? **a** When I am reminded to. **b** Without being told. **c** I don't like to. **d** I never wear them.

Valuing Level Acceptance of the worth of adhering to health and safety procedures; commitment to the value of practicing good health and safety habits

The school-crossing guard should not be obeyed if he or she is not one of your friends. **a** Yes. **b** No. **c** I'm not sure.

FOLLOW-UP ACTIVITIES AND PROJECTS

1 Identify two or three health or safety hazards in your community. Next, under each hazard list the following as has been done in the examples presented in this chapter:

Main idea _____

Teaching Objective _____

Content _____

2 Make a brief teaching plan to illustrate how you might use one of the following in providing instruction on a health topic of your choice: **a** demonstration **b** field trip **c** interview **d** experiment

3 Write four or five inquiry-conceptual questions, using concepts presented in this chapter. Identify the inquiry process emphasized in each question.

4 Examine a course of study in health education and note the following:
  a examples of contributions to major goals of education
  b objectives that are different from those mentioned in this chapter
  c major units or topics that are recommended for elementary grades
  d suggestions for evaluating children's learning.

BIBLIOGRAPHY

Ellena, William J. (ed.). *Curriculum Handbook for School Executives*. Arlington,

Va.: American Association of School Administrators, 1973. Chapter on health education.

Fulton, Gene B., and William V. Fassbender. *Health Education in the Elementary School.* Pacific Palisades, Calif.: Goodyear Publishing Co., 1972. Chapters on drug abuse education and illustrative teaching units.

Henrie, Samuel N. (senior ed.). *Sourcebook of Elementary Curricula Programs and Projects.* Washington, D.C.: U.S. Government Printing Office, 1972. Chapters on drug education, and health and physical education.

Jones, Kenneth L., L.W. Shainberg, and C.O. Byer. *Critical Issues in Health.* New York: Harper & Row, 1972. Information on environment, mental health, drugs, diseases.

————. *Environmental Health.* New York: Harper and Row, 1971. Population and pollution problems.

Miller, Dean F. *School Health Programs: Their Basis in Law.* New York: A.S. Barnes Co., 1972. School health programs in relation to law.

Oberteuffer, Delbert, and Marion B. Pollock. *School Health Education.* New York: Harper and Row, 1972. Basic principles and practices.

"Report of the Joint Committee on Health Education Terminology," *Journal of School Health,* **44**: 33–37, January, 1974. Definitions of selected terms.

Scott, Gwendolyn D., and Mona W. Carlo. *On Becoming a Health Educator.* Dubuque, Iowa: Wm. C. Brown Publishers, 1973. Teaching suggestions and sample lessons.

Willgoose, Carl E. *Health Education in the Elementary School.* Philadelphia: W.B. Saunders Co., 1969. Complete treatment of health education.

Yost, Charles P. *Teaching Safety in the Elementary School.* Washington, D.C.: American Association for Health, Physical Education, and Recreation, 1972. Guidelines for developing a safety education program.

Chapter 15

Physical Education

Physical movement is the subject matter of physical education. Movement of some sort is a characteristic of human activity. It is directly related to human development, not only physiological development, but also social, emotional, and intellectual development. Consistent with these wide-ranging ramifications, such topics as neuromuscular coordination, small-muscle movement, voluntary and involuntary movement, perceptual-motor development, balance, large-muscle movement, coordination, timing, oxygen balance, sportsmanship, respect for oneself and for others, and regard for rules are given attention in the program. The ultimate aim of the program is optimal and insightful physical fitness for every individual.

The relationship between physical fitness and productive human activity is well established and unquestioned today. Concern has been expressed at the national level that a rising living standard and greater affluence seem to be accompanied by some decline in the mean level of physical fitness in the population at large. The inference is easily drawn that such decline also will be followed by a decline in average productivity of the population. Projections based upon such inference have been viewed with sufficient alarm in the centers of government that special efforts have been launched to impede a progressive decline in physical fitness. The President's Council on Physical Fitness has done much to draw attention to the need for physical fitness and for systematic physical education, within and outside the school. Care has been taken to regard fitness on broad terms, so that physical fitness is viewed as a part of general fitness including social, emotional, and mental components as well. Concerted and continuing attention at all levels is required if individual and national physical fitness are to be assured. A good part of this attention is prescribed for the elementary physical education program.

CONTRIBUTION TO BASIC GOALS

The broad-ranging influence of physical education is revealed in contributions to the major goals of education. Besides, the contribution to general mental health, *thinking ability* is directly influenced as children learn to analyze relationships between physical development and physical performance and as they learn the need for quick thinking and quick response in competitive games. *Self-realization* is enhanced as children gain control of their own bodies and achieve desired goals through their own physical efforts. Desirable *human relationships* are established through the give and take in individual and team sports and through the interdependencies that are an integral part of team activities. Contribution to *economic competence* may be found in the realization that nearly all productive work for renumeration is dependent on physical movement of some kind; thus physical fitness and competence may be valued in economic as well as other terms. *Civic responsibility* is taught through sportsmanship, respect for the physical attainments of others, and valuing the unique individual contributions to group activities. *Learning how to learn* is inherent within the many strategic practice exercises that underlie performance in any physical specialization.

OBJECTIVES OF PHYSICAL EDUCATION

Although physical education has a broad, general impact in the child's total education, the objectives of the program are direct and concrete. First, the unique contribution of physical education is tied directly to physical development.

Basically, physical education is included in the curriculum to develop children's movement abilities properly and to increase their physical fitness. When these primary and unique objectives are obscured or diffused by other objectives, justifications for physical education are properly challenged. It is held that the secondary objectives of physical education may be met by other areas of study, but the unique objectives are not so easily transferred. Therefore, recent program changes in elementary physical education tend to reemphasize and reaffirm the primacy of these two objectives.

However, this does not mean that curriculum developers have lost sight of other objectives. On the contrary, well-planned, developmentally appropriate movement experiences for children make positive contributions to total child development.

A recently published taxonomy of the psychomotor domain includes the following categories of objectives (Harrow, 1972):

Fundamental movements such as running, jumping, and pulling

Perceptual abilities such as kinesthetic, visual, and tactile

Physical abilities such as endurance, strength, agility, and dexterity

Skilled movements such as playing games, dancing, and engaging in various sports

Nondiscursive communication through posture, gestures, and facial expressions

The typical physical education program includes the above plus other objectives as noted below.

Conceptual Objectives

To develop understanding of movement activities and the relationships between movement and concepts from biological, physical, and social sciences so that the child is able to do the following:

Explain how physiological structures of the body are related to posture and movement.

Tell what physical skills are involved in various movements.

Demonstrate exercise routines that contribute to physical fitness.

Demonstrate the basic principles of movement in standard exercise routines.

Demonstrate and explain safety rules and precautions for the prevention of accidents resulting from physical activity.

Process Objectives

To demonstrate functional competency in the following:

Observing activities to learn movement patterns

Comparing movement patterns in different activities

Defining terms related to games, sports, and exercises

Interpreting rhythmic patterns in response to changing tempos

Analyzing folk games and dances to identify rhythmic patterns

Predicting the outcome of games

Skill Objectives

To develop the separate skills needed in basic motor activities, fitness, maintenance, and self-awareness so the child is able to demonstrate the following:

Competence in chosen individual and group activities
Increasing ability in locomotor, manipulative, and stability tasks
Developing physical strength, endurance, flexibility, and power
Competence in judging one's own physical strength and weaknesses
Ability to effectively lead and follow
Competence in planning and engaging in worthwhile leisure-time activities

Affective Objectives

To develop an appreciation of the role of movement and physical activity in human development so that the child demonstrates the following:

An attitude of inquiry toward body capabilities and movement
Appreciation of the importance of developing competence in physical activities
Appreciation of the competence of others and of creative self-expression through physical activity
Interest in undertaking new activities and in developing new skills
Respect for individuals who differ in ability, who are handicapped, and who do not meet or who exceed achievements of the group
Appreciation of physical skill and performance from the viewpoint of a spectator
Willingness to submit to the discipline of team effort and to assess group activity in the light of rules and standards

ORGANIZATION OF THE CURRICULUM

Scope and sequence outlines for modern physical education programs reflect three major influences: (1) strands of foundation activities developed around central purposes of physical education, (2) developmental characteristics of children according to chronological age, and (3) types of activities. The idea of movement is central to program development, regardless of which of these foci is paramount in a given program framework. Likewise, the view that physical education is a vital part of a total elementary school curriculum and intimately associated with the total development of the child is reflected in most recommended activities.

Strands of Foundation Activities

Programs organized principally around major strands of foundation activities vary somewhat in number and nature of strands, but the following is a rather typical pattern:

Neuromuscular Skill Development Included in this strand are those locomotor, manipulative, and stability skills which constitute the essence of movement. Developmental activities are viewed as vehicles for the achievement of the several disparate goals of elementary physical education because they are the basic movement activities. They usually are introduced and sequenced according to children's maturation and experience. For example, activities for children in the early elementary grades are not designed to develop high degrees of skill in specific games, sports, or rhythmic activities. They are selected so that (1) the child's physical maturation level is sufficient to assure benefit from instruction and (2) the child's learning will proceed from simple to complex movements. The program is centered upon developing the child's ability to move in an acceptable manner and in a variety of ways.

Activities recommended for intermediate and upper-grade children tend to be pointed toward the development of form, skill, and accuracy in movements in selected games, sports, and dances. Children at this level are able to refine movements and skills to high levels of perfection. Activities involving complex combinations of movements are introduced, and practice routines are outlined and implemented. In general, the program is focused on refinement and perfection along a continuum of increasingly complex movements.

Fitness Development Physical fitness is an avenue for, but only a part of, total fitness. Fitness results from planned movement activity and regularity of exercise, amount and pattern of sleep; rest, quality, and quantity of diet; nature and regularity of recreation; and the maintenance of emotional well-being. Activities are selected so as to (1) create understanding of and good attitudes toward physical fitness, (2) motivate children sufficiently to develop a fitness regimen in their own lives, (3) provide children with a comprehensive repertoire of movement activities, and (4) actually help children improve their fitness.

Perceptual-motor Development In recent years the term *perceptual-motor development* has come into vogue, and in many modern programs a developmental strand is devoted to this aspect of physical education. In general, it is based on the realization that (1) efficient movement is dependent upon accurate perceptions of the environment and (2) perceptual acuity is dependent, in part, upon movement. Activities are included which develop children's eye-hand and eye-foot coordination, muscular kinesthesis, and responses to perceptions of imbalance. Activities are selected also which give recognition to what may be called the children's perceptual readiness. It is recognized that perceptual readiness may be advanced to some extent through properly chosen movement activities.

Social-emotional Development This strand is included to increase children's abilities to interact effectively with other people and to develop positive and accurate appraisals of themselves. Through movement the children learn a great deal about themselves. The view of the movement potential of their bodies has been shown to be directly related to their self-concepts, and activities are chosen to exploit this relationship. Furthermore, the sequence of activities in this strand takes advantage of the fertile opportunity offered in group physical activities to have children develop appreciation for rights, privileges, and responsibilities of others.

Development of Academic Understanding   The relationships between physical education and other curriculum areas in the elementary school are at the root of this strand. Beyond the general observation that learning proficiency is influenced by fitness, there are opportunities to coordinate activities in physical education with other ongoing activities. For example, children's understanding of social studies concepts can be enhanced through integrating games and dances of different nations, cultures, and historic periods. The understanding of simple machines and forces included in physical science study can be improved through movement examples and related physiological structures. Simple mathematical skills may be practiced in games and sports. In general, those activities which offer motivation for academic study and which fit the recommended sequence for neuromuscular and fitness development are included in the program.

Development of Constructive Leisure Time Use   The idea of play is fundamental to this strand. The physical education program not only includes activities for the refinement of movement, but also often embeds these activities in a repertoire of games and recreational skills which serve children as well as adults. The constructive use of leisure time is of growing importance to individuals at all age levels. The balance between time spent in gainful employment and leisure is shifted toward leisure. Activities are selected for the elementary physical education program which may be directly transplanted to adult-leisure time pursuits or which may serve as the foundation for further development.

The framework for organization around strands of foundation activities may be better appreciated when associated with expected outcomes as in the following summary:

Strands	Outcomes
Neuromuscular	Increased locomotor, manipulative, and stability abilities
Fitness	Enhanced strength, endurance, flexibility, and power
Perceptual-motor	Greater body, directional, and temporal awareness
Social-emotional	Increased emotional well-being and social skills
Academic	Enhanced academic understandings
Leisure time	Increased ability to entertain oneself constructively, play well and with enjoyment, gain skills in lifetime sports

Inherent within the strand organization is the idea that activities may be clustered about unifying purposes in the total program. In different curriculum frameworks, these clusters may range from those related to common physical needs of human beings to types of physical activity believed to be essential in a complete program of instruction. Many of the clusters appropriate in health education are directly related to physical education and will not be repeated in this section. The following examples highlight concepts that are typically included in materials for teachers:

Motor skills Movement, as in running, jumping, and dodging; eye-hand coordination, as in throwing, catching, and bouncing a ball; eye-foot coordination, as in kicking and punting a ball; balance, as in hopping and stunts; timing, as in rhythms and dances; kinesthetic perception, as in awareness of position of arms, legs, and other body parts in an activity

Play Types: active, passive, intellectual; contributions: new experience, adventure, recognition, security, participation, satisfaction, learning

Total fitness Physical, mental, emotional social, and spiritual well-being

Paths to physical fitness Proper diet, exercise, play and recreation, rest and relaxation, medical and dental care, satisfying work

Activities Individual, dual, group, team; games and sports, dances and rhythms, developmental or conditioning, self-testing, stunts, story, classroom, aquatics, track and field, camping and outdoor, social-recreational, leisure time

Dances and rhythms Fundamental, dramatized, folk dances, singing games, creative or interpretive dances, mimetics

Leisure-time activities Camping, fishing, hiking, swimming, riding, dancing, bicycling, sailing, skating, bowling, tennis, golf, archery, softball, badminton

Posture faults Forward head, round upper back, round shoulders, hollow back, lateral deviation

Infrequently, generalizations that are drawn from supporting disciplines are put to use in organizing and developing the physical education program, for example, discussion sessions may be built around modules of movement activities so as to stress ideas such as the following:

For every action, such as batting or kicking a ball, there is an equal and opposite reaction.

The amount of oxygen needed by the body is directly proportional to the amount of energy released by the body.

Muscles become stronger through use; they become weaker with disuse.

Mental health is influenced by one's state of physical well-being.

Man's cognitive, affective, and psychomotor capacities are interrelated in physical education activities.

Play is a means of learning, adjusting, and satisfying personal-social needs in cultures around the world.

Guided cooperation and competition contribute to individual development and group accomplishment.

Performance in games and other activities involves such aesthetic qualities as form, style, taste, and organization.

Self-activity, self-analysis, and practice are key elements in the attainment of motor skills.

Children's Developmental Characteristics

Children's physical, social-emotional, and mental growth characteristics serve as a basis for drawing implications which are used as guidelines for organizing physical education activities. Typical of such guidelines are those summarized below (Vannier, Foster, and Gallahue, 1973).

Kindergarten

Physical Characteristics

Growing about 2½ inches and 4½ pounds per year

Legs grow faster than arms, arms faster than trunk, and trunk faster than head.

Bone-cell formation is active

Walking and running are well established, balance is not always secure, eye-hand coordination rudimentary, fine focus not refined

Climbing is natural and easy, can jump down, learning small, long jump

Socio-emotional Characteristics

Emotions relatively uncontrolled, often complex

Crying diminishes, frustration and anger increase as causes

Some generalized fears apparent (being left alone, dark, unfamiliar situations)

Humor is associated with slapstick, physical sensations, etc.

Dependent on adults, but seeking some independence, some negativism evident, self-assertive, possessive

Children with especially good bodily skills tend to be dominant; competition and rivalry with others much affected by environment

Mental Characteristics

Openly curious, flits from one curiosity to another, short attention span

Responds to and needs adult direction

Can handle only one idea at a time, only one variable per idea, not susceptible to abstraction

Attracted by bright colors and unusual forms and likes simple stories, fairy tales, and flights and fancy

Very short chains of logic related to real things, learns through sense impingements

Implications for Physical Education

Stress use of arms and legs (climbing, hanging, pulling, pushing, kicking, running, hopping, jumping).

Playground balls should be fairly large, objects to be caught should be susceptible to rudimentary clasping motion.

Movement activities should stress gross movements, large muscle skills, including a good mixture of rhythms and dramatic play.

Excessive adult assistance with physical tasks should be avoided.

Parallel play should be used with different kinds of movement (light running, tiptoe, and crouch, walking, walking in zigzag lines, running in circles, etc.)

Small group rhythms and play should stress adjustment to others.

Grades 1–3

Physical Characteristics

Enjoys rugged big-muscle activities, hand-eye and foot-eye coordination poor, rapid growth (average 5½ pounds, 2 inches)

Loses baby fat if heavy, also loses weight if thin

Motor skills are important for acceptance and leadership, shows gradual increase in speed and accuracy, slow reaction time

Shows daring exploratory behavior, little attention to cleanliness

Can throw medium-sized balls with full arm swing; can bounce and catch a ball and kick a ball on the run, can learn to swim

Girls excel in stunts and tumbling, boys excel in throwing, batting, and combative games

Social-emotional Characteristics

Ego centered, sensitive, seeks and gives affection, cries easily

Fearful of being left alone, of failure, and loss of adult approval

Displays aggressive behavior, emotional outbursts

Sex roles and identities insecure

Mental Characteristics

Curious, creative, imaginative, serious about school

Likes definite directions, but also inattentive and talkative at times

Short attention span but good memory

Girls excel in reading and writing skills, boys in number concepts

Implications for Physical Education

Stress rhythmic activities and combinations of locomotor movements such as hops with runs.

Provide for many large-group games and a happy, secure, noncompetitive social climate.

Use a wide variety of exploratory movement skills with many kinds of equipment, such as climbing, jumping rope, jumping from various heights, the balance beam and stilts.

Use graduated-sized balls for throwing and catching skill development.

Stress big-muscle activities such as running, jumping, hopping, and skipping in grades 1 and 2; begin some skill refinement in grade 3.

Introduce a variety of small-group games such as Crows and Cranes or Frog in the Sea.

Stress climbing, hanging, and balancing activities.

Developing arm strength in stunts and tumbling activities such as wheelbarrow races, kneeling-position half pushups, and inchworm relays.

Use dual and combative stunts to develop strength, such as pull across the line, Indian leg and arm wrestle.

Stress creative play; provide for free play periodically in grades 1 and 2.

Avoid highly competitive activities, for children during these formative years will often push themselves too far.

In the second and third grade introduce chasing and fleeing games that require agility and change of direction.

Have children discuss and consider "cheating," taking turns, assisting others, accepting decisions.

Stress good posture, good health habits, and desirable social behavior.

Grades 4-6

Physical Characteristics

Developing rapidly, heart slowly increasing in size, growth spurts (average gain 7 pounds, 2 inches)

Rapid increase in strength, endurance, coordination

Robust, active, noisy, large appetitites

Slowly developing skill in use of small muscles, arms and hands growing longer and bigger, long bones and hips susceptible to injury

Girls often taller and heavier than boys, physical performance equal

Poor posture begins to develop and should be corrected

Locomotion steady, grace and skill increase

Sex differences increasingly noticeable

Social-emotional Characteristics

Some emotional instability, less attachment to adults, strong peer ties, some gangs

Increasingly conscious of others, sensitive to criticism, inquisitive about human relationships

Slowly developing interest in opposite sex

Peer acceptance paramount, quick to detect insincerity, hero worship

Accepts responsibility and wishes to be considered trustworthy

Likes self challenges

Increased need for independence and recognition, adult influence marked

Values good sportsmanship, loyalty, moral conduct, and strives to do the right thing

Mental Characteristics

Restless; discouraged easily at learning attempts

Shows initiative; is creative and curious

Idealistic and likes to read about great people, concerned with justice

Enjoys learning new things, concerned about adult approval of school work

Preoccupied often with thoughts of opposite sex

Implications for Physical Education

Provide longer activity periods in which skill instruction gradually receives more stress.

Provide opportunities for groups and individuals to release emotions and tensions through more rugged physical activities and cheering for one's team.

Stress vigorous exercise; help pupils know how exercise assists growth; alternate strenuous activities with less active ones.

Stress good body mechanics, posture, and movement in daily life as well as in sports.

Gradually emphasize movement accuracy and good form; use a wide variety of throwing, catching, and hitting activities through leadup games to softball, volleyball, and basketball.

Avoid highly competitive activities, stress good sportsmanship, player consideration, team loyalty.

Provide many activities that involve rhythm and balancing, and teach social, folk, and square dance to coed classes.

Give as much individual attention and help to each pupil as possible in skill-development tasks; develop good group rapport.

Provide a variety of activities using apparatus for chinning, vaulting, balancing, and hand traveling.

Keep competition at the children's level; provide intramural activities for all pupils.

Stress track and field events for both sexes, tumbling, rhythmics.

Seize upon all "teachable moments" in class for health and safety instruction and shaping life values.

Refinement of these organizational guidelines to provide even greater direction in the selection of particular movement activities often takes the form of prescription of particular competencies to be developed at various grade levels. It is recognized that competency development is a matter of continuous growth so a code such as the one shown in Chart 15-1 is employed to indicate expected level of competence according to grade.

Types of Activity

Programs representing this type organization commonly classify activities of the physical education program itself into various categories, then select from these categories to achieve balance, proper developmental sequence and consonance with children's developmental characteristics. For example, a program developed around types of activity may delineate three types or categories: locomotor activities, manipulative activities, and stabilizing activities. Then under each of these categories would be listed the more specific activity types, suitable for an elementary school physical education program and fitting the cateogry. This stage may appear as follows:

Locomotor activities	Manipulative activities	Stabilizing activities
Walking	Kicking	Standing
Running	Striking	Sitting
Skipping	Throwing	Bending
Galloping	Catching	Stretching
Jumping	Bouncing	Twisting
Leaping	Trapping	Turning
Climbing	Rolling	Swinging

Finally discrete activities would be chosen (1) to give representation to each of the categories and (2) to develop an organized sequence within each activity type. Of course, selection of separate activities would be influenced by the need to build a progression from simple to complex and by the necessity of selecting activities appropriate to the developmental level of the children under consideration.

A similar organizational emphasis may be seen in the following outline.

Chart 15-1 Competencies to be Developed

		GRADES					
	K	1	2	3	4	5	6
OPTIMUM PHYSICAL QUALITIES OF FITNESS (DEVELOPED TO MAXIMUM CAPACITY)		*	*	*	*	*	*
Strength	S	S	S	M	M	Ex	Ex
Power	S	S	S	M	M	Ex	Ex
Endurance		S	S	M	M	Ex	Ex
Flexibility	S	S	S	M	M	Ex	Ex
Agility	S	S	S	M	M	Ex	Ex
Functional Skill and Coordination		*	*	*	*	*	*
Locomotion (walking, running, skipping, hopping, jumping, climbing, galloping, sliding)	S	M	M	Ex	Ex	Ex	Ex
Balancing	S	M	M	M	Ex	Ex	Ex
Rhythmic Response in Movement							
Moving to a rhythmic sound	S	M	M	M	Ex	Ex	Ex
Moving in simple patterns	S	M	M	Ex	Ex	Ex	Ex
Skip, slide, polka, schottische, step-hop, waltz, fox-trot, two-step		S	S	M	M	Ex	Ex
Patterns—honor, swing, circle, allemande, do-si-do, grand right and left balance, promenade, ladies' chain, right and left through				S	M	Ex	Ex
Ball Skills							
Rolling	S	S	S	M	M	Ex	Ex
Tossing	S	S	S	M	M	Ex	Ex
Throwing—distance and accuracy	S	S	S	M	M	Ex	Ex
Dribbling and juggling				S	S	M	M
Volleying				S	S	M	M
Goal shooting				S	S	M	M
Kicking, dribbling, trapping			S	S	M	M	M
Striking—hand, bat, club			S	S	S	M	M
Rope Jumping		S	M	Ex	Ex	Ex	Ex
Beginning Swimming					S	M	M
Creativity, Exploration, and Self-Expression		*	*	*	*	*	*
Efficient and Attractive Posture		*	*	*	*	*	*
Standing	M	M	M	M	Ex	Ex	Ex
Sitting	M	M	M	M	Ex	Ex	Ex
Moving	M	M	M	M	Ex	Ex	Ex
Increasing Emotional Maturity		*	*	*	*	*	*
Social Adaptability		*	*	*	*	*	*

Key: S — Some competency
      M — Much competency
      Ex — Excellent competency
Source: The President's Council Program, *Youth Fitness.*

Note that a greater number of activity types have been defined following a different orientation. Some illustrative activities are included.

Dances and rhythms Fundamental movements; creative, folk, square, social
Mimetics Imitation of animals, wooden soldiers, bucking horses
Story plays On Halloween, a turkey for Thanksgiving, Easter bunnies
Activities on equipment Jungle gym, ladder, rings, bar, swings, slides, seesaws

Low-organization games Dodge ball, circle tag, endball, ringmaster
Individual and dual Hopscotch, ball bouncing, rope jump, tetherball
Self-testing Dog walk, elephant walk, rabbit jump, jumping jack
Relays Circular, shuttle, line, kangaroo, basketball, soccer dribble
Classroom games Yarn ball, dodge ball, lone ranger, Simon says
Developmental Jumping jack, wheelbarrow, pull-ups, push-ups
Lead-up games Circle kickball leading to soccer; paddle ball leading to badminton and tennis; netball leading to volleyball; bat ball leading to baseball; captain ball leading to basketball
Team sports Softball, soccer, touch football, speedball, volleyball
Track and field Broad jump, softball throw, dash, basketball free throw
Stunts and tumbling Stick jump, animal walks, headstand, making a bridge
Holidays and special events The witch, turkey pass, reindeer, May Day
Intramural Activities drawn from the instructional program, as well as special activities, organized into play days, sports days, tournaments

To the extent possible, a developmental series of activities representing all categories would be prescribed at each grade level. The range of recommended movement activities within each activity type is considerable, permitting the tailoring of the physical education program to the needs of a particular group of children. For example, in a typical outline for grade 4, the single activity-type "games of low organization" may have as many as twenty-four recommended activities, with a similar number for this activity type at each of the other grade levels.

Games of Low Organization

Paddle ball	Pom, pom pullaway	Sidewalk tennis
May I?	Ribbon tag	Duck on the rock
Tether ball	Red light	Four square
Block wolf	Merry-go-round	Vis-à-vis
Animal chase	Ante over	Charades
Skin the snake	Streets and alleys	Bombardment
Balloon ball	Hook on	Red rover
Keep away	Dodgeball	Prisoner's base

Additionally, emphasis upon particular activity types at the various levels may be indicated by recommended yearly time percentages. Instead of an equal selection from each type at all grade levels, variable selections are recommended. The recommendations in Chart 15-2 are based upon analysis of activities and knowledge of children's developmental characteristics (Vannier, Foster, and Gallahue, 1973).

In recent years it has become increasingly common to include camping and outing or outdoor activities as a type in program outlines. Activities within this type are those undertaken away from the school site under organized and supervised field experience. The experiences are designed to integrate with environmental education in science and social studies. Such activities as hiking, bicycle trip camping, use of a two-handed axe, making tools with knife and hatchet,

Chart 15-2 Suggested Yearly Time Percentages for the Elementary Physical Education Program

	K	1	2	3	4	5	6
GAMES AND SPORTS	10%	15%	25%	30%	40%	50%	50%
Low organized games	10	15	20	10	10	0	0
Relays	0	0	5	10	5	5	5
Lead-up games	0	0	0	10	25	45	45
Official sports	0	0	0	0	0	0	0
RHYTHMICS	30%	25%	25%	25%	20%	20%	20%
Fundamentals	15	10	10	5	5	5	5
Creative rhythm	15	10	10	10	5	5	5
Folk and square dance	0	5	5	10	10	10	10
SELF-TESTING	60%	60%	50%	45%	40%	30%	30%
Conditioning	0	5	5	10	10	10	10
Movement exploration	40	30	30	15	10	0	0
Stunts	10	10	5	5	0	0	0
Tumbling	0	5	5	5	10	10	10
Hand apparatus	10	10	5	5	0	0	0
Large apparatus	0	0	5	5	10	10	10

cooking in the woods, fire building, wood chopping, blanket rolls, fishing, shelter construction, lashing are included among those recommended.

It is clear that the organizational patterns discussed here extend only to the gross features of the organizational outline. Within each, the separate considerations of strands or clusters, child development characteristics, and activity type are integrated into a cohesive physical education program.

INSTRUCTIONAL MEDIA

A comprehensive organization of movement activities requires that some special physical education materials be available. Although many worthwhile activities call for no special materials, others depend upon the availability of prescribed supplies or equipment. There is general agreement on the minimum list of materials needed to carry out an adequate elementary school physical education program. The amount of each item necessary depends upon whether the school maintains a central storage and dispersal facility for these materials, school and class size, and historic usage patterns.

Supplies

Rubber balls 5, 6, 8, 10 inch
Soccerball, rubber
Soccerball, official
Football, rubber
Football, official
Basketball, rubber
Basketball, official
Volleyball, official
Softballs, 8, 12 inch

Jumpropes 3-foot 8-inch sashcord
Individual 6, 7, 8 foot
Long 12, 15, 20, 25 foot
Beanbags, 6 x 6, and targets
Indian clubs
Five-pin bowling sets
Hula hoop rings
Squad cards
Jump-off boxes

Catchers' mask, chest protector	Shuffleboard sets
Softball bats	Broomsticks of various lengths

Equipment

Game nets	Steel bars, vertical and horizontal
Hurdles 12, 15, 18, 20 inch	Ball inflator
Whistle	Swim fins, masks
Stopwatch	Bases
Tape measure, 100 feet	Canvas bags
Balance beams	Game nets
Low parallel bars	Lime and markers
Teeter boards	Targets
Table hockey	Swings
Jungle gym	Slides
Mats 3 x 5, 4 x 6 feet	Net standards

Camping and outing activities require special appropriate equipment. It is customary to expect children to furnish the basic essentials for this type activity.

Beyond the use of special equipment and supplies, the physical education program is enriched by the incorporation of a variety of audio-visual materials. Movement activities are especially susceptible to vivid portrayal through motion pictures and video tapes, and these materials along with other projective learning aids are being used with increasing frequency in the modern program.

TEACHING STRATEGIES

Over the years and until recently there has been little change in the conception of how physical skills are best communicated from teacher to child. In general terms, the teaching approach has been expository and didactic. Demonstration has been the key strategy. Ideally, the teacher has been able to demonstrate the physical skill being taught and the children have attempted to duplicate the model performance under the watchful eye and guiding hand of the teacher. Teaching steps in the expository, demonstration mode follow a sequence such as the following:

1 Explanation of movement
2 Demonstration of movement
3 Student trial of movement
4 Teacher diagnosis of performance
5 Teacher clarification submovement
6 Student practice of movement
7 Individualized assistance with movement
8 Using movement in total activity

Rules and procedures for games, camping, rhythms, dances, aquatics, sports, and even sportsmanship may be taught using most of the same steps.

Other strategies incorporate discovery as an important ingredient, even though most other features of the expository, demonstration approach are maintained. Active inquiry, exploration, discovery, and application on the part of children are stimulated. Observation skills, a sense of timing, direct involvement, and immediate feedback are involved as children learn to experiment and use physical skills in different activities. Probably no other area of the curriculum exceeds physical education in the degree of direct involvement of students, although active discovery is only rarely evident in teaching practice.

A pattern of demonstration, time for exploration and discovery, application of new learnings, and practice through activities distinguish those strategies which build upon discovery. The example that follows is illustrative of such a modified discovery strategy (Boyer, 1965).

Explore Children are scattered in play area to explore vertical jumping. They enjoy having their own "little space," "home," "garage," "hanger" to which they frequently return throughout the exploratory period. (This aids in class control without formal organization.) "Can you bounce like a ball and still keep your feet on the ground? (floor)." "Good!" "What helped you to be so bouncy?"

Discover Discussion leads to the use of the knees, "toes" (balls of the feet), ankles. Typical responses: "My knees bend and push." "My toes push." "My knees are springy." "They all bend and push."

Teacher "Now try to bounce lightly. Let your feet leave the floor. Bounce, bounce, bounce, bounce. Some of you sound like small rubber balls and some like big, heavy basketballs. Listen to the sound of this ball." (Use a small rubber ball to hear its sound.) "Now — a big basketball." (Use a basketball so they can hear it.) "What do you suppose caused the difference in sound?"

Discover Discussion leads to first learnings. "Too big a jump." "Knees did not bend when I was a basketball hitting the floor." "I landed on my toes when I was the little ball but forgot when I was the big ball."

Explore Continue the exploration to help children understand how the principles of jumping apply to various kinds of jumps, big or little.

Suggestions Look for spring from the feet. A common problem on the big jump is kicking feet up behind and then landing flatfooted. Emphasize springing, bouncing. Use further imagery to help to develop vertical jumping. Asking, "What else goes up and down in a jumpy way," produces responses such as these: "Jack in the box." "A pogo stick." "A Mexican jumping bean." "A jumping jack."

Note The question may also introduce animal jumps which then leads into horizontal jumps or jumping for distance. If this happens, use it. It is considered later in this design, but if it comes up here, it is a good place for the children to examine the difference.

Use Jumping up and over an object.

Teacher "Pretend you have a small block. Place it in front of you. Jump over it. Walk a few steps forward and put a medium-sized block down. Show us how high it is. Jump over it. Now walk a few more steps and put down a bigger block. Can you jump over it? Run back to your own little space. Now walk to the first block, stop, and jump over it. Walk to the medium-sized block, stop, and jump over it. On to the big block, stop, and jump over it. What did you have to do each time your jump became higher?"

Discover In addition to continued need for use of feet, ankles, knees, and hips, the children discover the importance of swinging the arms up, to help pull the body up, and after swinging up the arms go out and down, which helps to give balance to the landing.

Use in game Jack Be Nimble.

Of increasing importance in modern teaching, approaches to physical education is the strategy which has been named the exploratory strategy. In some sense it generalizes both discovery and physical activity. It underscores the philosophical orientation to the teaching of movement and fitness maintenance rather than more limited or diffuse topics. It is designed to free the children more completely to learn about themselves and their bodies.

In its purest form it originated in British Infant Schools and has been modified and adapted for use in this country. The uniqueness of the approach is free exploration of movement through what may be called a situational approach. Usually the teacher structures situations, conditions, or questions and the children are encouraged to freely explore and experiment in responding to these situations. There is no *correct* model of response and no standards of precision, strength, or endurance are set. All children are given opportunity (1) to explore and experience through kinesthesis the movement potential of their bodies, (2) to develop basic movement skills, (3) to know success in physical performance within the limits of their physical abilities, and (4) to express themselves creatively. The key to effective use of the exploratory strategy is selection of movement situations which permit a large variety of responses from the children, yet remain within the range of appropriate activity according to the developmental sequence. The following example in diary style characterizes the use of a guided exploratory approach at the second grade level.

As the second graders entered the classroom the exuberance and physical vitality so characteristic of this age was immediately obvious. I stood near the doorway and as they passed by individually or in small groups, I asked them to remember the buzzards we saw in our movie the other day. I said, "See if you can soar to your space silently, smoothly, without touching anything." I was pleased and amused with the variety of interpretations of this situation. Some children spread their wings and revolved in a series of small circles, others swayed from side to side as they challenged the individual pieces of furniture to spoil their record of no contact, and others flew in larger circles around the perimeter of the room. A few children challenged others either by moving in unsympathetic directions or patterns or directly causing others to change direction to avoid collision. In a short time, I gained attention with a tom-tom beat and urged them to settle into their spaces. I then asked them to show me whether they were taller than the last time and they stretched and reached and stood on tiptoes until I said, "Yes, you seem to be taller today." I then suggested that they become as large as they could, and this was followed by a great variety of stretching, extension movements both vertically and horizontally (on the floor). Next, I gave the instruction "Now see how small you can be." Most children doubled up, lowering their heads and clasping knees. As they assumed this sort of position, I remarked that they looked like tiny playground balls. I asked them to roll around like a ball but without leaving their spaces, and they delighted in the difficulty they found in controlling direction and distance as they tried to roll. We had some minor collisions, all accepted and enjoyed as a part of the ball-rolling experiment. To explore other movements, I asked them to *think strong* — "How do you feel when you feel real strong." Few muscles escaped this demonstration, although most attention expectedly centered on the use of the biceps. I followed this suggestion with the instruction to *think light,* "like a feather or a soap bubble." The movements again ranged broadly from light, elf-like, small movements on tiptoe through ballet-type total body involvements to crawling, sliding movements on the floor. The last situation I gave them today was the most difficult of all. I asked them to be driving along and have a flat tire and fix it. I was again reminded of the great creativity present in children this age, the great power of bodily movement as a medium for expressing ideas and the marvelous mechanisms of the human body. I was not able to interpret all of their movements, of course. Some children probably had very poor images of fixing a tire, but I knew that the exploratory opportunity offered by this situation and those earlier helped the children realize some of the same things at which I marveled.

Although individualized attention is important in all instruction within curriculum areas and at all levels, it is crucial to successful physical education teaching. Wide ranging differences in physical development and physical ability are immediately clear to the physical education teacher and are susceptible to adaptive instructional moves. Beyond normal ranges there are physical handicaps to which instruction must be adjusted. Therefore, a necessary and crucial aspect of all teaching in this area is the strategic planning of movement activities which are tailored to perceived individual needs and which assure an optimum progress toward movement efficiency and fitness.

Guidelines for the Teacher

The following guiding principles are indicative of key responsibilities of the teacher in providing high-quality instruction in physical education.

Emphasize Movement and Fitness While physical education is properly a multiobjective part of the elementary school curriculum, the unique responsibilities of movement education and fitness have received special emphasis in modern frameworks. Special teaching focus in these two areas is appropriate and necessary.

Give Attention to Broad Goals Keep the social, biological, and integrative functions in mind, selecting and adapting both indoor and outdoor activities that contribute to the development of the objectives specified for physical education. Include attention to neuromuscular skills, fitness, perceptual motor skills, social-emotional development, academic understanding, and constructive leisure time use, as long-range and daily plans are made. Check plans systematically to insure a well-rounded program of physical activities for all children.

Provide for Progression The progressive development of motor skills and other outcomes of physical education should be emphasized within grades as specific activities are taught and between grades as children's capabilities are brought to increasingly higher levels. Plan and guide activities that are linked to the child's capabilities and past experience and lead to higher levels of competence. Use conditioning and rhythmic lead-up and other activities to provide a sequence of development as outlined in current teaching guides.

Adapt and Individualize the Program Meet individual differences of children through adaptation of activities, teaching techniques, and evaluation of outcomes. Select activities in terms of observed characteristics and needs of children. Provide for differing interests and abilities of boys and girls as they mature and for different rates and levels of development of all children.

Use Strategies That Maximize Student Involvement Movement exploration, creativity, discovery, application, practice, and self-evaluation should be facilitated. Selected procedures and techniques that fit each type of activity and use them in ways that develop self-responsibility and initiative. Involve students in the planning, demonstrating, and evaluating of activities so that they will learn from one another.

Begin Activities Without Undue Delay Situations, explanations, demonstrations, directions, and background information should be clear and to the point. Motivation may be lowered, learning through discovery may be hampered, and the benefits of the activity may be decreased if preliminary activities are overextended. After clear and brief instructions, children need to learn through doing, obtaining further instruction as they get a feeling for the activity and as questions and problems arise.

Use Positive and Intrinsic Motivation Constructive suggestions, praise for effort and accomplishment, and encouragement should be given as needed by individual children. Comparisons, embarrassment, and a series of failures should be avoided. Each child will find activities to be intrinsically interesting and enjoyable if he has the opportunity to develop skills, make improvement, and play with others in an atmosphere of mutual respect. Because of children's natural interest in physical activities, there is no need for extrinsic rewards.

Direct the Use of Equipment and Facilities Close direction should be provided to maximize learning and to minimize accidents. Instructions on use, safety first, adherence to rules, staying in designated areas, removal of glasses and jewelry, appropriate dress, and supervision at all times are essential. All equipment and facilities should be inspected regularly, repaired or replaced as needed, and used in accordance with the purposes they are designed to serve.

Relate the Program to Other Areas The close links between physical education and other aspects of the complete school health program have been mentioned. Attention should be given to such items as games and rhythms in other lands in social studies, measuring distance and time in arithmetic, and concepts of force and momentum in science. Related activities in art and music should be identified as May Day activities, play days, folk dances, singing games, and rhythmic activities are undertaken. Reading can be used to gather ideas on games, sports, and other activities and to participate vicariously in the play experiences of other children and in the activities of athletes admired by students. Oral and written expression can be used to share the excitement and joy of children's own experiences, as well as those of others, and to report on ideas gleaned through reading, observation, and firsthand participation.

Seek Assistance on Special Problems Children with physical deficiencies should have adapted or corrective programs. The advice of doctors and other specialists should be obtained and used in planning adequate programs for them. In some cases, there may be need for a broad program of development that includes dietary changes, special therapy, and other provisions. The teacher's role is to make referrals, help in gathering data, and carry out the recommendations of specialists.

Assist in Intramural Programs The competitive tendency that emerges as children progress through school should be guided constructively through intramural competition, not interschool competition. Play and sports days that include individual, dual, and group activities from the regular physical education program are recommended. Grouping of children according to age and size, getting maximum participation of all children, providing a variety of activities, stressing teamwork and sportsmanship, and supervising of events are key ingredients in successful play days and tournaments. The assistance of teachers is needed in planning and conducting intramural programs to assure beneficial outcomes for all participants.

EVALUATION OF OUTCOMES OF INSTRUCTION

Evaluation of outcomes of the physical education program is greatly facilitated by the heavy emphasis on movement. Directly observable changes in behavior may be noted by both the teacher and students. Informal observation during activities, directed observation guided by charts and checklists, and systematic observation during special testing and self-testing activities are dominant features of evaluation.

Self-evaluation by students is another feature of evaluation that is prominent in physical education. Because of the direct involvement of students, the nature of physical activities, the responsibility each student has for his own performance, and the individual form and style that are developed, students themselves inevitably make continuing assessments of their progress. As in art education, the student is expressing himself in a highly individualized way and is making changes and adjustments in terms of his own evaluation. Self-assessment, therefore, in which the teacher promotes each student's ability to explore, discover, and use his movement potential creatively and effectively is a hallmark of sound evaluation.

Both informal and formal testing to assess knowledge, attitudes, and skills are included in complete programs of evaluation. Standardized and teacher-made tests and inventories geared to the instructional program make it possible to assess specific objectives that are being emphasized.

Positive and constructive approaches are essential in all phases of evaluation. During sharing and discussion of movement abilities, attention should be given to ways to improve, to promising beginning movements that can be nurtured, and to steps to be taken to develop motor skills. Students themselves may well share in commending others for their successes, demonstrating ways to improve, and suggesting procedures that they have found to be most helpful. By all means, realistic objectives should be set for each child so that at no time is he faced with insurmountable tasks that can only result in negative and defeatist attitudes and a turning away from physical activities. Furthermore, each child should be judged on his effort and progress, not on performance deriving from skills already at hand prior to instruction.

Illustrative Evaluation Devices

The checklist given below is illustrative of the sort of device that may be used successfully in recordkeeping for individual students. Note that specific movements are listed as guides to observation. Check marks may be made beside movements in which growth has been observed, letter or numeral ratings may be used as judgments are made, or check marks may be used to indicate movements in need of improvement. Notice that examples contain a cluster of related movements, thus showing how clusters can be used to devise evaluative devices.

A variety of charts, checklists, and rating devices can be constructed by the teacher and by the children. A key principle is to identify the specific behaviors that are to be assessed. This may be done by checking courses of study, teaching manuals, and other sources. Key behaviors also may be identified through discussions in which students suggest items to be evaluated. The following summary of key behaviors related to various activities includes examples that can be used in their present form for evaluating outcomes or can be incorporated in charts and other evaluative devices.

Muscular coordination in story plays: _____ Throws _____
Bends _____ Twists _____ Runs _____ Jumps
_____ Stretches

Balance Beam: _____ Walks forward _____ Walks back-
ward _____ Makes turns _____ Kneels _____ Cat
walks _____ Balances object on head while walking
_____ Tosses and catches ball while walking

Rhythmic movements: _____ Walks _____ Runs _____
Jumps _____ Hops _____ Slides _____ Claps
_____ Trots _____ Gallops _____ Marches _____
Waltzes _____ Two-steps

Ball control: _____ Tosses _____ Rolls _____ Bounces
_____ Throws _____ Kicks _____ Uses arm catch
_____ Uses hand catch _____ Bats _____ Serves
_____ Bats with hand

Zone soccer: _____ Kicks moving ball _____ Blocks _____
Passes _____ Punts

Zone basketball: _____ Shoots from field of play _____
Passes _____ Catches _____ Guards _____
Makes free throws

Bat ball: _____ Bats with fist _____ Throws _____
Catches _____ Runs bases _____ Tags a moving target
_____ Dodges

Softball: _____ Throws overhand _____ Throws under-
hand _____ Throws side arm _____ Catches _____
Fields ground ball _____ Fields fly ball _____ Pitches
_____ Bats _____ Runs bases

Pass touch football: _____ Passes forward _____ Passes
laterally _____ Punts _____ Place kicks _____
Centers the ball _____ Runs _____ Feints _____
Dodges

Volleyball: _____ Serves _____ Returns _____ Hits
returned ball _____ Shifts _____ Develops strategy

Basketball: _____ Shoots _____ Makes free throws
_____ Passes _____ Pivots _____ Dribbles _____
Catches _____ Guards _____ Uses pattern plays _____
Develops plays _____ Plays position

Soccer: _____ Kicks _____ Punts _____ Blocks
_____ Passes _____ Dribbles _____ Develops plays

Passing skills: _____ Passes underhand _____ Passes overhand _____ Passes from chest _____ Passes from shoul-
der _____ Passes overhead _____ _____ Bounce passes
_____ Hook passes

Charts 15-3, 15-4, and 15-5 include examples of checklists and rating devices which may be used for recording teacher observations and judgments on a variety of behaviors of importance in the well-rounded physical education program.

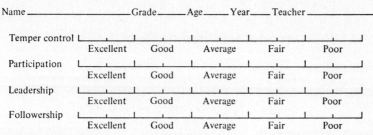

Name _____ Grade _____ Age _____ Year ____ Teacher _____

Temper control L__|____|____|____|____|___J
            Excellent   Good   Average   Fair   Poor

Participation   L__|____|____|____|____|___J
            Excellent   Good   Average   Fair   Poor

Leadership   L__|____|____|____|____|___J
            Excellent   Good   Average   Fair   Poor

Followership   L__|____|____|____|____|___J
            Excellent   Good   Average   Fair   Poor

Chart 15-3 A rating device.

	Names of students
Sportsmanship	
Accepts decisions	
Obeys the rules	
Has self-control	
Respects others	
Participation	
Begins promptly	
Tries to improve	
Encourages others	
Takes his turn	
Team Effort	
Plays for the team	
Plays own position	
Follows instructions	
Wins or loses gracefully	

Chart 15-4 Checklist for evaluating team sports.

Leadership	Sportsmanship	Bat Ball
_____ Are directions clear?	_____ Do I play fairly?	_____ Bat with fist?
_____ Is safety emphasized?	_____ Do I look out for others?	_____ Throw accurately?
_____ Are all treated fairly?	_____ Do I follow the rules?	_____ Catch the ball?
_____ Are rights respected?	_____ Do I accept decisions?	_____ Tag a moving target?
_____ Do all have turns?		_____ Dodge effectively?

Chart 15-5 Charts for self-evaluation.

Physical Fitness

Many tests of physical fitness have been developed during the past several years. Among others, the President's Council on Physical Fitness, The Canadian Air Force, AAHPER (American Association of Health, Physical Education and Recreation), and the Kraus-Weber Test are prominently mentioned. All these tests rate physical fitness according to several components. Within each component children's (and adult's) fitness is revealed by performance on selected tasks. A summary of components and selected tests is as follows (Hunsicker, 1963).

Table 15-3 Physical Fitness Components and Tests

Components	Selected tests[1]
1 Arm and shoulder length	Pull-ups, push-ups, parallel bar, dips, rope climb
2 Speed	50-yard dash, 100-yard dash
3 Agility	Shuttle run, agility run
4 Abdominal and hip strength	2-minute sit-ups
5 Flexibility	Trunk flexion standing, trunk flexion sitting, trunk extension (prone position)
6 Cardiorespiratory	600-yard run, half-mile run, mile run, 5-minute step step test
7 Explosive power	Standing broad jump, vertical jump
8 Static strength	Grip strength, back lift, leg lift
9 Balance	Bass test, brace test, tests on balance beam
10 Muscular endurance	Push-ups, chest raising (prone position, hands behind neck, legs held down), V-sit (against time)

[1] Norms for many of these tests for various ages appear in the citations on tests and measurements and the articles in the Selected Research References.

A preliminary screening test is recommended by the President's Council on Physical Fitness for identifying students who need special attention. Three tests are included: pull-ups (modified for girls), sit-ups, and squat thrusts. A normal boy in the ten- to thirteen-years age range should be able to do one pull-up, fourteen sit-ups, and four squat thrusts (in ten seconds).

The AAHPER test includes seven items: pull-ups (modified for girls), sit-ups, shuttle run, standing broad jump, 50-yard dash, softball throw for distance, and 600-yard run-walk. Norms are available for ten- to seventeen-year-olds. For example, to score "excellent" a ten-year-old boy must do six pull-ups, do sixty sit-ups, throw a softball 122 feet, do the 600-yard run-walk in 2 minutes and 15 seconds, do the shuttle run in 10.3 seconds, do a standing broad jump of 5 feet and 6 inches, and run the 50-yard dash in 7.6 seconds. A ten-year-old girl to score "excellent" must do forty-five modified pull-ups, do fifty sit-ups, throw a softball 69 feet, do the 600-yard run-walk in 2 minutes and 30 seconds, do the shuttle run in 11.2 seconds, do a standing broad jump of 5 feet and 4 inches, and run the 50-yard dash in 8.0 seconds.

Cognitive and affective outcomes of physical education may be assessed through use of the taxonomies of educational objectives (Bloom 1956; Krathwohl, Bloom and Masia, 1964). The following questions and test items according to taxonomic levels are illustrative.

Cognitive Domain

Knowledge Level Who can name three movement exercises that will help all boys and girls our age keep physically fit? Check a skill; the balance beam helps us learn: (1) throwing, (2) hopping, (3) eating, (4) bouncing a ball.

Comprehension Level Explain why muscles get tired. True or false: Kicking movements depend upon balance.

Application Level Keep a record of the number of sit-ups you do every day this week. Remember to follow through with arm movement when you shoot the basketball.

Analysis Level How did your running speed affect your performance in tennis? What movement drills are you going to use to improve the height of your jumps?

Synthesis Level What drills do you recommend for the basketball team? Check three games which require running, throwing, and kicking movements.

Evaluation Level Is exercise A better than exercise B for improving strength of back muscles? Check the list of movements suggested by Mr. Burling. Are they the best ones for you to practice?

Affective Domain

Receiving Level How did everyone contribute to our performance in the relay? Did you notice what good sports the members of the other team were?

Responding Level How do you feel about not winning the soccer match? Do you feel that we can do better next time?

Valuing Level Which is more important? (1) winning, (2) having fun, (3) good sportsmanship, (4) improving performance. What about team members who do not give their best?

FOLLOW UP ACTIVITIES AND PROJECTS

1 Examine a modern course of study for physical education. Note the specific suggestions for teaching:
   a Neuromuscular skills
   b Fitness
   c Perceptual-motor skills
   d Social-emotional development
   e Academic concepts
   f Constructive leisure-time use
2 Prepare a lesson plan for teaching the long jump using an exploratory strategy.
3 Select or create six low organization games for use in a grade level of your choice. Sequence the games for progressive development of a particular movement skill.

4 Select six features that you consider fundamental to a modern physical education program. Rank the features according to importance from your viewpoint. Defend your rankings.

5 Discuss movement. Include dimensions of physiology, philosophy, and psychology.

6 Discuss the value of play and leisure-time physical activity.

7 What is the role of organized competitive sports in the elementary school? Consider physical and social-emotional factors.

BIBLIOGRAPHY

American Association for Health, Physical Education and Recreation, *Essentials of a Quality Elementary School Physical Education Program.* Washington, D.C.: The Association, 1970. Guidelines for the development of a modern movement and fitness-centered physical education program at the elementary level.

American Association for Health, Physical Education and Recreation, *Foundations and Practices in Perceptual-motor Learning – A Quest for Understanding.* Washington, D.C.: The Association, 1971. The case for a strong perceptual motor strand in physical education; multidisciplinary implications.

Bloom, Benjamin S. (Ed.) *Taxonomy of Educational Objectives: Cognitive Domain.* New York: McKay, 1956. A classification of educational objectives into an hierarchy of complexity.

Boyer, Madeline H. *The Teaching of Elementary School Physical Education.* New York: J. Lovell Pratt, 1966. A handbook of activities for elementary teaching.

Bucher, C. *Foundations of Physical Education* (5th ed.). Saint Louis: Mosby, 1972. A classic, practical guide to planning and teaching physical education in the elementary school.

Gallehue, D. L., P. H. Werner, and G. Luedke. *Moving and Learning: A Conceptual Approach to the Physical Education of Young Children.* Dubuque, Iowa: Kendall-Hunt, 1972. Newer trends in physical education presented in a practical framework.

Halsey, E. and L. Porter. *Physical Education for Children.* New York: Holt, 1963. A general guide to teaching physical education with some especially detailed guides to teacher planning.

Harrow, Anita J. *Taxonomy of the Psychomotor Domain: A Guide for Developing Behavioral Objectives.* New York: McKay, 1972. Observable movement behaviors arranged from simple to complex.

Hunsicker, Paul. *Physical Fitness.* Washington, D.C.: National Educational Association. 1963. A summary of key factors in fitness.

Krathwohl, D. R., B. S. Bloom, and B. S. Masia. *Taxonomy of Educational Objectives: Affective Domain.* New York: McKay, 1964. A classification of affective objectives according to degree of internalization.

MacKenzie, M. M. *Toward A New Curriculum in Physical Education.* New York: McGraw-Hill, 1969. Theoretical underpinnings for the modern program with emphasis upon reasons for changing the traditional program.

MacLean, J. *Leisure and the Year 2000 – Recreation in Modern Society,*

Boston: Holbrook Press, 1972. Presents the case for significant attention to constructive use of leisure time as a part of physical education.

North, M. *Movement Education: Child Development Through Body Motion.* New York: Dutton, 1973. Theory and practice of movement education in British Infant, Junior, and Middle Schools.

President's Council on Youth Fitness. *Youth Physical Fitness: Suggested Elements of a School Centered Program.* Washington, D.C.: Government Printing Office, 1961. Guidelines for providing fitness activities and for testing achievement.

Sweeney, R. T. (Ed.) *Selected Readings in Movement Education.* Reading, Mass.: Addison-Wesley, 1970. Well-known authorities discuss aspects of the trend toward movement education.

Vannier, M., M. Foster, and D. L. Gallahue. *Teaching Physical Education in Elementary Schools.* (5th ed.) Philadelphia: Saunders, 1973. A complete handbook for the teacher of physical education in the elementary school; theory and practice.

Chapter 16

Aesthetic Education:
Art Education

Aesthetic education includes learning experiences in the arts—art, music, dance, literature, and other artistic modes of expression. Aesthetic education brings together cognitive, affective, and psychomotor aspects of learning. Performance is called for and creative problem solving and critical thinking are hallmarks of aesthetic expression. Through aesthetic education students discover nonverbal or nondiscursive ways of knowing, feeling, and doing. Other outcomes include deepened understanding and appreciation of contributions of the arts to the enrichment of culture and ways in which daily living can be enhanced.

Two projects illustrate the emerging emphasis on aesthetic education (Henrie, 1972). The *Aesthetic Education Program* is designed to make the arts a basic part of general elementary and intermediate education. Included in this program are units in visual arts, music, literature, dance, film, and theater arts tested for use at second and third grade levels but recommended for use in upper elementary and intermediate grades as well. The aim of experiences in these units is to develop both cognitive aesthetic knowledge and judgment and to develop affective outcomes through pupils' creative expression. Multimedia materials and teacher's guides were produced by CEMREL, Inc. in consultation with educational scholars and Lincoln Center for the Performing Arts under the title of *The Five Sense Store.** *The Arts in Education Project* is designed to improve the competence of teachers in visual art, drama, music, theater, dance, film, and poetry. A special feature of this project is the workshop program involving teachers, students, and artists. Each workshop is viewed as a laboratory for improving the competence of participating teachers.**

An aesthetic component may be found in all areas of the curriculum. Examples are the arts as aspects of cultures investigated in the social studies, the elegance of geometric and other patterns in mathematics education, the beauty of expression in the language arts, creative aspects of discoveries and inventions included in science education, and examples of creative thinking throughout the curriculum. But it is through the expressive arts that primary attention is given to aesthetic education.

Art and music are considered in the following two chapters. Literature is treated in the chapter on reading, and the dance is considered in the chapter on physical education. Art and music should be given an important place in the total curriculum for two fundamental reasons. First are the contributions they make to children's needs for aesthetic expression and to society's need for clarification of the feeling side of significant issues, problems, and events. Experiences in art and music add dimensions of meaning and feeling to the development of creative ability, self-esteem, appreciation of aesthetic expression in individual and group endeavors, understanding of what is valued by society, and greater sensitivity to human reactions to issues and events. The second major reason is related to the unique nature of art and music as modes of personal expression that contribute to human experience and understanding. Both highlight particular aspects of life, revealing hopes, aspirations, values, visions, and other thoughts and feelings that go beyond verbal expression and reflect the styles of their creators.

CONTRIBUTIONS TO MAJOR GOALS

Aesthetic education in general, and art and music in particular, make a variety of contributions to basic goals of education. *Thinking ability* is sharpened as visual, tactile, and aural perception are developed, intellectual bases for making aesthetic judgments are cultivated, and affective dimensions of thinking are combined with cognitive and physical elements. *Self-realization* is enhanced as children develop expressive and perceptual abilities, nurture interests and talents, enjoy aesthetic expression in different modes, and respond aesthetically to the great heritage of art and music and to experiences in and out of school. *Human relationships* take on new significance as children gain insights into the universality of aesthetic expression and discover how hopes, aspirations, values, conflicts, problems, love, and joy are expressed in various aesthetic modes in

---

*The Viking Press, 625 Madison Avenue, New York 10022
**Rhode Island State Council of the Arts, East Greenwich, Rhode Island

this and other cultures, currently and in the past. *Economic competence* may be made more humane and well-rounded as students develop understanding and appreciation of the impact of art and music on many economic activities, uses and misuses of them, and their importance in the world of work and industry, and in the constructed environment. *Civic responsibility* is given new dimensions of both feeling and meaning as students discover uses of art and music in civic rituals, ceremonies, and meetings, and as they analyze or participate in activities in which art and music are used to stir the emotions and arouse action to attain civic purposes. *Learning how to learn* calls for growth in the ability to inquire into the aesthetic side of human activities and to develop the competencies needed to use and enjoy the arts and to continually improve one's sense of appreciation throughout life. Other contributions may be noted in the following section on objectives of art education and in the later section on objectives of music education.

ART EDUCATION

Visual art is the creative organization of visual elements to express thoughts and feelings. The visual arts include such forms as painting, drawing, printmaking, sculpture, architecture, industrial design, and types of filmmaking. Visual art forms may be classified as those which are considered the "fine arts," usually singular creations in comparatively enduring form, and the "applied arts," which produce multiple reproductions of comparatively nonendurable forms. Painting, sculpture, and architecture are examples that would be considered fine arts; industrial design and weaving would be applied arts. The objectives of art education programs call for inclusion of a broad range of both fine and applied arts in pupils' activities.

OBJECTIVES OF ART EDUCATION

Objectives may be stated in terms of major areas of instruction—visual/tactile perception, creative expression, aesthetic judgment, and art heritage. Statements organized around such areas are helpful in making the point that concepts, inquiry processes, skills, and values are unified in many art activities. Furthermore, they provide a focus for instructional planning in terms of the area selected for study at a given time. The following are illustrative of this approach (adapted from California, 1971).

Objectives in Visual/Tactile Perception

Children's perceptual abilities should be developed so that they are able to do the following:

Recognize, discriminate, and describe different colors, shapes, and textures in constructed and natural forms, distinctions between value and hue, and negative and positive shapes

Demonstrate through art activities their awareness of visual qualities (unity, clarity, harmony) in various objects and art works, the use of line, space, color, texture, and form, and principles of design such as emphasis, contrast, balance, proportion, and rhythm

Demonstrate visual literacy by recognizing and describing ways in which color, size, shape, symbols, and position are used to convey feelings and messages in visual advertisements, mass media programs, and building design

Objectives in Creative Expression

As children grow in the ability to draw, paint, model, photograph, and use other media they should be able to do the following:

Demonstrate ways in which line, texture, color contrast, and the like can be used in their own art activities

Create two- and three-dimensional art forms, using a variety of media

Describe sources of inspiration and content for their art activities and demonstrate why resistance to stereotypes and emphasis on originality are important

Incorporate various forms of aesthetic expression in their individual range of expressive activities, and express positive feelings about self in relation to satisfaction in expressive activities.

Objectives in Art Heritage

Students should conceptualize basic ideas and appreciate art of others so that they are able to do the following:

Describe similarities and differences among artworks in different times and places, other cultures, social activities and rituals, and art that reflects beliefs and values, different views of events, and different styles

Describe uses of art in daily activities, mass media, business and industry, differing ethnic groups, other cultures, historical periods

Demonstrate how resource materials can be used to gather data on artists, changes in artistic expression, contributions of ethnic groups and other cultures, vocations in art, and the place of art and artists in society

Objectives in Aesthetic Sensitivity and Judgment

Students should develop competence in analyzing and evaluating art and nonart forms so that they will be able to do the following:

Describe artworks in terms of line, texture, and other elements; emphasis, contrast, and other principles; unity, clarity, and other qualities; and contrast them with nonart works

State the characteristics of art; state why one work of art may be preferred to another and give reasons for the choice, and describe aesthetic qualities of the environment and how it might be improved

State how design and function are related, how expressiveness in the visual arts is alike and different from other modes, and how art can be used to enrich daily living

Develop their own criteria for aesthetic evaluation of objects, structures, and use of space in the constructed environment

ORGANIZATION OF THE CURRICULUM

Organization of curriculum and instruction in art education is directly related to three basic factors. The first includes knowledge of stages of child development in artistic expression, a rich source of information and guidelines that can be used in all phases of the program. The second includes the different types of art activities that serve as strands or components that define the breadth and sequence of media and processes provided in the program. The third includes the conceptual structure—art elements, principles, qualities—that are developed and put to use in art activities in school and in the enrichment of daily living.

Developmental Stages

Programs of instruction in art have been in the forefront in relating instruction to stages of child development. Although writers have used different terms to describe specific stages, the sections that follow include the characteristics of development most commonly cited. It should be recognized that stages do not coincide with grades or ages in an exact manner. Rather, each child has a growth pattern and may be at one stage in painting and another in construction.

Manipulative, Exploratory, Scribble Stage

During the first stage children of two to five years of age begin with what is referred to as scribbling and exploration and manipulation of materials to get the feel of them. The motor activity is more important to them than the visual result. The child strokes with a whole-arm movement, making a tangle of line and using masses of color. Longitudinal strokes followed by a circular emphasis emerge after some experience. Clay is pounded, kneaded, rolled, and smoothed as the child experiments with different shapes. Blocks and pieces of wood are piled, stacked, and arranged in different ways. The child's manipulation and exploration are his way of learning how to handle various media. Although children have no conscious design in mind, the day soon arrives when they comment on their work or name it. Their comments should be accepted and received without interpretations by the teacher. Any comments or questions from the teacher should be in the direction of the child's story or remarks about his work. Encouragement to experiment with materials should be given. Materials should be selected that involve the use of large motions by the child. Appropriate activities widely used during this stage include water painting at the chalkboard with a wide brush, easel painting with one color at first and others added as needs arise, use of large black crayons and, then, colored crayons, block building, torn and cut paper work, and modeling with plasticine.

Preschematic, Presymbolic, Intuitive Design Stage

During the ages of five to seven, children typically move to a beginning semblance of order or intuitive design. A shape such as a circle may be used in drawing or painting to represent a person, an orange, or some other object. Lines may be attached to represent arms and legs. Shapes may be repeated in drawings; large masses of color appear in paintings; and clay work may consist of simple arrangements with varied surface treatments. Colors are used in terms of the child's desires, not in terms of reality. Designs that are related to real or imagined objects are evident in the work of some children. Content is related primarily to the child's self. Self-expression is helped by a discussion of experiences and of ideas of interest to the child. Appropriate activities include finger and easel painting, drawing with chalk and crayons, painting with tempera, simple stenciling, paper and wood construction, simple weaving, and clay modeling. Large thick brushes and large pieces of absorbent paper should be provided for painting.

Schematic, Symbolic, Conscious Design Stage

During the schematic or symbolic stage characteristic of many seven- to nine-year-olds, children use circles, ovals, and rectangles to portray people, houses, trees, and other objects. Lines and shapes are used in a repetitive manner, and colors are selected in relation to objects. Some children begin to bring out realistic details, others give subjective interpretations, and some use a combination of the two. Features important to the child may be exaggerated, e.g., a truck driver proportionally larger than the truck. Features unimportant to the child may be omitted entirely, e.g., the steering wheel of a car. Details important to the child may be shown even though they cannot be seen in reality as they are drawn, e.g., houses on both sides of the street, a table top "folded up" to show what is on it, and "x-ray" or transparent pictures to show both the inside and outside of a house. The base line is discovered and used, although objects may be placed along it without clear reference to size and space relationships. Objects made of clay show greater variation in shape, proportion, and surface treatment. Work with paper and cloth is indicative of a shift toward conscious design, as assorted colors and textures are used and varied shapes are created. Children are beginning to perceive their environment more clearly and tend to portray objects in accord with their perceptions. They are stimulated as they discuss their experiences, share their reactions, and respond to such questions related to their work as: What did you do? Where did it happen? What took place? What was most exciting? Essential materials and activities include colored crayons, chalks, large paper, tempera and poster paints, clay, sponge and potato printing, simple stenciling, paper and wood construction, work with cloth and yarn, simple weaving, the making of collages, and poster making.

Preplanning, Representational, Beginning Realism Stage

Nine- to eleven-year-olds grow in their ability to observe and visualize their environment with greater realism. The urge to portray perceptions realistically increases, but clarity of detail may be lacking and can be noticed in clothing drawn without folds or wrinkles, parts missing from objects, and the like. The attempts of some children to draw photographically and without creativity should be guided in such a way that freedom of expression of former years is retained. Copying, routine repetition, and somewhat rigid representation may be evident in the work of some children; this may be due to a lack of confidence, a desire to please others, an overemphasis upon the product, or failure of others to accept the child's own work. An important discovery for many children is the space between the base line and the horizon. Objects are placed within this space in better relationship to each other, and the sky is brought down to the base line. Space and distance relationships are given more attention, as indicated by children's efforts to show objects that are near and far. This may be done by having some objects overlap others. Lights and darks, textures, and colors are used by some children to highlight the overlapped parts. Lines are used with increasing effectiveness to show perspective, to emphasize central features, and to give a feeling of rhythm. Colors are selected more deliberately for realism and expression of the child's emotional responses. Decorative touches may be added to designs. A tendency develops to select materials that fit the child's purpose and are appropriate in terms of function. A variety of materials and activities are useful at this stage, including crayon etching, crayon batik, watercolors and tempera painting, colored chalks, poster making, collages, murals, block printing, monoprinting, stenciling, weaving, stitchery, papier-mache, plaster crafts, soap and wood carving, clay, wire and metal crafts, paper and wood construction, and the making of mobiles and stabiles.

Increasing Realism, Expressive Design Stage

From eleven to thirteen years of age, children grow in the ability to perceive and portray realism, although they are not fully aware of many details. The human body takes on more realistic proportions, arms and legs are jointed, bodily action is more definite, and clothing is colored, shaded, and draped more realistically. Line, form, color, texture, and shading are used with greater control and meaning to show action, space, distance, and mood. Composition, perspective, proportions, and foreshortening become significant problems for some children. More meaningful use of the horizontal line is evident and three-dimensional relationships are shown with greater clarity. Colors are selected more conventionally to express moods and ideas. Crafts are approached with great interest and provide rich opportunities to develop concepts of design. Self-criticism, techniques, content, and the product assume greater importance, and guidance and assistance from the teacher are needed to maintain confidence, emphasis on the process, and continuing growth to higher levels. Children are stimulated by dramatic situations, descriptions of action, posing to highlight bodily movements, demonstrations of processes, sharing and discussion of work, questions that clarify problems, guided observation, preplanning and experimentation, consideration of color in relation to feelings, and wide experience with the artwork of others. Watercolors, poster paints, mixed techniques, such as watercolor and tempera, pen and ink drawings, crayon resist, cartooning, poster making, charcoal, chalk, and group murals are effective for a variety of purposes. Printing activities include linoleum and wood block, stenciling, silk screen, monoprints, and rolling pin and rubber. Other activities include weaving, ceramics, sculpture, marionettes, mosaics, mobiles, stabiles, collages, montages, leather work, and wood construction.

ORGANIZATION AROUND ART ACTIVITIES

Art activities are widely used to structure the breadth and sequence of the curriculum. Although programs vary considerably in actual grade placement of activities the sequences presented below may be noted in many guides. The activities are outlined in a developmental sequence that begins with manipulative and exploratory experiences that help children gain control of materials. Subsequent activities may be characterized as involving intuitive design followed by those involving deliberate design, preplanned design, more refined design, and increasing realism coupled with expressive design. Development of skill in using different media and an understanding of elements and principles of design are an inherent part of each activity.

Drawing

Prekindergarten-2 Emphasis is given to free drawing with crayons on manila paper. As children gain control and experience, opportunities are provided for drawing to tell stories, design drawing, and use of chalk on wet paper.

Grades 3-4 Crayons are widely used and skill in using them is refined. Chalk is widely used in such activities as wet-chalk drawing, using chalk and powder paint, making texture rubbings, blending chalk and cotton, and using chalk with cut paper to make designs. New ways of using crayons (on tissue paper, with water color or poster paint) are explored along with stenciling and using the side of crayons for special effects.

Grades 5-6 The above are refined and new experiences are provided in combining chalk and India ink, scratchboard with crayons, and color on color.

Painting

Prekindergarten-2 Painting at an easel or on paper on the floor with water, one or two colors, and easy-to-handle brushes along with finger painting and sponge painting are suggested in many guides.

Grades 3-4 Opportunities are provided for two- and three-color painting, experimenting with color mixing, use of a variety of colors and brushes to achieve different effects, design painting, dry method of painting, and telling stories through painting. Children with adequate manual dexterity may be introduced to water colors.

Grades 5-6 Learning is extended as children continue the above with refinement of color experimentation and mixing, storytelling painting, design painting, and use of painting to make murals. New activities such as powder paint stenciling, spatter technique, collage and tempera, and tempera on cloth may be introduced.

Clay Modeling

Prekindergarten-2 First experiences include the manipulating of clay to make objects and shapes as the child wishes. Later, children make animals and figures, use slip to join parts, and may have some pieces fired and glazed by the teacher.

Grades 3-4 Experimentation and free modeling are continued. Opportunities for more refined modeling are provided to include designing with lumps of clay, using slabs, and welding and scoring.

Grades 5-6 Added to the above are coil method and the combining of lump, slab, and coil methods.

Making Murals and Posters

Prekindergarten-2 Simple murals may be arranged by grouping individual drawings or paintings on butcher roll or the bulletin board. Paper or cloth may be cut or torn and pasted on butcher paper. By grade 2 some students may cooperate in painting directly on paper to make a mural.

Grades 3-4 Emphasis is given to simple posters with one or two words, deliberate design of murals, cut paper posters and murals, and collage murals with many materials.

Grades 5-6 Murals and posters are preplanned with sketches, enriched with three-dimensional effects, and made with varied materials such as tempera on the cloth side of oil cloth.

Creating with Paper

Prekindergarten-2 Children experiment with a few shapes and strips, folding, curling, bending, twisting, pleating, cutting, and making simple favors. Cutting, tearing, and pasting along with the use of large strips to make designs and to weave simple mats are also suggested.

Grades 3-4 The above are continued with experiences in fanfolding, fringing, scalloping, notching, and the making of boxes, masks, paper bag figures, booklets, and other articles.

Grades 5-6 In addition to the above, opportunities are provided for creating stage properties, costume accessories for plays and puppets, paper sculpture, mosaics, and collages.

Stitchery and Weaving

Prekindergarten-2 Simple stitchery is done with burlap, monk's cloth, fabrics, ribbons, yarns, beads, and buttons. Simple cardboard loom activities may be initiated.

Grades 3-4 Stitchery is continued and weaving is done with rafia, cords, and leather or plastic strips on cardboard looms, looms made by children, and on Indian looms.

Grades 5-6 The above are continued and frame looms are used. Children are introduced to hooking on burlap and monk's cloth.

Printing

Prekindergarten-2 Vegetables and fruits cut in half (with no design cut in them) are used with young children to print various patterns.

Grades 3-4 Designs cut in potatoes and inner tubes are used for printing along with string prints and cardboard stencil prints.

Grades 5-6 The above are continued; stenciling, linoleum block, and monoprints are introduced.

Construction

Prekindergarten-2 Block building is widely used in nursery schools and kindergarten. Block building may be used in later grades for construction of items needed in the social studies and for extension of three-dimensional concepts and creativity in the art program. Simple construction of objects is also provided, using precut wood, popsicle sticks, beads, disks, and plastic containers. Simple carpenter's tools are used to make trucks, boats, and other objects.

Grades 3-4 Children construct more refined objects for gifts, personal use, creative expression, and use in social studies and other subjects. Use is made of wood, cardboard, wire and paper, papier mâché over corrugated cardboard, forms, and wire mesh, and cut paper and string.

Grades 5-6 A variety of objects are made and children try different finishes on them. Mobiles, mosaics, and papier mâché on stick armatures are included in some teaching guides.

Puppetry

Prekindergarten-2 Provision is made for dramatic play and experimentation with paper bag, sock, mitten, and other simple puppets.

Grades 3-4 A variety of dramatic activities may be provided, calling for the use of simple puppets, papier mâché puppet heads, puppet painting, costumes, and staging.

Grades 5-6 The above are continued and extended to include jointed puppet construction and refinements in painting, costuming, and staging.

Discovering the Heritage of Art

Prekindergarten-2 Children choose and use colors that look well together (harmonize), arrange and rearrange items to get effects that please them, react spontaneously to pictures and illustrations, and respond freely to other aspects of art around them to nurture appreciation.

Grades 3-4 The above are extended to include reactions to selected modern paintings, mosaics, and other items enjoyed by children, experimenting with and using patterns and shadings in arrangements, floral arranging, color schemes and arrangements for activities, uses of art at home and in the community, Indian art, and art in other cultures under study.

Grades 5-6 The above are continued with the addition of other types of painting, and an introduction to aspects of design in photography, architecture, textiles, pottery, and architecture.

Using Art Activities in Other Areas

Prekindergarten-2 Drawing and painting related to activities in units on Families, Schools, Communities, and Holidays are provided along with related modeling, construction, weaving, and paperwork.

Grades 3-4 Extensive use in all subjects and units may be provided. For example, in science and environment studies use may be made of crayon rubbing of leaves, seed collages, tempera leaf prints, landscape design, photographs or films made by students, posters, murals, and construction of planters, terrariums and dioramas.

Grades 5-6 Unlimited use is possible. For example, in a unit on Japan may be included calligraphy, origami, No and Kabuki masks, architecture, tatami mat and shoji screen designs and decorations, and the art concepts hade, iki, jimi, and shibui. (See Michaelis, 1972, for other examples at all levels.)

CONCEPTUAL STRUCTURE

Two major sets of concepts are widely used in art education. The first includes those concepts directly related to specific art activities. These include concepts related to the tools, equipment, and media used in painting, modeling, puppetry, and other activities as noted in the preceding section. The second set includes concepts of design that are useful in all phases of art education. They include three basic concept clusters:

Elements Line, color, light, form, space, texture, movement
Principles Balance, rhythm, contrast, emphasis, proportion
Qualities Unity, clarity, harmony

Concepts such as these are of critical importance in design which is at the very heart of artistic expression and criticism. Art educators tend to view design in terms of these concepts and children grow in the ability to use them through guided experiences in the art program. Briefly, design may be defined as the use of elements in accordance with principles and qualities to create works by means of specific processes and materials. Definitions of each concept follow.

Elements

Elements have a tangible or objective existence and visible or tactile characteristics such as hue, size, and texture. Principles and qualities are statements about relationships among such elements as the following:

Line refers to the path of vision and the direction it takes: vertical, horizontal, oblique, or spiral. Lines may be curved, straight, broken, continuous, delicate, bold, dynamic, static, precise, blurred, tense, relaxed.
Texture is the "feel" or appearance, real or apparent, of surface treatment, which may be rough, smooth, furrowed, wrinkled, even, irregular, soft, shiny, dull.
Light in two-dimensional design is the pattern of light and dark referred to as "chiaroscuro." In three-dimensional design, it is the pattern of light, shade, and

shadow without which form could not be perceived. The element of light is used even more directly in such forms as stage design, architecture, films, stained glass, and sculptures that include incandescent lamps or neon tubing as part of their construction. Light may be intense, dim, steady, varying, direct, diffused.

Color refers to the reflection of light and is described in terms of hue (name), intensity (brightness or dullness), and value (lightness or darkness of the color). The colors of natural light are classified as primary (red, yellow, blue), secondary (orange, green, violet), and intermediate. Neutral colors are black and white. Colors may also be referred to as complementary (opposite), analogous (adjacent), warm, or cool.

Form refers to the shapes seen in two-dimensional design and to the shape of a three-dimensional object or its component parts. Form may be solid, amorphous, suggested, defined, simple, complex.

Space refers to the area between and around forms. In two-dimensional design, an illusion of three-dimensional space may be provided by means of perspective, positional relation of forms, or "advancing" and "receding" colors. In three-dimensional design, space is defined by form, and in kinetic or mobile sculpture, by form and motion. The relationship of space, form, and motion may be referred to as *volume*. Space may be real, apparent, open, closed, static, dynamic.

Movement is the direction of vision over or around the work, directed by line, color, and form in two-dimensional design, and form itself in sculpture and architecture. In kinetic sculpture, air currents or motors produce movement as a change of position of the total work or its component parts. Movement may be rhythmic, repetitious, sporadic, smooth, abrupt, intersecting, oscillating, revolving, radiating.

Although works of art are observed in time, the duration of *time* usually depends upon the observer. However, in kinetic sculpture and films, time is an integral element because its duration, or the duration of movement patterns, is fixed by the artwork, not the observer.

Principles

Principles of design are concepts relating to the ways in which elements are employed to create art objects that possess design qualities. *Emphasis* refers to the use of dominance and subordination to make some colors, shapes, or line directions stand out while others are subdued. *Contrast* refers to opposition: dark against light, differing colors, change in planes, difference in form or texture. *Balance* refers to the distribution of each element in an artwork and the degree to which this distribution, in connection with emphasis and contrast, maintains equilibrium within the work. *Proportion* refers to the relation of parts to the whole and of parts to each other within the physical limits of the work. *Rhythm* refers to apparent movement within the work and may be expressed through repetition of lines, forms, colors, and other elements, or continuity of direction of vision between components of the work.

Qualities

Qualities are concepts which go beyond elements and relationships to include the materials and function of the art object. *Unity* refers to integrity in the use of materials and the relation of form to function. *Clarity* refers to the idea that all functional parts should be visible, all visible parts functional—effects achieved in the unification of form and function. *Harmony* refers to the relationships within and between the components of a work, the degree to which parts fit together, and the way in which the work fits into a larger ensemble.

USING ART CONCEPTS TO PLAN QUESTIONS AND ACTIVITIES

The elements, principles, and qualities above serve as a framework for planning questions and activities. In the following examples the key concept is italicized and the inquiry process that is being emphasized is in parenthesis.

Describe how the *texture* of this material feels to you (interpreting).

Look at the *form* of this object. How are the different parts tied together to give it unity (analyzing)?

How are *lines* used to show the road disappearing in the distance (interpreting)?

How might *line* and *space* be used together to give *perspective* to the objects in our mural (synthesizing)?

Which arrangement is best in terms of *balance* (evaluating)?

In general, how is *rhythm* expressed in these pictures (generalizing)?

What *values* and *hopes* do you think are expressed in this mural (inferring)?

How have the parts been fitted together to achieve *clarity* (interpreting)?

INSTRUCTIONAL MEDIA

Essential media have already been identified in the earlier sections on developmental stages and art activities. Below is a summary that may be used as a checklist of media included in a well-rounded program.

Drawing Crayons, chalk, pencils, ink, pens, assorted papers, cloth, tagboard

Painting Assorted brushes and papers, tempera, powder, poster, sponges, fingerpaint, watercolor, easels

Modeling Regular and nonhardening clay, papier mache, glaze, paints, storage containers

Paper work Assorted papers, paste, scissors, cardboard, butcher roll, boxes, sacks

Stitchery and weaving Assorted needles, yarn, thread, burlap, monk's cloth, assorted cloths, rafia, leather and plastic strips, looms, hooking device

Printing Sponges, cut vegetables and fruits, cardboard, inner tubes, linoleum blocks

Puppetry Sacks, socks, mittens, papier mâché, armature material

Art heritage Vases and other art objects, reproductions of paintings, drawings and etchings, textiles, realia and pictures from various cultures

Recycled materials Sacks for masks, stuffed animals and other objects, puppets; plastic containers for papier mâché armature, flower pots, collage base; styrofoam meat trays for printing block, loom, collage, or stitchery base; egg cartons and carton lids for collage or stitchery base, trays; styrofoam packing scraps for doll furniture, printing blocks, trucks, models; frozen food pans for curled metal flowers, repoussé (tooled) designs, chimes

Photography Suitable cameras and film for prints, slides, and motion pictures; materials for noncamera impressions on film

Construction Wood and wood scraps, heavy cardboard, styrofoam and plastic scraps

TEACHING STRATEGIES

Discovery approaches have long been used in art education along with direct instruction to develop skills and concepts needed in creative expression, criticism, and uses of art in daily living. The following strategies illustrate procedures to use in connection with each of the major objectives noted earlier. Each strategy should be used flexibly and creatively in a way that sparks original expression on the part of children.

Developing Visual/Tactile Perception

This strategy is used to improve children's observation of objects, works of art, and their own products. Concepts of line, form, color, and others noted above are used as needed to guide observation, interpretation, and analysis. The strategy begins with free response to a selected item or items and the setting of a focus for observation. This is followed by guided questions to evoke responses, to identify similar elements in responses, and to interpret and put to use what has been perceived and interpreted. Although the following example is based on the perceptions of *lines*, it may be used with any element, principle, or quality.

1 Begin with free response to the item and then move to set a focus. *Example:* Look at these pictures of modern buildings. What is your reaction to them? Now, look at them to identify vertical lines. Can you also find horizontal lines?

2 Identify and interpret similar elements in responses. *Example:* What uses of vertical lines did several of us observe? Of horizontal lines?

3 Identify possible uses of what has been discovered or extended. *Example:* Which uses of lines in these pictures are suggestive of how we might use lines creatively? How might we make original applications in our own work?

Developing Creative Expression

The creative process in art leads to the production of works that constitute unique forms or organization of knowledge. The process may well be referred to as divergent problem solving because the artist's creative effort is a unique response to a recognized problem. The problem may be to determine the design possibilities inherent in a material, to obtain a special effect by mixing colors, to convey a feeling of rhythm, to produce a design or pattern, to express a message, to exaggerate an important feature, or a host of other intentions. To meet the problem, the artist works intuitively or in terms of hypotheses that may or may not be explicit, selects materials, uses processes, sometimes experimenting and other times moving ahead according to a design, and creates a solution that is unique. Art skills and techniques are used in the process and brought to higher levels of development through actual use and through instruction, whether the artist is an adult working with a master or a child working with a teacher. As children participate in the creative process, they come into direct contact with the structure of art and develop insights into design concepts.

Aspects of the creative process include such activities and thinking skills as the following:

Observation, imagination, visualization
Perception, analysis, spatial organization
Classification and utilization of elements and principles
Invention and utilization of symbols
Exploration and experimentation with various processes and media
Evaluation of results of expression according to criteria developed by children

Essential to creative expression is the development of skill in using various media and related processes. The strategy below is indicative of an approach that may be used to develop skills and at the same time emphasize the importance of creativity. The strategy begins with exploration and experimentation by the children which is followed by the sharing of discoveries, reactions, and problems or questions they encountered. Next, a demonstration is given by the teacher (or artist) that is directly related to reactions, questions, or problems of children. Finally, students return to their own work, emphasizing creative use of the material and of individual ideas gleaned from the demonstration.

1 Provide opportunity to experiment with and explore the materials. *Example:* Provide opportunity to explore the use of watercolors.

2 Have children share reactions, questions, problems. *Example:* How did you use them? Let's share and talk about them. What questions do you have? Any problems?

3 Provide a demonstration related to reactions, questions, and problems. *Example:* Demonstrate use of brushes, controlling amount of water.

4 Provide for further use of the materials. *Example:* Let's try them again. Use them in your own way to create what you wish.

With some materials (cutting and pasting, stitchery, hooking) it is necessary to give preliminary directions so that they will be used safely and appropriately.

This is done as children are introduced to the activity and followed by exploratory use, demonstration, and further activity.

An important trend in art education is the inclusion of an artist-in-residence as a key person in the program. The artist may be a painter, potter, or photographer. He or she usually spends time in an elementary school working directly with children, demonstrating techniques, explaining his or her aesthetic views and work procedures and carrying out art activities with children using strategies like those included here. The artist-in-residence may also serve as a resource for classroom teachers.

Developing Understanding and Appreciation of Art Heritage

Understandings and appreciations are developed through art activities, through creative expression, and in the making of aesthetic judgments. At times there is a specific focus on art in daily living and the works of artists, the objective being to deepen understanding and appreciation. Guiding questions may be used to direct observation, interpretation, and analysis. For example, useful questions in connection with the study of an artist's pictures are What subject is depicted? Why do you think he selected this subject or topic? What elements are dominant? How are they used?

The illustrative strategy that follows may be used with any work of art. Both cognitive and affective aspects of understanding and appreciation are given attention. Special attention is given to the clarification of values reflected in the work of art being studied. The strategy begins with children's own reactions and moves to a discussion of both familiar and new features. This is followed by identification of special or distinctive features and a consideration of values reflected in the work.

1 Invite free and informal reaction to the work. *Example:* Show a reproduction of a Matisse painting and invite comments.

2 Discuss both familiar and new elements discovered by children. *Example:* What use of color have you seen before? What new ways of using colors are evident?

3 Identify distinctive or special features. *Example:* What is special or distinctive in his work? Let's find out by looking at others.

4 Infer values reflected in the work. *Example:* What do you think is prized or valued by this artist? First, in the use of color? Second, in what is depicted?

Reproductions bring a variety of artwork to the classroom, but they should be supplemented with visits to museums and galleries, particularly in the case of art objects such as sculpture and folk art which cannot be adequately represented by a two-dimensional photograph, or which lend themselves to handling by observers.

Developing Aesthetic Judgment

The attainment of aesthetic judgment involves critical thinking—the use of standards or criteria to make decisions about the worth, aesthetic quality, suitability, usefulness, or other value of a work of art. Criteria may be developed through discussion, observation, comparative analysis, or recommendation of experts and typically include one or more of the following:

The suitability of materials selected by the artist
The compatibility of medium and technique used by the artist
The relationship of form to function
How well the design unifies all parts of the work
How well the work commands and holds interest

How color, line, and movement are used to convey mood
The quality of the work in comparison with similar works
The quality of the work in terms of personal or social uses
The characteristics of the work in light of the artist's intentions
The originality of the work or its components

The strategy below involves the process of evaluating and thus requires thorough understanding of what is to be appraised. After clarification of the focus of evaluation, standards or criteria are defined and related evidence or reasons are collected in relation to each standard. The judgment is made on the basis of supporting reasons or evidence.

1 Clarify the focus of evaluation. *Example:* Which color scheme do you prefer for our exhibit?
2 Define standards of appraisal. *Example:* How shall we decide? What colors will be most suitable in terms of attracting attention? Highlighting items?
3 Gather related evidence or reasons. *Example:* What color combinations best meet our standards? Why?
4 Make the judgment. *Example:* Everything considered, which one(s) shall we use?

Walking trips in the neighborhood of the school can be utilized to call children's attention to design of buildings, bridges, signs, and decorative details on lampposts, park benches, and so on. Aesthetic criteria developed by the children can be applied to these observations of art elements in their environment.

GUIDELINES FOR THE TEACHER

Although skill, understanding, and appreciation can only be developed as a result of the child's direct and active involvement in art activities, the teacher has a definite role to play. The teacher makes plans for appropriate activities, observes children as they work in order to raise suggestive questions, make encouraging comments, help children clarify problems through discussion, or demonstrate a process in order to add to children's knowledge after their own explorations. However, there is no place for overdirection in which problems are set for the child, he is told what technique to use and how to use it, or, even worse, difficult aspects of the work are done for him. A key principle that must be kept in mind is that genuine art is the creative expression of the artist; it is his very own. The teacher's role should be defined in accord with this idea. Although art educators differ somewhat on details, a review of their writings reveals several guidelines for teachers:

Create an atmosphere that encourages creativity Work with the children to maintain a classroom atmosphere that stimulates creativeness in both expressive and appreciative activities. Children and teacher should accept, respect, and encourage honest expression in artwork and recognize that, in art education activities, the experiences of the creative process are more important than the product. Confidence and creative ability grow and enjoyment and understanding of the work of others increase in an atmosphere of respect and acceptance of individual differences in ability and expressive choices.

Use knowledge of developmental stages for planning and evaluation General overall planning is most effective when consideration is given to characteristics and interests of children at various developmental levels. In each class, this consideration should be augmented by the teacher's recognition of individual deviations from general growth patterns. Be sensitive to these differences, and provide experiences that nurture individuality.

Pace introduction of materials with children's development Introduce materials and processes as children evidence readiness for them, but avoid introducing too much at one time or children will become confused. Ample time must be provided for children to manipulate and explore materials and experiment with processes. Bear in mind that there will be variations in the amount of time most suitable for each child.

Plan working time and space effectively In early grades, arrange materials, tools, work space, and time allotments so that routine management problems are minimized and children are free to do creative work. In the upper grades, children can assume more of a share in such planning. Workmanship skills and responsibility for the care of tools and materials are valuable concomitant learnings.

Utilize children's work constructively to develop design understandings Techniques and design concepts become more meaningful to children when seen in relation to their own work, rather than in an abstract presentation. Use guiding questions to help children to note similarities and make constructive comparisons in order to attain concepts, and to help them to clarify design problems and discover solutions.

Emphasize enjoyment of art Guide children to discover the use of art products in daily living. Provide experiences in which they encounter varieties of forms and styles in art. Encourage them to observe and comment constructively on the best or most appealing features of each other's work.

Use a multimedia approach to stimulate interest and inspiration Take the children on study trips to museums, galleries, and studios. Provide prior classroom experiences that will prepare them for the exhibits they will see. Discuss and evaluate observations after the trip. Invite artists and craftsmen to the school to demonstrate processes and display their works. Have classroom exhibits of art books, magazines, art objects from different cultures, reproductions representing different styles and periods, and examples of natural objects with aesthetic qualities. Other examples of natural and cultural objects may be shown through films, slides, filmstrips, and overhead projections.

EVALUATION OF ARTISTIC DEVELOPMENT

Evaluation of artistic expression is informal, highly individualized, and very closely integrated with all phases of instruction. Emphasis is on self-evaluation and other constructive techniques that help each student solve problems and discover ways to achieve his intentions. A fundamental principle is to guide self-evaluation so that each student develops confidence, self-reliance, and constructive attitudes. The teacher helps each student to consider his work in terms of what he wishes to accomplish with the media he is using and the background of experience and skill that he has developed. Close identification with the student is essential so that his work may be seen from the student-artist's point of view. Questions and comments made by the teacher are framed in relation to problems confronting the individual student, problems which the student recognizes and needs to solve in order to continue his growth in artistic expression. Therefore, guided self-evaluation which the teacher utilizes to promote each student's ability to explore, experiment, and create in his own way is a hallmark of effective evaluation.

The role of the teacher in guiding self-evaluation varies with the artistic maturation of the child. Young children are guided in the selection of media, given praise and recognition, encouraged to experiment, guided to share work constructively, and assisted in learning basic routines that facilitate creativity. The teacher is a keen observer who notes the child's needs for suitable materials: a wider brush, a larger paper, a different color, a change of subject or media. Samples of children's work may be kept at all grade levels and periodically reviewed by the teacher to discover growth and to identify needs for additional experiences with certain media, processes, and problems. Self-evaluation is sharpened in later grades as the teacher continues to stress positive, constructive attitudes. Care must be taken to prevent self-evaluation from slipping into destructive self-criticism. Special attention should be given to helping each child to recognize his successes, to develop new skills and techniques commensurate with his aspirations and abilities, and to set realistic goals in terms of his capabilities and the limitations of available media, for when the level of aspiration far exceeds one's capabilities, there is a tendency to turn away from art. It is extremely important to guide students to set standards for themselves that are children's, not adults', standards. As each student faces a problem he should have the opportunity to discuss it with the group, to invite suggestions, and to choose and adapt suggestions to his individual modes of expression.

A similar stance is taken during group discussions of artwork. Each individual plays a leading role as his work is shared with the group. Emphasis is Placed on his intentions, the ways in which he has expressed his thoughts and feelings, his solutions to problems, and discoveries he has made. Unique and distinctive qualities are highlighted in much the same manner as when professional artists exchange ideas related to their work. Respect for self-expression, self-reliance, ingenuity, and integrity of expression are nurtured. The teacher's role in maintaining a constructive and creative atmosphere is of critical importance if genuine and useful evaluation is to be attained.

Emphasis in group discussion is given to successful aspects of creative expression of ideas or feelings in each work. The successful and distinctive characteristics of a particular work are discovered, noted, and shared in appreciative terms that stimulate further creativity but do not convey the notion that others should copy these characteristics or techniques. It is highly unrealistic and out of step with the character of creative expression to engage in such activities as finding "the *best* picture" or selecting "the *best* artist." Such arbitrary and meaningless judgments have no place in the effective art education program. Instead, each individual's work is viewed in light of its distinctive qualities, and each child is encouraged to explore the use of elements, arrangements, and media in ways that he, as an artist, feels are appropriate for himself. Thus goodness or badness, right or wrong, are not judgments handed down by the class serving as a jury; they are highly *personal* judgments that the artist makes in light of his own intentions and capabilities.

Although evaluation in art education is primarily informal and individualized, the teacher may structure evaluation of pupil growth and understanding in terms of the objectives of the program or the use of taxonomies of objectives (Bloom, 1956; Krathwohl, Bloom, and Masia, 1964). The following illustrate how specific performance objectives may be stated on different levels in connection with different art activities.

Cognitive Domain

Knowledge Given three pictures representing different art styles, the child will state the style each one represents.

What are three characteristics of primitive art?

Underline the three terms among those presented below that are art qualities.

Light Clarity Form Shape Unity Space Color Harmony

Comprehension Given a drawing, the child will state in his own words how texture is represented.

Describe how texture can be used in a design of your choice.

Which picture (A, B, or C) illustrates the use of texture?

Application Given charcoal and paper, the child will demonstrate how vertical lines can be used to give a feeling of height.

Paint a picture that shows how color can be used to highlight an object.
Make a bowl using the coil method.

Analysis Given a work of art, the child will analyze it by describing the
main parts in terms of the use of art elements.

State at least two differences between paintings A and B regarding ways in
which balance, contrast, and proportion have been used.

Point to the parts of the mural that most clearly reflect the artist's intention
to convey the people's desire for freedom.

Synthesis Given materials for making a flower arrangement, the child will
make one that accurately represents principles of Japanese flower arranging, as
judged by the teacher.

How shall we arrange these materials in a display?

Make a mural that brings together ,the three main types of art objects made
during the colonial period, as noted in the reference on colonial art.

Evaluation Given a work of art, the child will make a judgment about it in
terms of criteria developed in class, giving at least three acceptable reasons for
the judgment as determined by the teacher.

How can we improve the way in which stitchery is used to make geometric
designs?

Rank order these three works of art in terms of their appeal to you for use
as a part of room decoration, giving at least two reasons for the order of
preference.

Affective Domain

Receiving Given the opportunity to learn a new process, the child listens
to directions for using the work center.

Responding Given the opportunity to engage in an art activity, the child
responds by creating a product of his own design.

Valuing When given a choice, the child selects an art activity and gives
acceptable reasons for the choice, as judged by the teacher.

FOLLOW-UP ACTIVITIES AND PROJECTS

1 Evaluate a curriculum bulletin in art education in terms of the following:

   a Are objectives appropriate? Clearly defined? Do they include all aspects
   of a comprehensive, balanced art program?
   b Is the sequence of activities related to children's developmental levels?
   What provisions are made in choice of media and in sequence for individual differences?

    c Does the program emphasize direct experience, varied use of media, and creativity?
    d What instructional strategies are suggested?
    e What aesthetic concepts are developed?
    f What forms of evaluation are suggested?
    g What aspects of the program meet the needs of your students?

2 Obtain several examples of children's paintings or drawings at each age level in your school. Analyze them in terms of the developmental levels described in this chapter. Note differences in levels among children of a given chronological age. What are the implications of your analysis for the planning of your own program in visual arts?

3 Develop a list or directory of community resources for art education. These would include museums, galleries, libraries, community members who can teach crafts of different cultures, studios of painters, sculptors, potters, weavers, photographers, and others who can provide demonstrations for school children, magazines with articles and reproductions, books on visual arts, special television programs, and the like. Give an example of a learning experience for your children utilizing one or more of these resources.

4 Outline a unit plan or set of lessons for a particular group of learners for evaluation of use of visual arts in mass media: "mood" or "theme" set by magazine illustrations of short stories; uses of illustrations or photographs in advertising; use of camera angles, cropping, selection of images in magazine photo essays; and analysis of illustrations in trade books and basal readers.

5 Plan a walking trip of your school neighborhood or area to have children note aesthetic elements of the natural and built environment. Give an example of a creative activity that would be an appropriate follow-up to this trip for children in early grades, and an example suitable for children in the upper elementary or middle school years.

BIBLIOGRAPHY

Anderson, W. A. *Art Learning Situations for Elementary Education*. Belmont, Calif.: Wadsworth, 1965. Practical suggestions for activities, with attention to concept formation related to structure in art.

Barkan, Manuel. *Through Art to Creativity*. Boston: Allyn and Bacon, 1960. Specific suggestions for developing creative experiences in relation to levels of development.

Bloom, Benjamin S. (Ed.) *The Taxonomy of Educational Objectives: Cognitive Domain*. New York: McKay, 1956. Classification of objectives and examples of test items.

California. *Art Framework, Kindergarten Through Grade Twelve*. Sacramento: California State Department of Education, 1971. Broad guidelines for instruction.

Croft, Doreen J., and Robert D. Hess. *An Activities Handbook for Teachers of Young Children*. Boston: Houghton Mifflin, 1972. Sections on art and music activities.

Dewey, John. *Art as Experience*. New York: Minton, 1934. A classic statement which highlights the relationships between art and life.

Dimondstein, Geraldine. *Exploring the Arts with Children*. New York: Macmillan, 1974. Suggestions for various art forms such as painting, sculpture, dance, and poetry.

Eisner, Elliot W. *Educating Artistic Vision*. New York: Macmillan, 1972. Philosophy, principles, and procedures of art education in elementary and secondary schools.

Gardner, Helen. *Art through the Ages*. (6th ed.), to be published. New York: Harcourt Brace Jovanovich, 1976. Background information on art history and principles.

Henrie, Samuel N. (Senior Ed.) *Sourcebook of Elementary Curricula Programs and Projects*. Washington, D.C.: U.S.: Government Printing Office, 1972. Chapter on aesthetics and arts.

Hess, Robert D., and Doreen J. Croft. *Teachers of Young Children*. Boston: Houghton Mifflin, 1972. Chapter on the arts in a preschool program.

Kaufman, Irving. *Art and Education in Contemporary Culture*. New York: Macmillan, 1966. Discussion of cultural influences on artwork of children and professional artists and suggestions for art instruction and development of good taste in contemporary culture.

Krathwohl, David R., Bloom, Benjamin S., and Masia, Bertram A. *Taxonomy of Educational Objectives: Affective Domain*. New York: McKay, 1964. A classification of objectives and sample test items in the area of attitude and value development.

Lark-Horovitz, Betty. *Graphic Work Diagnosis*. Cleveland: Museum of Art, 1939. A classic study of developmental stages.

Lark-Horovitz, Betty, Lewis, Hilda, and Luca, Mark. *Understanding Children's Art for Better Teaching*. (2nd ed.) Columbus, Ohio: Merrill, 1973. Development of instructional guidelines drawn from the characteristics of artwork and aesthetic responsiveness of average, disadvantaged, and exceptional elementary school children.

Lewis, Hilda. (Ed.) *Child Art: The Beginnings of Self-affirmation*. Berkeley: Diablo Press, 1966. Contributions by Read, Kellog, Arnheim, Schaefer-Simmern, Stern, Barron, Lowenfeld, D'Amico, and Heckscher; examples of children's work in various countries and at various stages of development.

Lowenfeld, Viktor, and Brittain, W. L. *Creative and Mental Growth* (5th ed.) New York: Macmillan, 1970. Detailed analysis of stages of development.

McFee, June K. *Preparation for Art*. Belmont, Calif.: Wadsworth, 1961. Discussion of cultural and psychological aspects of art as well as art activities.

Merritt, Helen. *Guiding Free Expression in Children's Art*. New York: Holt, 1964. Techniques for providing varied activities.

Michael, John A. (Ed.) *Art Education in the Junior High School*. Washington, D.C.: National Education Association, 1964. Rationale and suggestions for art instruction useful to the teacher in middle or intermediate schools and in the upper elementary grades.

National Society for the Study of Education. *Art Education*. Sixty-fourth Yearbook, Part II. Chicago: University of Chicago Press, 1965. Background information and useful discussions of various aspects of art education.

New York Graphic Society. *Man through his Art*. Greenwich, Conn.: 1965. A series of volumes utilizing artworks as sources of information and understanding about man, his history, culture, and activities.

Read, Herbert. *Education Through Art*. New York: Pantheon, 1947. A classic work that continues to influence art education.

Smith, Ralph A. (Ed.) *Aesthetics and Criticism in Art Education*. Chicago: Rand McNally, 1966. Essays on aesthetics and art-criticism, and guidelines for critical evaluation of artworks useful for teachers and planners of art education at all grade levels.

Templeton, David E. The Arts: Sources for Affective Learning. *Educ. Leadership*, April, 1965, 22, 465–468. Discussion of inquiry in art and of the learner as artist and inquirer.

Chapter 17

Aesthetic Education: Music Education

Music is the creative organization of tonal elements to express thoughts and feelings. Sounds serve as the clues to meaning and feeling. Such tonal elements as melody, harmony, and rhythm are arranged in an aesthetic sequence that expresses the composer's intention. A musical experience for the listener involves direct perception of the particular form or composition that is being presented. The experience is marked by immediate response or reaction to what is heard. Thoughts and feelings well up within the listener in highly personalized ways that are linked to past musical experience. The contributions of music education to major goals of education have been noted in the preceding chapter. These contributions may be elaborated by considering the objectives presented in the following section.

OBJECTIVES OF MUSIC EDUCATION

As with art education, a central goal of music education is to develop aesthetic sensitivity. The focus in music education is on the concepts, processes, skills, and affective elements that are related to sensitivity to music. It is recognized that the cognitive, affective, and psychomotor domains are tightly interrelated in both performing and listening activities. The following illustrative objectives are separated to highlight specific outcomes and to serve as guides for the planning of learning experiences.

Conceptual Objectives

To develop understanding of concepts and principles so that students are able to identify, recognize, describe, and demonstrate, in performing or composing, the use of the following:

Concepts of tone, melody, rhythm, harmony, form or design, tempo, dynamics, tone color, style, notation

Principles based on concepts, such as "Melodies may be based on scale patterns, chord patterns, or repeated tones"

Inquiry Process Objectives

To develop skill in using processes of inquiry so students are able to do the following:

Demonstrate in music activities how classifying, interpreting, analyzing, and other processes may be used

State how the music of others and music in daily life may be classified, analyzed, and evaluated

Skill Objectives

To develop psychomotor skills needed in different types of musical activities so that students are able to do the following:

Express thoughts and feelings through singing, playing instruments, moving to rhythm, composing, and notating music

Respond to music and demonstrate the ability to react to different types of music as they participate in listening, singing, playing, reading, and bodily movement activities

Affective Objectives

To demonstrate in music activities the values, attitudes, and appreciations of individuals who:

Are sensitive and responsive to tone, rhythm, form, and other elements of music, and to a variety of styles in our and other cultures

Use valuing strategies to clarify values inherent in musical expression as experienced in and out of school

Additional specific objectives may be noted in the following section in which different music activities are discussed.

ORGANIZATION OF THE CURRICULUM

The organization of curriculum and instruction in music education is directly related to children's developmental characteristics. First experiences are exploratory and involve rhythmic movement, recognition of skipping and other movement patterns, responding to changes in tempo, and the learning of singing games, simple action songs, and interpretive activities descriptive of people, animals, and objects. As children mature and develop aesthetic sensitivity, they are able to build on their own firsthand experiences in music and move toward the development of concepts, processes, and skills involved in both performing and analytic/evaluative music activities. The following section illustrates how the program is adapted to developmental characteristics in addition to showing the breadth and sequence of the curriculum.

Organization Around Music Activities

The music activities that are widely used to structure the curriculum are presented in Chart 17-1.

Performing may be broken down into singing, playing of instruments, and reading of music. Composing includes vocal, instrumental, and rhythmic creative activities and the writing of musical notation. Listening includes a variety of ear-training activities ranging from sensitivity to simple rhythmic patterns to discrimination of various musical forms. Rhythmic activities include creative and spontaneous response to music as well as various dance forms. Related to each of these musical activities are uses of music in other subjects and the investigation of topics in music, such as music in the lives of other peoples, how musical sounds are produced, characteristics of instruments, and stories about composers.

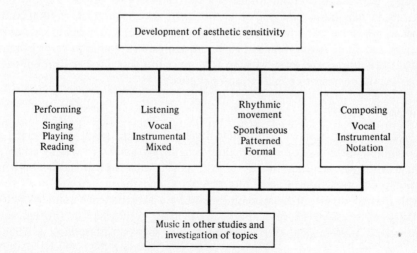

Figure 17-1 Phases of a complete program of music education.

Rhythmic Activities

Rhythmic experiences are an inseparable part of activities in each area of music education. Clustered around the major concept of rhythm are meter, pace, pulse, phrase, duration, accent, pattern, and syncopation. Rhythmic movement is used as a vehicle to improve enjoyment and to deepen understanding of rhythm as a basic element of music. Spontaneous, patterned, and formal activities are included as shown in the following summary.

Prekindergarten-1 Children engage in free rhythmic movement as the teacher claps or plays a simple accompaniment. Children learn simple singing games, action songs, and movement patterns such as skipping and galloping. They demonstrate awareness of pulse, pace, and accent through movement, play rhythm instruments and use them to accompany movement and songs, and participate in interpretive activities descriptive of people, animals, and objects.

Grades 2-3 Increasing rhythmic awareness is developed as children move in march time and waltz time and clap, tap, and step movement patterns. Simple folk dances and new rhythmic patterns such as the polka (step-close-step-hop) are introduced, children learn to conduct in 2/4, 3/4, and 4/4 time, and grow in the ability to select music to accompany different movements. Children identify common rhythmic patterns by notation, such as quarter notes for walking and eighth notes for skipping, discover relationships among phrase, accent, meter and form, and create movements to use in dramatic play, singing, and other activities.

Grades 4-6 Improved expressiveness emerges in interpreting singing games, creating movements, folk dancing, and the learning of new dance forms. Children change movements without losing time as frequently as before, identify basic meters in folk music and poetry, demonstrate syncopation on rhythm instruments, recognize patterns in notation, and notate. They also create new movements and floor patterns, investigate and compare rhythmic patterns in music of other cultures, and learn to substitute inner response for overt movement in reacting to beat, measure, phrase, and patterns.

Singing

Through singing experiences students develop increasing sensitivity to tonal relationships, melody, harmony, rhythm, song forms, and voice classification. As their repertoire increases, steady growth may be noticed in tonal quality, free voice production, use of the full vocal range, and the blending of one's voice with that of others. With increasing maturity and experience come growth in clarity of enunciation, intonation, and diction, confidence in singing, voice projection, part singing, and use of symbols to improve interpretation. Singing experiences contribute much to the development of aesthetic sensitivity as activities such as the following are provided:

Prekindergarten-1 Children find their singing voices by listening and matching tones in calls, tone games, and songs. They develop sensitivity to changes in pitch, volume, and melody, distinguishing loud and soft, up and down, and high and low tones. They learn to sing by phrases, change the voice to fit the mood, and by the end of grade 1 have extended their vocal range. They like to interpret songs through rhythmic, dramatic, and other activities, use rhythm instruments to accompany familiar songs, and sing with piano accompaniment. Most children learn to recognize familiar melodies, marches, lullabies, and uncomplicated tonal and rhythmic patterns in familiar songs. Some are able to create simple songs and play them on tone bells.

Grades 2-3 There is improvement in tonal quality, accuracy of pitch, sensitivity to rhythm, and clarity of enunciation. Children recognize like and unlike phrases, accent, underlying beat, fast and slow tempo, differing time values, and notation of familiar tonal patterns. Many are able to add introductions and endings (codas) to songs, play a descant to accompany known songs, sing simple rounds and descants, play one- and two-chord accompaniments on the autoharp, and begin to build a repertoire of songs.

Grades 4-6 Children develop tonal quality, increased sensitivity to phrasing, tempo and dynamics, pitch discrimination, interpretation of mood, and breath control and intonation. Many learn common key and meter signatures, how to find the key chord (do) and the starting tone for a song, how to harmonize by ear and to do vocal chording. Two- and three-part singing are included in a well-rounded program along with school chorus. Basic skills and processes are developed as students sing from notation, play accompaniments on the autoharp, piano, and other instruments, investigate favorite composers, and put concepts and skills to use in creating original songs and descants. Concepts of melody are extended as students discover horizontal movement, intervals, patterns or motifs, phrases, and sequences in songs of our own and other cultures.

Playing Instruments

Effective programs include the playing of a variety of instruments in all grades as an extension of singing and rhythmic experiences. At first, opportunities are provided for children to experiment with instruments and to discover the sounds that can be made by playing them. This is typically followed by experiences in which simple instruments are used to produce rhythms, melodies, and accompaniments. Group instruction is provided in some schools in piano and instrument classes. Concepts and concept clusters are developed, links to other phases of the program are highlighted, and growth in musicality is extended as shown in the following summary of instrumental activities:

Prekindergarten-1 Children discover sounds that can be made with their hands and feet and by striking metal, wooden, and glass objects. They experiment with melody bells, tuned bottles and glasses, and percussion instruments. They learn to play rhythmic patterns appropriate for walking, running, skipping, and other basic movements. They play tunes on melody bells and accompaniments to songs on percussion instruments. They begin to strum the autoharp, learn to recognize common instruments by sight and sound, and select and play rhythm instruments to accompany songs and movements.

Grades 2-3 Children play accompaniments, melodies, and tonal patterns with greater skill, find the pitch, and demonstrate up and down, high and low, stepwise and skipwise intervals, and repeated tones. They use percussion and melody instruments to add introductions, interludes, and codas to songs, rhythmic activities, and dramatizations. Some are able to play descants while the class sings. Instruction is provided in reading notation while playing simple instruments. Children are introduced to additional band and orchestral instruments, ways in which harmony is produced, how instruments may be used to embellish and accompany activities, and how simple instruments may be constructed.

Grades 4-6 Children develop increasing skill in playing percussion, melody, harmony, recorder-type, and other instruments. They use melody bells or the piano to check pitch, find the starting tone, improve part singing, play descants and deepen understanding of intervals, harmony, and other concepts. Many children recognize and identify the tone and timbre of band and orchestral instruments, and develop sensitivity to forms of music ranging from solo and chamber to band and orchestral. They investigate instruments used in other lands, make and play such instruments as claves, bongo drums, guiros, maracas, and cabacas.

Listening

Listening is a part of all musical experiences because music is a tonal art. Getting the beginning tone, sensing a rhythmic pattern, improvising a coda, identifying instruments, and discovering harmonic changes are illustrative of the importance of listening. Of utmost importance is listening to music for sheer enjoyment. The developmental listening program includes such activities as the following:

Prekindergarten-1 Children are guided to discover and identify sounds and tones, to match tones, and to develop sensitivity to high and low, loud and soft, and fast and slow. They interpret the feeling, mood, or story through rhythmic movement. They listen to Saint-Saen's *The Swan*, Brahms' *Lullaby*, and other great music that is enjoyed by young children. They also listen to percussion, melody, the violin, and other instruments.

Grades 2-3 Children grow in the ability to listen for tones, rhythms, tempo, and patterns. They interpret mood and other qualities with more feeling and develop greater understanding and appreciation of descriptions and stories in program music. Their listening repertoire grows as they experience Debussy's *Corner Suite,* Grieg's *March of the Dwarfs,* Haydn's *Surprise Symphony,* and other great literature.

Grades 4-6 Listening ability is greatly extended as children follow melodic lines, recognize themes and their variation and repetition, and distinguish major and minor mode. Many can recognize the different parts, identify voices in part singing, detect harmony in vocal and instrumental music, and identify instruments according to tone. Many opportunities are provided to interpret mood, develop understanding of melody, harmony, dynamics, arrangement, form, and style, and to learn to concentrate on the music itself without extramusical stimulation. Children's listening repertoire is enriched through program and absolute music that includes a rich selection in terms of composers, styles, periods, themes, and forms of composition.

Creative Activities

Creativity takes many forms including self-expression through music activities, improvisation of melodies and rhythmic patterns, arrangement of accompaniments, construction of instruments, and interpretation of the music of others. Most completely creative of all activities is the composition of original songs for which words, music, and accompaniment are created by children. The following are illustrative of the many opportunities for creative expression.

Prekindergarten-1 First experiences involve free response to different rhythms, rhythmic movement and impersonation, interpretation of music about people, animals, and activities, and free expression on simple melody and rhythm instruments. Other creative activities range from selecting rhythm instruments to accompany rhythmic movement and improvising a jingle or chant to use with a rhythmic pattern to creating a tune for a rhyme and composing words and music for a short song after a study trip or other exciting experience.

Grades 2-3 Children creatively interpret folk and other music, devise introductions, interludes, and codas, and respond to moods and descriptions in music through art, language and movement activities. Original expression is also developed by devising and combining rhythmic patterns and movements, producing special effects on instruments, making instruments, and arranging accompaniments. Creativity flowers as children create songs, movements, and melodies, and improvise on tone bells, the piano, and other instruments.

Grades 4-6 Songs are interpreted with greater originality and understanding of the composer's intentions, and children's ability to create songs can be brought to high levels. Children devise variations, embellishments, movements, dance steps, accompaniments, and the like with a flair and delight that should be nurtured. They set poems or stories to music, improvise melodies on instruments, make and play instruments for use in the social studies, combine selections and dramatizations into playlets, and create chants, rounds, and other music if a supportive climate and teacher guidance are provided.

Understanding and Reading Music

Concepts of music are clarified and understanding of notation is developed as visual perception of terms and symbols is used to enrich aural perception of melody, rhythm, harmony, and form. Experiences in listening, singing, and other activities are the context in which understanding and reading of music are developed. Planned activities are used to develop insight into the structure of music and ways in which musical ideas are communicated.

Prekindergarten–1 Readiness is developed through singing, playing, rhythmic, and other activities, associating tonal direction with high and low tones as demonstrated by arm movements, associating rhythmic patterns with movements, playing tunes on tone bells by ear and later by numerals, and other exploratory experiences. By grade 1 children discover that notes are written on lines and in spaces, and they develop the meanings of such terms as fast and slow, soft and loud, high and low, starting tone, tune, melody, and others related to different activities.

Grades 2–3 Children follow notes in textbooks and on charts or the chalkboard while singing, recognizing notes of differing duration, associating notes and syllables, comparing numeral and letter notation, and identifying meter in music that moves twos, threes, and fours. They use notation to play phrases and melodies, relate note and chord sequences to piano chording, and learn notation in group instrumental instruction. They notate phrases and simple songs on charts and the chalkboard with assistance as needed. Their vocabulary of music grows as they learn and use such terms as chord, beat, staff, stanza, measure, signature, and clef.

Grades 4–6 The above are extended to include playing instruments by reading notation, using notation for writing, singing and playing original music, and following parts in two- and three-part songs. Specific attention is given to increasing facility in independent sight reading, investigating and comparing different scales such as diatonic and pentatonic, notating melodies, descants, thirds, sixths, basic chords and chord sequences, and learning the meaning of such terms as descant, coda, interlude, theme, harmony, modulation.

Music in Other Studies

People everywhere have made music a significant part of activities ranging from ceremonies and dancing to politics and warfare. There is music of work, play, love, worship, rest, travel, heroes, battles, hopes, fears, and a myriad of other human activities, thoughts, and feelings. Because music is such an important part of the lives of people, it inevitably is made a part of learning experiences in the social studies. Because of its many links to other arts and to science it is appropriately included in studies outside the developmental program of music education. A guiding principle is to include musical experiences in ways that contribute to the development of aesthetic sensitivity. The following examples are illustrative.

Social Studies Learning lullabies, folk and art songs, and work and recreation songs related to family and community studies; exploring music of Indians, Hawaiians, and others; learning state and national songs and folk games and dances; learning to utilize ethnic and national music and the music of differing periods as sources for information and understanding of other times and cultures; making and playing authentic instruments; hearing recordings, seeing dances, and hearing music performed by local, national, and international artists; selecting music for culminating activities, discovering that the capacity for musicality is universal; discovering intercultural influences in music.

Language Arts Writing creatively as music is played, selecting background music for individual or choral reading and storytelling, selecting music to fit the mood of poems and stories, composing music to use in singing original poems, hearing great works related to heroes in literature, hearing poems that have been set to music.

Science Learning how pitch is changed in relation to length of a bar, string, or tube, discovering how thickness of bars and strings alters tone, finding how heat, moisture, and paint change the tone produced by striking drumheads, bars, clay pots, and gourds, learning how a megaphone, violin box, or gourd reinforces vibrations and gives resonance.

Art Drawing, painting, or sketching as music is played, using drawings, paintings or pictures to illustrate songs, using pictorial materials to direct and motivate listening, making and decorating musical instruments of different cultures, discovering that rhythm is a basic element in art as well as in music and poetry, discovering that there are similar styles in both art and music, sometimes within a time period, as in the paintings of Watteau and the music of Mozart, and sometimes cutting across periods, as in the paintings of Mondrian and the music of Bach.

CONCEPTUAL STRUCTURE

Selected concepts and concept clusters are used extensively in planning, carrying out, and evaluating music activities. Experiences provided in early childhood education programs provide readiness for direct and systematic attention to the use of concepts in later grades. As noted earlier, each concept is developed in the context of activities in which children are involved. The following concept clusters are widely used in contemporary materials. Examples of questions and activities on different cognitive levels are given to illustrate how the concepts are made a part of activities.

Rhythm Pulse, pace, accent, meter, duration, pattern, phrase, syncopation
Illustrative questions and activities Let's demonstrate the *pulse* by clapping (interpreting). Can you demonstrate *accent* by clapping louder on the strong beat (interpreting)? How can we combine these *patterns* to make a *phrase* (synthesizing)? Which rhythm is best for fast movement? Why (evaluating)?

Melody Tone, range, duration, horizontal movement, interval, tonal center, pattern or motif, phrase, sequence
Illustrative questions and activities Who can match this tone by singing it (interpreting)? Let's break this melody down into *phrases* (analyzing). Who can tell what sequence means, or play one on the tone bells (defining, interpreting)?

Harmony Rounds, chants, descants, canon, vertical interval, chord, vertical structure, chord change, homophonic, polyphonic
Illustrative questions and activities Now, let's play and sing the *round*, with each group coming in as planned (synthesizing). Which *chord change* will be most pleasing for this part of the accompaniment? Why (evaluating)? Let's create a *descant* to sing above the melody (synthesizing).

Design and Form Phrase, section, two-part and three-part song form, section, introduction, interlude, coda, rondo, suite, theme, variation, tone poem, symphony
Illustrative questions and activities Who can define a *phrase* and play an example (defining)? How are these two *suites* alike and different: *Le Cid* and *Peer Gynt* (comparing/contrasting)? Which of these three codas do you prefer? Why (evaluating)?

GENERALIZATIONS

Generalizations that are developed as children gain experience in using the concepts noted above constitute an important part of the conceptual structure of music education. The following are illustrative of those included in teaching guides.

The rhythm in a melody is different from its pulse.
Tones may form phrases as words form phrases or sentences.
Melody, rhythm, and harmony may be combined in a variety of forms.
Pitch, rhythm, and tone quality may be used to produce different effects.

Folk music is a basic mode of expression in cultures around the world.

Notation is used to communicate melody, rhythm, and harmony in a variety of musical forms.

Standards for judging music vary greatly from situation to situation and culture to culture.

Characteristic styles of music may be identified in various countries and periods of time.

INSTRUCTIONAL MEDIA

In addition to textbooks, a well-rounded music education program includes the use of recordings, charts, notation materials, and a variety of instruments. Basic classroom equipment should include songbooks and accompanying albums of records, pitch pipe, record player, tape recorder, rhythm instruments, song bells, resonator bells, autoharp, material for notation, and, if possible, a piano. The variety of instruments to which access should be available is great, ranging from such simple wind instruments as the tonette, flutaphone, and songflute to band and orchestral instruments. Varieties of instruments may be made by students. Also viewed as part of the total instructional resources are live concerts in the community and music available through television, radio, and motion pictures.

TEACHING STRATEGIES

Many different teaching strategies are used in music education, ranging from directed rote singing and listening to guided discovery of elements of music and inquiry into selected topics. With increasing attention to elements of music as key concepts has come greater emphasis on strategies that highlight ways in which rhythm, melody, and harmony are organized in various forms to express musical ideas. The teacher's role is primarily one of guiding the learning of students in a series of performing, listening, creating, and investigating experiences. Throughout the program high premium is placed on creative expression and response as students are given opportunities to interpret, enjoy, and compose music in genuinely original ways. Specific teaching strategies are used to develop competence in various activities as shown in Chart 17-2.

Using Varied Approaches

The use of different approaches is recommended in teaching guides. In recognition of the fact that the various phases of music education are highly interrelated, teachers should begin with rhythmic or singing or other experiences and devise such sequences as the following:

1 Begin with rhythmic activity and move to related singing, playing of instruments, listening, and reading.

2 Begin with singing and move to related rhythmic activity, playing, listening, and playing of instruments.

Discovering rhythmic patterns	A folk dance
1. Have children demonstrate walking and running patterns as the class claps the rhythm.	1. Listen to catch the rhythm.
2. Have the class listen as a record with a galloping rhythm is played.	2. Clap the rhythm or play it on rhythm instruments.
3. Discuss how the rhythm is different from running and walking rhythms.	3. Watch the foot pattern as it is demonstrated.
4. Have a child demonstrate the movement he thinks is appropriate.	4. Match the foot pattern to the beat and accent.
5. Have others demonstrate the movement as the record is played.	5. Sing or say the rhythm steps as the music is played: Step-step-step-hop.
	6. Do the steps to music.
	7. Practice as needed.

Listening activities	Reading music
1. Know the music thoroughly.	1. Place several measures on the board.
2. Discuss purposes for listening.	2. Review the types of notes to be sung.
3. Present the selection.	3. Discuss the meter and clap the time.
4. Use pictures, poems, or other devices to highlight mood.	4. Clarify the time for different notes.
5. Discuss discoveries which students enjoyed.	5. Discuss the key signature and give the starting tone.
6. Provide for repetition to increase enjoyment and understanding.	6. Have a student give the syllables for each note in the first measure.
7. Provide for follow-up activities related to objectives.	7. Have one student sing a measure followed by others.
8. Respect the views of students.	8. Have the class sing the entire song from notation.

Rote singing	The autoharp
1. Use a pitch pipe to sound starting tone.	1. Use a single chord at first.
2. Sing the song for the class with a clear diction.	2. Locate the key to be depressed with the left hand.
3. Sing it again as children listen to note the time and phrases.	3. Get the rhythmic pattern.
4. Clarify the meaning of new words.	4. Depress the key with the left hand and strum with the right.
5. Have the group sing with you.	5. Try a two chord accompaniment, following a similar procedure.
6. Have the group sing each phrase.	
7. Listen as the group sings.	
8. Review and practice as needed.	

Chart 17-2 Illustrative teaching strategies

3 Begin with listening and move to rhythmic expression accompanied by playing of instruments.

4 Begin with the playing of instruments and move to related rhythmic movement and listening.

5 Begin with the notation of a pattern on a chart or on the chalkboard and move to singing and playing of the pattern.

6 Begin with a pattern created by the students and move to rhythmic movement, the playing of an accompaniment, and listening to a taped recording of the activity.

7 Begin with inquiry into a selected form of music and move to listening, singing, or playing of selected patterns, and on to further listening.

The beginning and the sequence may be varied as needed by the teacher. A guiding principle is to relate each succeeding activity to others so that various dimensions of understanding and feeling are engendered. When this is done children have opportunities to respond in a variety of ways and thus gain insight into the relationships among elements of music as a part of different activities. Furthermore, individual differences can be met as each child is guided to participate in the various activities that are included in the sequence.

Rhythmic Activities

Strategies in this phase of music education range from providing opportunities for spontaneous response to music through movement to direct teaching in which elements of music are emphasized. The following examples are illustrative.

Fundamental Rhythmic Movements Teachers of young children frequently provide opportunities for pupils to walk, skip, or gallop in a spontaneous manner as music is played. One or two children may respond to a selection and others join them as the music is played. The movement is changed as the tempo of the music changes. At other times, the music is changed to fit the movement of children. Rhythm instruments, clapping, the piano, the autoharp, or recordings may be used for accompaniment.

Creative Movement One strategy is based on creative response to music in which children create rhythmic movements that are sparked as music is played. One or two children, or a group of four or five, may initiate the activity by moving about the room or by swaying, bending, or using other axial movements. Later, other children create movements which they feel are expressive of the mood of the music. A second strategy is based on children's expression, and music is selected to fit the movements. Children create movements or dance steps, and an accompaniment is improvised on the piano, autoharp, or percussion instruments.

Discovering Rhythmic Elements The focus of this strategy is on the use of rhythmic activity to highlight patterns that are discovered through listening activities. Music is selected to reveal elements of music that can be expressed rhythmically. Children listen to discover ways in which they can express one or more of the following through rhythmic activity: story, mood, tempo, accent, metric beat, melodic and rhythmic patterns, and form. Individuals and small groups give interpretations, followed by others in the class.

Singing

The teaching of songs includes the use of both aural and visual approaches. In the aural approach children listen as the teacher or a child sings or as a recording or an instrument is played. Repeated listening experiences may be provided so that children can learn the melody and discover the rhythmic pattern. Special attention is given to phrases that are alike and different. Children then hum or sing the melody as they listen, sing repeated phrases, sing with and without music books, sing with and without listening to the teacher or recording.

In the visual approach, notation is provided to guide listening. Children watch the notation and listen critically in order to discover like and unlike phrases, ascending and descending passages, small and large melodic intervals, and rhythmic patterns. Selected parts may be highlighted as children watch the notation while someone sings or plays the song. This may be followed by having the class sing various phrases, clap the time, tap the rhythm of the melody, or play repeated patterns on simple instruments. The children next sing the song as accurately as they can as they watch the notation. As shown in the foregoing example, the visual approach is supplemented by aural and rhythmic activities. This appears to be essential in the early stages of the development of musicality. It probably should be stressed at all stages for most students, because music is primarily a tonal art.

Part singing calls for strategies that may combine both aural and visual approaches. Preparatory experiences should be provided in which children sing as a descant or alto part is sung or played, embellishments are added to familiar songs, rounds are sung or played, and harmonic accompaniments are provided by means of the piano, autoharp, or recordings. Instruction should include the singing of descants and rounds, harmonizing the ending of songs, listening to parts sung or played by others or played on a recording, singing in parallel thirds or sixths, listening to one or two parts while singing another, following the notation while listening and while singing, and the learning of several two- and three-part songs. Current textbooks contain a variety of part songs that have been graded in difficulty and can be used to develop competence to a high level.

Listening

Different strategies are used for program and absolute music. Listening to program music is guided so that children may discover ways in which stories or descriptions are portrayed. Listening to absolute music is guided so that they may discover melodic and rhythmic patterns, form, and other musical elements without reference to story or descriptive material. Both types of listening call for discovery on the part of children, and both are guided inductively to elicit responses from them.

Program Music After the teacher has made introductory comments regarding the selection and composer, children are asked to listen in order to find out how a story or description is suggested through the use of rhythm, melody, or other elements. Questions about the selection are asked in a way that does not give clues to the answer so that children themselves will use the music for clues. If a story is suggested, children are asked to tell which parts are the best clues and to explain why they chose them. Replaying may be done as needed as children discover and tell in their own words the story suggested by such a selection as Weber's *Invitation to the Dance* in which the first measures suggest an invitation and later measures indicate acceptance, the dance, and the ending.

Absolute Music   Children are asked to listen to musical content in order to discover creative ways in which selected elements of music are used. Introductory comments may include information on the selection and the composer in order to set the stage for listening. Themes to be heard may be played, and attention may be called to rhythmic, melodic, or harmonic characteristics of special importance in the selection. The teacher or student may identify the theme or other elements as they appear if such behavior does not detract from listening. Children express their reactions, demonstrate patterns they have discovered, and discuss other elements after the listening experience. For example, after listening to a selection they may play or hum the theme and discuss the variations that resulted as different instruments or varied accompaniments were used in the composition.

Instrumental Activities

Strategies in this phase include a combination of creative experimentation and direct instruction. Self-instruction through practice is a key to continuing progress. Strategies vary somewhat for rhythm, melody, and other instruments as shown in the following examples.

Rhythm Instruments   The introduction of rhythm instruments typically begins with exploratory activities so that children can discover the clicking, rattling, swishing, clanging, and booming qualities of sticks, claves, blocks, maracas, triangles, cymbals, drums, and gourds. Opportunities are provided for children to select and use them to accompany activities, to set the mood for activities, to improvise rhythmic patterns, and to demonstrate patterns discovered through listening.

Melody Instruments   Diatonic and chromatic bells fastened to a frame and resonator bells on separate blocks may be introduced by playing the starting tone of songs, playing a phrase, or playing a simple tune. Children need opportunities to experiment with them and, after discovering how they are played, to use them for a variety of purposes. Simple melodies, descants, rounds, duets, and embellishments may be played. Pitch may be checked, new melodies may be created, melodies may be played by ear, and chords may be played to strengthen harmonic concepts. Reading letters and numerals in order to play melodies and chords is helpful in developing understandings and skills that are useful in playing other instruments.

Other Instruments   Instruction on the autoharp includes guidance in following chord markings in song books, playing a single chord and then two or more different chords for accompaniment, changing chords, and stroking to fit rhythmic patterns, the metric beat, and fast and slow tempo. Simple wind instruments (recorders, tonettes, song flutes) are used in individual and group instruction to teach concepts of melodic movement, to improve music reading, to help uncertain singers, to clarify a part in part singing, to create interest in learning to play orchestral instruments. Individual and group instruction in orchestral and band instruments is provided in a systematic sequence by a teacher who has had appropriate preparation. Various instruments are used in the classroom to acquaint children with their sound and appearance, produce different musical effects, demonstrate phrasing and rhythmic patterns, play obbligatos and parts, improve music reading, accompany musical activities, and introduce transposition.

GUIDELINES FOR THE TEACHER

The teacher has a specialized role to play in music education. Teachers who carry out this role effectively are well grounded in music as a field of study, have insight into the structure of music, plan and carry out a variety of musical experiences, and are continually developing higher and higher levels of musicality as individuals. No longer should it be assumed that anyone can be a teacher of music. Rather, the view is dominant that special preparation is needed if music education is to reach a level of quality that is essential to the attainment of current objectives. Among the guidelines which teachers may use to reach a high level of quality are the following which are drawn from teaching guides and professional textbooks.

Provide a planned program of musical experiences designed to develop musicality to higher and higher levels throughout the year and from year to year. Contributions to the objectives of music education may be made by providing developmental activities in seven basic areas: singing, listening, rhythmic expression, playing instruments, creating music, reading music, and music in other subjects. The overall program in the elementary and secondary schools should be designed as a whole. The integrity of music as a tonal art should be maintained throughout the program as every effort is made to develop attitudes, appreciations, interests, understandings, and abilities that will have lasting value in the lives of students.

Select music of different types in relation to its intrinsic worth and its value in contributing to the development of musicality. Different kinds of music are needed to acquaint children with man's rich musical heritage, to provide a broad base for the development of tastes and appreciations, and to take children far beyond the musical fare that they experience at home.

Employ creative approaches to musical experiences in ways that involve children actively as both producers and consumers of music. Avoid the exclusive use of a "consumer's approach" which inevitably limits learning. Through creative approaches to producing, performing, and enjoying music, children bring out their own thoughts and feelings, express them in different ways, begin to understand that music is a means of communication, develop a desire to learn how others have expressed their ideas, and are motivated to develop understanding and skills that are essential to growth in musicality.

Develop concepts, skills, and appreciations in the context of the music the children are experiencing under the guidance of the teacher. The development of musicality should be rooted in musical experiences appropriate to students' backgrounds at each level of instruction. In the context of such experiences it is possible to guide students to develop insight into the structure of music, learn to read music for purposes important to them, and use terms and symbols to interpret the music of others and to express their own thoughts and feelings. Appreciation and enjoyment may be extended and new avenues of learning may be opened as children develop increasing understanding of the basic elements of music and increasing ability to read notation.

Challenge each student to develop in all dimensions of musicality. Well-rounded musical growth can be attained by providing varied experiences even though some children are more successful in one mode of expression or enjoyment than another. At the same time, differing aptitudes for music and for particular modes of expression should be accepted, satisfying participation should be provided for each student, and every student should be challenged to the limit of his capabilities. Both individual and group activities should be used to meet individual differences.

Encourage students to use what has been learned in music education and to engage in musical activities outside the classroom. A desired outcome for students is sensitivity to the wealth of music that is around them and how it can enrich daily living. This may take a variety of forms, such as keener interest in one or more types of music, greater discrimination in selecting musical fare, participation in community activities, taking private lessons, making a record collection, and enjoying music on radio and television.

Seek the assistance of specialists in order to provide for continuing improvement of instruction in all phases of music education. Consultants in music education can demonstrate effective techniques, assist in obtaining equipment and instructional media, advise on special problems, and suggest creative approaches to teaching. Special teachers who give instruction on band and orchestral instruments, group piano lessons, and the school choir are a valuable source of ideas and help. Many classroom teachers have special musical competence that can be tapped through the use of team teaching, the swapping of classes, and the combining of classes for various musical activities.

EVALUATION OF INSTRUCTIONAL OUTCOMES

A primary mode of evaluation in music education is direct observation of each student's musical performance and his responses to music. The behavior of students as they sing, play, engage in rhythmic activities, and express musical ideas is immediately perceivable by the teacher. How students respond to music in listening activities is less directly perceivable but may be assessed by observing reactions and by providing follow-up discussion and rhythmic and other expressive activities.

Evaluation may be facilitated through the use of observational guidelines as noted in the following section in which behaviorally stated outcomes are listed under different activities. A key principle to keep in mind is that observation checklists should be designed to fit instruction in each classroom. The following sample checklists illustrate the range of objectives in music education; they conclude with the heading "other," which is followed by space to write in other outcomes sought by the teacher.

Rhythmic activities _____ Knows fundamental rhythms _____ Recognizes different patterns _____ Moves to music _____ Selects music to fit movement _____ Creates movements _____ Recognizes beat, meter, and accent _____ Plays and distinguishes rhythm instruments _____ Selects accompaniments _____ Knows dance patterns _____ Substitutes inner response for overt movement _____ Other _____

Singing _____ Matches tones _____ Is sensitive to changes in pitch, melody, and volume _____ Is sensitive to phrasing _____ Sings with accompaniment and selects accompaniment _____ Interprets mood _____ Enunciates clearly _____ Recognizes lullabies, marches, and other types of music _____ Sings rounds, descants, parts _____ Sings from notation _____ Is building a singing repertoire _____ Other _____

Playing instruments _____ Plays simple melody and percussion instruments _____ Selects instruments for use in other activities _____ Uses autoharp for accompaniments _____ Adds introductions and codas _____ Enjoys group and individual instruction _____ Recognizes woodwinds and other types of instruments _____ Identifies instruments by sound and sight _____ Investigates how sounds are produced and other topics _____ Other _____

Listening _____ Identifies sounds and tones _____ Interprets feeling or mood _____ Enjoys listening to music _____ Responds in various ways _____ Catches the mood _____ Discusses listening out of school _____ Detects rhythm, melody, harmony _____ Identifies instruments _____ Detects phrases, beat, independent melodies _____ Recognizes overture and other forms _____ Is building a listening repertoire _____ Investigates composers and other topics _____ Other _____

Creative activities _____ Responds to music in original ways _____ Expresses responses through art and other activities _____ Improvises tunes and rhythmic patterns _____ Experiments with instruments to devise special effects _____ _____ Creates embellishments _____ Creates songs and related accompaniment _____ Sets poems and stories to music _____ Other _____

Reading music _____ Associates tonal direction with arm movements _____ Associates rhythmic patterns with fundamental movements _____ Recognizes notes of varying duration _____ Associates notes with syllables _____ Associates notes with numeral and letter notation _____ Plays tunes by ear, numeral and letter notation _____ Uses notation to sing and to play _____ Notates phrases and original music _____ Understands musical terms _____ Reads by sight _____ Other _____

Using the Taxonomies to Improve Evaluation

The taxonomies of educational objectives (Bloom, 1956; Krathwohl, Bloom, and Masia, 1964) are suggestive of items and questions that may be used to improve evaluation. With increasing recognition of the importance of the cognitive side of music education has come increased attention to assessment of conceptual outcomes. Assessment of affective components of the program can be sharpened by devising evaluative items and questions on the various levels identified in the taxonomy. The cognitive and affective domains are intimately interrelated.

Cognitive Domain

Knowledge Level Knowledge of musical terminology, information, and forms of music; knowledge of vocal music; recognition of musical works

What instruments are included among woodwinds? Mark a W under each of the pictures that shows a woodwind instrument.

Comprehension Level Ability to read music and to understand and explain musical principles

Can you explain how sound is created by a violin? Make a sketch or drawing that shows how sounds are produced on a string.

Application Level Ability to apply musical knowledge and comprehension to the selection of appropriate music in varying situations; ability to understand and classify new musical works or instruments when these are heard

What rhythmic pattern is best for marching? Listen to the following rhythmic patterns and select the one that is best for marching.

Analysis Level Understanding of the relationships of parts of musical forms

In what ways is the melodic phrase varied in this composition?

Keep a record of the following as you listen: (1) the number of times the melodic phrase is repeated and (2) the number of times it is varied.

Synthesis Level Production of original musical works or creative organization and utilization of existing works

How shall we combine the songs, rhythms, and accompaniments in our program on Indians?

Play on the melody bells a tune that can be used to set this poem to music.

Evaluation Level Use of criteria to evaluate quality of a composition or performance

How can we improve the accompaniment to the folk dance?

Listen critically and rank the following compositions according to the power of the underlying rhythmic pattern.

Affective Domain

Receiving (attending) Level Can you tell when the music sounds like a rooster crowing?

Change from walking to skipping as the music changes.

Responding Level What parts of the recording made you feel happy? Sad?

Make a check by each of the following that you would like to have more time to do: _____ Singing _____ Playing instruments _____ Folk dancing _____ Listening to records

Valuing Level After hearing a song that you enjoy very much, do you try to find out about the singer? The composer?

List the main reasons you would include in a letter to a radio station to convince them to play the kind of music you like.

FOLLOW-UP ACTIVITIES AND PROJECTS

1 Evaluate a curriculum bulletin in music education in terms of the following:

   a Are objectives appropriate? Clearly defined? Do they include all aspects of a comprehensive, balanced music program?
   b What concepts and skills are included?
   c What sequence of activities is suggested?
   d Does the program emphasize direct experience, varied forms of music, and encouragement of creative expression?
   e What instructional strategies are suggested?
   f How is music related to movement education and to other subject areas?
   g What forms of evaluation are suggested?
   h What aspects of the program are appropriate for your students?

2 Have children in your class make percussion, string, and wind instruments of "recycled" materials. Form groups that include each type of instrument, and have the children in each group compose an eight-measure composition for their combination of instruments. Record these on tape to share with fellow students. If you are not in a classroom, work with at least two other fellow students to make at least one of each type of instrument, and perform your own composition.

3 Develop a list or directory of community resources for music education, such as children's concerts, musicians offering school performances, library record collections and books, community members who can perform or teach music or dances of different cultures, and the like. Give an example of a learning experience for your children utilizing one or more of these resources.

4 Develop a list of songs and instrumental music relevant to a unit or theme in your social studies program. (For example, lullabies or work songs from different cultures, music of colonial times, music of Japan.) Where possible,

obtain authentic or facsimile musical instruments, or pictures of them. Plan and describe a set of experiences for children in learning the songs, listening to (and responding to) the music, and if possible, playing the appropriate instruments. What conclusions do you anticipate the children will arrive at in areas of understandings and attitudes as a result of these experiences?

5 Plan and describe a set of experiences for your children that includes rhythmic activity, listening, composing, singing, and performing, based on activities and sounds in the children's community, or, for older children, their own activities in the community. For example, summer activities: rhythmic movement and "beat" of different sports; sounds of water splashing, hydrants opened, ice cream cart bells, etc.; a "musical" of songs and dances depicting summer activities, and the like.

BIBLIOGRAPHY

Beer, Alice S., and Mary E. Hoffman. *Teaching Music: What, How, Why*. New York: General Learning Corporation, 1973. Principles and procedures.

Bloom, Benjamin S. (Ed.) *Taxonomy of Educational Objectives: Cognitive Domain*. MacKay, 1956. Objectives and test items on levels of complexity.

California. *Music Framework, Kindergarten through Grade Twelve*. Sacramento: California State Department of Education, 1971. Broad guidelines to instruction.

Choksy, Lois. *The Kodaly Method*. Englewood Cliffs, N.J.: Prentice Hall, 1974. Historical background, problems, and procedures on Kodaly's method.

Gelineau, Phyllis R. *Experiences in Music*. New York: McGraw-Hill, 1970. Practical procedures of instruction.

Greenberg, Marvin, and Beatrix McGregor. *Music Handbook for the Elementary School*. West Nyack, N.J.: Parker Publishing Co., 1972. Activities and techniques for various areas of music education.

Jarrett, James L. *The Humanities and Humanistic Education*. Reading, Mass.: Addison-Wesley, 1973. Historical and philosophical treatment of the humanities in the curriculum.

Klotman, Robert R. *The School Music Administrator and Supervisor: Catalyst for Change in Music Education*. Englewood Cliffs, N.J.: Prentice Hall, 1973. Guidelines for administration, supervision, and curriculum development.

Krathwohl, David R., Benjamin S. Bloom, and Bertram B. Masia. *Taxonomy of Educational Objectives: Affective Domain*. New York: McKay, 1964. Objectives and test items grouped by degree of internalization.

Land, Lois R., and Mary A. Vaughn. *Music in Today's Classroom: Creating, Listening, Performing*. New York: Harcourt, Brace, Jovanovich, 1973. Background information on music, development of skills, and teaching procedures.

Music Educators National Conference. Vienna, Va. Bulletins on concepts in music, the music specialist, and other topics.

"Music in Open Education," *Music Educator's Journal*, 1974 **60**:20–81, Issue on open education; extensive bibliography on all aspects of open education.

Nye, Robert, and Vernine. *Essentials of Teaching Music*. Englewood Cliffs, N.J.: Prentice Hall, 1974. Practical guide to development of concept and skills.

Reimer, Bennett. (Chairman) *Toward an Aesthetic Education*. Vienna, Va.: Music Educators National Conference, 1971. Essays on definition, development, and resources of aesthetic education.

Sidnell, Robert. *Building Instructional Programs in Music Education*. Englewood Cliffs, N.J.: Prentice Hall, 1973. Definition of objectives, design of instructional systems, evaluation, and accountability.

Part Three

Looking Ahead

Chapter 18

Planning
and Implementation:
Challenges and Questions

Increasingly rapid social and technological changes, persistent social and political concerns and pressures, and the multiplicity of available curricular alternatives, pose challenges and problems for the curriculum planner today. This chapter reviews the curriculum planning process presented in the model outlined in Chapter 1 and expanded in Chapters 2 through 8, with questions raised related to the curricular implications of some of these challenges and problems. The first section deals with the use of educational foundations to develop goals and objectives. Planning of content, strategies, and pupil evaluation to meet these goals and objectives are discussed in the second section with attention to analysis and adaptation of curriculum plans or materials developed outside the school or school system. The third section focuses on implementation of curriculum designs. The chapter concludes with guidelines for evaluation and modification of curriculum designs.

Planning of the total elementary curriculum is done on several levels. At the district-wide level, participants may include administrators, curriculum supervisors, teachers, psychologists, scholars in education and academic disciplines, and other resource people. Community members are increasingly included. In the future, more people in business, industry, and the arts, and the staff of such institutions as museums, libraries, and hospitals will participate in curriculum planning as offices, factories, and other community facilities are utilized as learning environments. Planning on a district-wide level usually results in production of curriculum guides for one or more areas of learning. Chapter 5 includes an outline of elements included in a complete guide.

Planning may also be done within a single school, on a schoolwide basis, or for such subunits as one grade, one subject area across all age or grade levels, a cross-grade cluster of classes, or a group of learners with a specified instructional team. School administrators, support personnel, teachers, and parents are the participants at this level. Although high school students are included in planning for secondary school curriculum, elementary school pupils would not be likely to make effective contributions in the context of adult meetings. Their participation might be more productively obtained by means of interviews, interest inventories, questionnaires, or essays on preferences for types of learning activities, reactions to new materials or procedures, responses to the physical environment of the school, and the like.

Curriculum planning always takes place at the classroom level, both in the deliberate preplanning of content and strategies for the year, a unit, or a lesson, and in the daily, minute-by-minute decisions made in the process of teaching. Here teachers have the central responsibility, although they may include other school or resource personnel in their planning. The children, of course, are the ultimate curriculum makers, for curriculum is determined by what the child actually experiences and learns. However, even in the most open or unstructured classroom setting, the teacher plans for the provision of specific materials and experiences available for children's individual choices and sequences and makes decisions to intervene in ways that take advantage of potential learning opportunities in unplanned experiences or events. In both open and comparatively structured settings, teachers also need to evaluate and adapt curricular programs or materials produced by regional or national curriculum development centers or commercial publishers and the curriculum guides developed at the state-wide or district-wide level.

Some school systems are setting up teacher centers: facilities where teachers can meet, exchange ideas, examine and evaluate new programs and materials, engage in workshops, or participate in other professional activities. Such centers would also serve as locales for joint curriculum-planning efforts as well as resource centers for professional publications and curricular materials available to individual teachers. An important problem, of course, is the provision of time needed for thoughtful and detailed curriculum planning.

At all these levels, the following sequence of procedures provides a means for effective curriculum development:

Assessment of conditions in foundations areas as a basis for generating goals
Formulation of broad goals and specific objectives
Planning and organization of curriculum content, instructional strategies, and

media; adaptation of "outside" programs and materials; provision for continuous evaluation of instructional outcomes

Implementation of curriculum designs: teacher preparation, utilization of support services, utilization of facilities and equipment, carrying out instructional strategies

Evaluation, feedback, and modification of curriculum design

FOUNDATIONS FOR DETERMINING GOALS

Philosophical, social, psychological, and discipline foundations of education provide a framework for gathering information on present conditions relevant to curriculum planning and for estimating possible and probable conditions in the emerging and more remote future.

Shane (1971) suggests procedures for what he terms "*future*-planning." The first stage of this process involves the participation of experts from a variety of fields in the identification of future trends and developments in their respective fields and the estimation of the probability of the occurrence of each. At the next stage, educators join some or all of the preceding participants to assign positive or negative values to each trend or development according to their judgment of its estimated social consequences. Next, the probability of occurrence of a particular trend and the anticipated ease or difficulty of promoting or impeding it through educational means are worked out as a weighted score to determine priorities for educational efforts: how school resources might be invested to support desirable trends, resist undesirable ones, and avoid wasting efforts on procedures, materials, or programs that prepare children "for a world that either will no longer exist or should no longer exist (Shane, 1971, p. 213)." This leads to the fourth stage, hypothetical exploration of possible curriculum designs relevant to the priorities established in the third stage. The purpose of all these procedures is not merely to anticipate the future but to participate in shaping it. The process concludes with periodic assessments of the procedures used in each of the four stages and of the coherency of efforts and results from one stage to another. To be useful and realistic, the "*future*-planning" process needs to be utilized periodically.

Of course, the personnel and efforts involved are available only at the district or statewide levels of planning, but the procedures can be adapted for use on schoolwide, subunit, or individual levels. Expert opinion about future developments expressed in such publications as those identified in the end-of-chapter bibliography can be used as sources of information and, in some cases, for value judgments of various trends. Curriculum planners can then use these predictions to develop priorities and curriculum decisions. Alternative designs can be explored hypothetically. The most promising plans can then be implemented and evaluated.

Another procedure in estimating future possibilities would be helpful at the local level. This would involve identification of social trends in terms of the ways in which they are likely to affect the local community. This effort would parallel the first stage of the more nationally oriented "*future*-planning" process and would probably be most productive and relevant if qualified community representatives as well as scholars in education and the social sciences participate along with school personnel.

Some emerging trends and possible future developments will be identified in this chapter, as starting points for projections by curriculum planners. However, future-estimation techniques such as those suggested above should be utilized for periodic reappraisal, updating, and extension of views of the world as it may be when your pupils reach voting age, enter the work force, and engage in other adult roles and responsibilities.

Philosophical Foundations

The educational philosophies discussed in Chapter 2 will continue to be theoretical sources for a variety of approaches or emphases in education. Existentialism may have increasing influence as humanistic curriculum designs emphasize "personalized" education in which most, if not all, choices of content and sequence are made by the learner. Maintenance of democratic values and ideals will continue to require educational support. The values and educational priorities of community members will be expressed through decentralized school boards and community groups in urban centers, as they have been in smaller communities. Pluralism of values may impede or prevent consensus for educational priorities on a national, state, or even local level. Alternative schools will be developed within, as well as outside, public school systems to provide for different philosophies and priorities. This might provide more opportunity for development and exploration of varied curriculum designs.

Some questions that might be raised in order to gather data relevant to curriculum planning include the following:

What are the predominant views of the purposes of education held by educators and laypersons in the school's community? What are your views?

What are the aspirations of parents for their children? What are the children's aspirations and expectations? What role is seen for education in meeting these aspirations?

What types of school programs would meet the values and priorities of community members? What types of alternative schools might be supported in the community?

What is the role of the curriculum planner in proposing and advocating curriculum alternatives? What procedures should be used to involve or inform community members?

What learning experiences will enable children to cope with rapid and pervasive change, value conflicts, and ideological pluralism? How can children become future planners?

What content and experiences are needed for future-directed education?

Social Foundations

Curriculum planners need to take into account such social considerations as the nature of the school population, change in the community, political influences on education, changing social roles, changing work roles, and persistent as well as emerging social, political, and economic problems. The questions below supplement the full discussion of social foundations in Chapter 2.

Pupil population

What is the ethnic composition? How does it compare with that of the community as a whole? If there are differences, what educational experiences are needed to promote interaction and understanding?

Is enrollment increasing or decreasing? What impact would changing enrollment have on class size, deployment of school personnel, and support for various programs?

Are there special needs for bilingual-bicultural programs, "compensatory" prekindergarten programs, enrichment programs, and the like?

What are the children's daily out-of-school experiences? How do these experiences mesh with those in school to provide continuity of learning and consistency in promotion of specified educational, social, and personal goals?

Social roles

What changes are occurring in definitions of male and female roles? What aspects of the planned and "hidden" curriculum promote or prevent development of sex-role stereotypes?

What social responsibilities will children of today have in the context of future changes in social groups, institutions, and mores? What learning experiences build attitudes of responsibility? How is value clarification incorporated in different types of school programs or curriculum designs? What social action experiences are appropriate for children at different age levels?

What are the areas of the individual's social development that are the unique, complementary, or joint responsibilities of the school and various social, political, economic, or religious agencies? What learning experiences should be provided in nonschool settings to foster development of skills or attitudes relevant to social roles?

Citizenship

How is citizenship defined? What learning experiences build skills and attitudes for rational participatory citizenship?

How is cultural pluralism reflected in curriculum designs? What provisions are needed for development of understanding of the full range of ethnic, religious, and cultural diversity in the United States?

What are the international dimensions of citizenship in the present and future? What knowledge, skills, and attitudes may be needed for the responsibilities of citizenship in a world characterized by diversity, interdependence, and conflicts of interest?

Community changes

What changes (see checklist in Chapter 2) are occurring in the community? How do these changes compare with national trends?

What "conserving" forces are apparent in the community?

What curricular provisions reinforce traditions or conserving trends?

What curriculum changes may be needed to accommodate or promote desirable or inevitable changes in the community?

Economic conditions

What changes in work rules are likely? What knowledge and skills are likely to be continuously useful? What content and experiences are needed for relevant career education?

What level of "economic literacy" will be needed by people in the late twentieth and early twenty-first century?

What provisions should be made for consumer education? What contributions can education make to use of increased leisure time?

Persistent problems

What ecological concerns are likely to persist? How can educational experiences in and out of school build needed knowledge, skills, and attitudes of responsibility? What nonschool agencies can contribute to environmental education?

What are the views, issues, or procedures in the community in regard to integration? What have the children experienced relevant to these issues, procedures, or conditions? What forms of grouping of pupils would be appropriate? If the school population is ethnically or racially homogeneous, what learning experiences are needed to develop multicultural understandings and positive intergroup attitudes?

Political influences on schools; Accountability

What local political structures or interest groups influence educational policies or control funding or staffing? What is the interaction of education personnel with local school boards, political leaders, and groups? What influences are exerted on curriculum decisions?

How can teachers, administrators, school board members, and community representatives work jointly to develop goals and procedures for accountability that are consistent with the full range of educational goals? What procedures and criteria are needed to assess citizenship skills and attitudes, thinking and learning skills, creativity, human relations, or values?

How are educational responsibilities defined? Does accountability include measurement of effective school board operations and administrative functions? Who is accountable for provision or lack of supplies, class size, condition of school facilities, and other factors beyond the classroom teacher's control?

How are accountability procedures utilized to provide constructive input into continuous improvement of instruction? (See Chapter 8 for guidelines and criteria for effective accountability programs.)

What aspects of national assessment are relevant to educational objectives in your community? How can national assessment results be utilized in local curriculum planning? What inputs can community educators make in determination of objectives and content of national or state assessment instruments?

What steps need to be taken in curriculum planning processes to avoid determination or limitation of curriculum scope and sequence in conformity with the content and the age or grade level criteria of tests or other assessment devices?

What curricular influences are exerted by state laws, funding procedures, or provision of educational services or materials? What influences are exerted by federal agency funding? What input can be made by community members and education personnel to effect local, state, or federal support for curriculum planning and implementation?

Psychological Foundations

Ongoing study of child development and learning has been stimulated in recent years by the work of Piaget and Skinner. Educators are exploring the implications of their theories. Curriculum planners need to keep informed about current thinking, research findings, and opposing as well as supportive opinions on these and other positions. An important area of research will probably be the study of the effects of environmental factors, health care and diet, and early educational experiences on intellectual development.

The theory that the earliest years are most crucial for intellectual development will continue to provide impetus for exploration of appropriate early learning experiences. A variety of viewpoints are being expressed in regard to this, a variety of instructional designs are in use, and a variety of nonschool agencies are vying to offer preschool services. Educators are challenged to identify appropriate objectives for prekindergarten experiences, to evaluate varied instructional procedures objectively, to determine appropriate curricula to meet agreed-upon objectives, and to identify the appropriate responsibilities of schools and of private, industrial, or government agencies outside the school system in the provision of experiential environments or directed learning activities for young children.

Reexamination of child development in the context of the contemporary environment has led to identification of the common characteristics of the "transescent," the child from the age of about ten to thirteen or fourteen, and the movement toward organization of middle or intermediate schools to replace junior high schools as the link between elementary and high school education. Educators are challenged to design programs, learning procedures, and patterns of pupil organization that will fit the developmental needs of this group of learners. All too often the junior high school has followed the organization of the departmentalized, graded high school. What is needed is an approach to planning that will avert the imposition of this junior high school model on the middle or intermediate school. Consistency of objectives and continuity of learning and development are essential for an effective continuum of educational experiences from prekindergarten through secondary or post-secondary levels.

The trend toward individualization of learning will continue, with a movement toward personalizing education by means of increased participation of learners in determination of content, sequence, and pace of learning experiences. This increases the curricular responsibilities of teachers, instructional-team members, and support personnel, all of whom are challenged to provide a broad range of possible learning experiences and instructional materials.

Scientific and technological developments will continue to have an impact on learning. Computer models of intellectual functions may be refined for use in the study of learning processes and testing of learning procedures. Research into chemical effects on brain function will have implications for education in the future. Increasing automation and an increasing population will necessitate continued attention to development of self-identification in an impersonal universe. Ethnic heritage studies, bilingual-bicultural education, and career education can be curricular contributions to development of positive self-concepts and self-identification. Provision for development of varied physical and aesthetic skills, strategies for individual value clarification, environmental studies, personalization of education, and utilization of out-of-school locations, institutions, and resource personnel for learning experiences are also likely, if well planned, to promote self-realization and aid development of children's understandings of themselves in relation to others, and in the context of their social, political, economic, technological, and physical environment. Educators are challenged to help children integrate these diverse curricular provisions or to develop comprehensive curriculum designs to meet these objectives now and in the future.

Chapter 3 provides guidelines for interpretation and application of developmental and learning theories in curriculum planning.

Discipline Foundations

The totality of human knowledge, organized by scholars into discipline areas, will, of course, continue to be a foundation for curricula. However, the parameters of discipline areas may change as areas of overlap between two disciplines emerge as distinct fields of knowledge and inquiry or a new focus of inquiry is identified that draws on knowledge from several disciplines (social psychology and ecology are examples).

Satellite television and other mass media are literally deliverying a world of ideas and information to children. However, the manner of delivery lacks the organization or appropriate sequencing needed to optimize children's learning. The bits and pieces children encounter need to be cemented with sound understandings derived from discipline-based programs and materials. Curriculum planners face the challenge, in a world in which human knowledge is continuously expanding, of determining what content will be most useful for children. Use of substantive elements to organize content and of methodological elements to derive learning experiences, as discussed in Chapter 3, can provide a foundation for understandings and inquiry skills that can be generalized and applied in new situations children will encounter.

The following model for analysis and use of current or evolving disciplines may be used in planning new programs as well as in evaluating the discipline base of curriculum projects, textbooks, or media kits.

What is anthropology? (or botany, geometry, etc.) Provide a succinct definition that clarifies the domain of study. In some cases, scholars use more than a single definition.

Why study the discipline? Indicate reasons, objectives, or major values to be attained; include values from the student's as well as the scholar's point of view.

What basic questions are investigated? Indicate the major questions of concern in this domain of study.

How may the substantive elements be specified? Explore various ways in which key concepts, concepts clusters, generalizations, and themes may be presented. Select the way or ways that are most useful in organizing content.

How may the methodological elements be indicated? Outline modes of inquiry and techniques of investigation that are used, giving examples that can be used in children's learning experiences.

What are the relationships between this and other disciplines? Indicate relationships to other disciplines both within the same broad field and those in other categories. Include examples of substantive or methodological similarities, or areas of concern, that can be used in cross-disciplinary studies.

What applications can be made at various levels of instruction? Suggest actual examples of how concepts, clusters, generalizations, and modes of inquiry may be used in units and courses. Include examples both for separate-discipline and cross-discipline units.

What conditions of instruction are basic? Indicate teaching strategies, instructional media, organizational patterns, and evaluation procedures that are believed to be most useful.

What references are recommended for further study? Suggest references for background information that will be most useful to curriculum builders.

Notice that this model includes curriculum planning elements as well as elements for analyzing a discipline.

Formulating Goals and Objectives

Specific guidelines for identification of broad goals and formulation of learning objectives are provided in Chapter 4. In this process, the following questions should be kept in mind:

How are the six major goals of education defined in regard to changes in educational foundations? Should other goals be added? Should emphases be changed, or the categories reorganized?

How do the goals of development of thinking skills and learning skills promote self-identification, individuality, and self-reliance in a rapidly changing, impersonal, and interdependent world?

How is self-realization defined? What learning experiences and instructional strategies are appropriate for each objective in this category? How do changes in personal and social roles affect definition of this goal?

How are the goals of human relationships and civic responsibility defined at every level of interaction from family and peer groups to national and international responsibilities? What models of school organization or teacher-pupil interaction are conducive to development of these goals?

How do technological changes and current economic concerns affect definitions of economic competence? How may direct learning experiences and use of labor and business resources in the community contribute to attainment of this goal?

PLANNING CONTENT, INSTRUCTIONAL STRATEGIES, AND EVALUATION

Chapters 5 through 8 provide detailed guidelines for these aspects of curriculum planning. In this section, some questions are raised in regard to relevant emerging trends, and guidelines are provided for assessment and incorporation of curriculum projects and materials developed outside the school system.

Organization of Curriculum Content

How can mass media sources be utilized at home and in school in meaningful and ongoing studies of current affairs? How can studies of current happenings and conditions be linked to past developments and future projections?

What social concerns and forms of social action are appropriate elements of elementary and middle school programs? What resources and locations in the community can be utilized for useful learning experiences in this area?

How is self-knowledge developed? What content area studies contribute to self-understanding?

Instructional Strategies and Instructional Media

What learning processes are utilized in out-of-school learning experiences? What instructional strategies are appropriate for effective guided or independent learning in community resource locations?

What is the role of the classroom teacher or instructional team leader in planning or coordinating learning experiences in school, home, and community settings?

What areas of learning (usually acquisition of factual information and development of learning skills) are effectively developed by programmed, computer-assisted, or educational television instruction? How can educational technology be utilized to facilitate diagnosis of individual pupil needs and progress?

How may mass media and computer-assisted instruction be utilized in the future to extend the range of learning experiences in the home?

If students spend some time in out-of-school settings, what scheduling plans might be possible for in-school procedures such as more extensive individual teacher-pupil conferences, group work, and use of shared (and presumably more accessible) school facilities?

Extensions of the Learning Environment

What forms of staffing would be most effective in meeting new objectives or implementing new designs? What roles or skills are needed for a specific instructional team? What in-service activities would afford preparation for changes in instructional roles or tasks?

How can paraprofessionals or other classroom aides be deployed effectively? Are there some subjects or skills that might require instruction by specialists? What needs for particular support services are current, or anticipated, in your school? How does the availability of aides and specialists affect your curriculum design?

What additional facilities will be needed in new schools designed to serve as community learning centers? How might such facilities (pools, media centers, health information centers, conference rooms, music practice rooms, industrial arts workshops, and the like) extend learning experiences for elementary and middle school children?

How can existing buildings be adapted for use in open education, multi-grade, or continuous progress programs? What instructional groupings and strategies are facilitated in buildings with open plans or with clusters of classrooms? What suggestions would you make for design of learning spaces? How can your present facilities be utilized in the implementation of new curriculum designs?

Evaluation of Instructional Outcomes

What formal, informal, and self-evaluation procedures are appropriate for evaluation of out-of-school or pupil-planned learning experiences?

What forms of evaluation are suitable for each of the six major goals of education? Is care taken to avoid limiting evaluation to tests of factual knowledge at the classroom, school, or district-wide level?

Utilization of Curriculum Projects and Materials

Prior to the 1950s, curriculum planning was the responsibility of school superintendants, principals, curriculum supervisors, and teachers. After these participants developed curriculum guides for a particular school system, the next step was usually adoption of a textbook for each subject area. This, in effect, made textbook publishers another major source of curriculum design.

During the curriculum reform movement of the fifties and sixties, scholars in education and the academic disciplines engaged in curriculum evaluation and design at university-based or regional curriculum development centers. Resulting programs or materials, sometimes supported with in-service preparation for teachers, have been made available to schools, sometimes in commercially published forms. It is likely that regional centers will continue to share curriculum development responsibility with school system personnel, because the setting, resources, time, and funding available at this level can enable more experts from all relevant fields to participate in curriculum design than would usually be possible at the school or system-wide level.

Thus, school system curriculum planners will probably find that their time and efforts would be most productive if primary attention is given to specification of goals and objectives appropriate to the particular system and to development of broad guidelines for curriculum organization and instructional strategies to meet these objectives. This would be followed by evaluation of projects, multimedia programs or kits, and materials, to select those that contribute toward the school's or system's objectives. A number of projects and materials are described in Henrie (1972) and other sources in bibliographies of Chapters 9 through 17.

Of course, no matter how well conceived these curriculum designs and materials may be, they are not necessarily comprehensive enough to meet all your objectives, even within a single subject, topic, or skill-development area. Nor are they planned to relate to the other components of the educational program of a particular school. Therefore, teachers must provide the additional experiences needed to meet all objectives, relate content and skill development across subject areas, and adapt the program or materials for use by different learners.

With so many sources and materials to choose from, curriculum planners need to develop criteria for assuring balance in the total curriculum. One useful framework would be the six major goals of education suggested in this volume or the major goals of your school system. Does the total program at any age or grade level contribute in appropriate ways to each goal? Additional criteria can be derived from taxonomies of inquiry processes, or categories of areas of knowledge, and used as checklists for comprehensiveness and balance in the curriculum. An example is the identification by Phenix (1964) of six realms of meaning: symbolics, including mathematic, verbal, and nonverbal symbol systems; empirics, meanings based on observation and experimentation; aesthetics, meanings derived and expressed through the arts; synoptics or personal knowledge; ethics or moral meanings; and synoptics, the integration of meanings from other realms in the comprehensive structures of history, philosophy, and religion.

New curriculum designs and related materials need to be scrutinized in regard to the nature of their objectives, planning, utilization of foundation disciplines, scope and sequence, teaching strategies and materials, evaluation of instructional outcomes, relation to total curriculum, and feasibility of use. Problems and questions in each area will be considered below in this sequence. Useful sources of criteria for evaluation of new curriculum projects and designs will be found in several end-of-chapter references (Ammons and Gilchrist, 1965; Gilchrist, 1963, pp. 1-10; Fraser, 1962; Michaelis, 1972, p. 61; Payne, 1974).

Objectives Curriculum builders will need to identify the objectives of new designs and materials, compare them with those of the school system, and consider their suitability for the school population. Such questions as the following should be raised:

What are the objectives of the design? Are they specified in behavioral terms that include understandings in a structural framework related to the disciplines; skills in the areas of thinking, inquiring, learning; and attitudes? Are the objectives meaningful to teachers? Will teachers encounter difficulties in their implementation?

In what ways, or to what extent, do the objectives fit in with and support the overall educational objectives of the school system? How do they match or augment specific objectives for each grade level or curriculum area?

How does the school population compare with tryout groups (if any were used)? For what groups or types of learners are project or materials objectives best suited? What modifications can be made to suit new designs to the needs of specific groups within the school system?

Planning of Designs and Materials Criteria related to the planning and production of new curriculum designs are reflected in such questions as these:

How was the design initiated? Under whose auspices (foundations, public institutions, commercial organizations, etc.) was the design produced? What are the qualifications of those who planned the design or materials? Were diverse specialists (scholars in academic disciplines and education, teachers, curriculum specialists) involved? To what extent was each of these special competencies represented?

Have the designs or materials been tried out in appropriate classroom settings? What evaluative information is available? Is further information needed?

What assistance is available from scholars and other curriculum producers for implementation of new designs? How can the benefits of their assistance be maximized or maintained over long periods of time? If revisions are planned, how are these communicated to the school system?

Foundation Disciplines, Scope, and Sequence In analyzing or planning the sequential organization of the curriculum, designers should employ both logical and psychological aspects of curriculum planning, giving increasing attention to logical sequencing of instructional materials. There is no need for any debate over logical versus psychological planning. Both aspects are evident and mutually supportive in new curriculum designs. Logical planning should be evident in the arranging of facts, concepts, generalizations, skills, and methods of inquiry in sequences related to outlines of the structure of disciplines. The use of logical processes should be apparent in the modes of instruction in many designs, involving such elements as deducing hypotheses, categorizing and classifying data in terms of criteria, systematic testing of conclusions, and critical analysis of evidence and proof. Psychological aspects of planning should be evident in the attention given to such cognitive processes as classifying, generalizing, and evaluating, and in using methods that move students to higher levels of thinking in a teaching sequence.

It is strongly recommended that intensive efforts be made to identify key concepts, concept clusters, and generalizations that are used in units of study as well as those which outline the overall structure of a discipline or a program of instruction.

Special efforts should be made to draw out the major modes of inquiry (experimental, historical, case study, survey, etc.) that constitute the methodological aspects of structure. Specific methods of investigation employed (interviewing, mapping, observing, etc.) should also be identified. If the focus in curriculum design is exclusively on the substantive, conceptual aspects, the dynamic processes that are key ingredients in inquiry may be neglected. Both content and process should be considered, as disciplines are reviewed and curriculum is planned.

Closely related to these considerations is the problem of making appropriate forms of inquiry an *integral* part of instruction. A variety of proposals have been made, ranging from inquiry based on questions posed by students, to which the teacher should reply either yes or no, to free-wheeling experimentation in which little or no teacher direction is provided. The authors take the stand that primary attention should be given to the use of modes and techniques of inquiry drawn directly from the disciplines. Special inquiry procedures designed outside the context of fundamental ways of knowing and producing knowledge cannot be expected to pay off in the long run. Nor will a single mode of inquiry, anymore than a single view of learning, have much mileage in curriculum planning. In short, the view is taken that curriculum builders should draw upon the full array of processes of inquiry in current use in disciplinary and cross-disciplinary studies in order to select and use the most appropriate modes and techniques of inquiry as units or programs of study are planned.

The following questions, then, might be used to evaluate the structural aspects, scope, and sequence of new curriculum designs:

What outlines of structure are found in curriculum designs and materials? Are there conflicts between the approaches of various designs, or are differences reconcilable as the content of one design supplements that of another? Are substantive frameworks suitable to the learning needs of children for whom the designs or materials are intended?

What inquiry modes and specific techniques are incorporated in the design? How appropriate are these procedures for classroom use at intended grade or learning levels? Are suggested inquiry procedures clearly described and consistent with the methodological structure of foundation disciplines, or are they vaguely set forth, overly generalized, or not stated at all?

Is the content organized in a framework and sequence that will enhance children's understandings and encourage inquiry and independence in learning?

Does the content represent an improvement over present programs in the effectiveness of its organization? Does it replace outmoded content?

Are provisions made for modification of scope and pace of sequence to meet the needs of individual learning differences? Are special materials provided for various groups of learners?

Teaching Strategies and Instructional Media   Some new curriculum designs include a coordinated "package" of content outlines, teaching plans, and instructional media. All designs specify appropriate supportive media, even when these are not included within the project materials themselves. Other materials are produced independently Guidelines for teaching strategies and use of materials are provided, to varying extents, in the form of manuals and unit or lesson plans. These guidelines for teachers should be, in general, directive without being prescriptive. Teachers should be free to alter and improve them to meet local needs and conditions. Guidelines and directives should be set up to highlight relationships among objectives, content, key concepts and generalizations, learning activities, instructional media, and evaluation.

Teaching strategies should involve inductive approaches in which students are guided in analyzing and synthesizing information. New programs should employ some form of inductive approach in which questions embodying key concepts are used to guide study, problems are analyzed, independent study is emphasized, and students themselves organize data and formulate generalizations. Conceptual models in the form of questions should be used to guide study of different problems or topics. Cognitive processes involved in handling content and values should be stressed. Processes of conceptualizing, hypothesizing, inferring, generalizing, and evaluating should be emphasized. Taxonomies of cognitive objectives may be used to identify process objectives and to build a series of questions on varying levels of cognition.

New developments in the design and use of instructional media have posed a further set of challenges and problems to curriculum workers. In the past, teachers and administrators have evolved ways of utilizing new materials in support of instructional programs within an approach that regarded each new item as a supplementary aid to the central components of instruction, the teacher and the textbook. There is a growing tendency now for curriculum planners to go beyond listing recommended materials and to produce a package of materials that constitutes an integral, not a supplementary, part of the total curriculum design. When the design is implemented, the teacher, employing the materials in the sequence and manner prescribed in the curriculum design, is functioning as a part of a total instructional system. The teacher needs to understand the rationale for the organization of the system in order to be able to utilize it most effectively, and this means knowing how to modify the system to meet specific, local instructional needs. Attention should be given to pre-service and in-service programs that acquaint the teacher with appropriate approaches to the uses of educational media systems and permit teacher selection and coordination of separate materials to reach more effective levels.

Some relevant questions include the following:

What strategies are suggested? How clearly are these described? Are they based on teaching/learning theories consistent with those of the school system? What balance is there between adequate guidance for teachers and freedom to adapt to special needs?

What materials are required? Do they support the goals of the overall curriculum design? Do they develop content in a form consistent with structural outlines? Do they develop inquiry processes?

What materials are provided with the overall design? Are other suitable materials available? Are any materials called for which are already utilized in local programs? Are the materials provided in new designs and projects appropriate to the needs of learners for whom they are intended?

Evaluation of Instructional Outcomes Evaluation of instructional outcomes should be concerned with the full range of possible outcomes beyond the measurement of academic achievement. Attention should be given to assessment techniques that will reveal data on development of skills, attitudes, and values. Evaluation may be improved as projects and designs build appraisal devices into instructional materials and as new instruments are developed. A variety of techniques and devices for evaluating outcomes of instruction may be found in project materials: summarizing questions and test items in students' materials, self-checking programmed material, checklists, charts, questions to guide self-evaluation, questions and items to guide teacher evaluation of learning, and end-of-unit tests. The preceding chapters present examples of evaluative procedures and instruments.

Questions such as the following may be used in reviewing evaluation provisions in new designs:

What instructional objectives are identified for evaluation? Are tests and other instruments provided? Are guidelines given for construction of evaluative materials?

Does the design provide activities and materials that permit continuous evaluation? Are materials provided for pupil self-evaluation?

What outcomes may be anticipated, in addition to those identified in design or project materials?

Feasibility of Adoption and Implementation Important considerations in the analysis and review of new curriculum designs are those related to the feasibility of their use in the local school system. Of course, all the preceding questions refer to the suitability of the design or materials for the learners in a particular system, and suitability is the primary requisite for adoption. However, that which is desirable must also be feasible to implement if it is to be adopted. Questions such as the following should be considered:

What competencies are required of teachers? What relevant background preparation do the system's teachers have? Will teachers be able to understand, and be willing to meet, the changes to be made?

What in-service training will be necessary? What assistance for such training is provided by curriculum producers? What time, facilities, and personnel are available in the system to meet in-service training needs?

What organizational changes, if any, need to be made? Are changes required in class size, vertical school organization, responsibilities of teachers? Are adequate plant facilities and equipment available?

To what extent is the local community aware of needs for curriculum change? What changes does the community favor? What efforts must be made to inform the community about proposed changes? Is there sufficient financial support to thoroughly implement the program?

Are administrative and supervisory personnel available to guide implementation of the program? Can the program be given an experimental tryout? Are time, instruments, and personnel available for adequate evaluation of all aspects of the program?

IMPLEMENTATION OF NEW CURRICULUM DESIGNS

Implementation of instructional programs is not a single activity. It is an interwoven network of varying activities involved in translating curriculum designs into classroom practice. The implementation phase of curriculum development is defined by questions such as these: What must teachers do to carry out this particular program or effectively utilize these materials? What do they need to know to do this? How can they be prepared? What supportive personnel are needed? What kinds of instructional materials and facilities are most helpful? What forms of school and class organization are required?

Curriculum change is most effectively implemented when the community understands and supports it, when facilities are available for desirable school organization and learning activities, when appropriate materials are at hand, and when supportive personnel assist teachers. But it is the classroom teacher who is the key to curriculum implementation, for in the last analysis, in plain terms, the curriculum is what the teacher makes of it. The curriculum is described in the teacher-pupil interaction of each classroom. Therefore, aspects of teacher preparation will be considered first in this discussion, although it is understood that all the other elements of implementation contribute to what the teacher does with curriculum designs in the classroom.

Teacher Preparation

An important problem for in-service education is the preparation of the teacher for changes in instructional roles. Traditionally, the teacher has been prepared for the role of sole (or at least primary) determiner of all curricular activities in all subjects in a single classroom at a specified grade level. This role is changing in many ways. To begin with, the teacher who genuinely develops children's inquiry skills has assumed a role of less-than-complete determination of all phases of the child's learning experiences. Another example of change is seen in the greater attention being given to utilization of special competencies of teachers who have depth of preparation in different school subjects, as teachers are grouped into teaching teams. The responsibilities of the team teacher are at once limited and extended in comparison with the traditional role — limited to one, or just a few, of the school subjects and extended to the instruction of varying groups of children in a wider range of grade or achievement levels.

As new curriculum designs are adopted (or adapted), resultant needs for in-service education must be assessed.

What specific skills or understandings need to be developed? Do all teachers need the same program? What provisions should be made for differing teacher backgrounds and needs?

What are the most effective procedures for the in-service program? What time allotment is required in the teacher's day and school year?

What materials are needed? Are materials and guidelines for in-service activities supplied by the curriculum producers? Are members of curriculum planning groups available for consultation if needed? Can demonstrations or observations of classroom activities be arranged? Are adequate reference materials available in the system's professional or school libraries?

In-service education is only one aspect of adequate teacher preparation. No less than their pupils, teachers differ in regard to their academic and experiential backgrounds and in the specific talents they bring to the instructional task. Self-directed activities can greatly augment each teacher's competencies. In addition, teachers may explore new ideas and materials even when no system-wide revision is in progress. The following are possible ways of developing insight into the content and processes needed to utilize new developments:

Obtain, examine, and try out (if feasible) materials still under development in various projects. Administrators may write to project directors to obtain materials and be placed on the mailing list for project bulletins.

Formulate objectives in behavioral or operational terms. Study examples presented in current materials, such as those cited in the preceding chapters. Use behavioral statements in unit and lesson plans.

Begin now to make the classroom a laboratory for the development of competence in inquiry. If there is one common element in the many new curriculum developments across the board, it is the emphasis on the involvement of students in inquiry.

Examine current materials to find examples of structure and inquiry. Look for key concepts, concept clusters, generalizations, modes of inquiry, and specific techniques of inquiry in new units of study, textbooks, films, and other materials. Begin to guide students to use concepts, clusters, and generalizations to structure their learning.

Examine so-called teacher-proof or teacher-safe materials for the express purpose of finding out how specialists structure ideas, ask questions, stimulate inquiry, and assess outcomes. Much can be gained by analyzing these materials for good ideas; much can be lost by condemning them for being assertedly teacher-proof.

Try out selected teaching strategies presented in this volume and in new curriculum materials. Modify and adapt them to fit your style, the capacities of your students, and local conditions. By all means, try to keep in mind that the spirit and intent of various strategies is to involve students as intensively as possible in learning experiences.

Give particular attention to the kinds of questions used, striving for those which spur inquiry on the part of students. Study guidelines for framing questions as reported in current materials and cited in examples in the preceding chapters.

Assume the role of teacher-observer in the classroom in order to diagnose needs, to plan next learning experiences, to evaluate outcomes of instruction, and to study ways in which children carry on inquiry and cluster ideas.

Make evaluation a basic part of instruction from initial through concluding phases. Use a variety of devices and procedures ranging from questions and items on various levels of the taxonomies of educational objectives to check lists and tasks related to multiple outcomes. Give attention to both cognitive and affective outcomes.

Participate in professional activities that bear directly on new developments. Identify courses (both academic and professional), institutes, workshops, meetings, and conferences that are specifically designed to familiarize school personnel with new programs and materials in various areas of the elementary curriculum.

While the needs of teachers in service are met by in-service and self-directed activities, the needs of the school system require a third vital aspect of teacher preparation: the pre-service education of teachers. In-service programs will always serve the function of keeping experienced teachers abreast of new developments, but the demands on the school system's in-service personnel and resources are less staggering when preservice education provides the beginning teacher with an understanding of the rationale underlying curricular innovations in addition to providing contact with specific new designs and materials.

Supportive Personnel and Services

Preservice and in-service education provide preparation for effective program implementation, but supervision and consultation must take up implementation responsibilities where these leave off, in the continuous assistance and provision of supportive services needed daily in the classroom. The challenge to supervisors and principals has been especially great because the national curriculum projects have not dealt with problems of supervision and consultation to any great extent.

One aspect of this challenge is the identification of the types of supportive services needed and the provision of suitable training for the personnel who will provide these services. Just as the role of the teacher has undergone changes, the responsibilities and roles of supervisors, curriculum specialists, school administrators, and central staff personnel are being redefined as new curriculum developments affect the kinds of leadership each one provides in all phases of curriculum planning and implementation. For example, the roles of the school librarian and audiovisual coordinator tend to merge as the impact of new designs and materials turns the school library into an instructional materials center where children find books, films, tapes, or programmed materials for individual or group study and teachers obtain resource materials and equipment for classroom use.

Other ways in which school systems have met the challenges posed by new designs have included provision of such supportive services as closed-circuit or intersystem educational TV, institution of team-teaching procedures and non-graded organization, construction of elementary schools with flexible interior partitions to permit varying groupings and activities, and exploration of ways in which programmed instruction and computer technology can free teachers to devote more of their time to creative and individualized aspects of instruction.

The Community and Curriculum Implementation

Effective implementation of new curriculum designs is dependent on at least two factors related to the neighborhood and school system community. First, financial support, despite state, federal, or foundational assistance, is still requisite for the provision of needed educational facilities and services. Second, though equal in importance, is the community's theoretical support for changes. Educators can bring about changes most effectively if a climate of understanding and encouragement prevails in the community. Especially important are the attitudes held by parents, for these are invariably transmitted to the children for whom the changes are intended. Preceding sections have touched on the tremendous range and accelerating pace of new developments in curriculum design and materials and the challenges to educators to keep abreast of these developments and, of course, to go beyond merely maintaining such awareness by initiating curriculum innovation activities themselves. But at the same time, school personnel should recognize that the supportive community must not be left behind. Despite the time and effort devoted to information and curriculum development within the school system, some time and effort must be expended to keep the community aware of the changing conditions and needs perceived by educators. School-community communication should go beyond mere information; it should include the maintenance of a continuous dialogue that enables the community to understand rationales for change, to understand the educational problems and procedures involved, and in many instances to provide direct assistance for curriculum implementation in the form of resource persons, school volunteers and aides, and any number of other personal forms of contribution to the efforts of the schools.

EVALUATION OF NEW INSTRUCTIONAL PROGRAMS

After curriculum designs and materials are developed, they are tried out in the classroom, critical reactions are obtained, test data are analyzed, and needed revisions are made. This process, a subsystem in the total implementation process, may be conducted in the ways diagrammed in Chart 18-1.

Following this phase, more formal evaluation is developed and is conducted along the lines diagrammed in Chart 18-2.

There is a need to identify all the objectives and outcomes that may be evaluated. This means going beyond mere assessment of pupil achievement as measured by paper-pencil tests, to an evaluation of a full range of cognitive, affective, and psychomotor outcomes through a variety of instruments. The attitudes and effectiveness of teachers and other supportive personnel, the value of various materials, media systems, and strategies, the extent to which better scope and balance have been achieved in the total curriculum — all need to be clearly defined and properly assessed before any sound judgment can be made of the effectiveness of new curriculum designs and innovations. Under limited procedures and techniques of evaluation, comparisons between old and new programs have in general revealed that students do about as well on traditional

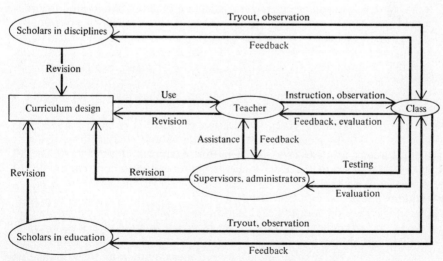

Chart 18-1 Preliminary classroom evaluation of new curriculum designs

Chart 18-2   Formal evaluation of new curriculum designs

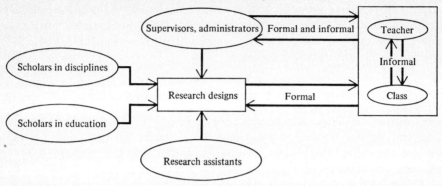

learning in either type of program and that students in new programs "gain additional insights and understandings." A key difficulty is to get measurement instruments that are "fair" to both new and traditional programs. Because objectives are quite different, it is not possible to define appraisal criteria that are equally applicable to both old and new programs.

The preceding chapters include checklists of questions for the evaluation of curriculum improvement in specific curriculum areas. Other lists that aid in definition of questions to be evaluated may be found in end-of-chapter references. There is agreement on the part of all concerned with program evaluation that, to be meaningful, evaluation must be continuous.

FOLLOW-UP ACTIVITIES AND PROJECTS

1 Use the guidelines in this chapter to evaluate a textbook, a curriculum project or a media kit, and a curriculum guide or bulletin. What modifications would you make in each of these to adapt it to the needs of your pupils?
2 Analyze and evaluate your present program in terms of contributions to the six major goals of education or to the major goals of your school system. Identify some types of changes that need to be made, explain why these changes are needed, and describe two or three examples of specific changes you would make in curriculum organization, instructional strategies, organization of learners, or evaluation.
3 Select one of the major goals of education and identify specific content areas and instructional procedures that contribute to that goal in the program at a specific age or grade level. Then outline examples of ways in which this goal is developed in the total kindergarten-secondary school continuum of your school system.
4 Content and experiences in different areas of the curriculum may be integrated to develop a specific objective, to develop and apply or transfer related understandings or skills, or to motivate interest in a learning task.
    a State an objective for your learners and describe specific content and experiences in two or more subject areas that would be integrated in order to contribute to that objective.

   b Describe an example of a learning skill or conceptual (substantive) understandings developed in one subject area and indicate how the skill or understandings would be transferred or applied in another area.

   c Describe an example of the use of content or experiences in one subject area to motivate interest in acquiring learning skills or understandings in another area.

5 Individually, or with a team of fellow students (or other teachers in your school), develop a detailed description of a school in your community twenty years from now. Describe the facilities, philosophy of the total program, examples of curriculum organization and learning experiences, staffing, organization of learners, examples of use of instructional media, and evaluation techniques. You may want to use drawings, floor plans or models, charts, diagrams, or dramatization in developing this description and sharing it with others. Give reasons for the examples you describe and for the forms of staffing and pupil organization your plan requires.

BIBLIOGRAPHY

Ammons, Margaret, and Robert S. Gilchrist. *Assessing and Using Curriculum Content.* Washington, D.C.: Association for Supervision and Curriculum Development, 1965. Useful guidelines for curriculum workers.

Combs, Arthur W. *Educational Accountability — Beyond Behavioral Objectives.* Washington, D.C.: Association for Supervision and Curriculum Development, 1972. Discussion of humanistic objectives in education.

Cook, Ruth C., and Ronald C. Doll. *The Elementary School Curriculum.* Boston: Allyn and Bacon, 1973. Chapter on education in the future.

Curriculum Theory Network. Toronto, Ontario, Canada: The Ontario Institute for Studies in Education. Periodically published journal on curriculum theory, development, and evaluation.

Eisner, Elliot W., and Elizabeth Vallance. (Eds.) *Conflicting Conceptions of Curriculum.* Berkeley, Calif.: McCutchan Publishing Corporation, 1974. Articles on five conceptual views of curriculum.

Fraser, Dorothy M. *Current Curriculum Studies in Academic Subjects.* Washington, D.C.: National Education Association, 1962. Guidelines for using curriculum projects in last chapter.

Frazier, Alexander. Making use of national curriculum studies, *Educational Leadership,* November, 1964, **22**, 101–106. Analysis of steps in developing new curriculum materials.

———. (Ed.) *A Curriculum for Children.* Washington, D.C.: Association for Supervision and Curriculum Development, 1969. Contemporary conditions and future trends relevant to curriculum decisions.

Gilchrist, Robert S. (Ed.) *Using Current Curriculum Developments.* Washington, D.C.: Association for Supervision and Curriculum Development, 1963. Guidelines for curriculum workers, review of curriculum developments.

Goodlad, John I., and Harold G. Shane. (Eds.) *The Elementary School in the United States.* 72d Yearbook, Part II. Chicago: National Society for the Study of Education, 1973. Influences on curriculum development in elementary education.

Gordon, C. Wayne. (Ed.) *Uses of the Sociology of Education.* 73d Yearbook, Part II. Chicago: National Society for the Study of Education, 1974. Discussion of curricular implications of youth culture, evaluation and accountability, desegregation, and federal government influences.

Hass, Glen, Joseph Bondi, and Jon Wiles. *Curriculum Planning – A New Approach.* Boston: Allyn and Bacon, 1974. Collection of readings in all areas of curriculum development.

Henrie, Samuel N. (Senior Ed.). *A Sourcebook of Elementary Curricula Programs and Projects.* Washington, D.C.: Government Printing Office, 1972. Chapters on programs and materials for affective education and personal development, career education, ethnic education and intergroup relations, and general systems and resources (special school plans).

Jackson, Philip W. *Life in Classrooms.* New York: Holt, 1968. Discussion of effects of the "hidden" curriculum.

Kahn, Herman, and Anthony J. Weiner. *The Year 2,000: A Framework for Speculation on the Next Thirty-Three Years.* New York: Macmillan, 1967. Projections of future developments.

Lange, Phil C. (Ed.) *Programmed Instruction.* 66th Yearbook, Part II. Chicago: National society for the Study of Education, 1967. Critical review of principles and procedures of programmed instruction.

Leeper, Robert R. (Ed.) *Curricular Concerns in a Revolutionary Era.* Washington, D.C.: Association for Supervision and Curriculum Development, 1971. Articles on all areas of curriculum development.

———. (Ed.) *Curriculum Decisions – Social Realities.* Washington, D.C.: Association for Supervision and Curriculum Development, 1968. Papers on social influences on curriculum.

Macdonald, James B., Bernice J. Wolfson, and Esther Zaret. *Reschooling Society: A Conceptual Model.* Washington, D.C.: Association for Supervision and Curriculum Development, 1973. Pamphlet outlining proposals for a personalized, humanistic curriculum.

McClure, Robert M. (Ed.) *The Curriculum: Retrospect and Prospect.* 70th Yearbook, Part I. Chicago: National Society for the Study of Education, 1971. Historical background of curriculum development and chapters on future directions and trends in education.

Michaelis, John U. "Educating children for change" in *Readings in Curriculum,* Glen Hass and Kimball Wiles (Eds.) Boston: Allyn and Bacon, 1965. Suggestions for curricular provisions that enable children to cope with rapid change and value conflicts.

———. *Social Studies for Children in a Democracy.* 5th Edition. Englewood Cliffs, N.J.: Prentice-Hall, 1972. Guidelines for project evaluation on page 61, and chapter on developing values and attitudes.

Nelson, Jack L., Kenneth Carlson, and Thomas E. Linton. (Eds.) *Radical Ideas and the Schools.* New York: Holt, 1972. Collection of papers representing a broad spectrum of ideas from right to left.

Nelson, Ralph T. "Helpful Hints for Your High School's Alternative Programs," *Educational Leadership,* May, 1974, **31**:8, pp. 716–721. Down-to-earth guidelines applicable to elementary and middle school curriculum implementation on a schoolwide or subunit level.

Olson, Arthur V., and Joe A. Richardson. *Accountability: Curricular Applications*. Scranton, Pa.: Intext Educational Publishers, 1972. Articles representing different views of the uses of accountability processes; those by Lopez, Barro, and Walberg, particularly, stress cooperative goal determination, constructive feedback, and attention to affective and humanistic goals.

Overly, Norman V. (Ed.) *The Unstudied Curriculum*. Washington, D.C.: Association for Supervision and Curriculum Development, 1970. Curricular implication of the "hidden" curriculum.

Payne, David A. (Ed.) *Curriculum Evaluation*. Boston: Heath, 1974. Readings in curriculum development and project evaluation.

Phenix, Philip H. *Realms of Meaning*. New York: McGraw-Hill, 1964. Discussion of six areas of cognitive understanding as a basis for balance in the curriculum.

Ragan, William B., and Gene D. Shepherd. *Modern Elementary Curriculum*. New York: Holt, 1971. Chapter on education in the future.

Review of Educational Research, June, 1969, **39**:3. Entire issue devoted to review of studies and papers on curriculum development.

Saylor, J. Galen. (Ed.) *The School of the Future Now*. Washington, D.C.: Association for Supervision and Curriculum Development, 1972. Curriculum proposals for early childhood education and for elementary, middle, and high school levels.

————, and William M. Alexander. *Planning Curriculum for Schools*. New York: Holt, 1974. Chapters on curriculum planning procedures and future trends.

Shane, Harold G. *"Future*-planning as a means of shaping educational change," *The Curriculum: Retrospect and Prospect*. Chicago: National Society for the Study of Education, 1971. Guidelines for estimating relevant future developments and applying estimates to curriculum development.

Short, Edmund C., and George D. Marconnit. (Eds.) *Contemporary Thought on Public School Curriculum*. Dubuque, Iowa: Wm. C. Brown, 1968. Collection of readings on all areas of curriculum development.

Thoreson, Carl E. (Ed.) *Behavior Modification in Education*. 72d Yearbook, Part I. Chicago: National Society for the Study of Education, 1973. Philosophy of behavior modification and chapter on applications to elementary classroom situations.

Toffler, Alvin (Ed.) *Learning for Tomorrow: The Role of the Future in Education*. New York: Random House, 1974. Articles on education for the future.

Witty, Paul A. (Ed.) *The Educationally Retarded and Disadvantaged*. 66th Yearbook, Part I. Chicago: National Society for the Study of Education, 1967. Guidelines for improving programs of instruction.

Index

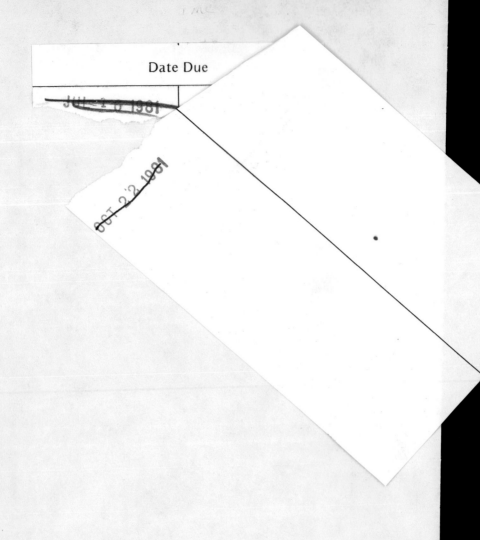